# The ESL Miscellany

Cherokee basket

## A Treasury of Cultural and Linguistic Information

### Fifth Edition

Raymond C. Clark • Patrick R. Moran • Arthur A. Burrows

# PRO LINGUA ☯ ASSOCIATES

# Pro Lingua Associates, Publishers

P.O. Box 1348
Brattleboro, Vermont 05302-1348 USA

Office: 802 257 7779
Orders: 800 366 4775
Fax: 802 257 5117
Webstore: www.ProLinguaAssociates.com
Email: info@ProLinguaAssociates.com
SAN: 216-0579

*Pennsylvania Dutch plaque of heart and birds*

At Pro Lingua
our objective is to foster
an approach to learning and teaching
that we call **interplay**, the **inter**action
of language learners and teachers with their materials,
with the language and culture,
and with each other in active,
creative and productive
**play**.

Copyright © 1981, 1991, 2000, 2001, 2003, 2007, 2008, 2015 by Pro Lingua Associates, Inc.

ISBN 0-86647-367-X; 978-0-86647-367-X

This book was designed and set in Adobe Century Schoolbook type by Arthur A. Burrows; the cover uses the Monotype Corsiva and Palatino faces. The photographs of American gestures are by Michael Jerald. The maps are from MapArt by Cartesia. Original drawings are by Patrick Moran. The road signs are copyright © 2005 Richard C. Moeur were rendered by (http://www.trafficsign.us/). The folk art and other illustration are from the Dreamstime.com catalogue as follows: page i © Czalewski, ii © Connie Larsen, v © Konstantinkirov, viii © Andrey Arkusha, xi © Mark Hryciw, xii © Tangibleday, 6 © Murphy81, 60 © Reid Dallard, 75 © Andreirybachuk, 86 © Dinorah Alejandra Valdés, 93 © Flynt, 174 © Jirkaejc, 271 © Smirno, 310 © Eric Krouse, 334 © Bounder32h, 338 © Sivanova. The front cover art, "Earth Perspective" is copyright © Vampy1 | Dreamstime.com - Space View Of Earth – Europe, Africa, and America.
This book was printed and bound by Gasch Printing in Odenton, Maryland.

Printed in the United States of America

Fifth edition, first printing 2015.
34,100 copies in print.

# Acknowledgements

As we became involved in the revision of our ESL Miscellany, we inevitably were reminded of the many people who contributed in one way or another since the very first edition in 1981. Our acknowledgement for all this help must be made in a very general way. However, we do want to express our thanks to a few people who have made a special contribution.

First and foremost of these has been the late **Richard Yorkey** of St. Michael's College in Vermont. Dick sent us many useful ideas and resources as we developed the first few editions. In constructing many of our word lists, we borrowed heavily from Dick's collection of lists.

At the very beginning of the first edition, we had considerable help from **Eleanor Boone, Rick Gildea, Mike Jerald,** and **Mary Clark.** We also had help from **Marilyn Funk** and **John Croes.** In the first edition, **Peg Clement** contributed her collection of American gestures, on which the selection in this book is based; for this most recent edition, we again thank **Mike Jerald** for his photography and **Adrienne Major, Liza Aldana, Veronica McKay,** and **Cole Madden** for their modeling.

**Susannah Clark** was our chief editorial assistant for the first edition, and **Mary Clark** suggested the title for the book. **Diane Larsen-Freeman** looked over the first rendition of the Linguistic Aspect. **Bonnie Mennell** and **Karen Kale** reviewed our list of communicative topics. **Anders Burrows** helped develop the topics on photography, cinema, and video and the media. **Thor Carlson** added to the topic on automobiles and compiled the list of computer acronyms. **Thomas Dunbar** up-dated our computer and internet information.

Now that our fifth edition is a reality, we invite you to contact us with your suggestions for the next edition.

*RCC, AAB, PRM*

## Pronouncement on Pronouns

In this book, we at Pro Lingua Associates are offering a solution to the vexing "he/she" pronoun problem. We have come to the conclusion that when a reference is made to third person singular, and that person is indefinite (and hence gender is unknown or unimportant), we will use the third person plural forms, they, them, their(s). We are fully aware that historically these forms represent grammatical plurality. However, there are clear instances in the English language where the third person plural form is used to refer to a preceding indefinite, grammatically singular pronoun. Examples:

Everyone says this, don't **they?**
Nobody agrees with us, but we will ignore **them.**

If you will accept the examples above, it is not a major step to find the following acceptable:

The user of this book should find this easier because **they** can avoid the confusion of *he* or *she*, the awkwardness of *he or she*, and the implicit sexism of using *he* for everybody.

So in this book, you will find statements such as, . . . *the teacher who is using this book to prepare **their** own lessons.* The reader of our text may disagree with our solution, but we ask them to consider that it is time to change the usage of gender-marked pronouns when they are clearly inappropriate. This is our solution, and we encourage you to try it out. And we invite your comments.

# Contents

*American carved duck decoy*

## Grammar

# THE COMMUNICATIVE ASPECT

Contents

*American Crazy Quilt*

# THE CULTURAL ASPECT

# THE METALINGUSITIC ASPECT AND MISCELLANEOUS MATERIALS

# THE PARALINGUISTIC ASPECT

# The ESL Miscellany

*Eagle totem pole in Vancouver, BC*

*American tinware pitcher and cup*

# Introduction

## *The Purpose and Contents of the Miscellany*

This book is a compendium of useful and interesting information for teachers and learners of English as a Second Language. Although the book focuses on North American English, it will also be useful to teachers and students of other varieties of English. Teachers will find this book useful as a resource for developing material as they supplement, expand, replace, adapt, or develop from scratch a complete curriculum. This one book does not contain everything that the teacher/materials developer needs to know, but we believe it is the most comprehensive one-volume reference available to the lesson writer.

In addition to its usefulness in developing materials, this book offers another function as a guideline/checklist for teachers who teach "a little of this and a little of that." The problem with this kind of eclecticism, of course, is that it is not always easy to know if everything is being covered. This book will not be able to tell teachers everything they need to know about North American English, but it can serve as a comprehensive outline. By consulting the list of Situations, for example, the teacher can rather quickly review which conversational situations have been covered and what remains to be covered.

A third use for this book is that many of the lists can be copied and used as hand-outs. For example, the summary of religions in the U.S. and Canada could be copied and given to the students as the point of reference for a question-answer practice or discussion of religion. For that reason we encourage copying of these lists for classroom use.

We suggested earlier that students of North American English will also find this book useful, but it is likely that it will be especially valuable to advanced students of North American English who are in need of a one-volume guide that will help them determine what they already know and what they should focus their study on. We think this book will be of particular interest to advanced students who are preparing to be teachers of English as a Second Language.

The **Miscellany** is divided into five parts. Parts I and II contain information about the language itself. This information is classified as two major aspects: Linguistic and Communicative. The linguistic aspect contains information that in some way deals with what is commonly called the phonology, lexicon, and grammar of the language. However, this linguistic aspect is not a grammar, but rather a series of lists of words and forms that exemplify some grammar point. For example, under Phrasal Verbs, there will be no rules for the use of these verbs.

1

Instead, there will be a list of separable and inseparable phrasal verbs. In other words, it is assumed that the user will have some understanding of how phrasal verbs function in English.

The communicative aspect does not deal with linguistic forms such as "go, went, gone" but outlines ways in which the language is used to send and receive messages. We have included lists of *functions* such as asking, introducing, telling, etc. Also in the communicative aspect section, we have included vocabulary lists that outline potential *topics* of conversations and *situations,* the contexts in which communicative functions and topics of conversation are carried out.

In Part III we have compiled several lists that form an outline of North American culture. Each list can be used as the basic data upon which can be based a discussion or controlled conversation about some facet of North American culture. Part III can be used as the basis for an orientation to immigration and resettlement in the United States and Canada.

Part IV is a pot-pourri of information that is, in general, metalinguistic. In other words, the information in this part will help the teacher and the learner facilitate the teaching/learning process. But there is also information that does not fit neatly into any of the other categories and is best labeled as miscellaneous.

Part V needs little explanation. It contains some examples of communicative systems that parallel the language itself. Hence, we have called it the paralinguistic aspect. Of greatest interest is a photographic catalog of 61 gestures that are commonly recognized and understood in North America. We have provided titles and minimal explanations for the gestures, but otherwise we leave it up to you, the user of this book, to discuss, compare, practice, and even add to this listing.

We will be the first to admit that this volume is far from complete. The information is such that it changes almost as fast as it is updated. As we prepare for the next edition, we welcome your comments and suggestions.

In preparing this fifth edition, some of the material from previous editions no longer seemed as relevant and appropriate as it once did. Since we have added new material, it seemed reasonable to drop some, too. However, we know that each topic we have dropped will be missed by some teachers who have found the material, for example, on nursery rhymes, contraception, human and animal body parts, curses, and vulgarities, useful in working with specific students. So that we don't disappoint these teachers, we are making this information available for free at our webstore, ProLinguaAssociates.com, linked to the *ESL Miscellany* announcement.

*PRO LINGUA ASSOCIATES*
*Brattleboro, 2015*

# The Interplay Lesson Plan

On the next page we offer a lesson plan that may be helpful to the teacher who is using material from this book to prepare their own lessons. For that matter, this lesson plan can be used for most teaching activities.

The plan is based on Pro Lingua's concept of **Interplay**: The **inter**action of the teacher and learner with the material, with the language and the culture, and with each other in active, creative, and productive **play**.

The basic format comprises three stages in the implementation of most lessons: **Before**, **During** and **After**. *Before* teaching, the typical lesson is based on the students (who), the context of the teaching (when and where), the objective of the lesson (why), and the lesson content (what). *During* is the time in which the teacher and the students are actively involved face-to-face in teaching and learning. *After* focuses on assessing the lesson and looking forward to review and future lessons.

A few brief definitions may be useful.

**Students**: Although it is usually unnecessary to state explicitly who the students are, it is, nevertheless, always useful to consider, as the lesson is planned, the age, proficiency level, and goals of the students.

**Context**: For purposes of maintaining a record of the lesson for future reference, it may be helpful to state the time and place of the teaching.

**Objective(s)**: In simple terms, the objective is a statement of *what the students should be able to do* as a result of the lesson. There may be more than one objective, but unless there is at least one objective for the lesson, it may lack focus, and the assessment of the objective may be difficult to carry out.

**Linguistic Content**: The lesson may or may not have a specific linguistic content, but if it does, it will be in the area of *pronunciation, vocabulary,* or *grammar.*

**Functional/Strategic Content**: This aspect of the content is concerned with communicative competence. Typically, functional content involves "-ing words," such as *asking, demanding, explaining,* and strategic skills, such as *rejoindering, interrupting, confirming,* and *clarifying.*

**Topical Content**: This involves the "message," especially the vocabulary associated with topics, such as *clothing, restaurants, business, sports,* and *music.*

**Cultural Content**: There may be a cultural content to the lesson. For example, *a holiday, a folktale, family structure,* and *rites of passage, from birth to death.*

**Presentation**: Typically, this part of the lesson is teacher-centered as the teacher *introduces the material* to the students. The presentation of the new material is often preceded by review of old material or schema-building in which the teacher sets the stage for the introduction of the new material.

**Practice**: Once the material is presented, the teacher and students engage in relatively *controlled interaction* with error correction so that the students will gain skill in using the new material.

**Production**: The final part of the lesson features the students *using* the material with each other to accomplish a communicative task. Typically, the teacher stands aside and observes and encourages the students as they become more fluent at manipulating the material in real or realistic communication.

**Assessment**: At the end of the lesson, or shortly thereafter, the teacher looks back at the objective *to measure* the success of the lesson. This can be done formally as a quiz or informally as monitoring the students and noting successes and errors.

**Assignment**: The teacher may ask the students to do *homework* that is based on the content of the lesson.

**Follow-up**: The teacher notes how and when the lesson content can or should be *reviewed or recycled* in future lessons.

*American gargoyle on Bradley Hall. Bradley University, Peoria, Illinois. 2011*

# *The Lesson Plan*

**Before**

    Students:

    Teaching/Learning Context:

    Objective:

    Content

        Linguistic:

        Functional/Strategic:

        Topical:

        Cultural:

**During**

    Presentation:

    Practice:

    Production:

**After**

    Assessment:

    Assignment:

    Follow-up:

*American tribal wolf tattoo*

# The Linguistic Aspect

**A Note on the Alphabet:**

There are 26 letters in the English alphabet. However, there are (depending on how you classify them) at least 38 distinct sounds in spoken English. Complicating the picture, some of the letters of the English alphabet are really not necessary, for example, the letters **c**, **q**, and **x**.

> **c** could be replaced by **s** or **k**: city = sity and cake = kake
> **q**, which is normally followed by **u**, could be replaced by **kw**: quit = kwit
> **x** could be **ks**: box = boks

But, of course, in standard English spelling, **c**, **q**, and **x** are used. Another complication is the use of consonant clusters, two or more letters that represent one blended sound, for example, **sp** and **ct** in *aspect*. See the chart of common consonant clusters on page 9.

**A Note on Phonetic Symbols:**

Some letters have to do double duty in standard English spelling. For example, in addition to the use of **c** and **h** as single consonants, the final consonant sound in the word "much" is a single sound spelled with two letters, **ch**. In many ESL texts, this sound is represented by ʧ or č. In this book, however, we will use CH simply because we do not want to use special phonetic symbols. We think our students have enough of a problem learning the 26 letters that they will see in their everyday lives. Therefore, on page 10, "Basic Sounds of English," we offer our phonetic spelling of English using the ordinary symbols of the alphabet. We use upper case in spelling these phonemes to make them distinct from the more commonly seen lower case. For your information, on page 267 in the Metalinguistic Aspect, we have included two other phonetic alphabets.

**A note on "A Grammar Sequence":**

There are 50 steps in the grammar sequence. There is much more to the grammar of English than the series of steps presented here. However, the learner who has encountered the grammatical features in these 50 steps will be well along toward a basic mastery of the grammar of English. The particular sequence presented here is, of course, only one possible sequence to be used as the basis for a grammatical syllabus. Nevertheless, it is our hope that our sequence will be a useful guide for what grammatical features are usually taught before others.

# 1: The Alphabet

A B C D E F G

H I J K L M N O P

Q R S T U V

W X Y Z

a b c d e f g

h i j k l m n o p

q r s t u v w x y z

*a b c d e f g*

*h i j k l m n o p*

*q r s t u v*

*w x y z*

*a b c d e f g*

*h i j k l m n o p*

*q r s t u v w x y z*

# 2: Common Consonant Clusters
## Standard English Spelling

**Initial Consonant Clusters (two or more sounds)**

| **bl** | **br** | **cl** | **cr** | **dr** | **dw** | **fl** | **fr** | **gl** | **gr** | **pl** | **pr** |
|--------|--------|--------|--------|--------|--------|--------|--------|--------|--------|--------|--------|
| **qu** | **sc** | **sch** | **scr** | **sk** | **sl** | **sm** | **sn** | **sp** | **spl** | **spr** | **st** |
| **str** | **sw** | **tr** | **tw** | | | | | | | | |

**Final Consonant Clusters (two sounds)**

| **bl** able | **ct** act | **ft** left | **ld** old | **lf** shelf | **lk** bulk |
|-------------|------------|-------------|------------|--------------|-------------|
| **lp** help | **lt** halt | **mp** lamp | **nc** since | **nch** lunch | **nd** hand |
| **ng** orange | **nk** ink | **nt** hunt | **rd** hard | **rg** large | **rk** park |
| **rl** girl | **rm** arm | **rn** corn | **rp** tarp | **rt** art | **sk** ask |
| **sp** clasp | **st** must | | | | |

**Consonant Digraphs (two or three letters representing one sound)**

| **ch** much | **ck** luck | **dg** edge | **gu** guard | **gh** ghost, laugh |
|-------------|-------------|-------------|--------------|---------------------|
| **gn** sign | **kn** knife | **lk** walk | **mb** thumb | **ng** sing |
| **ph** phone | **sh** shut | **tch** watch | **th** thigh, thy | |
| **ti** action | **wh** where, whose | | **wr** write | |

# 1: Basic Sounds of English (phonemes)

## *Vowels*

| Symbol | Example | Symbol | Example |
|--------|---------|--------|---------|
| EE | beet | AH | bot |
| I | bit | AY | bite |
| AI | bait | OU | bout |
| E | bet | OO | boot |
| A | bat | U | bull |
| Er | Burt | O | boat |
| UH | abut | OY | boy |
| uh | abut | AW | bawl |

## *Consonants*

| Symbol | Example | Symbol | Example |
|--------|---------|--------|---------|
| P | pin | B | bin |
| T | tin | D | din |
| K | kin | G | begin |
| F | fin | V | vim |
| th | thin | TH | this |
| S | sin | Z | zig |
| SH | shin | ZH | Asia |
| CH | chin | J | jin |
| M | mill | | |
| N | nil | | |
| NG | ring | | |
| L | lip | | |
| R | rip | | |
| W | will | | |
| Y | yip | | |
| H | hip | | |

NOTE: Pro Lingua's phonemic transcription system uses (mostly) uppercase letters to distinguish the representation of sound from the normal spelling.

Only familiar letters are used to avoid the non-alphabetic symbols such as ∫ (SH) and æ (A). Also see page 267 for a comparison with other systems.

# 2: Major Phoneme-Grapheme (sound-letter) Correspondences in English

## *Vowels*

| Symbol | Example | Symbol | Example |
|--------|---------|--------|---------|
| EE | beet, beat, he, here, please, either, brief, city, key | uh | abut, problem, capitol, question |
| I | bit | AH | botch, father |
| AI | bait, cake, day, great, eight | AY | by, bite, lie, high |
| E | bet | OO | boot, blue, new, rule |
| A | bat | U | book, bull, would |
| Er | her, fur, word, bird | O | boat, no, slow, hope |
| UH | but, son, double, love | OY | boy, oil |
|  |  | AW | bawl, ball, haul |

## *Consonants*

| | | | |
|--------|---------|--------|---------|
| P | pepper | B | bubble |
| T | tattle, talked | D | din, middle, lived |
| K | kin, can, black | G | begin, luggage |
| F | fin, phone | V | vim |
| th | thin | TH | this |
| S | sin, city, glass | Z | zig, has, jazz |
| SH | shin, action, sugar | ZH | Asia, azure |
| CH | chin, catch | J | jin, ridge, gin |

| | |
|---|---|
| M | mill, bummer, comb |
| N | nil, banner |
| NG | ring, think |
| L | lip, will |
| R | rip, arrive, write |
| W | will, quit |
| Y | yip, unit |
| H | hip, who |

# 3: Pronunciation of English Consonants

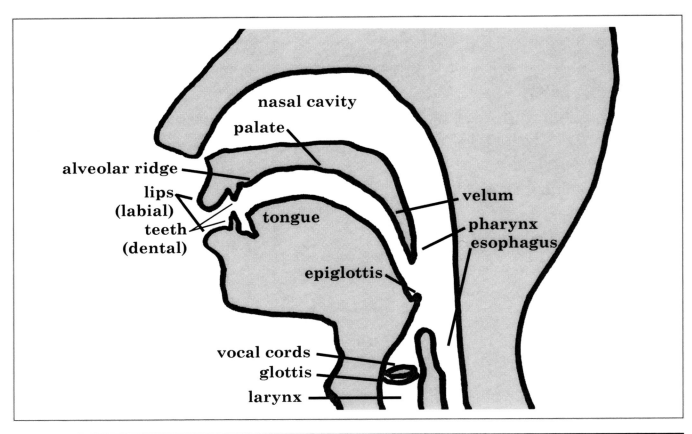

| Point of Articulation | labial | labial-dental | dental | alveolar | palatal | velar | glottal |
|---|---|---|---|---|---|---|---|
| stops  vl | P | | | T | | K | |
| vd | B | | | D | | G | |
| fricatives  vl | | F | th | S | SH | | H |
| vd | | V | TH | Z | ZH | | |
| affricatives  vl | | | | | CH | | |
| vd | | | | | J | | |
| nasals  vd | M | | | N | | NG | |
| liquids  vd | | | | L, R | | | |
| glides  vd | W | | | | Y | | |

# 4: Common Spellings of Vowel Sounds

## EE

beat
cheap
clean
cream
deal
dream
each
east
heal
heat
lead
leaf
lean
least
leave
meal
mean
meat
neat
reach
read
real
sea
seat
speak
steam
stream
tea
teach
weak

deed
deep
feed
feel
free
green
greet
keep
knee

meet
queen
see
seed
seem
sheep
sheet
sleep
speed
steel
steep
street
sweet
tree
weed
week

be
he
me
she
we

chief
field
piece
thief
yield

seize
cheese
these

## I

big
bill
bit
dig
dip
dish
ditch

fill
film
fish
fit
fix
gift
give
hill
him
his
hit
if
ill
in
inch
inn
it
kick
kill
kiss
lid
lift
lip
list
live
milk
mill
miss
mix
pick
pig
pin
print
quick
rich
ship
silk
since
sit

skill
spit
split
stick
still
strip
swim
thick
thin
this
trick
trip
win
wind
wish
with
wrist

## AI

age
base
cage
cake
cape
case
date
face
fade
flame
grave
hate
lake
late
make
male
name
pale
paste
plate

race
rage
rake
safe
sale
same
scale
shade
shake
shame
shape
snake
space
stage
state
strange
take
tame
taste
trade
wage
wake
wave

aid
claim
fail
faint
faith
gain
mail
nail
paid
pain
paint
plain
rail
rain
raise
sail

stain
tail

bay
clay
day
gray
hay
lay
may
pay
pray
ray
say
stay
tray
way

they
weigh

## E

bed
beg
bell
belt
bend
best
cent
check
chest
debt
desk
dress
egg
end
fresh
get
help

left
leg
lend
less
let
melt
mend
neck
net
next
pen
pet
press
red
rent
rest
self
sell
send
sense
set
shelf
smell
spell
spend
swell
tell
tent
test
them
then
well
west
wet
when
yes
yet

bread
breath

13

dead
deaf
death
head
health
sweat
wealth

edge
else
friend

**A**

act
add
am
as
ask
at
bck
bad
bag
band
bank
bath
black
camp
cat
catch
chance
class
crack
crash
damp
dance
drag
fact
fan
fast
fat
flag
flat
gap

gas
glad
glass
grand
grass
half
hang
hat
have
lack
lamp
land
last
mad
map
mass
mat
pack
pad
pan
pass
past
path
sad
sand
staff
stamp
stand
tap
tax
thank
that
trap
wrap

**UH**

brush
bunch
bus
but
club
cup
cut

drum
duck
dull
dust
fun
gun
hunt
hut
judge
jump
just
luck
lump
lunch
lung
much
mud
must
nut
pump
rub
rug
run
rush
rust
shut
such
suck
sun
thumb
thus
trunk
trust
up

from
front
love
month
none
of
once
some
son
ton

rough
touch
tough
young

blood
flood

**U**

book
brook
cook
crook
foot
good
hook
look
shook
took
wood
wool

bush
full
pull
push
put

could
should
would

**OO**

boot
broom
cool
food
fool
hoop
loop
mood
moon

noon
pool
roof
room
shoot
smooth
soon
spoon
too
tool
tooth

choose
loose
lose
move
prove
shoe

blew
crew
few
new
screw
stew
threw

rude
rule
tube
tune
use

group
soup
through
wound
youth

fruit
juice
suit

due
true
truth

do
to
who

view

**OW**

bone
close
hole
home
hope
joke
nose
note
owe
rope
stone
stove
vote
whole

bold
both
clothes
cold
comb
fold
gold
hold
host
most
old
post
roll

boat
coal
coast
coat
float
goat
load
loan

road
roast
soap
throat

blow
bow
bowl
flow
grow
know
own
row
show
slow
snow
throw

go
no
so

though
toe

**OY**

boil
boy
coin
join
joint
joy
noise
oil
point
soil
spoil
toy
voice

## AW

all
ball
call
chalk
fall
false
hall
salt
small
talk
tall

cloth
cost
cross
dog
long
loss
off
soft
strong
wrong

draw
law
paw
raw
saw
straw

cause
fault
pause
sauce

cough
ought
thought

broad

## OU

cloud
count
doubt
ground
hour
house
loud
mouse
mouth
noun
ounce
our
out
proud
round
shout
sound
sour
south

bow
brown
cow
crowd
down
drown
how
now
town

## AH

block
box
clock
dot
drop
lock
lot
not
on
pot
rock

shop
spot
top

## AY

bite
crime
die
dine
dive
drive
fine
fire
hide
ice
knife
life
like
line
live
mine
nice
pile
pipe
price
pride
rice
ride
ripe
shine
side
size
slide
smile
strike
tide
time
tribe
while
white
wide
wife
wine

wipe
wise
write

bind
blind
bright
child
fight
find
high
kind
light
mild
mind
night
right
sight
sign
tight
wild

by
cry
dry
fly
fry
my
sky
try
type
why

buy
die
lie
tie
eye
I

## AHr

arm
art
bar

car
card
charge
dark
far
farm
hard
harm
march
mark
park
part
sharp
star
start
yard

heart
guard

## AIr

air
chair
fair
hair
pair
stairs

bare
care
dare
rare
share

bear
swear
tear
wear

their
there
where

## EEr

beard
clear
dear
ear
fear
hear
near
tear
year

cheer
steer
fierce
here

## Er

bird
birth
dirt
firm
first
girl
shirt
sir
skirt
stir
thirst

burn
church
curve
fur
hurt
nurse
turn
urge

word
work
world
worm
worse
worth

earn
earth
learn
search

her
serve
term
verb

## Or

born
cork
corn
for
fork
form
lord
nor
north
or
sort
storm

force
horse
more
shore
sore
store

course
court
pour

board
oar
roar

war
warm
warn

door
floor

# 5: Basic Lexical Stress Patterns

/ —

| | | | | | |
|---|---|---|---|---|---|
| able | double | heavy | morning | pretty | stranger |
| agent | early | honest | mountain | prison | subject |
| always | effort | hurry | music | profit | summer |
| answer | either | keyboard | nation | promise | supper |
| beauty | empty | lady | neighbor | question | system |
| better | enter | landlord | never | rapid | table |
| brother | equal | language | noisy | rather | teacher |
| busy | ever | lawyer | nothing | ready | ticket |
| careful | father | leader | number | river | travel |
| carry | favor | lesson | office | rubber | under |
| center | fellow | listen | often | ruler | useful |
| circle | finger | market | owner | safety | valley |
| college | flower | matter | paper | science | village |
| corner | follow | measure | parent | second | visit |
| danger | foreign | member | pencil | sister | window |
| daughter | freedom | middle | person | sleepy | woman |
| distance | garden | mixer | poison | speaker | yellow |
| dollar | happy | monster | practice | stomach | zero |

— /

| | | | | | |
|---|---|---|---|---|---|
| about | arrive | contain | hotel | prepare | review |
| above | attend | control | improve | pretend | succeed |
| accept | because | decide | include | produce | success |
| account | become | degree | inform | pronounce | suggest |
| across | before | delay | instead | protect | supply |
| admit | begin | depend | intend | receive | surround |
| adopt | behind | describe | machine | refer | today |
| afraid | believe | destroy | mistake | refuse | tonight |
| again | belong | direct | observe | regret | unite |
| ago | below | discuss | omit | remain | unless |
| agree | beside | disease | oppose | remind | until |
| allow | between | employ | perform | reply | without |
| alone | beyond | event | perhaps | report | |
| along | collect | exact | police | respect | |
| among | complete | except | polite | result | |
| around | connect | explain | prefer | return | |

## — / —

| | | | | | |
|---|---|---|---|---|---|
| acceptance | apartment | companion | description | imagine | religion |
| admission | appearance | condition | destruction | important | remember |
| advantage | appointment | consider | develop | invention | reporter |
| adventure | approval | container | dictation | mechanic | solution |
| advisor | arrival | December | diploma | musician | successful |
| agreement | attendance | decision | effective | opinion | suggestion |
| already | attractive | delighted | election | perfection | together |
| ambition | banana | deliver | exactly | performance | tomorrow |
| amusement | collection | department | familiar | possession | umbrella |
| another | commuter | departure | idea | relation | whoever |

## / — —

| | | | | | |
|---|---|---|---|---|---|
| animal | curious | generous | mystery | possible | satisfy |
| article | difficult | gentleman | nowadays | prejudice | substitute |
| beautiful | document | government | numeral | president | sympathy |
| capital | embassy | grandfather/ | opposite | probable | tendency |
| century | enemy | mother | origin | property | valuable |
| certainly | energy | industry | passenger | quality | various |
| character | excellent | institute | personal | quantity | visitor |
| citizen | exercise | interview | politics | radio | wonderful |
| company | frequently | liberty | poverty | recently | yesterday |
| criminal | funeral | medicine | powerful | relative | |

## \ — / —

| | | | | |
|---|---|---|---|---|
| accidental | cancellation | democratic | independent | population |
| accusation | combination | energetic | interruption | reproduction |
| advertisement | competition | explanation | observation | recognition |
| admiration | conscientious | exploration | occupation | sympathetic |
| application | correspondence | horizontal | operation | systematic |
| calculation | declaration | imitation | politician | substitution |

# 6: Noun-Verb Stress Patterns

| *Noun* | *Verb* |
|--------|--------|
| / — | — / |
| address | address |
| annex | annex |
| conduct | conduct |
| conflict | conflict |
| contract | contract |
| contrast | contrast |
| convert | convert |
| decrease | decrease |
| defect | defect |
| extract | extract |
| object | object |
| increase | increase |
| insult | insult |
| intrigue | intrigue |
| permit | permit |
| produce | produce |
| progress | progress |
| project | project |
| protest | protest |
| rebel | rebel |
| record | record |
| reject | reject |
| subject | subject |
| suspect | suspect |

# 7: Pronunciation of -s Suffix

| _Voiceless /S/_ | _Voiced /Z/_ | _Voiced /ɪZ/_ |
|---|---|---|

## Nouns

| | | |
|---|---|---|
| banks | brothers | bridges |
| books | cars | buses |
| cents | days | classes |
| clocks | dollars | colleges |
| exits | doors | garages |
| minutes | friends | glasses |
| mistakes | girls | houses |
| months | homes | inches |
| nights | hotels | languages |
| parents | lessons | lunches |
| pints | mornings | offices |
| quarts | planes | ounces |
| seats | problems | packages |
| shops | roads | pages |
| stamps | rooms | pieces |
| streets | schools | places |
| tickets | taxis | prices |
| weeks | words | sentences |

## Verbs

| | | |
|---|---|---|
| asks | buys | catches |
| drinks | gives | changes |
| gets | goes | closes |
| helps | knows | finishes |
| likes | leaves | fixes |
| makes | listens | freezes |
| puts | lives | guesses |
| sits | needs | kisses |
| sleeps | opens | loses |
| speaks | pulls | notices |
| stops | reads | practices |
| takes | returns | pronounces |
| talks | says | pushes |
| thanks | sees | reaches |
| thinks | spells | realizes |
| waits | studies | uses |
| walks | turns | watches |
| wants | understands | wishes |

# 8: Pronunciation of -ed Suffix

| _Voiceless /T/_ | _Voiced /D/_ | _Voiced /ID/_ |
|---|---|---|
| asked | answered | accepted |
| checked | believed | assisted |
| discussed | called | corrected |
| dropped | changed | counted |
| finished | cleaned | decided |
| helped | closed | departed |
| hoped | enjoyed | divided |
| introduced | explained | doubted |
| jumped | filled | ended |
| liked | learned | expected |
| looked | listened | folded |
| missed | lived | handed |
| picked | loved | hated |
| placed | moved | included |
| practiced | played | invited |
| pushed | pulled | needed |
| shopped | returned | noticed |
| stopped | showed | pointed |
| talked | spelled | repeated |
| thanked | studied | started |
| walked | tried | visited |
| washed | turned | waited |
| watched | used | wanted |

All words have been selected from Pro Lingua's _Learner's Lexicon_, 1200-word level.

# 9: Basic Intonation Patterns

1. I bought a new com|pu|ter. — Statement (final word is multisyllabic)

2. Did you get it at|Office Shop? — Yes/No question

3. I bought it at|Brown's. — Statement (final word is one syllable)

4. When did you|buy|it? — WH question

5. You like to shop there,|don't|you? — Tag question expecting agreement

6. So, you got another HT,|didn't you? — Tag question for information or clarification

7. Don't you like the new Bells? — Negative question expressing surprise

8. I looked at a|Bell,|an HT,|and a|Trac. — Series

9. So, did you get an H|T|or a|Trac? — Alternative

10. I bought a|used|HT. — Focused information

11. If I have enough|money,|I'll get a|printer. — Continuation of a phrase or clause. (Here, in the 'result' clause.)

# 10: Minimal Pairs

## Vowels

**/EE/**    **/I /**

| sheep | ship |
|-------|------|
| leave | live |
| seat  | sit  |
| green | grin |

**/EE/**    **/AI/**

| eat   | ate   |
|-------|-------|
| see   | say   |
| week  | wake  |
| creep | crepe |

**/EE/**    **/E/**

| meet  | met  |
|-------|------|
| mean  | men  |
| seeks | sex  |
| beast | best |

**/I/**    **/AI /**

| it   | ate   |
|------|-------|
| kick | cake  |
| chin | chain |
| give | gave  |

**/I/**    **/E/**

| pick | peck |
|------|------|
| did  | dead |
| sit  | set  |
| knit | net  |

**/I/**    **/A/**

| big | bag |
|-----|-----|
| it  | at  |
| sit | sat |
| zig | zag |

**/I /**    **/UH/**

| big  | bug  |
|------|------|
| live | love |
| sick | suck |
| rib  | rub  |

**/AI/**    **/E/**

| wait | wet  |
|------|------|
| date | debt |
| pain | pen  |
| raid | red  |

**/AI/**    **/A/**

| snake | snack |
|-------|-------|
| ate   | at    |
| made  | mad   |
| hate  | hat   |

**/AI /**    **/UH /**

| ape  | up   |
|------|------|
| lake | luck |
| rain | run  |
| came | come |

**/AI /**    **/O/**

| taste | toast |
|-------|-------|
| say   | so    |
| break | broke |
| wake  | woke  |

**/E/**    **/A/**

| dead | dad |
|------|-----|
| said | sad |
| men  | man |
| bed  | bad |

**/E/**    **/UH /**

| beg  | bug   |
|------|-------|
| ten  | ton   |
| many | money |
| net  | nut   |

**/E/**    **/AH/**

| get  | got  |
|------|------|
| step | stop |
| red  | rod  |
| net  | not  |

**/A/**    **/UH/**

| grab | grub |
|------|------|
| swam | swum |
| mad  | mud  |
| cap  | cup  |

## Vowels (Continued)

| /A/ | /AH/ |
|-----|------|
| an | on |
| map | mop |
| cat | cot |
| lack | lock |

| /A/ | /AY/ |
|-----|------|
| am | I'm |
| sad | side |
| dad | died |
| back | bike |

| /UH/ | /AH/ |
|------|------|
| hug | hog |
| cup | cop |
| luck | lock |
| nut | not |

| /UH/ | /U/ |
|------|-----|
| luck | look |
| buck | book |
| stud | stood |
| tuck | took |

| /UH/ | /O/ |
|------|-----|
| cut | coat |
| must | most |
| come | comb |
| but | boat |

| /UH/ | /AW/ |
|------|------|
| gun | gone |
| cut | caught |
| bus | boss |
| dug | dog |

| /AH/ | /U/ |
|------|-----|
| lock | look |
| pot | put |
| cod | could |
| shock | shook |

| /AH/ | /O/ |
|------|-----|
| hop | hope |
| got | goat |
| want | won't |
| rod | road |

| /AH/ | /AW/ |
|------|------|
| cot | caught |
| sod | sawed |
| pa | paw |
| tock | talk |

| /AH/ | /OU/ |
|------|------|
| are | hour |
| shot | shout |
| dot | doubt |
| got | gout |

| /AW/ | /OY/ |
|------|------|
| all | oil |
| jaw | joy |
| ball | boil |
| bald | boiled |

| /U/ | /OO/ |
|-----|------|
| full | fool |
| pull | pool |
| soot | suit |
| could | cooed |

| /U/ | /O/ |
|-----|-----|
| bull | bowl |
| cook | coke |
| should | showed |
| brook | broke |

| /O/ | /OY/ |
|-----|------|
| toe | toy |
| old | oiled |
| bold | boiled |
| cone | coin |

| /OU/ | /AY/ |
|------|------|
| mouse | mice |
| tower | tire |
| proud | pride |
| found | find |

| /OU/ | /OY/ |
|------|------|
| owl | oil |
| vowed | void |
| sow | soy |
| bough | boy |

| /OY/ | /AY/ |
|------|------|
| toy | tie |
| boy | buy |
| voice | vice |
| alloy | ally |

## Consonants

**/P/**      **/B/**

| | |
|---|---|
| pig | big |
| cap | cab |
| pie | buy |
| rapid | rabid |

**/B/**      **/V/**

| | |
|---|---|
| boat | vote |
| best | vest |
| curb | curve |
| cupboard | covered |

**/L/**      **/R/**

| | |
|---|---|
| light | right |
| bowl | boar |
| collect | correct |
| lead | read |

**/CH/**      **/SH/**

| | |
|---|---|
| cheap | sheep |
| catch | cash |
| watch | wash |
| cheese | she's |

**/J/**      **/SH/**

| | |
|---|---|
| jeep | sheep |
| jade | shade |
| jack | shack |
| gyp | ship |

**/J/**      **/CH/**

| | |
|---|---|
| gin | chin |
| joke | choke |
| jeer | cheer |
| junk | chunk |

**/J/**      **/Y/**

| | |
|---|---|
| juice | use |
| jet | yet |
| jam | yam |
| wage | weigh |

**/G/**      **/K/**

| | |
|---|---|
| bag | back |
| grape | crepe |
| glass | class |
| gap | cap |

**/th/**      **/T/**

| | |
|---|---|
| death | debt |
| thigh | tie |
| thin | tin |
| three | tree |

**/th/**      **/S/**

| | |
|---|---|
| think | sink |
| thing | sing |
| mouth | mouse |
| thin | sin |

**/TH/**      **/D/**

| | |
|---|---|
| they | day |
| lather | ladder |
| their | dare |
| breathe | breed |

**/F/**      **/V/**

| | |
|---|---|
| fine | vine |
| fail | veil |
| life | live |
| safe | save |

**/V/**      **/W/**

| | |
|---|---|
| vine | wine |
| veered | weird |
| veal | we'll |
| over | ower |

# 11: Pronunciation Problem Areas
## for Selected Learners

VOWELS. Virtually all learners will have difficulty distinguishing the /I/EE/ and the /E/A/ vowel contrasts. Many will also have difficulty with the lower vowels: /A/AH/UH/AW/, and the back vowels /U/OO/. Other vowel problem areas are noted in the list below.

CONSONANTS. Very few languages use /th ~ **TH**/, therefore these sounds are troublesome for all. Otherwise, language-specific consonant problems are listed below.

| | | | | | |
|---|---|---|---|---|---|
| Arabic: | E/I | P/B | F/V | | |
| Chinese: | A/E | L/N | L/W | R/W/L | W/V |
| Czech: | A/E | th/T | D/TH | | |
| Farsi: | W/V | R | | | |
| French: | CH/J | R | H | | |
| German: | O | W/V | R | | |
| Greek: | S/SH | S/Z | R | H | |
| Hindi: | A/E | F/P | V/B | W/V | |
| Italian: | H | R | | | |
| Japanese: | S/SH | T/CH | V/B | L/R | |
| Korean: | P/F | B/V | S/SH | L/R | |
| Polish: | W/V | L/W | R | NG | |
| Portuguese: | SH/CH | J/ZH | S/SH | L/W | |
| Russian: | A/E | ER | W | NG | |
| Serbo-Croation: | | A/E | W/V | | |
| Spanish: | B/V | CH/SH | J/Y | S/Z | R |
| Thai: | I/E | AI/E | P/F | W/V | SH/CH L/R |
| Turkish: | A/E | V/W | | | |
| Vietnamese: | A/E | P/F/B | | | |

# 1: Affix Chart

| Prefixes | | Function/ Meaning |
|---|---|---|
| un-    non- in- anti-   mal- a-      mis- dis- | | Negative |
| uni-    multi- mono-  semi- bi-      poly- tri-     equi- pan- | | Quantity |
| en-     be- | | Verb |
| pre-    intra- post-   extra- inter- | | Position |
| super- sub- sur- epi-     hypo- hyper- para- | | Relationship |
| ex-     ab- in-      trans- ad-     pro- de-     se- re- | | Movement |
| syn-    contra- co- | | With or Against |

| Suffixes | | Function/ Meaning |
|---|---|---|
| -er -ist    -ant -ian    -ary | | "Doer" Noun |
| -en     -ate -ify     -ize | | Verb |
| -ance  -ship -ity     -ness -hood -ion     -age -ment   -dom -ism | | Noun |
| -able    -al -less    -en -ful     -ous -y        -ary -ish     -ive -ic | | Adjective |
| -ly       -wise -ward | | Adverb |

# 2: Common Affixes
## PREFIXES

| Prefix | Meaning | Example |
|---|---|---|
| a-, an- | not | amoral, atypical, amorphous |
| ab- | away from | abnormal, abrupt, abstain |
| ad- | toward, to | administer, adhere, adapt |
| ante- | before, in front of | anteroom, antecedent, antedate |
| anti- | against, opposite | antidote, antipathy, antiseptic |
| arch- | chief, prime | archbishop, archangel, archenemy |
| auto- | self | automatic, automobile |
| be- | to cause, intensely | belittle, befriend, beware, bedecked, befuddled |
| bene- | well | benefactor, benefit, benevolent |
| bi- | two | bisect, bifocal, bigamy |
| circum- | around, on all sides | circumscribe, circumnavigate, circumvent |
| con- | with | conversation, confound, convoy |
| col- | with | collage, collateral, collapse |
| cor- | with | correlate, correspond, correct |
| co- | with | co-worker, co-exist, co-author |
| contra- | against, opposite | contradict, contraband, contravene |
| counter- | against, opposite | counteract, counterbalance, countermand |
| de- | not, away from, down from | descend, deflate, deviate |
| di- | apart, away, not | diverge, diminish, dilute, divorce |
| di- | twice, two-fold, double | dichotomy, digraph, dilemma |
| dia- | through, completely | diameter, diaper, diaphanous, diaspora |
| dif- | apart, away, not | diffuse, differ, difficult |
| dis- | apart, away, not | distrust, disinterested, disorder |
| en- | make, create | engage, enact, entrust |
| epi- | above, around, additional | epicenter, epidemic, epidermis |
| equi- | equal | equivalent, equinox, equilibrium |
| ex-, e- | out from, former | exit, excavate, ex-governor, egress, exhale |
| extra- | outside, beyond | extraordinary, extrasensory, extravagant |
| hetero- | different | heterogeneous, heterosexual |
| homo- | same | homogeneous, homosexual |
| hyper- | extremely | hyperactive, hyperventilate, hyperbole |
| hypo- | below, beneath | hypodermic, hypocrisy, hypotenuse |
| in- | into, not | inhale, inept, innocent |
| im- | into, not | impel, imbalance, immoral |
| il- | into, not | illuminate, illiterate, illegal, illegible |
| ir- | into, not | irradiate, irregular, irresponsible, irresolute |
| inter- | between, at intervals | intersperse, intermittent, intervene |
| intra- | within | intracellular, intramural |
| intro- | motion inward | introduce, introspective, introvert |
| macro | large | macrocosm, macrobiotics, macro-organism |
| mal- | ill, badly, bad, wrong | malfunction, malnutrition, malevolent |
| mega- | big | megaphone, megaton, megalopolis, megabyte |
| micro- | small | microscope, microphone, micro-organism |
| mini- | small, little | minivan, miniskirt, minimal |
| mis- | wrong, wrongly, not | misunderstanding, misuse, mistrust |

| Prefix | Meaning | Example |
|---|---|---|
| mono- | single, one | monophonic, monologue, monomania |
| multi- | many | multisided, multiplex, multivitamin |
| neo- | new | neophyte, neoclassical, neonatal |
| non- | not | nonexistent, nonpayment, nonconformist |
| ob- | against | obstinate, obscure, object |
| pan- | all, whole, completely | Pan African, panorama, pandemic |
| para- | beyond, outside, near | parabola, paramilitary, paradox, paramedic |
| pen- | almost | peninsula, penultimate |
| per- | motion through, thoroughly | percolate, perfect, perceive |
| peri- | around, about, enclosing | perimeter, periscope, periphery |
| poly- | many | polygamy, polyglot, polychrome |
| post- | behind, after | posterity, posthumous, postscript |
| pre- | before, earlier, in front of | preconceived, premonition, predict |
| pro- | forward, before, in favor of | propulsion, prologue, project |
| proto- | earliest, first, original | prototype, proto-American, protocol |
| re- | back, again | reappear, recapture, reclaim, return |
| retro- | backwards | retrospect, retroactive, retroflex |
| se- | aside, apart | seclusion, secede, seduce |
| semi- | half, partly | semiannual, semicircle, semiprecious |
| sub- | under, below | subway, submarine, subnormal, submerge |
| super- | over, above, extra | superimpose, supernatural, superfluous |
| sur- | above, additional | survey, surtax, surface |
| syn-, sym- | together | synchronize, synthesis, sympathy |
| tele- | distant | telegraph, telepathy, television |
| trans- | across, over, through, beyond | transition, transcend, transgress |
| tri- | three | trimester, trilateral, trillion |
| ultra- | beyond, excessively | ultraliberal, ultramodern, ultraviolet |
| un- | not | unimportant, unflattering, unattractive |
| uni- | one | uniform, unicameral, unique |
| vice- | one who takes the place of another | vice-president, viceroy, vice-consul |

## NOUN SUFFIXES

| Suffix | Meaning | Example |
|---|---|---|
| -ance, -ence | act of | attendance, precedence, reliance |
| -ancy, -ency | state of | hesitancy, presidency, consistency |
| -age | action, condition, collection | message, bondage, marriage, postage, baggage |
| -ant, -ent | one who, that which | stimulant, participant, student, president |
| -ar | one who | bursar, liar, beggar |
| -ary, -ory, -ery, -ry | one who, place where, study of | secretary, library, history, conservatory, winery, bakery, chemistry |
| -dom | domain, condition of | freedom, wisdom, kingdom |
| -ee | one who is | employee, refugee, absentee |
| -eer | one who | profiteer, racketeer, pamphleteer |
| -er | one who | painter, receiver, baker |
| -ess | one who (female) | actress, poetess, lioness |
| -hood | state of | boyhood, falsehood, manhood |
| -ian | one who | beautician, musician, librarian |

| Suffix | Meaning | Example |
|---|---|---|
| -ics | science, art, or practice of | graphics, mathematics, athletics, dramatics |
| -ion, -ation, -sion, -tion | state, action, institution | fixation, exploration, starvation, foundation, organization, preservation, suspension, competition |
| -ism | doctrine, point of view | mannerism, idealism, realism |
| -ist | one who, believer | segregationist, realist, cyclist |
| -ity | state, quality | sanity, rapidity, elasticity |
| -ment | state, quality, act of | amazement, payment, embodiment |
| -ness | state of | fullness, shyness, sickness |
| -ocracy | system, style of government | democracy, autocracy, plutocracy |
| -or | one who | actor, governor, inspector |
| -ship | state, condition | friendship, dictatorship, membership |

## ADJECTIVE SUFFIXES

| Suffix | Meaning | Example |
|---|---|---|
| -able, -ible | capable of | capable, edible, visible |
| -al | like, pertaining to | criminal, practical, musical |
| -ary, -ory | connected with, engaged in | ordinary, budgetary, compensatory |
| -ed | covered with, affected by | wooded, clothed, blessed |
| -en | made of, resembling | wooden, ashen, silken |
| -ful | full of, having | useful, hopeful, successful |
| -ic | like, pertaining to | democratic, heroic, specific |
| -ish | like, pertaining to | foolish, childish, selfish |
| -ive | like, pertaining to | active, explosive, sensitive |
| -less | without | speechless, childless, harmless |
| -like | having the qualities of | childlike, cowlike, statesmanlike |
| -ly | having the qualities of | beastly, manly, worldly |
| -oid | like, resembling | spheroid, humanoid, paranoid |
| -ous | like, pertaining to | courageous, ambitious, grievous |
| -ward | manner, position | awkward, backward, forward |

## ADVERB SUFFIXES

| Suffix | Meaning | Example |
|---|---|---|
| -ly | in a _ manner | happily, strangely, comically |
| -ward(s) | direction of movement | backward(s), earthward, homeward |
| -wise | in the manner of, as far as _ is concerned | crabwise, clockwise, corkscrew-wise, education-wise, weather-wise |

## VERB SUFFIXES

| Suffix | Meaning | Example |
|---|---|---|
| -ate | to cause, to make | placate, indicate, irritate |
| -en | to become, to make | deafen, ripen, widen |
| -ify | to cause, to make | beautify, diversify, simplify |
| -ize | to cause, to make | symbolize, hospitalize, publicize |

# 3: Common Roots

| Root | Meaning | Example |
|------|---------|---------|
| agr | field, farm | agriculture, agronomy |
| anthro | man | anthropoid, misanthrope |
| aqua | water | aquatic, aqueduct |
| astro | star | astrology, astronaut |
| aud | hear | auditorium, audience |
| | | |
| biblio | book | bibliography, bibliophile |
| bio | life | biology, biography |
| | | |
| celer | speed, hasten | accelerate, celerity |
| chronos | time | chronicle, chronology |
| cap, capt, cip | take | capture, reciprocate |
| cep, cept, ceive | take | reception, conceive |
| ced, cess, cede | go, move along | success, proceed |
| | | |
| cid | kill | suicide, genocide |
| clud, clus | close, shut | seclusion, include |
| cosmo | world | cosmopolitan, cosmonaut |
| crat | power | democrat, autocrat |
| cred | believe, trust | credit, incredulous |
| cur, curr | run | incur, current |
| demo | people | democrat, demography |
| dict | say | diction, contradict |
| duc, duct | lead | induce, abduct, educate |
| | | |
| fac, fact | make, do | manufacture, factory |
| fec, fect | make, do | infect, effect |
| fer | carry, bear | infer, conference |
| fic, fict | make, do | efficacious, fiction |
| flect | bend | inflection, deflect |
| frater | brother | fraternal, fratricide |
| fund, fus | pour | refund, effusive |
| | | |
| gen, gener | birth, race | generation, regenerate |
| geo | earth | geology, geography |
| glot | tongue | polyglot, glottal |
| gram | written | telegram, grammar |
| graph | write | autograph, biography |
| gress, grad | go, step | progress, gradual |
| | | |
| hydr | water | dehydrate, hydrant |
| | | |
| ject, jact | throw | project, rejection |
| jud | judgement | judicial, judicious |
| | | |
| lect, leg | read, choose | collect, legend, elect |
| logo, log, logy | study, word | anthropology, chronology, analog |
| loq, loc | speak | eloquent, locution |

| Root | Meaning | Example |
|------|---------|---------|
| manu, mani | hand | manuscript, manicure |
| mar | sea | maritime, submarine |
| mater | mother | maternal, matriarch |
| med | middle | intermediary, medium |
| min | smaller, less | diminish, minute |
| mit, mis | send, let go | transmit, missile, missionary |
| mort | death | mortician, mortal |
| mot, mob, mo | move, start | motion, motivate |
| | | |
| naut | sailor | astronaut, nautical |
| necro | death | necromancer, necropolis |
| neuro | nerve | neurology, neurotic |
| nom | name | nomenclature, nominal |
| nom | knowledge, law | autonomy, astronomy |
| | | |
| pater | father | paternal, patriotic |
| path | suffering, ill | pathetic, pathology |
| ped, pod | foot | pedal, tripod |
| pend | hang, weigh | depend, ponderous, pending |
| phil | love | philosophy, philanthropist |
| phob | fear | hydrophobia, phobia |
| phon | sound, voice | phonology, telephone |
| photo | light | photography, photosynthesis |
| plex, pli, ply | fold | complexity, pliant, plywood |
| plic | fold | complicate, duplicate, implicate |
| poli | city | cosmopolitan, politician |
| port | carry | portable, import |
| pos, pon | place, put | postpone, position |
| psych | of the mind | psychic, psychology |
| | | |
| reg, rect | rule, manage | direct, regulate |
| rupt | break | rupture, disrupt |
| | | |
| scop | watch/look at | microscopic, telescope |
| scrib, scrip | write | inscribe, conscription |
| soph | wise | sophisticated, philosophy |
| spec, spic | see, watch | inspect, despicable |
| sta, stat | stand | stable, station |
| stit, sist | to set up, establish | constitution, insist |
| | | |
| tact, tang | touch | tactile, tangible |
| ten, tain, tin | hold, keep | contain, tenacious |
| tend, tens, tent | stretch, weaken | extend, tenuous |
| typ | image | typical, typewriter |
| | | |
| vacu | empty | vacuum, evacuate |
| ven | love | venerate, venereal |
| ven | come | prevent, convene, intervene |
| voca | call | vocal, invocation |
| vor | eat, devour | voracious, carnivorous |

# 4: Common Suffixed Words

## Noun

action
completion
condition
connection
decision
definition
description
direction
discussion
division
introduction
permission
prediction
preposition
production
question
station
television
translation

conversation
demonstration
examination
explanation
identification
invitation
location
occupation
preparation
pronounciation
reservation
taxation

brother
computer
container
doctor
employer
eraser
father
mother
lawyer
leader
marker
neighbor
owner
refrigerator
robber
ruler
sister
stranger
sweater
teacher
typewriter
waiter
worker

musician
patient
president
artist
dentist
dictionary
vocabulary
discovery
laundry

absence
acceptance
assistance
difference
distance
entrance
license
patience
preference

agency
emergency

departure
failure
furniture
measure
mixture
picture
signature
temperature

advertisement
agreement
apartment
argument
assignment
employment
government
requirement

baggage
college
garage
marriage
package

approval
arrival
criminal
decimal
terminal

ability
activity
electricity
reality
relationship
freedom
business

## Verb

advertise
memorize
realize
identify
frighten
demonstrate
translate

## Adjective

busy
chilly
cloudy
dirty
easy
empty
foggy
healthy
heavy
hungry
icy
muddy
noisy
oily
rainy
shiny
stormy
tasty
thirsty
windy

awful
beautiful
careful
successful
wonderful

nervous
various
careless
considerable
enjoyable
possible
probable
artistic
electric
public
expensive
conditional
national
natural

## Adverb

actually
awfully
certainly
closely
fairly
finally
partly
probably
quickly
quietly
really
simply
slowly
specially
successfully
suddenly
usually

Words are taken from Pro Lingua's *Learner's Lexicon,* 1200-word level.

# 5: Irregular Noun Plurals

## A. Vowel change

man > men
woman > women

foot > feet
tooth > teeth

goose > geese
mouse > mice

## B. *-en* Suffix

child > children

ox > oxen

brother > brethren

## C. f > v

thief > thieves
wife > wives
life > lives
knife > knives
calf > calves

half > halves
hoof > hooves
leaf > leaves
loaf > loaves
self > selves

sheaf > sheaves
shelf > shelves
wolf > wolves

## D. Same

sheep > sheep
deer > deer
moose > moose
fish > fish
trout > trout

salmon > salmon
bass > bass
series > series
means > means
species > species

Chinese > Chinese
Japanese > Japanese
Swiss > Swiss

## E. No singular

scissors
tweezers
tongs
trousers
slacks

shorts
pants
pajamas
(eye) glasses
spectacles

binoculars
clothes
people

## F. Borrowed Greek and Latin words

analysis > analyses
basis > bases
hypothesis > hypotheses
parenthesis > parentheses
synopsis > synopses
thesis > theses
crisis > crises

stimulus > stimuli
nucleus > nuclei
alumnus > alumni
radius > radii
syllabus > syllabi
medium > media
memorandum > memoranda

curriculum > curricula
phenomenon > phenomena
criterion > criteria
vortex > vortices
matrix > matrices
index > indices

# 6: Compound Word Chart

| | | |
|---|---|---|
| **N = N+N**<br>fireplace<br>raincoat<br>keyboard | **N = N + V-ing**<br>bookkeeping<br>sightseeing<br>shoplifting | **ADJ = ADV/ADJ + V-en**<br>new born<br>quick frozen<br>absent minded |
| **N = ADJ+N**<br>blackbird<br>software<br>short circuit | **N = V + N**<br>push button<br>pickpocket<br>cookbook | **ADJ = ADJ + ADJ**<br>audio-visual<br>deaf mute<br>African-American |
| **N = N +V-er**<br>baby sitter<br>stockholder<br>bus driver | **ADJ = N + ADJ**<br>age-old<br>jet black<br>duty-free | **ADJ = NUM + N**<br>ten-foot<br>seven-member<br>two-dollar |
| **N = V + part**<br>breakdown<br>grownup<br>drop-off | **ADJ = N + V-ing**<br>man eating<br>fact-finding<br>breathtaking | **V = PART + V**<br>overcome<br>outdo<br>input |
| **N = N + V**<br>handshake<br>lifeguard<br>headache | **ADJ = N + V-en**<br>typewritten<br>bow-legged<br>heart broken | **V = N + V**<br>window shop<br>brainwash<br>sleepwalk |
| **N = V-ing + N**<br>dining room<br>firing squad<br>chewing gum | **ADJ = ADV/ADJ + V-ing**<br>far reaching<br>good looking<br>well-meaning | **V = ADV/ADJ + V**<br>download<br>dry clean<br>fast forward |

The boxes have been half-filled to allow you to insert other compound words

# 7: Common Antonyms

| | | | |
|---|---|---|---|
| above ·· below | far ·· near | long ·· short | send ·· receive |
| absent ·· present | fat ·· thin | lose ·· find | shallow ·· deep |
| add ·· subtract | few ·· many | loud ·· soft | sick ·· well |
| ahead ·· behind | former ·· latter | man ·· woman | sink ·· swim |
| all ·· none | first ·· last | major ·· minor | sit ·· stand |
| apart ·· together | friend ·· enemy | male ·· female | slow ·· fast |
| always ·· never | for ·· against | narrow ·· wide | soft ·· hard |
| arrive ·· depart | front ·· back | near ·· far | smooth ·· rough |
| awake ·· asleep | full ·· empty | neat ·· messy | speak ·· listen |
| beautiful ·· ugly | give ·· take | new ·· old | stop ·· go |
| before ·· after | good ·· bad | night ·· day | strong ·· weak |
| begin ·· end | happy ·· sad | noon ·· midnight | sweet ·· sour |
| best ·· worst | hard ·· easy | offense ·· defense | succeed ·· fail |
| big ·· little | hit ·· miss | on ·· off | sun ·· shade |
| bitter ·· sweet | here ·· there | open ·· close | sunrise ·· sunset |
| black ·· white | high ·· low | over ·· under | tall ·· short |
| borrow ·· loan | hot ·· cold | noisy ·· quiet | take off ·· land |
| both ·· neither | huge ·· tiny | plain ·· fancy | take off ·· put on |
| boy ·· girl | in ·· out | plural ·· singular | terrible ·· terrific |
| bring ·· take | inbound ·· out- | polite ·· rude | then ·· now |
| buy ·· sell | bound | private ·· public | thick ·· thin |
| catch ·· miss | inside ·· outside | push ·· pull | throw ·· catch |
| cheap ·· expensive | interesting ·· boring | put ·· take | tight ·· loose |
| city ·· country | into ·· out of | question ·· answer | top ·· bottom |
| clean ·· dirty | large ·· small | raw ·· cooked | true ·· false |
| cool ·· warm | late ·· early | remember ·· forget | turn on ·· turn off |
| crooked ·· straight | laugh ·· cry | rich ·· poor | turn down ·· turn up |
| dangerous ·· safe | lead ·· follow | right ·· wrong | upper ·· lower |
| dark ·· light | least ·· most | round trip ·· one way | wet ·· dry |
| dull ·· bright | left ·· right | run ·· walk | win ·· lose |
| easy ·· difficult | like ·· hate | same ·· different | work ·· play |
| exit ·· enter | live ·· die | save ·· delete | yes ·· no |
| export ·· import | log on ·· log out | save ·· spend | young ·· old |

# 8: A Collection of Common Collocations

## Food Pairs with *AND*

bacon and eggs
bacon, lettuce,
   and tomato
bread and butter
fish and chips

half and half
meat and potatoes
milk and honey
pork and beans
salt and pepper

soup and sandwich
spaghetti and
   meatballs
sugar and spice
surf and turf

## Noun Pairs with *AND*

aches and pains
brothers and sisters
cats and dogs
cops and robbers
cowboys and Indians

dos and don'ts
fame and fortune
husband and wife
ladies and gentlemen
life and death

peace and prosperity
odds and ends
sticks and stones
supply and demand
thunder and lightning

## Other Pairs with *AND*

back and forth
betwixt and between
down and out
each and every
far and away
fast and furious
few and far between
first and foremost
forever and ever
forgive and forget
front and center
fun and games
hard and fast

high and mighty
hit and run
hot and bothered
lost and found
more and more
nice and easy
now and forever
off and on
out and out
over and done with
over and over
pure and simple
rise and shine

rough and tumble
safe and sound
sick and tired
spick and span
stop and go
straight and narrow
thick and thin
time and again
tried and true
up and coming
up and down
war and peace
wear and tear

## Pairs with *OR*

dead or alive
do or die
double or nothing
feast or famine
friend or foe
give or take

hit or miss
life or death
more or less
no ifs, ands, or buts
on or about
plus or minus

rain or shine
ready or not
right or wrong
sink or swim
trick or treat
win or lose

## Adjective + Noun

confirmed bachelor
happy ending
inveterate smoker

moldy bread
rancid butter

rotten apple
sonic boom

## Adjectives

bare naked
bone dry
dirt cheap
freezing cold
hard headed

hard hit
high powered
picture perfect
razor sharp
red hot

slap happy
sound asleep
stark naked
tough minded
wide awake

## Containers, etc.

a bag of potatoes
a bottle of wine
a bouquet of flowers
a box of cereal
a bunch of bananas
a bushel of apples
a can of soup
a clove of garlic

a dozen eggs
an ear of corn
a head of lettuce
a jar of honey
a jug of cider
a loaf of bread
a pack of gum

a pound of meat
a quart of milk
a roll of toilet paper
a six-pack of beer
a stick of butter
a tub of butter
a tube of toothpaste

## Animal Sounds

a bird chirps
a cat meows
a chick peeps
a cow moos
a dog barks

a duck quacks
a frog croaks
a hen clucks
a horse neighs
a lion roars

a mouse squeaks
an owl hoots
a pig grunts
a rooster crows
a snake hisses

## Animal Similes

blind as a bat
busy as a bee
crazy as a loon
free as a bird

happy as a clam
proud as a peacock
silly as a goose
slippery as an eel

sly as a fox
strong as an ox
stubborn as a mule
wise as an owl

## Similes with *LIKE*

cry like a baby
drink like a fish
drive like a maniac
eat like a pig
hop like a bunny

purr like a kitten
roar like a lion
run like a deer
sell like hotcakes

shake like a leaf
sleep like a log
smell like a rose
work like a dog

## More Similes with *AS*

American as apple pie
bright as a button
cool as a cucumber
dead as a doornail

easy as pie
flat as a pancake
high as a kite
old as the hills

naked as a jaybird
nutty as a fruitcake
pretty as a picture
sober as a judge

## Verb + Noun

catch a cold
commit suicide
do a favor
   an assignment
   homework
   housework
   the dishes
drive a car
fly a flag
   a kite
   a plane
get busy
   dressed
   even
   going
   involved
   lost
   mad
   pregnant
   sick
   tired
   to sleep
   some/nowhere
   well
   with it
give directions
   a gift
   a hand
   permission

have an advantage
   a baby
   children
   a drink
   a good/bad time
   an excuse
   a headache
   an idea
   a job
   a seat
   the time
   time
make an appointment
   a bed
   a bet
   a copy
   a date
   a decision
   do
   friends
   love
   money
   a phone call
   progress
   a request
   sense
   waves
operate an elevator
paddle a canoe
play ball
   cards
   dead
   a game
   possum

sail a boat
take advantage of
   a bath
   the blame
   a break
   a bus
   care
   dictation
   a drink
   effect
   one's medicine
   a nap
   notes
   offense
   a picture
   place
   a plane
   responsibility
   a seat
   a shower
   a swim
   a train
   someone's word
say one's prayers
   grace
   hello/goodbye (for me)
tell one's fortune
   a joke
   a lie
   a secret
   a story
   the truth

# 9: Nationality and Place Words
## Members of the United Nations

| Place | Person | Adjective |
|---|---|---|
| Afghanistan | Afghan(s), Afghanistani | Afghan, Afghani |
| Albania | Albanian(s) | Albanian |
| Algeria | Algerian(s) | Algerian |
| Andorra | Andorran(s) | Andorran |
| Angola | Angolan(s) | Angolan |
| Antigua and Barbuda | Antiguan(s), Barbudan(s) | Antiguan, Barbudan |
| Argentina | Argentine(s), Argentinean(s) | Argentine, Argentinean |
| Armenia | Armenian(s) | Armenian |
| Australia | Australian(s), Aussie(s) (colloq.) | Australian |
| Austria | Austrian(s) | Austrian |
| Azerbaijan | Azerbaijani(s) | Azerbaijan, Azerbaijani |
| Bahamas, The | Bahamian(s) | Bahamian |
| Bahrain | Bahraini(s) | Bahraini |
| Bangladesh | Bangladeshi(s) | Bangladeshi |
| Barbados | Barbadian(s) | Barbadian |
| Belarus | Belarussian(s) | Belarus |
| Belgium | Belgian(s) | Belgian |
| Belize | Belizean(s) | Belizean |
| Benin | Beninese | Beninese |
| Bhutan | Bhutanese, Bhutani(s) | Bhutanese, Bhutani |
| Bolivia | Bolivian(s) | Bolivian |
| Bosnia and Herzegovina | Bosnian(s) | Bosnian |
| Botswana | Motswana (sing.), Batswana (pl.) | Motswana (sing.), Batswana (pl.) |
| Brazil | Brazilian(s) | Brazilian |
| Brunei | Bruneian(s) | Bruneian |
| Bulgaria | Bulgarian(s) | Bulgarian |
| Burkina Faso (Upper Volta) | Burkinabe (Voltan(s) | Burkinabe (Voltan) |
| Burundi | Murundi (sing.) Burundi (pl.) | Burundi, Kirundi (lang.) |
| Cambodia (Kampuchea) | Cambodian(s) | Cambodian |
| Cameroon/Cameroun | Cameroonian(s) | Cameroonian |
| Canada | Canadian(s) | Canadian |
| Cape Verde | Cape Verdean(s) | Cape Verdean |
| Central African Republic | Central African(s), Centrafrican(s) | Central African, Centrafrican |
| Chad | Chadian(s) | Chadian |
| Chile | Chilean(s) | Chilean |
| China, Peoples Republic of | Chinese | Chinese |
| Colombia | Colombian(s) | Colombian |
| Comoros | Comorian(s) | Comorian |
| Congo, Dem. Republic (Zaire) | Congolese | Congolese |
| Congo, Republic of | Congolese | Congolese (Zairean) |
| Costa Rica | Costa Rican(s) | Costa Rican |
| Côte d'Ivoire (Ivory Coast) | Ivorian(s) | Ivorian |
| Croatia | Croatian(s) | Croatians |
| Cuba | Cuban(s) | Cuban |
| Cyprus | Cypriot(s) | Cypriot |
| Czech Republic | Czech(s) | Czech |

| Place | Person | Adjective |
|---|---|---|
| Denmark | Dane(s) | Danish |
| Djibouti | Djibouti(s) | Djibouti |
| Dominica | Dominican(s) | Dominican |
| Dominican Republic | Dominican(s) | Dominican |
| East Timor | Timorese | East Timorese |
| Ecuador | Ecuadorian(s) | Ecuadorian |
| Egypt | Egyptian(s) | Egyptian |
| El Salvador | Salvadoran(s) | Salvadoran |
| Equatorial Guinea | Equatorial Guinean(s) | Equatorial Guinean |
| Eritrea | Eritrean | Eritrean |
| Estonia | Estonian(s) | Estonian |
| Ethiopia | Ethiopian(s) | Ethiopian |
| Fiji | Fijian(s), Fiji Islander(s) | Fijian |
| Finland | Finn(s) | Finnish |
| France | Frenchman/woman (men/women) | French |
| Gabon | Gabonese | Gabonese |
| Gambia, The | Gambian | Gambian |
| Georgia | Georgian | Georgian |
| Germany | German | German |
| Ghana | Ghanaian | Ghanaian |
| Greece | Greek | Greek |
| Grenada | Grenadian | Grenadian |
| Guatemala | Guatemalan | Guatemalan |
| Guinea | Guinean | Guinean |
| Guinea-Bissau | Guinean | Guinean |
| Guyana | Guyanese | Guyanese |
| Haiti | Haitian(s) | Haitian |
| Honduras | Honduran(s) | Honduran |
| Hungary | Hungarian(s) | Hungarian |
| Iceland | Icelander(s) | Icelandic |
| India | Indian(s) | Indian |
| Indonesia | Indonesian(s) | Indonesian |
| Iran | Iranian(s) | Iranian |
| Iraq | Iraqi(s) | Iraqi |
| Ireland | Irishman (-men, -women) | Irish |
| Israel | Israeli(s) | Israeli |
| Italy | Italian(s) | Italian |
| Jamaica | Jamaican(s) | Jamaican |
| Japan | Japanese | Japanese |
| Jordan | Jordanian(s) | Jordanian |
| Kazakhstan | Kazakh(s) | Kazakh |
| Kenya | Kenyan(s) | Kenyan(s) |
| Kiribati (Gilbert Islands) | Kiribati(s) | Kiribati (Gilbertese) |
| Korea, North | North Korean(s) | North Korean |
| Korea, South | South Korean(s) | South Korean |
| Kuwait | Kuwaiti(s) | Kuwaiti |
| Kyrgyzstan | Kirgiz(es) | Kirgiz |
| Laos | Lao(s), Laotian(s) | Lao, Laotian |
| Latvia | Latvian(s) | Latvian |

| Place | Person | Adjective |
|---|---|---|
| Lebanon | Lebanese | Lebanese |
| Lesotho | Mosotho (sing.), Basotho (pl.) | Basotho, Sesotho (lang.) |
| Liberia | Liberian(s) | Liberian |
| Libya | Libyan(s) | Libyan |
| Liechtenstein | Liechtensteiner(s) | Liechtenstein |
| Lithuania | Lithuanian(s) | Lithuanian |
| Luxembourg | Luxembourger(s), Luxembourgian(s) | Luxembourgish, Luxembourgian |
| Macedonia | Macedonian(s) | Macedonian |
| Madagascar | Malagasy(ies) | Malagasy |
| Malawi | Malawian(s) | Malawian |
| Malaysia | Malaysian(s) | Malaysian |
| Maldives | Maldivian(s) | Maldivian |
| Mali | Malian(s) | Malian |
| Malta | Maltese | Maltese |
| Marshall Islands | Marshall Islanders | Marshallese |
| Mauritania | Mauritanian(s) | Mauritanian |
| Mauritius | Mauritian(s) | Mauritian |
| Mexico | Mexican(s) | Mexican |
| Micronesia | Micronesian(s) | Micronesian |
| Moldova | Moldovan(s) | Moldovan |
| Monaco | Monegasque(s) | Monegasque |
| Mongolia | Mongolian(s) | Mongolian |
| Montenegro | Montenegran(s) | Montenegran |
| Morocco | Moroccan(s) | Moroccan |
| Mozambique | Mozambican(s) | Mozambican |
| Myanmar (Burma) | Burmese | Burmese |
| Namibia | Namibian(s) | Namibian |
| Nauru | Nauruan(s) | Nauruan |
| Nepal | Nepalese | Nepalese, Nepali |
| Netherlands, The (Holland) | Dutchman (men, women) | Dutch |
| New Zealand | New Zealander(s) | New Zealand |
| Nicaragua | Nicaraguan(s) | Nicaraguan |
| Niger | Nigerien(s) | Nigerien |
| Nigeria | Nigerian(s) | Nigerian |
| Norway | Norwegian(s) | Norwegian |
| Oman | Omani(s) | Omani |
| Pakistan | Pakistani(s) | Pakistani |
| Palau | Palauan(s) | Palauan |
| Panama | Panamanian(s) | Panamanian |
| Papua New Guinea | Papua New Guinean(s) | Papua New Guinean |
| Paraguay | Paraguayan(s) | Paraguayan |
| Peru | Peruvian(s) | Peruvian |
| Philippines | Filipino(s) (-a(s)) | Filipino |
| Poland | Pole(s) | Polish |
| Portugal | Portuguese | Portuguese |
| Qatar | Qatari(s) | Qatari |
| Romania, Rumania | Romanian(s) | Romanian |
| Russia | Russian(s) | Russian |
| Rwanda | Rwandan(s) | Rwandan |

| Place | Person | Adjective |
|---|---|---|
| St. Kitts and Nevis | St. Kittitian(s), Nevisian(s) | St. Kittitian, Nevisian |
| St. Lucia | St. Lucian(s) | St. Lucian |
| St. Vincent and the Grenadines | Vincentian(s) | Vincentian |
| Samoa | Samoan(s) | Samoan |
| San Marino | Sammarinese (sing.) (-inesi (pl.)) | Sammarinese (sing.) (-inesi (pl.)) |
| Sao Tome and Principe | Sao Tomean(s) | Sao Tomean |
| Saudi Arabia | Saudi(s) | Saudi (Saudi Arabian) |
| Senegal | Senegalese | Senegalese |
| Serbia | Serb(s) | Serbian |
| Seychelles | Seychellois | Seychellois |
| Sierra Leone | Sierra Leonean(s) | Sierra Leonean |
| Singapore | Singaporean(s) | Singaporean |
| Slovakia | Slovakian(s) | Slovakian |
| Slovenia | Slovenian(s) | Slovenian |
| Solomon Islands | Solomon Islander(s) | Solomon Islander |
| Somalia | Somali(s) | Somali |
| South Africa | South African(s) | South African |
| South Sudan | South Sudanese | South Sudanese |
| Spain | Spaniard(s) | Spanish |
| Sri Lanka (Ceylon) | Sri Lankan(s) (Ceylonese) | Sri Lankan (Ceylonese) |
| Sudan | Sudanese | Sudanese |
| Surinam | Surinamer(s) | Surinamer |
| Swaziland | Swazi(s) | Swazi |
| Sweden | Swede(s) | Swedish |
| Switzerland | Swiss | Swiss |
| Syria | Syrian(s) | Syrian |
| Tajikistan | Tajik(s) | Tajik |
| Tanzania | Tanzanian(s) | Tanzanian |
| Thailand | Thai(s) | Thai |
| Togo | Togolese | Togolese |
| Tonga | Tongan(s) | Tongan |
| Trinidad and Tobago | Trinidadian(s), Tobagonian(s) | Trinidadian, Tobagonian |
| Tunisia | Tunisian(s) | Tunisian |
| Turkey | Turk(s) | Turkish |
| Turkmenistan | Turkoman (-men) | Turkoman |
| Tuvalu (Ellice Islands) | Tuvaluan(s) | Tuvaluan |
| Uganda | Ugandan(s) | Ugandan |
| Ukraine | Ukrainian(s), | Ukrainian |
| United Arab Emirates | Emirati(s) | Emirati(s) |
| United Kingdom of Great Britain | Briton(s), Brits | British |
| United States of America | American(s) | American |
| Uruguay | Uruguayan(s) | Uruguayan |
| Uzbekistan | Uzbeki(s), Uzbek(s) | Uzbeki, Uzbek |
| Vanuatu | ni-Vanuatu | ni-Vanuatu |
| Venezuela | Venezuelan(s) | Venezuelan(s) |
| Vietnam | Vietnamese | Vietnamese |
| Yemen | Yemeni(s) | Yemeni |
| Zambia | Zambian(s) | Zambian |
| Zimbabwe | Zimbabwean(s) | Zimbabwean |

This list includes all the members of the United Nations as of the publication of this edition.

# 1: A Summary of Basic Sentence Types

## Key

| | | | |
|---|---|---|---|
| S | sentence | DO | direct object |
| SUBJ | subject | IDO | indirect object |
| V | verb | PP | prepositional phrase |
| VP | verb phrase | ADJ | adjective |
| N | noun | ADVL | adverbial |
| NP | noun phrase | ADVL CL | adverbial clause |
| BE | copular be | WHQ | information question with WH |
| LV | linking verb | RCL | relative clause |
| COMP | complement | POSS RCL | possessive relative clause |

1. SUBJ  BE  N  COMP
She   is   a teacher.

   SUBJ  BE  PP  COMP
She   is   in room 203.

   SUBJ  BE/LV  ADJ COMP
She   is     busy.
She   seems  friendly.

2. SUBJ  V       IDO        DO        ADVL(PP) --TRANSITIVE
She   teaches  my friend  English   in the morning.

   SUBJ  V       DO        PP (IDO)       ADVL(PP)
She   teaches  English   to my friend   in the morning.

   SUBJ  V  ADVL (PP)  -- INTRANSITIVE
She   lives  in Chicago.

3. SUBJ  BE NOT  COMP  -- NEGATED BE
She   is   not   an American.

   SUBJ  AUX  NOT  V     DO/ADVL  -- NEGATED V
She   does  not  know  Russian.
She   does  not  teach  in the afternoon.

4. BE  SUBJ  COMP    YES/NO QUESTION WITH BE
  Is   she   a Canadian?

  AUX  SUBJ V   DO YES/NO QUESTION WITH TRANSITIVE V
  Does  she  speak French?

  AUX  SUBJ  V  ADVL YES/NO QUESTION WITH INTRANSITIVE V
  Does  she  live  alone?

5. WHQ BE  COMP
  Who  is   he?
  Where
  What
  How

  WHQ V   DO
  Who  knows him?

  WHQ  AUX  SUBJ  V
  Who(m) does  he   know?

6, SUBJ V   ADVL   ADVL CL
  She  lives  there   <u>because</u> it is near the school.
  She  drives here    <u>if</u> it rains.
  She  rides  in the bus  <u>although</u> she prefers to walk.
  She  taught in Korea  <u>before</u> she came here.

7. SUBJ   RC      VP
  My teacher, who lives in Oak Lawn, drives to work. NONRESTRICTIVE CL
  The teacher who lives in Skokie  takes the bus. RESTRICTIVE CL

  SUBJ V  DO    RC
  I   know the teacher  who lives in Evanston.

  SUBJ V  IO   RC      DO
  She  gives my friend who lives in Skokie a ride

  SUBJ  POSS RC     VP
  The boy whose bike was stolen is my friend

  SUBJ V  DO   POSS RC
  I   know the boy whose bike was stolen.

44

| SUBJ | V | IDO | RC | DO |
|------|---|-----|-----|-----|
| I | gave | my friend | whose bike was stolen | a ride. |

| SUBJ | V | ADVL RC |
|------|---|---------|
| I | know | where she lives. |
| | | when she leaves. |
| | | why she takes the bus. |
| | | what she teaches. |
| | | who she teaches. |

8.
| SUBJ | V | COMP GERUND AND/OR INFINITIVE |
|------|---|-------------------------------|
| She | likes | teaching here. |
| She | likes | to teach in the morning |

| SUBJ | V | THAT COMP |
|------|---|-----------|
| I | think | (that) she is busy. |

# 2: Words Grow on Trees

The tree diagram commonly used to illustrate the basic phrase structure of language is a useful analogy for illustrating how language is used. First, however, the usual basic tree on the left needs to be turned upside down, so that the tree on the right becomes our diagram:

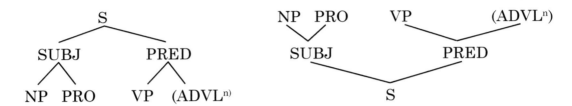

Now, referring to the illustration, the analogy goes like this. In the earth where the tree is anchored, pre-linguistic thought occurs like the roots of the tree below the surface. As these thoughts are formed into a physical expression, they are forced to confine themselves to a single trunk, the sentence (S).

The English sentence has two major limbs, the SUBJ (subject) and the PRED (predicate). The subject branches into a NP (noun phrase) or a PRO (pronoun). The predicate has two branches, the VP (verb phrase), and an optional (ADVL$^n$) (adverbial, possibly several).

Each limb has branches, and at the end of the branches are buds (morphemes). There are processes within the buds (inflections, derivations, compounding) that will turn the bud into a leaf (lexeme, or word).

But before the tree begins to form its leaves, there may be some "winds of change" that cause the branches to move. In effect, the basic tree structure may be modified by negative or question "winds" and other form and movement winds such as contraction and fronting (an adverbial is moved to the front of a sentence).

The tree in its final form is situated in a physical context where a sun brings the leaves to their final shape and sound. Thus, a South African sun produces a pronunciation that will be slightly different from an Australian, or American, or British pronunciation.

Ultimately there is a sociocultural context (SCC) which influences final usage of the sentence and its parts (pragmatics). In effect, words and structure may be formal, informal, deleted, elided, and otherwise modified according to the appropriateness of the sociocultural context.

For additional details on the nodes on the tree, consult the glossary on page 48.

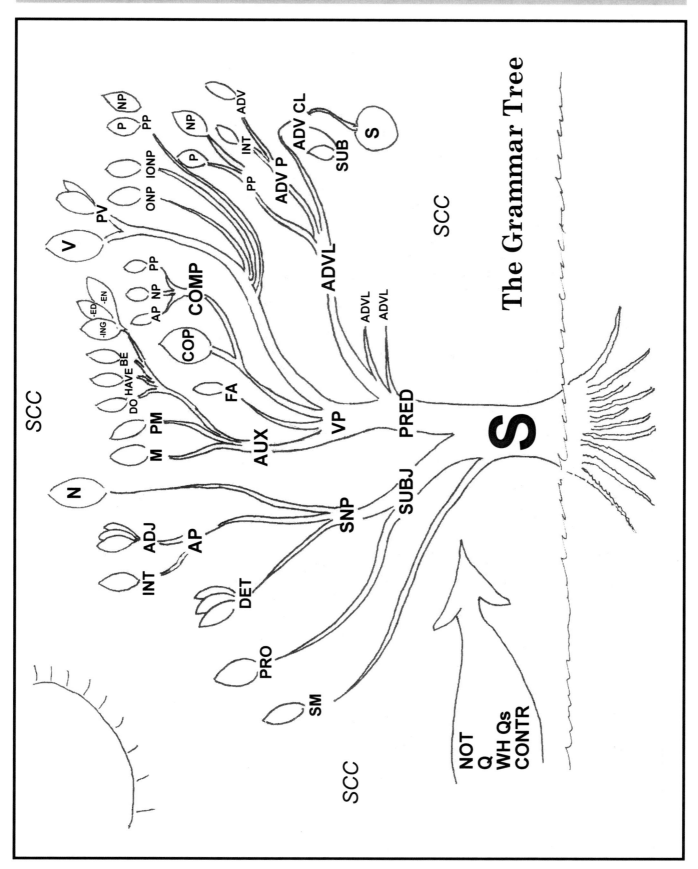

The Grammar Tree

# 3: Grammar Tree Glossary

**ADV – ADVERB.** A word that modifies a verb or an adjective. It frequently has the suffix *-ly*.

**ADVL- Adverbial.** An optional element whose default position in the S is final, although it can be moved to other positions, especially the first element in the S. There are three types: Prep P, Adv P, and Advl Cl. There can be more than one in a sentence, and they usually follow this default order: Manner, Direction, Position, Time, Frequency, Purpose, Reason (see SUB).

**ADVL CL – Adverbial Clause.** A dependent clause that contains a subordinator and a S.

**ADV P – Adverb Phrase.** A modifying element that can modify an adjective or a verb. It can have an optional intensifier.

**AP – Adjective Phrase.** The core is an adjective. There may be as many as seven adjectives usually following the order: Opinion, Size, Shape, Condition, Age, Color, Origin: *beautiful, large, square, frayed, antique, red, Turkish (carpet).* There may be an optional intensifier.

**AUX – Auxiliary Verb.** It refers to one of the three "helping" verbs – *do, be, have* with the inflections *–ing, -ed, -en,* and the modals.

**Auxiliary *do*.** It is used to form yes/no questions and syntactic negation. There is also a main verb "do."

**be . . (V)en.** An auxiliary construction that uses auxiliary *be* and the past participle. It is the passive voice. It may also be in the perfective and progressive aspect.

**be . . (V) ing.** An auxiliary construction that uses auxiliary *be* and the present participle *-ing.* It is called the progressive (or continuous) aspect.

**COMP – Complement.** A phrasal structure that completes the meaning and form of a S. It follows a copula. Another type of complement is like a NP or noun clause. I know *the answer.* I know *what you mean.*

**COP – Copula.** A type of verb that links the SUBJ and a Complement. The copular BE is the most common. It can be followed by one of three complements: Prep P, AP, or NP.

**Clause** – A structure that has both a SUBJ and a PRED. It may be an independent S or a dependent S that is subordinated to a main clause.

**DET – Determiner**. Like adjectives, determiners modify the N in some way. There are four types of determiners: articles, possessive adjectives, demonstratives, and quantifiers. The first three are mutually exclusive. There may be up to three determiners in a NP.
Example: *All my many* (friends)

**FA – Frequency Adverb**. A small list of adverbs that describe how often, from *never* to *always*.

**have .. (V) en**. An auxiliary construction that uses auxiliary *have* and the past participle form of the verb. The form can be: *–en (broken), -ed (walked)*, or irregular *bought, drunk*. Ît is called the perfective aspect.

**have be .. en (V) ing**. An auxiliary construction that uses auxiliary *have* with *been* and the verb followed by the *-ing* suffix. It is the perfect progressive aspect.

**Int – Intensifier**. A kind of adverb that modifies an adjective or aadverb. Key intensifiers are *very, rather, quite, somewhat*, and many adverbs ending in –ly (*intensely*)

**IONP – Indirect Object Noun Phrase**. A noun phrase (frequently a pronoun) that is the beneficiary of the verb.

**M – Pure Modal Verb**. There are nine (*can, could, will, would, shall, should, may, might, must*). *Ought to* is often considered a M, but it may also be called a PM. They are auxiliary (helping) verbs that modify the main verb.

**NP – Noun Phrase**. The core is a noun (N). It may have other elements.

**ONP – (Direct) Object Noun Phrase**. A noun phrase which follows a transitive verb. It is affected directly by the action of the verb.

**Phrase** – Two or more words that function as a unit, but do not have a SUBJ and a PRED.

**PM – Phrasal Modal**. Like a modal it modifies the verb. The most important ones are: *be going to, be able to, be about to, be supposed to, have to, have got to, used to*. Unlike the M, they may take tense and they may conjugate: *She has to*.

**PP – Prepositional Phrase.** There are two main parts: a preposition and a NP. In some cases the preposition may be omitted: *I'll see you (on) Friday.*

**PRED – Predicate.** The second major element in a S. Its core is a verb.

**PRO – Pronoun.** Pronouns may be personal: *me*, etc; impersonal: *everyone*; demonstrative: *this*; relative: (the man) *who*; interrogative: *why*; and reflexive: *myself*. Pronouns inflect for case (subject, object, possessive).

**PV – Phrasal Verb.** Often called a two-word verb, it has a V followed by a particle – a word that is like a preposition or an adverb. She *looked up* the word. They can be transitive or intransitive. If transitive they can be separable: She *looked* the word *up*.

**S – Sentence.** The basic grammatical structure. All aspects of the grammar are contained in a S.

**SM – Sentence Modifier.** An optional element such as *perhaps* that modifies the meaning of the entire S.

**SNP** – Subject noun phrase. A noun with optional determiners and adjective phrase.

**SUB – Adverbial Subordinator.** A word that precedes a S and makes the S dependent on a main clause. There are four main types: Causal (*because*), Temporal (*when*), Conditional (*if*), and Concessive (*although*).

**SUBJ – Subject.** Usually the first element in the S. It is a noun phrase or a pronoun, but not both.

**V – (Main) Verb.** All other verbs. They may be regular or irregular.

**VP – Verb Phrase.** A required element in the S along with the NP. There are three main types of verbs: Copula (COP), Phrasal Verb (PV), and all other verbs (V). The VP can include an ONP (direct object noun phrase), an IONP (indirect object noun phrase), and a Prep P: *(I live) in Brattleboro.*

# 4: A Grammar Sequence

This grammar sequence is only a handy guide to what can and should be covered in a basic English course. The list represents a series of steps from very basic phrase structures and transformations to increasingly complex or unusual structures. Some of the steps are large, and some small, and some will be easier than others. It is by no means a complete outline of the grammar of English. However, mastery of this list, along with commensurate progress in pronunciation, vocabulary development, and communicative skills would enable a student to function reasonably independently in an English-speaking world.

1. **Affirmative Statement Word Order**          *I am reading this sentence now.*
    Subject noun phrase + verb phrase + object noun phrase + adverbial
    **Subject Pronouns**          *I, you, he, she , we, they*
    **Present forms of** *BE*          *am, are , is*
    **Subject - verb agreement with** *BE*          *I am,* etc.
    **Present progressive aspect**          *am reading*
        *BE* + **V** *-ing*
    **Determiner + Object noun**          *this sentence*

2. **Negative Statement Word Order**          *I am not reading a French sentence.*
    Placement of *not* after 1st auxiliary
    **Determiner + adjective + noun**          *a French sentence*

3. **Yes/No Question**          *Are you learning English?*
    Inversion of subject and  1st auxiliary
    **Short answer**          *Yes, I am.*

4. **Simple Present Tense Aspect**
    **with Stative Verbs**
    **Affirmative statement**          *I need English.*
    **3rd person singular** *–S*          *She needs English.*
    **Negative statement**          *I do not know that word.*
        **Do insertion; placement of** *not* after *do*
    **3rd person singular with** *do*          *She does not know that word.*
    **Yes/No question with** *do*          *Do you like English?*
    *Do* **insertion and inversion of**
        **subject and** *do*
    **Short answer**          *Yes, I do. /Yes, she does.*
                   *No, I do not. /No he does not.*
    **Common Stative Verbs**          *cost, feel, have, hear, know, like,*
                   *need, want, understand*

51

5. **Simple Present with Copula *BE***       *He is a student.*
   **Affirmative statement**        *She is a teacher.*
   *BE* **+ noun phrase**          *is a teacher.*
   **Indefinite article**          *a teacher*
   **Definite article**            *The teacher is in the classroom.*
   *BE* **+ prepositional phrase**     *is in the classroom*
   *BE* **+ adjective**            *The students are busy.*
   **Regular plural** *–S*                *students*

6. **Yes/No Question and Negation**     *Are you an English teacher?*
   **with Copula *BE***            *I am not a teacher.*
   **Inversion of Subject and** *BE*      *Are you*
   **Placement of** *not* **after** *BE*      *am not*
   **Indefinite article** *an*           *an English teacher*

7A. **Contraction of** *Not*           *She isn't a math teacher.*
                                 *He isn't taking this course.*
                                 *They don't speak Spanish.*
                                 *She doesn't know the answer.*
    *AM* **exception**            *I'm not happy.*

7B. **Contraction of** *BE*           *She's a very good teacher.*
    **Intensifier**                *very*

8. **Simple Past Tense**           *I learned a new word.*
   **regular** *–ed* **suffix**
   **Did in questions and negatives**     *Did you like the class?*
                                 *We didn't know the answer.*
   **Common irregular past forms**      *I knew the answer.*
                                 *begin, bring, buy, cost, drink, eat, forget,*
                                 *go, have, make, read, say, see, sleep,*
                                 *speak, take, teach, tell, think*
   **Common adverbs of time**        *yesterday, last X,  ago*

9A. *WH* **subject Question Words with**    *Who is she?*
    **copula** *BE*                *What is he?*
                                 *Where is he?*

9B. *WH* **subject Question Words with**
    **Other Verbs**                *Who speaks Russian?*
                                 *What happened?*

9C. *WH* **Predicate Question Words**     *What do you want?*
                                 *Where are you going?*
                                 *Who did you see?*
                                 *When did you return?*

9D. *HOW:* formulaic

*How are you?*
*How do you do?*

10. **Locative and Temporal Prepositions** *at school, in the park, on the street,*
    **in Prepositional Phrases**          *to the bank, from the store, near the*
                                          *post office, under the desk,*
                                          *at three o'clock, on Monday, in 2008*

11. **Coordination with** *and, but, or*

*the bank <u>and</u> the post office*
*I went home <u>and</u> read the paper.*
*She knows the answer, <u>and</u> he does <u>too</u>.*
*She speaks well, <u>but</u> he <u>doesn't</u>.*

      **adverbs:** *also, too, either*

*I <u>also</u> need a pen <u>or</u> a pencil.*
*I need a pen, <u>too</u>.*
*She doesn't <u>need</u> a pen, <u>and</u> I don't <u>either</u>.*

      **Indefinite pronoun:** *one(s)*

*She likes the red <u>one</u>, but*
*I like the blue <u>ones</u>.*

12. **Modal Verbs:**
    *Can* **(ability)**                        *I <u>can</u> do that.*
    **Requests and permission**                 *<u>Can you</u> help me?*
    **with** *can, may*                         *<u>May I</u> go now?*
    **Polite requests with** *would, could*    *<u>Could</u> you give me a hand, <u>please</u>?*
        **and** *please.*                 *<u>Would</u> you <u>please</u> do me a favor?*

13. **Imperative (affirmative),**
    **Demonstratives and invitations**         *Give me <u>this</u> blue one.*
      **Negative imperative**                *Don't take <u>that</u> red one.*
      **Hortative**                          *<u>Let's buy</u> these pens.*
      **Negative hortative**                 *<u>Let's not buy</u> those pens.*
      **Invitation with** *shall* **and**   *<u>Shall we go</u> now?*
        *would you like (to)*            *<u>Would you like this</u> or <u>that</u>?*
      **Demonstratives as Pronouns:**        *I want <u>these</u>.*
      *this, that, these, those*            *She wants <u>those</u>.*

14. **Object Pronouns:** *me, you, him,*      *Please give <u>me</u> this one.*
    *her, it, us, them*
    **Direct and indirect object**             *Please give <u>it</u> to <u>me</u>.*
    **position**                               *Please give <u>me the book</u>.*

15. **Nonreferential** *there, here*          *<u>There</u> is a bus station on the corner.*
                                              *<u>Here</u> comes the bus.*

    *How* **+ adj and** <u>**nonreferential** *it*</u>    *<u>How far</u> is <u>it</u> to the station?*
                                              *<u>How long</u> does <u>it</u> take?*

    **Adverbial** *there, here*                *Is <u>it</u> raining <u>there</u>?*
                                              *<u>It</u>'s a nice day <u>here</u>.*

**16A. Phrasal Modal:** *have to, have got to*  *I have to go.*
     **Contraction of** *have*  *I've got to go home.*

**16B. Phrasal Modal:** *be going to*  *I'm going to take the bus.*

**16C. Future Predictive** *Will*  *I'll arrive at three o'clock.*
     **Contraction of** *will*  *I won't be late.*

**17.  Present Habitual Tense-Aspect**  *I go to work at 8 o'clock.*
     **With frequency adverbs:**  *I usually eat lunch at noon.*
       *always, usually, sometimes, never*
     **Position with copula BE and**  *I am always on time.*
       **auxiliaries**  *I can usually finish by four.*
     **Time expressions:**  *I do it every day.*
       *all* (day, month year, etc.)  *I don't do it all day, but*
       *every (other)*  *I do it every other day.*
     **Frequency questions:** *How often,*  *How often do you do that?*
       *ever*  *Do you ever do that?*
     **Fronting of** *usually* **and**  *Usually I leave at three.*
       *sometimes*  *Sometimes I go at two.*

**18.  Why with adverbial clause and**  *Why do you do that?*
     **subordinator** *because*  *I do it because I have to.*
       *How come* **and** *what ..for*  *How come you're late?*
         *What did you do that for?*

**19A . Tag questions:** Agreement  *It's a nice day, isn't it?*
       intonation
       Affirmative tag  *It isn't easy, is it?*

**19B. Tag questions:** Information  *You're leaving soon, aren't you?*
       intonation  *You aren't leaving now, are you?*

**20A. Possession:** *Whose*  *Whose book is this?*
     **Possessive adjectives:** *my, your,*  *That's my book.*
       *his, her, its, our, their*
       *–S* **suffix**  *That one is Maria's.*
       *of* **possessive phrase**  *in the middle of the book*

**20B. Possessive Pronouns:** *mine, yours,*  *That book is hers.*
       *his, hers, its, ours, theirs*
       *Which/what* **+ Noun**  *Which book is his?*
         *What book are you reading?*
       *Whose, which* **as pronouns**  *Whose is that?*
       **Idiomatic** *belongs to*  *That book belongs to me.*

21. **Comparison of Adjectives:** *–er, –est*
    *more, most*

    I need a *bigger* car.
    I don't want a *more expensive* car.
    Yoshi has *the fastest* car.
    Margot has *the most economical* car.

    **Comparative constructions:**
    *–er than, more X than*
    **Equative constructions:** *as .. as*
    *the same as, different from*

    *the same X as*

    His computer is *slower than* mine.
    My laptop is *more portable than* his.
    My cell phone is *as nice as* yours.
    Your mouse is *the same as* mine, but
       his is *different from* ours.
    My computer has *the same memory as* his.

22. **Present Perfect Tense Aspect**
    *Have + –en*
    **With adverbs:** *just, recently,*
    *since, already, yet, never,*
    *for (ten years, etc.), up to now*

    I have *seen* that film.
    She has *just* returned from Boston.
    I've *already* done that, but she hasn't
    done it *yet.*
    I have *never* been to Australia.
    I have *practiced yoga for several years.*
    *Up to now* I have *always* had a Ford.

23. **Noun Phrase: Count and**
    **noncount nouns**
    **With determiners: indefinite**
    **specific:** *a, some, ø*
    **Definite:** *the*

    Generic

    I'll have *a* vegetable *and* rice.

    I'd like *a* hot dog *and some*
    mustard, but I don't want *ø* relish.
    *The* hot dog was good, but *the* mustard
    wasn't.
    I like *ø* apples. *The* apple is very
    nutritious.

24. **Noun Phrase:**
    Quantifiers *much, many*

    **Statements, questions,**
       **and negatives**
    with *some, any*
    with count nouns: *few, a few,*
       *several*
    with noncounts: *little, much, a lot of*

    with count or noncount: *all, most,*
       *almost, no*

    I don't have *much* money, and
       I have *many* debts.

    I don't have *any* twenties. Do you have
       *any* tens? No, but I have *some* fives.
    There were *few* people there, and *a few*
    left early. However, *several* people stayed.
    She has *little* money, *a lot of* courage,
       but not *much* luck.
    Almost *all* the customers bought something.
    *Most* of them spent a lot of money. There
       were *no* complaints.

25A. **Modals: Prediction with** *will,*
    *might, may*

*The rain will be heavy, but it may end by evening. There might be more rain tomorrow.*

25B. **Modals: Probability with** *may,*
    *might, could, ought to, should,*
    *must*

*RRRRRRing! That may be Alfredo.*
*Yeah, but it might be Anna. And it could be Yukiko. No, it ought to be Franz. It's two o'clock; it should be Jon. You're all wrong. It must be Antonio. He promised to call at two.*

26. **Phrasal Verbs:**
    **Intransitive:**
    **Transitive Inseparable:**
    **with adverb/preposition:**
    **Transitive Separable:**
    **Pronoun object placement**

*My car broke down in the desert.*
*They broke into a store.*
*He broke up with her.*
*He broke the engine down into five sections.*
*He broke it down.*

27A. **Past Progressive Tense-Aspect**

*Yesterday at two o'clock I was driving home.*

    **Time expressions:** *at/on/in* **with**
    *o'clock, Monday, 2005*

*In 2003 I was studying for the TOEFL.*

27B. **Past Progressive with adverbial**
    **Time Clause with** *when*

I was taking a shower *when the phone rang.*

28. **Modals: Advice with** *should,*
    *ought to, had better*
    **Contraction of** *had*
    **Use of** *or else*
    **Ability with** *be able to*
    **Prohibition with** *cannot*
    **Obligation with** *have to, must*

    **No Obligation with** *don't have to*

*You should see a doctor.*
*You ought to take this medicine.*
*You'd better get some rest*
  *or (else) you won't*
  *be able to go with us.*
*I'm sorry, you cannot drive.*
*You have to use a seat belt.*
*You must yield to pedestrian.*
*You don't have to wear a helmet.*

29. **More Questions**
    **Embedded WH questions**
    **WH + infinitive**
    **Negative Questions**
    **Short answer**

*I know where he is.*
*Do you know where to go?*
*Don't you know the answer?*
*No, I don't.*

30. **Future Time**
    **with present progressive**　　*I am leaving tomorrow.*
    **with simple present**　　*I leave a two o' clock.*
    **with** *be about to*　　*We are about to leave.*
    **Future Progressive**　　*I will be taking the train.*
    **Time expressions:** *tomorrow,*　　*She's going tomorrow.*
    　*soon, at / on / in*　　*We're leaving soon.*
    　　*Tomorrow at two o'clock I'll be*
    　　*flying to Europe.*

31. **Infinitives and Gerunds**
    **Verbs followed by infinitives:**　　*I want to go.*
    　*want, learn, wait, teach, tell,*
    　*ask, need, prefer*
    **Verbs followed by Gerunds:**　　*I enjoy singing.*
    　*dislike, keep, miss, practice*
    **Verbs followed by either:**　　*I like singing.*
    　*begin, have, love, prefer, stop*　　*I stopped to look. I stopped looking.*
    **Verbs followed by object and**
    **simple verb:** *hear, notice, see, watch*　*We watched them leave.*

32. **Causative Verbs**　　*We made him go.*
    **Verbs followed by simple form**　　*We had him go by taxi.*
    　*make, have, let*　　*I didn't let her go.*
    **followed by infinitive** *get*　　*She got us to change our minds.*

33. **Noun Phrase word order**　　*both my two big brothers*
    **Pre-determiners:** *both, all, half*　*both brothers*
    **core determiners:** *a, the, some*　*a brother*
    　*my, your, his, her, its, our, their*　*my brother*
    　*this, that, these, those*　*that brother*
    　*each, every, some*　*every brother*
    **Post determiners:** *two, first, next,*　*two brothers*
    　*many, much, a lot of, several*
    **Intensifiers:** *very, quite, rather,*　*very big*
    　*somewhat, too, enough,* repetition　*too big, big enough, my big big brothers*
    **Adjective ordering:** *opinion, size,*　*beautiful, big, long, rusty, old,*
    　*shape, condition, age, color, origin*　*black, German Mercedes*

34. **Adverbials**
    Prepositional phrases            *to the city*
    Adverb phrases                  *very slowly*
    Adverbial clauses:
        time                        *after I go*
        cause                   *because I have to go*
        concession            *although I cannot go*
        condition             *if I go*
    Word order: Manner/direction,    *rapidly • to the mall • on Elm Street •*
        place/position, time/frequency,    *at two o' clock • every Friday • to shop •*
        purpose, reason             *because he gets paid on Friday*

35. **Conditional Verb Clauses**
    **Future Predictive**            *If it rains, I won't go, but she will.*
                              *If it should (happen to) stop, I'll go.*
    **Factual**                     *If I get up too early, I am grumpy.*
                              *Whenever it rains our roof leaks.*
    **Imaginative**              *If I had enough money I'd take a vacation.*
                              *If I were you, I'd go to Hawaii.*
                              *If I had gone to Hawaii, I would have gotten a nice tan.*

36. **Modal Verbs in Past Time**      *He had to do it, but you didn't have to.*
                              *Andy should have done it.*
                              *I couldn't have done it.*
                              *Cindy might have done it.*
                              *Bill must have done it.*

37. **Phrasal Modals**                   *We had better go.*
                              *We are supposed to go now.*
                              *I would rather go later.*
                              *She is willing to go later.*
                              *I am not able to go now.*

38. **Passive Voice**
    Simple past              *The flowers were planted yesterday.*
    With *by* phrase         *They were planted by the Garden Club.*
    Simple future           *More flowers will be planted tomorrow.*
    Simple present         *They are planted every spring.*

39. **Participles as Modifiers**
    *–ing* vs *–ed*            *The movie was boring. I was bored.*

**40. Other Past Time Verb Phrases**
Iterative *used to / would*                 *We <u>used to/would</u> swim every day.*
Noniterative *used to*                       *I <u>used to</u> like swimming.*

Interrupted future past                      *I <u>was going to</u> go to the beach, but it rained.*

**41. Reflexive/Emphatic Pronouns**
Reflexive                                    *I hurt <u>myself</u>.*
Emphatic                                     *I <u>myself</u> was not hurt.*
Unaided                                      *I did it all <u>by myself</u>.*

**42. Past and Future Perfect tense/aspects**
Past perfect                                 *I <u>had</u> never <u>done</u> that before.*
Future perfect                               *By next year I <u>will have done</u> that several times.*

**43. Perfect Progressive tense/aspects**
Present perfect progressive                  *She <u>has been studying</u> Spanish since 1999.*
Future perfect progressive                   *By next year she <u>will have been studying</u> Spanish for several years.*

Past perfect progressive                     *She <u>had been studying</u> Spanish for one year when she first went to Mexico.*

**44. Complementation**
Embedded *that* noun clause                  *I know <u>that he is here</u>.*
Embedded Yes/No question                     *Do you <u>know if/whether she is here</u>?*
Embedded negative clause                     *I don't know <u>if/whether he is here</u>.*
Embedded WH question                         *I don't know <u>where they are</u>.*

**45. Generalized *–ever***                  *<u>Wherever</u> he went he planted apple trees.*
                                             *<u>Whoever</u> saw him was amused.*
                                             *He wore <u>whatever</u> he pleased.*
                                             *He ate <u>whenever</u> he wanted to.*

**46. Impersonal Pronouns**
*you*                                        *<u>You</u> can't drive fast when it's slippery.*
*we*                                         *<u>We</u> should slow down in bad weather.*
*they*                                       *<u>They</u> usually salt the roads in the winter.*
*one*                                        *<u>One</u> should be careful driving when it snows.*

**47. Other Subjunctive**
 with "control" verbs      *He advised that <u>she take</u> only four courses.*
 with certain adjectives     *It is important <u>she pass</u> them.*
 with wish         *I wish that she <u>would listen</u> to him.*
 hope vs. wish        *I hope that she <u>will</u>.*

**48. Conjunctive Adverbs**
 addition         *I know that. <u>Moreover</u>, she does too.*
 result          *I know that. <u>Therefore</u>, I won't go.*
 concession/contrast      *I know that. <u>However</u>, I'll go anyway.*

**49. Relative Clauses**
 with *who/that*       *She is the person <u>who/that knows you</u>.*
            *She is the person <u>who(m)/that you know</u>.*
 with *when*        *I'll never forget the day <u>when we met</u>.*
 with *where*        *This is the place <u>where she lives</u>.*
 restrictive vs. nonrestrictive   *My friend who is <u>from New York</u> is here.*
            *My friend, who is from New York, is here.*

**50. Reported Speech**
 Statements        *He <u>said (that)</u> he was OK.*
 Questions        *He <u>asked if</u> I was OK.*
 Commands        *He <u>told me to tell</u> you he was OK.*

*Southwest American traditonal Pueblo Indian pot*

# 5: Tense/Aspect Chart

| | Simple | Perfect | Progressive | Perfect Progressive |
|---|---|---|---|---|
| | Active • Passive | Active • Passive | Active • Passive | Active |
| **Future** | I will teach English<br><br>English will be taught | I will have taught English<br><br>English will have been taught | I will be teaching English | I will have been teaching English |
| **Present** | I teach English<br><br>English is taught | I have taught English<br><br>English has been taught | I am teaching English<br><br>English is being taught | I have been teaching English |
| **Past** | I taught English<br><br>English was taught | I had taught English<br><br>English had been taught | I was teaching English<br><br>English was being taught | I had been teaching English |

# 6: Stative Verbs

| | | | | |
|---|---|---|---|---|
| agree | desire | hear | own | taste |
| appear | dislike | imagine | prefer | tend |
| appreciate | doubt | know | realize | think |
| be | dread | like | regret | trust |
| believe | equal | look like | remember | understand |
| belong | fear | love | require | want |
| care | feel | mean | resemble | weigh |
| consider | forget | need | see | wish |
| contain | guess | note | seem | |
| cost | hate | notice | smell | |
| depend | have | owe | suppose | |

# 7: Linking Verbs

| | |
|---|---|
| act | My cat is acting very strange nowadays. |
| appear | She appeared confused by his answer. |
| be | She is a teacher.<br>She is very skillful.<br>She is in her office now. |
| become | He became dissatisfied with his progress.<br>Eventually, he became a wonderful teacher. |
| feel | She feels quite pleased with the results. |
| get | She got angry when the company fired her. |
| go | This bottle of milk is going bad. |
| grow | It's growing darker with every minute. |
| look | You look terrible. |
| remain | This strange mystery remains unsolved. |
| seem | Our last assignment seemed quite easy. |
| smell | Your new perfume smells wonderful. |
| sound | Her explanation sounds very strange to me. |
| taste | Your oyster stew tastes great. |
| turn | The leaves in my yard have turned red. |

*Less common:* lie, rest, stand, come, fall, run

# 8: Irregular Verbs
## Past participle ends with *n:*

| | | | | | |
|---|---|---|---|---|---|
| arise | arose | arisen | mow | mowed | mown/mowed |
| awake | awoke | awoken/awaked | prove | proved | proven |
| be | was/were | been | ride | rode | ridden |
| bear | bore | born | rise | rose | risen |
| beat | beat | beaten | run | ran | ran |
| begin | began | begun | see | saw | seen |
| bite | bit | bitten | sew | sewed | sewn/sewed |
| blow | blew | blown | shake | shook | shaken |
| break | broke | broken | shine | shone/shined | shone/shined |
| choose | chose | chosen | show | showed | shown |
| do | did | done | slay | slew | slain |
| draw | drew | drawn | sow | sowed | sown/sowed |
| drive | drove | driven | speak | spoke | spoken |
| eat | ate | eaten | spin | spun | spun |
| fall | fell | fallen | steal | stole | stolen |
| fly | flew | flown | stride | strode | stridden |
| forbid | forbid/forbade | forbidden | strike | struck | stricken/struck |
| forget | forgot | forgotten | strive | strove | striven |
| forgive | forgave | forgiven | swear | swore | sworn |
| forsake | forsook | forsaken | swell | swelled | swollen/swelled |
| freeze | froze | frozen | take | took | taken |
| get | got | gotten | tear | tore | torn |
| give | gave | given | throw | threw | thrown |
| go | went | gone | undertake | undertook | undertaken |
| grow | grew | grown | wake | woke | woken/waked |
| hide | hid | hidden | wear | wore | worn |
| know | knew | known | weave | wove | woven |
| lie | lay | lain | win | won | won |
| mistake | mistook | mistaken | write | wrote | written |

## Past participle ends with *d:*

| | | | | | |
|---|---|---|---|---|---|
| bind | bound | bound | lead | led | led |
| bleed | bled | bled | make | made | made |
| breed | bred | bred | pay | paid | paid |
| dive | dove/dived | dove/dived | read | read | read |
| feed | fed | fed | say | said | said |
| flee | fled | fled | sell | sold | sold |
| find | found | found | slide | slid | slid |
| grind | ground | ground | speed | sped | sped |
| have | had | had | stand | stood | stood |
| hear | heard | heard | tell | told | told |
| hold | held | held | understand | understood | understood |
| lay | laid | laid | wind | wound | wound |

## Past participle ends with *t:*

| | | | | | |
|---|---|---|---|---|---|
| bend | bent | bent | lose | lost | lost |
| bring | brought | brought | mean | meant | meant |
| build | built | built | meet | met | met |
| buy | bought | bought | seek | sought | sought |
| catch | caught | caught | send | sent | sent |
| creep | crept | crept | shoot | shot | shot |
| deal | dealt | dealt | sit | sat | sat |
| feel | fought | fought | sleep | slept | slept |
| fight | felt | felt | spend | spent | spent |
| keep | kept | kept | spit | spat | spat |
| kneel | knelt | knelt | sweep | swept | swept |
| leave | left | left | teach | taught | taught |
| lend | lent | lent | think | thought | thought |
| light | lit | lit | weep | wept | wept |

## Past participle ends with *d* or *t,* but the verb does not change:

| | | | | | |
|---|---|---|---|---|---|
| bet | bet | bet | quit | quit | quit |
| bid | bid | bid | rid | rid | rid |
| burst | burst | burst | set | set | set |
| cast | cast | cast | shed | shed | shed |
| cost | cost | cost | shut | shut | shut |
| cut | cut | cut | slit | slit | slit |
| fit | fit | fit | split | split | split |
| hit | hit | hit | spread | spread | spread |
| hurt | hurt | hurt | thrust | thrust | thrust |
| let | let | let | wet | wet | wet |
| put | put | put | | | |

## Past participle ends with *m, g,* or *k:*

| | | | | | |
|---|---|---|---|---|---|
| become | became | become | sink | sank | sunk |
| come | came | come | sling | slung | slung |
| dig | dug | dug | spring | sprang | sprung |
| drink | drank | drunk | stink | stank/stunk | stunk |
| fling | flung | flung | strike | struck | struck |
| hang | hung/hanged* | hung/ hanged* | swim | swam | swum |
| ring | rang | rung | swing | swung | swung |
| shrink | shrank | shrunk | wring | wrung | wrung |
| sing | sang | sung | | | |

*different meanings

# 9: Intransitive and Transitive Verbs

Most English verbs can be used in either an intransitive or a transitive way. (Transitive verbs take a direct object.)

Example: (intransitive) *She writes every day.* (transitive) *She is writing a book.*

The verbs in the following lists are <u>usually</u> only intransitive or transitive.

Example: (intransitive) *He acted in Hamlet every night, and* (transitive) *every night he accepted a standing ovation.*

However, some of them may be used either way.

Example: (intransitive) *She lived in Manhattan, but* (transitive) *she lived a good life.*

## A. Intransitive Verbs

| | | | |
|---|---|---|---|
| act | dream | live | sit |
| agree | fall | look | sleep |
| appear | go | matter | stand |
| arrive | happen | occur | step |
| belong | laugh | rain | talk |
| care | lie | remain | think |
| come | listen | rise | wait |

## B. Transitive Verbs

| | | | |
|---|---|---|---|
| accept | cost | have | pick |
| admit | cover | hear | put |
| allow | demand | hold | raise |
| beat | destroy | include | realize |
| bring | discover | join | say |
| build | enjoy | kill | send |
| buy | expect | know | suppose |
| carry | express | lay | take |
| catch | feed | let | tell |
| cause | find | like | wear |
| consider | force | make | |
| contain | give | mean | |

# 10: Phrasal Verbs
## A. Separable Transitive

*Example:* (beat up)　She beat up Freddy. She beat Freddy up.

| Verb | Meaning | Example |
|------|---------|---------|
| beat up | hurt physically | She beat Freddy up. |
| blow out | extinguish | The children wanted to blow the matches out. |
| break down | disassemble | Max broke his bike down into sixty parts. |
| bring up | raise children | Their parents brought the children up to respect the law. |
| call off | cancel | The umpire called the game off. |
| call up | telephone | Call me up tomorrow. |
| do over | do again | The teacher asked me to do the assignment over. |
| fill out | complete | Fill these forms out and come back tomorrow. |
| get up | arouse from bed | Jane gets her children up by six every morning. |
| give back | return | The teacher gave the papers back. |
| give up | abandon | We had to give the puppy up to its real owner. |
| hand in | submit | The students handed their exams in late. |
| hang up | place on hook | He always hangs the phone up when I'm speaking. |
| keep up | maintain | It costs a lot to keep that car up. |
| leave out | omit | I've published; don't leave that out on my resume. |
| let down | lower | Let your hair down. |
| look over | review, examine | Look the test over before beginning. |
| look up | search for | I spent hours looking those words up. |
| make out | distinguish | The envelope was wet. He couldn't make her address out. |
| make up | compose, invent | They made a list up of people willing to contribute. |
| make up | use cosmetics | She made her daughter's face up for the party. |
| pack up | gather in a container | The carpenter packed his tools up at five o'clock sharp. |
| pass out | distribute | The captain passed aspirin tablets out to all of us. |
| pick out | choose | He picked a tie out to go with his shirt. |
| pick up | lift, collect | Someone picks the garbage up on Tuesday. |
| put away | put in the customary place | Put your toys away, children. |
| put off | postpone | Another meeting? Let's put it off. |
| put on | don | It's better to put your socks on before your shoes. |
| put out | extinguish | The fireman put the blaze out. |
| take back | return | My new radio doesn't work; I'm taking it back to the store. |
| take off | remove | They took their coats off when they entered. |
| take up | raise, discuss | Take that issue up with the manager. |
| talk over | discuss | The defendant talked his case over with lawyers. |
| throw away | discard | Don't throw those old magazines away. |
| try on | test the fit and appearance | She never tries clothes on when she shops. |
| try out | test | They tried the car out and decided not to buy it. |
| turn down | reject | The boss turned my request for a raise down. |
| turn down | lower the volume | Turn that television down! It's giving me a headache! |
| turn in | deliver, submit | The hub-cap thief turned himself in to the police. |
| turn off | stop power, shut off | Turn the lights off when you leave. |
| turn on | start power, put on | I turned the lights on to see better. |
| use up | finish | We've used all our sugar up. |

# B. Inseparable Transitive

*Example:* (get on)   She got on the bus as I was getting off.

| Verb | Meaning | Example |
|------|---------|---------|
| believe in | have faith in | He says he doesn't believe in God. |
| break up with | end a relationship | Betsy broke up with her boyfriend. |
| break into | enter forcibly | Somebody broke into our house yesterday. |
| call on | ask to respond | The teacher never calls on me. |
| call on | visit | We called on the Smiths last week. |
| catch up on | become up to date | It took me a day to catch up on my email. |
| come down with | get sick | My son came down with chicken pox. |
| come to | total | The bill came to one hundred dollars. |
| come up with | find | He always comes up with a good answer. |
| count on | depend on | You can count on me. I'll be there. |
| cut down on | reduce | She wants to cut down on her smoking. |
| dwell on | keep attention on | Please don't dwell on that. I've learned! |
| feel up to | be able | I'm tired, and I don't feel up to going out. |
| get along with | be friendly | He gets along with everybody. |
| get around | avoid | Somehow she gets around all the rules. |
| get out of | escape | We were lucky to get out of that mess. |
| get over | recover from | I finally got over my bad cold. |
| get through | finish | I couldn't get through the test in time. |
| go into | explain | He went into great detail when I asked him. |
| go over | review | Let's go over all the questions. |
| keep on | continue | He never stops – just keeps on talking. |
| look after | care for | My aunt looks after the kids on Monday. |
| look into | investigate | Detective Smith is looking into the murder. |
| look like | resemble | She looks like her grandmother. |
| look up to | respect | Young boys look up to famous athletes. |
| pick on | tease | That bully likes to pick on my friend. |
| put up with | tolerate | I won't put up with that rude behavior. |
| read up on | study | I read up on the history before I went there. |
| run into | meet accidentally | Guess who I ran into yesterday. |
| run across | find accidentally | She ran across the old letter and cried. |
| see in | find attractive | I don't know what she sees in him. |
| take after | resemble | He takes after his father. |
| take over | get control | John took over and calmed everyone down. |
| take up | begin | He took up the violin at the age of fifty. |
| talk back to | answer rudely | My children never talk back to me. |
| turn into | change into | Cinderella's coach turned into a pumpkin. |
| wait on | attend, serve | He waited on tables for a living. |

# C. Intransitive

| Verb | Meaning | Example |
|------|---------|---------|
| blow up | explode | What a disaster! The building blew up. |
| break down | stop working | The car broke down on the bridge. |
| break up | end a relationship | Maria and Ted broke up. |
| check in | arrive | We checked in at two o'clock. |
| check out | leave | It's 11 o'clock. It's time to check out. |
| come back | return | She never comes back from school on time. |
| come over | visit informally | Come over for lunch some time. |
| come to | regain consciousness | She fainted, but she soon came to. |
| come up | occur | I'm sorry I was late. Something came up. |
| fall apart | disintegrate | Her new toy suddenly fell apart. |
| foul up | make a mistake | I really fouled up and lost my job. |
| freak out | become hysterical | When I told her about Jim, she freaked out. |
| get by | barely succeed | His motto is do enough just to get by. |
| get in | arrive | My flight finally got in at 11 p.m. |
| get up | arise | He gets up early. |
| give in | surrender | We were losing, but we wouldn't give in. |
| give up | quit | Don't give up. We can still win. |
| go along | agree | She goes along with all his suggestions. |
| go away | leave | Please go away; I'm busy now. |
| go off | sound | I was late because my alarm didn't go off. |
| go on | happen | What's going on here? |
| grow up | mature | Grow up and act like an adult. |
| hang out | be with someone | I'm hanging out with my friends these days. |
| let up | decrease | The rain wouldn't let up. |
| log on | go on line | I logged on to your web site this morning. |
| look out | beware | Look out! There's a car coming. |
| look up | improve | Things are looking up. I have a new job. |
| make out | succeed | She made out well on those investments. |
| pan out | result | His big plan didn't pan out, and he failed. |
| pass out | faint | It was very hot, and she passed out. |
| settle down | become quiet | All right, kids, settle down and get to work. |
| shape up | improve | He shaped up and made a lot of progress. |
| ship out | leave | Shape up or ship out. |
| show up | appear | His ex-wife showed up at the ceremony. |
| sink in | realize | The truth finally sank in and he cried. |
| space out | forget | I spaced out and missed my appointment. |
| speak up | vocalize | If you don't speak up, you won't succeed. |
| take off | leave | I don't like this concert. Let's take off. |
| throw up | vomit | I don't feel well. I'm going to throw up. |

# 11: Modal Verb Chart

| Meaning | | Modal | Pre | Fut | Past | Expression | Examples |
|---|---|---|---|---|---|---|---|
| Obligation | unavoidable | **must** | ✓ | ✓ | had to | need to<br>have to | We must pay our taxes<br>    by the 15th of April.<br>You must be at school and<br>    at your desk before the<br>    bell rings. |
| | necessity | **must** | ✓ | ✓ | had to | need to<br>have to | We had to drink brackish<br>    water in order to survive.<br>The crops must have<br>    water or they will die. |
| | prohibition | **must not** | ✓ | ✓ | it was prohib- ited | be forbidden to | You must not smoke in<br>    an arsenal.<br>You must not play in<br>    the streets. |
| | no obligation | **not have to** | ✓ | ✓ | didn't have to | | She doesn't have to be at<br>    home before 10:00 p.m.<br>They don't have to come<br>    to class. |
| | avoidable obligation | **should** | ✓ | ✓ | should have | be supposed to | You should do your<br>    homework every day.<br>We should return these<br>    books to the library today. |
| | | **ought to** | ✓ | ✓ | ought to have | | |
| Advisability | | **should** | ✓ | ✓ | should have | | You look terrible, you<br>    should see a doctor.<br>You ought to have<br>    knocked before entering. |
| | | **ought to** | ✓ | ✓ | ought to have | | |
| | obligation with implied consequences | **had better** | ✓ | ✓ | had better have | | You had better pay me<br>    back before I leave.<br>She'd better watch<br>    her language. |
| | strong advisability, recom- mendation | **must not** | ✓ | ✓ | ✗ | should not | You mustn't go out alone.<br>    It's dangerous.<br>She mustn't drive so fast.<br>    She'll have an accident. |
| Preference | | **would rather** | ✓ | ✓ | would rather have | would prefer, would sooner | I'd rather do it myself.<br>He'd rather have read<br>    the book. |

✓ indicates that the modal is used in this time reference with no change in its form.
✗ indicates that the modal is not found in this time reference in any form.
Where the modal changes its form, the new form is indicated.

| Ability | ability | **can** | ✓ | ✓ | could | be able to, know how to | I can speak Russian.<br>He couldn't understand a word. |
|---|---|---|---|---|---|---|---|
| | former ability | **could** | ✗ | ✗ | could | used to be able to | He could run a 4-minute mile in those days.<br>I couldn't express myself then. |
| Possibility | theoretical and/or factual | **can** | ✓ | ✓ | could have | it is possible, maybe, perhaps | Any citizen can become a senator.<br>Could man have decended from apes?<br>We could go to the movies tonight.<br>The road may be blocked.<br>He may buy a new car next year.<br>He might have taken another road home. |
| | | **could** | ✓ | ✓ | could have | | |
| | | **may** | ✓ | ✓ | may have | | |
| | | **might** | ✓ | ✓ | might have | | |
| Probability | expectation | **should** | ✓ | ✓ | should have | expect | He should be here any minute now. |
| | | **ought to** | ✓ | ✓ | ought to have | | They ought to have finished now. |
| | inference | **must** | ✓ | ✗ | must have | have to, have got to | It's very muddy; it must have rained a lot. |
| | | **can't** | ✓ | ✗ | can't have | it is not possible | She can't be hungry; she just ate. |
| | | **couldn't** | ✓ | ✓ | couldn't have | | He couldn't have flown a plane; he died in 1512. |
| Willingness | | **will** | ✓ | ✓ | ✗ | not mind | Stay there, I'll do the dishes. |
| Invitation | you | **could** | ✓ | ✓ | ✗ | would like, can, will | Could you go to the dance with me? |
| | | **would** | ✓ | ✓ | ✗ | | Would you come to dinner tonight? |
| Request | he, she, we, they, I | **may** | ✓ | ✓ | ✗ | can, might | May I leave the room? |
| | | **could** | ✓ | ✓ | ✗ | | Could Johnny stay overnight? |
| | you | **would** | ✓ | ✓ | ✗ | can, will | Would you open the window?<br>Could you please lower your voice? |
| | | **could** | ✓ | ✓ | ✗ | | |
| Permission | | **may** | ✓ | ✓ | was allowed to, was permitted to | be allowed to, be permitted to | You may leave the room.<br>She may marry whomever she likes. |
| | | **can** | ✓ | ✓ | | | Johnny can't stay over. |

# 12: Direct and Indirect Objects

## A. Verbs that require the direct object before the indirect object

**Verbs that usually require *to*\***

    Example: *He admitted his mistake to his father*

| | | | |
|---|---|---|---|
| admit | explain | prove | report |
| announce | introduce | recommend | say |
| describe | mention | remember | speak |
| | | | suggest |

**Verbs that usually require *for***

    Example: *She answered the phone for me.*

| | | | |
|---|---|---|---|
| answer | correct | keep | pronounce |
| cash | design | open | repeat |
| change | fill | prepare | sign |
| close | fix | prescribe | translate |

## B. Verbs that can have the indirect object before the direct object\*\*

**Verbs that usually require *to* or Ø**

    Example: *He brought the apple to Eve. He brought Eve the apple.*

| | | | |
|---|---|---|---|
| bring | offer | sell | teach |
| deny | owe | send | tell |
| give | pass | show | throw |
| hand | pay | sign | write |
| lend | read | take | |

**Verbs that normally require *for* or Ø**

    Example: *She built a cage for her pet snake. She built her pet snake a cage.*

| | | | |
|---|---|---|---|
| build | cook | get | order |
| buy | do | hire | save |
| call | draw | leave | type |
| catch | find | make | |

\*Some verbs can be used with either **to** or **for,** but note the difference in meaning.
    Example: *He brought the apple to Eve. He brought an apple for Eve.*

\*\*The direct object is usually not a pronoun when it comes after the indirect object.
    Example: *He brought her the apple,* but not: *He brought Eve it.*

# 13: Verbs That Are Followed by an Infinitive

## A. No object

Example: *He agreed to meet at noon.*

| | | | |
|---|---|---|---|
| agree | deserve | learn | swear |
| appear | desire | manage | volunteer |
| arrange | fail | mean | offer |
| care | guarantee | tend | wait |
| claim | happen | promise | wish |
| consent | hesitate | refuse | |
| decide | hope | seem | |
| demand | know how | struggle | |

## B. With object

Example: *She advised the man to duck.*

| | | | |
|---|---|---|---|
| advise | dare | instruct | require |
| allow | encourage | invite | teach |
| authorize | forbid | oblige | tell |
| cause | force | order | train |
| challenge | get | permit | urge |
| command | help | persuade | warn |
| convince | hire | remind | |

## C. With or without object

Example: *He asked her to leave. He asked to be excused.*

| | | | |
|---|---|---|---|
| ask | expect | prefer | want |
| beg | need | prepare | would like |

# 14: Verbs Followed by Gerunds

Example: *She admits going to see the movie.*

| | | | |
|---|---|---|---|
| admit | discuss | mind | risk |
| anticipate | dislike | miss | suggest |
| appreciate | enjoy | postpone | tolerate |
| avoid | finish | practice | understand |
| can't help | get through | quit | |
| complete | give up | recall | |
| consider | imagine | recollect | |
| delay | keep | recommend | |
| deny | keep on | resent | |
| | mention | resist | |

# 15: Verbs Followed by Infinitives or Gerunds

Example: *He can afford to vacation in Italy. He can afford vacationing in Italy.*

| | | | |
|---|---|---|---|
| (can)afford | forget* | love | remember* |
| attempt | go | neglect | start |
| (can) bear | hate | plan | (can) stand |
| begin | hesitate | prefer | stop* |
| choose | intend | pretend | threaten |
| dread | like | regret* | try* |

# 16: Perception Verbs Followed by Simple Verbs**

Example: *She felt him approach.*

| | | | |
|---|---|---|---|
| feel | observe | see | watch |
| hear | overhear | sense | witness |
| notice | perceive | smell | |

*The meanings of these verbs are often slightly different when they are followed by an infinitive rather than a gerund.
  Example: *He stopped to listen to the speech. He stopped listening to the speech.*

**These verbs may also be followed by a gerund. Example: *She felt him approaching.*

# 17: Noun and Adjective Phrase Word Order

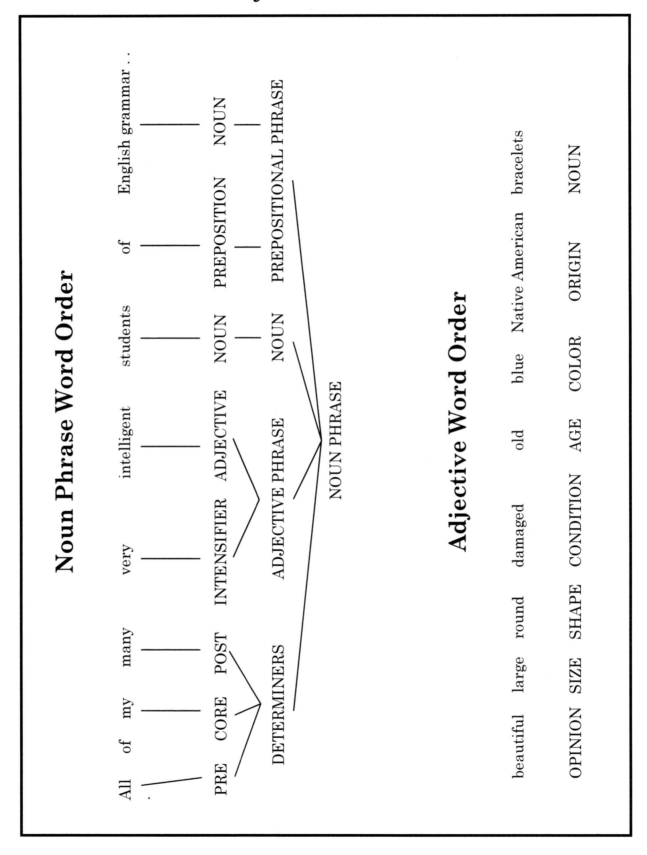

## Noun Phrase Word Order

All of my many very intelligent students of English grammar . .

PRE    CORE    POST    INTENSIFIER    ADJECTIVE    NOUN    PREPOSITION    NOUN

DETERMINERS    ADJECTIVE PHRASE    NOUN    PREPOSITIONAL PHRASE

NOUN PHRASE

## Adjective Word Order

beautiful    large    round    damaged    old    blue    Native American    bracelets

OPINION    SIZE    SHAPE    CONDITION    AGE    COLOR    ORIGIN    NOUN

# 18: Order of Determiners
# in the Noun Phrase

## Pre-Determiners

### Quantifiers
all
both
many of, a lot of
none of, two of

### Multipliers
double
twice
three times

### Fractions
(one) half (of)

## Core Determiners

### Articles
a/an
the
some

### Possessive Adjectives
my, your, his, her
our, your, their

### Possessive Noun
X's, Joe's

### Demonstratives
this, that, these, those

### Quantifiers
some/any
each, every
either, neither
no

## Post Determiners

### Cardinal Numbers
one, two, etc.

### Ordinals
first, second
next, last
another

### Quantifiers
many, much
few, a few
little, a little
more/less
most/least

*Turtle totem with three whales*

# 19: Pronouns

## *Personal Pronouns*

| Subject | Object | Possessive Adjective | Possessive | Reflexive/ Emphatic |
|---------|--------|----------------------|------------|---------------------|
| I | me | my | mine | myself |
| you | you | your | yours | yourself |
| he | him | his | his | himself |
| she | her | her | hers | herself |
| it | it | its | its | itself |
| we | us | our | ours | ourselves |
| you | you | your | yours | yourselves |
| they | them | their | theirs | themselves |

## *Impersonal Pronouns*

| | | | | |
|---|---|---|---|---|
| one | one | one's | | oneself |

## *Indefinite Pronouns*

| | –body | –one | –thing |
|---|-------|------|--------|
| **some–** | somebody | someone | something |
| **any–** | anybody | anyone | anything |
| **no–** | nobody | no one | nothing |
| **every–** | everybody | everyone | everything |

## *Interrogative Pronouns*          *As Adjectives*

| | | |
|---|---|---|
| **WHAT** | What hit me? | What color do you like? |
| **WHICH** | Which do you like? | Which car is yours? |
| **WHOSE** | Whose is this? | Whose car is that? |

# 20: Articles

|  | *Specific* | | *Generic* |
|---|---|---|---|
|  | **Indefinite** | **Definite** | |
| **Count Singular** | I ate **an** apple and **a** banana. | **The** apple was green.<br>**The** banana was black. | **An/The** apple is more nutritious than **a/the** banana. |
| **Count Plural** | I also ate (**some**) pears. | **The** pears were red. | Ø Pears are also nutritious. |
| **Noncount** | I ate (**some**) fruit. | **The** fruit was delicious. | I eat **ø** fruit for lunch. |
| **Proper** | | Apples are grown in **ø** Vermont. | |

# 21: Noncountable (Mass) Nouns*

| A. Abstract | B. Matter, material | C. Generic terms |
|---|---|---|
| advice | air | business |
| age | beer | change |
| beauty | blood | equipment |
| capitalism | bread | fruit |
| communism | butter | furniture |
| democracy | cake | jewelry |
| energy | chalk | luggage |
| fun | cheese | machinery |
| happiness | coal | mail |
| help | coffee | money |
| honesty | electricity | news |
| information | fog | propaganda |
| justice | fish | scenery |
| kindness | gold | slang |
| knowledge | grass | stationery |
| laughter | hair | traffic |
| liberty | ice | vegetation |
| life | ink | weather |
| play | iron | _____ |
| recreation | juice | _____ |
| strength | lumber | _____ |
| trouble | meat | _____ |
| truth | milk | _____ |
| virtue | oil | _____ |
| wisdom | oxygen | _____ |
| work | paper | _____ |
| youth | rain | _____ |
| _____ | rice | _____ |
| _____ | smoke | _____ |
| _____ | snow | _____ |
| _____ | soap | _____ |
| _____ | soup | _____ |
| _____ | sugar | _____ |
| _____ | tea | _____ |
| _____ | water | _____ |
| _____ | wine | _____ |
| _____ | wood | _____ |
| _____ | _____ | _____ |
| _____ | _____ | _____ |

* This list is far from complete; it is intended only to be suggestive. We have tried to include high frequency nouns. Add your own to our lists.

## D. Subject matter

architecture
art
chemistry
civics
economics
engineering
English
geology
grammar
history
literature
mathematics
music
philosophy
physics
science
technology
vocabulary

_____
_____
_____
_____
_____
_____
_____
_____
_____
_____
_____
_____
_____
_____
_____
_____
_____
_____
_____
_____

## E. Sports and recreation/activities

baseball
basketball
bridge
camping
dancing
drinking
football
golf
hiking
hockey
homework
hunting
opera
sailing
singing
softball
swimming
television
traveling
volleyball

_____
_____
_____
_____
_____
_____
_____
_____
_____
_____
_____
_____
_____
_____
_____
_____
_____
_____

## F. Countable and noncountable nouns*

age
baseball (and other balls)
beer (and other drinks)
business
change
company
dope
glass
iron
paper
play
room
smoke
tape
tea (party)
work
youth

_____
_____
_____
_____
_____
_____
_____
_____
_____
_____
_____
_____
_____
_____
_____
_____
_____
_____

*This list(F) contains words that can have dual meanings: one countable meaning and a different non-countable meaning. Example: _The game of American_ **_football_** _is played with an oddly shaped ball called a_ **_football._**

Many non-count nouns, if used to refer to items or units, can also be used as count nouns. Example: _We work at home and do a lot of business there. I run one business here and my wife runs two others._

# 22: Quantifiers with Count and Noncount Nouns

| Noncount only | Count or noncount | Count only |
|---|---|---|
| much | all | many |
| not much | almost all | several |
| a little | most | quite a few |
| little | a lot of | a few |
| | quite a lot of | just a few |
| | not all | not many |
| | some/any | a couple of |
| | hardly any | few |
| | scarcely any | |

# 23: Prepositions

| | | | |
|---|---|---|---|
| about | away from | from | out of |
| above | because of | in | outside |
| according to | before | in back of | over |
| across (from) | behind | in front of | past |
| against | below | inside | plus |
| along | beneath | in spite of | regardless of |
| alongside | beside | in the middle | since |
| among | between | like | through |
| around | but (for) | minus | to |
| as | by | near | toward(s) |
| as . . as | close to | next to | under |
| as far as | despite | of | underneath |
| as for | during | off | up |
| at the top/bottom of | down | on | up to |
| as to | except for | on the left/ | until/till |
| as well as | far from | right/corner of | with |
| at | for | opposite | within |

# 24: Verb + Preposition Combinations

## A. Verb + preposition + object

Example: *They agree on everything.*

| | | | |
|---|---|---|---|
| agree on | care for | hear about | succeed in |
| agree with | comment on | hear from | talk about |
| approve of | complain about | laugh at | talk to |
| argue with | consent to | listen to | think about |
| arrive at | consist of | look at | vote for |
| arrive in | count on | object to | wait for |
| believe in | decide on | pay for | wish for |
| belong to | depend on | rely on | work for |

## B. Verb + object + prepostion + object

Example: *She adds fertilizer to her garden soil.*

| | | |
|---|---|---|
| add ___ to/with ___ | explain ___ to ___ | prefer ___ to ___ |
| blame ___ for ___ | excuse ___ for ___ | remind ___ of ___ |
| compare ___ with/to ___ | introduce ___ to ___ | thank ___ for ___ |
| congratulate ___ on/for ___ | keep ___ for ___ | subtract ___ from ___ |

# 25: Participles As Modifiers

Example: *He thinks her work is amazing. He is amazed by her work.*

| | | | |
|---|---|---|---|
| amazing | amazed | fascinating | fascinated |
| amusing | amused | frightening | frightened |
| annoying | annoyed | interesting | interested |
| astonishing | astonished | intriguing | intrigued |
| boring | bored | irritating | irritated |
| challenging | challenged | pleasing | pleased |
| confusing | confused | satisfying | satisfied |
| convincing | convinced | shocking | shocked |
| disappointing | disappointed | surprising | surprised |
| disgusting | disgusted | terrifying | terrified |
| disturbing | disturbed | thrilling | thrilled |
| embarrassing | embarrassed | tiring | tired |
| exciting | excited | touching | touched |

# 26: Time Expressions
# for the 12 Tense-Aspect Constructions

## 1. Present Simple
| | | | |
|---|---|---|---|
| always | often | usually | sometimes |
| never | every (day) | once a (week) | at/on/in |

## 2. Past Simple
| | | | |
|---|---|---|---|
| yesterday | last (night/week/year) | at/on/in | ago |

## 3. Future Simple
| | | | |
|---|---|---|---|
| tomorrow | next (week) | soon | at/on/in |

## 4. Present Perfect
| | | | |
|---|---|---|---|
| for (ten years, etc.) | since (1968) | already | just |
| so far | up to now | until now | all her life | lately |
| yet | recently | finally | never/ever |

## 5. Past Perfect
| | | | |
|---|---|---|---|
| already . . when | just . . when | before | after |
| until | no sooner . . . than | as soon as | when |

## 6. Future Perfect
| | | | |
|---|---|---|---|
| by | by the time | before | already |

## 7. Present Progressive
| | | | | |
|---|---|---|---|---|
| now | at the moment | these days | still | at/on/in |

## 8. Past Progressive
| | | |
|---|---|---|
| already . . .when | just . . . when | at/on/in |

## 9. Future Progressive
| | | |
|---|---|---|
| tomorrow . . . when | soon | at/on/in |

## 10. Present Perfect Progressive
| | | | |
|---|---|---|---|
| for | since | lately | recently |

## 11. Past Perfect Progressive
| | | |
|---|---|---|
| for . . . when | before | after |

## 12. Future Perfect Progressive
for . . . by

# 27: Adverbials

## *Order of Adverbials*

**Mike walks to town very rapidly on Main Street every morning**
Direction Manner    Position    Frequency

**at eight for exercise because he's trying to get in shape.**
Time   Purpose    Reason

## Adverbial Subordinators

**TEMPORAL**

after
before
when
while
as
by the time (that)
since
until/till
as soon as
s/so long as
once
whenever
every time
the first time (that)
"   last   "   "
"   next   "   "
(at) the same time (that)
"   "   moment "
during the time (that)

**CONDITIONAL**

if
only if
if only
even if
unless
whether or not
providing (that)
provided (that)
in case
in the event that
except that

**MANNER**

as if
as though
as
however
in any way that

**CAUSAL**

because
since
now (that)
as
as/so long as
inasmuch as
insofar as

**PURPOSE**

so (that)
in order (that)
in the hope that
lest
for fear that

**CONCESSIVE**

although
though
even though
in spite of /despite
the fact that
regardless of
the fact that
whatever
however
no matter WH
while
whereas
when

**PLACE**

where(ver)

# 28: Preverbal Adverbs of Frequency

| 0% | 10% | 50% | 75% | 100% |
|---|---|---|---|---|
| never | rarely | sometimes | often | always |
| don't ever | seldom | occasionally | frequently | |
| never ever | hardly ever | | usually | |
| | scarcely ever | | generally | |
| | don't often | | regularly | |
| | | | nearly always | |
| | | | almost always | |

*Initial*                                                                      *Final*

| | | |
|---|---|---|
| sometimes | | sometimes |
| occasionally | | occasionally |
| frequently | | frequently |
| usually | | often |
| generally | | |

# 29: Adverbial Participles

## Present Participle (-ing)

   1. **Basic** – Working on his paper, X . . .
   2. **Perfective** – Having worked on his paper,  . . .
   3. **Perfective-progressive** – Having been working on his paper, X . . .

## Past Participle  (-en/-ed)

   1. **Basic** – Worn out from the work, X . . .
   2. **Perfective** – Being worn out from his work, X . . .
   3. **Perfective-progressive** – Having been worn out from the work, X . . .

# 30: Adjective + Preposition Combinations

Example: *She is interested in becoming a judge.*

| | | | |
|---|---|---|---|
| concerned about | slow at | conscious of | sure to |
| happy about | quick at | confident of | opposed to |
| angry about | lucky at | ashamed of | |
| enthusiastic about | surprised at | sure of | bored with |
| careful about | amazed at | afraid of | impressed with |
| excited about | | certain of | involved with |
| glad about | interested in | sick of | annoyed with |
| worried about | involved in | | delighted with |
| sorry about | disappointed in | upset over | satisfied with |
| disappointed about | | disturbed over | pleased with |
| pleased about | fond of | | disappointed with |
| | in favor of | accustomed to | |
| good at | tired of | slow to | |
| clever at | capable of | quick to | |
| bad at | aware of | resigned to | |

# 31: Verbs and Adjectives Taking Subjunctive

## Verbs

Example: *He **advised** that she **watch** the stock market very carefully. He said it is **important** that she **do** this immediately.*

| | | | |
|---|---|---|---|
| advise | propose | forbid | require |
| ask | recommend | desire | stipulate |
| beg | command | insist | suggest |
| demand | request | prefer | urge |

## Adjectives

| | | | |
|---|---|---|---|
| advisable | essential | desirable | important |
| best | good | mandatory | urgent |
| better | imperative | necessary | vital |
| critical | crucial | required | requisite |

# The Communicative Aspect

The communicative aspect does not deal with linguistic forms, such as *go, went, gone*, the **medium** of communication. It outlines ways in which the language is used to send and receive **messages.** We have further analyzed this communicative aspect into three sub-aspects that are usually present when a message is being communicated. First, there is a **situational context** in which the message is exchanged, the *where*. The **topical content** is the subject matter of the message, the *what,* and the **communicative function** is the-manner and purpose of the message, the *how* and *why.*

*Tiffany lamp*

## Contents

# Situational Context

The situational context, in its simplest sense, is a definite, identifiable place or setting where communication happens *(a bank,* for example). However, some of the situations in the following pages are not specific places. There are events or chains of events that are common and recurrent in everyday life (for example, a *wedding* or *asking for prices).* There are also contexts which are topics for discussion and cultural exploration (such as *planning nutritious meals).*

In order to communicate effectively in these situations, students need appropriate topical vocabulary, cultural information, and functional language. The materials in the following sections will be helpful.

This section amounts to a series of lists of suggested communicative contexts that could be used in presenting and practicing communicative language and cultural insights. In many cases, vocabulary topics relevant to these contexts are given in the next section. When they are, cross-references are given.

A teacher using this section as a planning guide selects a situation appropriate to the interests and needs of their students and then plans a lesson using any of the topics which seem relevant. For example, looking over the list, the teacher settles on *restaurant* from List 1. Basic Daily Needs. The reference is to topics 1–3, 24, and 32. The teacher finds that these lists suggest both vocabulary and cultural information students will need in a restaurant. They will need to know about *reservations, menus, waiters, orders, checks,* and *tips.* After teaching the lesson, the teacher may hand out photocopies of the relevant topic lists for further vocabulary enrichment.

Once the students have been given a handout, it can be used as the basis for pair work, writing assignments, situational role playing, and many other kinds of in-class and out-of-class activities.

The list of situations given in this section is in the form of an outline or checklist. It is intended to be suggestive rather than exhaustive. It is not intended as a situational sequence or syllabus, but it should help teachers develop sequences of their own appropriate for each class.

❑ 1. Basic Daily Needs  88
❑ 2. Transportation  88
❑ 3. Work  88
❑ 4. Health and Safety  89
❑ 5. Personal and Family Needs  89

❑ 6. Personal Finances  89
❑ 7. Education  90
❑ 8. Shopping and Service  90
❑ 9. Recreation  91
❑ 10. Citizenship  91

# 1: Basic Daily Needs

## Food
kitchen
dining room
cooking
restaurant
using a recipe
planning nutritious meals
storing food safely
grocery shopping
weights and measures
planning to save money
serving meals
eating and drinking

See topics 1–3, 24, 32

## Clothing
buying clothes, shoes
repairing clothes, sewing
using a washer, dryer
laundry/laundromat
cleaner

See topics 6, 7, 33

## Shelter
types of housing
rooms, including:
   living room
   bedroom
   bathroom
   kitchen
housekeeping
maintenance
yard work

See topic 4

# 2: Transportation

asking directions
using maps
getting lost
walking—when, where
subway station, subway

See topics 19, 29

bus stop, city bus
bus station, intercity bus
railway station, train
airport, plane
taxis

commuting
buying tickets, tokens
travel agent
customs/immigration
hitchhiking

# 3: Work

## The work place
  home
  work shop/factory
  warehouse
  shipping/freight terminal
  store/department store/mall
  office
  studio
  school
  hospital/clinic/nursing home
  daycare/eldercare center
  hotel
  restaurant
  construction site
  outdoors
  farm
  travel/transportation
See topics 34, 46–50

## Work procedures
  housekeeping
  cooking/doing dishes
  gardening/groundskeeping
  cleaning and maintenance
  doing repairs
  using the telephone
  taking messages
  making/keeping appointments
  placing/taking orders
  writing receipts
  making change
  packing/shipping
  dictating/taking dictation
  typing
  filing
  using computers
  planning/following plans

scheduling/following schedules
getting paid
cashing pay checks
supervising/being supervised
following instructions
scheduling staff meetings
following safety regulations
asking for help
dealing with mistakes
changing jobs
applying for work
employment office
job training
health insurance/benefits
social security
compensation insurance
labor unions/union dues
health and safety regulations

# 4: Health and Safety

advice on a healthy diet
advice on getting exercise
gym, athletics
taking vitamins
taking medicine
drug store
doctor's office

dentist's office
emergency services
   police
   fire
   ambulance
medical center
health clinic

hospital
   emergency
   visiting
medical insurance
personal hygiene
sex and contraception
personal safety

See topics 1–3, 27, 41, 42, 43

# 5: Personal and Family Needs

interpersonal relationships, roles
   work
   school
   sports
   friendship
   romance
family relationships
family planning
family counseling
children
   siblings
   discipline
   child care
   babysitting
   schooling
   afterschool activities
   birthdays/holidays
camp

See topics 8, 9, 26, 56–58, 63

adult education, training
elderly people
relatives
spiritual
wedding
   ceremony
   wedding party
   bridal dinner
   wedding gown, dress
   bachelor party
marriage
   anniversary
   counseling
   separation, divorce
civil union
living together
   as roommates
   out of wedlock
   common law partners

family activities
family trips
record keeping
retirement
elder care
hospice
death, burial
places of worship
community organizations
   ethnic
   religious
   civic
   service
   political
   cultural
social life, entertaining
dating
caring for pets
veterinarian

# 6: Personal Finances

spending money
   cash
   checks, cashing checks
   charging
   charge accounts
   credit cards
   interest costs
   loan payments

See topic 36

bank, savings and loan
planning a family budget
getting/making a loan
getting a mortgage
getting a second mortgage
home equity loan
educational loans, financial aid
planning investments
savings accounts

savings bonds
retirement accounts
buying stock, bonds
insurance
social security
work benefits
taxes
gambling
retirement

# 7: Education

**Expectations, routines**
classroom
schedules
being on time
assignments, homework
researching, writing papers
library
tests, quizzes
final exams
standardized tests
grades, records
tuition, room and board
scholarships
neatness
honesty/cheating

See topics 53, 57, 58; Culture topic 37

**At school, on campus**
registration
dean's office
adviser's office
    scheduling
    course change
teacher's office hours
    getting help
    planning a research paper
housing office
bursar's office
dormitory life
    rooms, roommates
    dorm rules
    laundry
off-campus housing

campus post office
book store
student center
cafeteria, dining hall
fraternity, sorority
chapel, chaplain's office
student health service
foreign student adviser
computer center
library
other campus services
gymnasium
team, coach
team spirit
locker room
drugs and sports

# 8: Shopping and Services

planning
making a shopping list
using the yellow pages
newspaper/magazine ads,
    junk mail
sales, come-on's
coupons, bargains
internet shopping
finding products in big stores
kinds of stores
    department store
    supermarket
    mall
    specialty shops
    main street
    boutiques
    copy center
getting advice about products
    from consumer services
    in specialty shops
        bakery
        optician
        book store
        camera store
        on the internet

*See topics 33, 34

unit pricing
asking for prices
fixed prices/bargaining
ordering from catalogues
ordering on the internet
paying for purchases
    cash
    charge
    credit cards
    time payments
    layaway plans
    lease-purchase
    rental
    getting change
    tipping
returning merchandise
choosing and getting services
    mechanic
    barber/hairdresser
    plumber
    electrician
    carpenter
    car mechanic
    doctor
    dentist
    lawyer
    accountant

tax preparation service
insurance agent
pastor/priest
real estate agent
getting help/public services
    police department
    court
    public defender/legal aid
    emergency services
    ambulance service
    hospital/emergency room
    fire department
    town offices/city hall
    local town officials
    extension agent
    post office
    state and congressional
        representatives
    school board
    IRS - internal revenue service
    INS - immigration and
        naturalization service
    public library
    childcare, eldercare
    adult center
    teen center
    YMCA

# 9: Recreation

**Athletics**
local team sports – seasonal
children's and adult leagues
  finding a team
  signing up
  schedules
exercising – working out
  walking, running
  swimming
games – tennis, golf
children's games
  capture the flag
  jumping rope
  dodge ball
  marbles/jacks
  hide and seek
  tag
  three-legged races

See topics 37–40

**Social**
dinner parties
cocktail/beer parties
dances
community events, socials
restaurants

**Entertainment**
movies
theater
opera, musicals
popular music concerts
classical music concerts
rock concerts
professional sports events
night clubs
coffee houses
dance performance/ballet

**Arts and crafts**
art classes
music lessons

art studios
galleries
craft shows
gift shops
museums

**At home**
TV, radio
games – cards, board games
  computer games,
  role playing games
parties – children's parties
  family parties
  holiday parties
special meals –
  barbecue
  picnic
  brunch
  potluck
  buffet
hobbies

# 10: Citizenship

town/city offices
police department
court
contacting government officials
  local and national
  getting help
  expressing opinions
election campaigns
voter registration
voting
discussing taxes
discussing immigration status
discussing work permits
discussing civil rights
discussing civil obligations
discussing national holidays
discussing historic landmarks
discussing corruption
  bribery
  protection money
  organized crime

discussing honor codes
  codes of conduct
  truth in advertising
  civic responsibility
discussing
  national anthem
  other patriotic songs
  Gettysburg address
  Dr. King's "I have a dream"
American history
  explaining important events
  leaders
  movements
  the Constitution
  functions of government
    local
    state
    national
    international
discussing the importance of
  dissent

getting involved
an informed electorate
The Bill of Rights
discussing what makes a
  community
  a good place to live
  a good place to work
  a good place to raise children
discussing the roles of
  organizations –
  civic
  political
  special interest
  religious
  cultural
  arts
  public and private education
  public and private/commercial
    broadcasting
local, state, federal taxes
volunteer work

See topics 34, 51, 52, 54, 59 and Culture topics 4-11, 22-23, 41-42 National Documents of the U.S.A. and Canada

# Topical Content

The topics of human conversation are virtually endless, but it is possible to predict a general list of topics that virtually every language learner will encounter at some time or other. The following lists are an attempt at a comprehensive list of **basic** topics. Each topic is outlined as a vocabulary list of the words, phrases, and idioms that might be encountered in a general conversation about the topic. In the case of the idioms, they are included not because they might appear in the context of a conversation, but rather because they have some semantic relationship to the topic, usually at the literal level, rather than the figurative.

It will again be obvious that the vocabulary collected under each topic is influenced by the cultural context of contemporary North America.

Finally, please bear in mind that these lists are far from complete. They should be seen as basic words of fairly high frequency. You will want to add your own discoveries to our lists, and once again we welcome your additions and comments. info@ProLinguaAssociates.com

## Topic checklist

*Jack O'Lantern*

# 1: Food  also see #2 *Cooking* and #3 *Eating*

## Vegetables

artichoke
asparagus
avocado
bean
beet
bok choy
broccoli
brussels sprouts
cabbage
carrot
cauliflower
celery
chard
Chinese cabbage
collard
corn
cucumber
eggplant

endive
garlic
jicama
kale
kohlrabi
leek
lettuce
lima beans
mushroom
okra
onion
parsnip
pickle
peas
pepper
  bell
  chili
plantain

potato
pumpkin
radish
rhubarb
rutabaga
salad
scallion
shallot
snow peas
spinach
squash
  summer
  winter
sweet potato
tomato
turnip
yam
zucchini

## Fruit

apple
apricot
banana
berry
blackberry
blueberry
cantaloupe
cherry
coconut
cranberry
date

fig
guava
grape
grapefruit
kiwi
lemon
lime
melon
orange
papaya
peach

pear
persimmon
pineapple
plum
pomegranate
prune
raspberry
raisin
strawberry
tangerine
watermelon

## Bread and Cereal

bagel
bread
burrito
biscuit
bun
cereal
  cold
  hot
cracker
Danish pastry
doughnut
dumpling
English muffin

French toast
grain
granola
grits
muffin
noodle
nut
oatmeal
pancake
pasta
pita
pizza

popcorn
potato chip
rice
roll
roll up
sandwich
spaghetti
sweet roll
toast
taco
tortilla
tortilla chip
waffle

## Meat and Poultry

| | | |
|---|---|---|
| meat | chicken | lamb |
|   dark | duck | pork |
|   red | egg | ribs |
|   white | game | sausage |
| bacon | goose | turkey |
| beef | ham | veal |

## Seafood

| | | |
|---|---|---|
| bass | mackerel | shark |
| catfish | mahi mahi | shellfish |
| caviar | mollusk | shrimp |
| clam | mussel | smelt |
| codfish | octopus | sole |
| crab | oyster | squid |
| crayfish | perch | sturgeon |
| fillet | pike | swordfish |
| fish | pollock | trout |
| haddock | red snapper | tuna fish |
| herring | salmon | walleye pike |
| lobster | scallop | whitefish |

## Dairy

| | | |
|---|---|---|
| butter | cream | skim/1%/2%/whole milk |
| cottage cheese | half and half | sour cream |
| cheese | margarine | whipped cream |
| ice cream | milk | yoghurt |

## Food Groups

| | | |
|---|---|---|
| fruits | meats, beans, fish, nuts, eggs | oils, fats |
| grains, breads, cereals | milk, dairy | vegetables |

## Dishes and Cuts

| | | |
|---|---|---|
| breast | hamburger | pie |
| chili | hash | ribs |
| chop | hot dog | roast |
| chop suey | leg | salad |
| cold cuts | leftover | sauerkraut |
| casserole | loaf | souffle |
| cocktail | meatball | soup |
| corned beef | meatloaf | steak |
| curry | meat patty | stew |
| fillet | mixed vegetables | stuffing |
| fondue | paté | wing |

## Desserts

| | | | |
|---|---|---|---|
| brownie | cupcake | Jello | sherbet. ice, sorbet |
| cake | custard | pastry | soufflé |
| cheesecake | fruit | pie | sundae |
| cookie | ice cream | pudding | tart |

## Herbs, Spices, and Other Flavoring

| | | | |
|---|---|---|---|
| allspice | coriander | mustard | sage |
| anise | clove | nutmeg | savory |
| basil | cocoa | oregano | salt |
| bay leaf | curry | paprika | syrup |
| cardamom seed | dill | parsley | sugar |
| caraway seed | fennel | pepper | brown |
| chervil | garlic | black | white |
| chive | ginger | cayenne | tarragon |
| chocolate | honey | chili | thyme |
| cilantro | marjoram | white | vinegar |
| cinnamon | mint | rosemary | |

## Condiments and Sauces

| | | | |
|---|---|---|---|
| bacon bits | hollandaise sauce | mayonnaise | salad dressing |
| barbecue sauce | horseradish | mustard | soy sauce |
| butterscotch | hot sauce | pepper | steak sauce |
| cheese | jelly, jam | pickle | sugar |
| chocolate sauce | ketchup | relish | tartar sauce |
| chutney | marshmallow | salsa | white sauce |
| cocktail sauce | marmalade | salt | worchestershire sauce |
| gravy | | | |

## Beverages, Drinks

| | | | |
|---|---|---|---|
| ale | coffee | liqueur | soda |
| beer | coke | liquor | soft drink |
| brandy | cola | milk | tea |
| cider | decafe coffee | mineral water | tonic water |
| club soda | ginger ale | punch | water |
| cocktail | juice | Sanka | whiskey |
| cocoa | lemonade | seltzer | wine |

## Idioms and Expressions

| | | | |
|---|---|---|---|
| baker's dozen | natural/organic food | food fit for the gods | fishy |
| baloney | to cry over spilled milk | gluten-free | sour grapes |
| to beef about | to have one's cake | to know which side one's | to spill the beans |
| to beef up | and eat it, too | bread is buttered on | square meal |
| to bring home the bacon | to not know beans | like two peas in a pod | to take the cake |
| corny | to pepper with questions | locavore | upper crust |
| cream of the crop | proof of the pudding | Variety is the spice of life. | Hot dog! |
| fast food | to put all one's eggs | not my cup of tea | |
| junk food | in one basket | to egg on | |

# 2: Cooking <small>also see #1 Food and #3 Eating</small>

## Equipment

| | | | | |
|---|---|---|---|---|
| baking pan | chef's knife | food processor | mixer | rolling pin |
| baster | chopping block | frying pan | mixing spoon | saucepan |
| blender | coffee maker | grater | oven | sifter |
| bowl | cookbook | grill | popcorn popper | skillet |
| bottle opener | colander | kettle | pan | spatula |
| bread pan | cover | ladle | pot | steamer |
| broiler | double boiler | lid | potato masher | stove |
| burner | dutch oven | measuring cup | pressure cooker | strainer |
| can opener | eggbeater | microwave oven | recipe | thermometer |
| casserole dish | | | | wisk |

## Processes

| | | | | | |
|---|---|---|---|---|---|
| add | broil | dice | knead | refrigerate | smoke |
| bake | brown | drain | mash | roast | spread |
| barbecue | can | dredge | marinate | roll out | sprinkle |
| beat | carve | dry | measure | salt | steam |
| blanch | chill | fold in | melt | sauce | stir |
| blend | chop | flour | mince | scorch | stir-fry |
| boil | coat | freeze | mix | season | stain |
| bone | combine | freeze dry | parboil | sift | steep |
| bottle | cook | fry | peel | simmer | toast |
| burn | cover | grate | pickle | skin | toss |
| braise | cure | grease | pour | slice | turn |
| brew | deep fry | grind | preserve | soak | whip |

## Ingredients

| | | | | | |
|---|---|---|---|---|---|
| baking powder | butter | dressing | lard | peanut butter | stock |
| baking soda | corn meal | filling | loaf | roast | stuffing |
| batter | cornstarch | flake | leftover | salad dressing | syrup |
| bread crumbs | crust | flavor | molasses | sauce | vinegar |
| brine | dash | flour | oil | seasoning | (egg) whites |
| broth | dough | | | shell | (egg) yolks |

## Dishes, Measures

| | | | | |
|---|---|---|---|---|
| bread basket | gallon | pinch | platter | tablespoon |
| casserole | measuring spoons | pint | quart | teaspoon |
| cup measure | pie plate | pitcher | serving dish | tureen |

## Adjectives

| | | | | |
|---|---|---|---|---|
| boiled | fresh | high, hot (oven) | rare | scalloped | steamed |
| broiled | fried | medium | raw | slow (oven) | tender |
| crisp | ground | moderate (oven) | ripe | soft-boiled | thickened |
| curdled | | | | | well-done |

## Idioms and Expressions

| | | | |
|---|---|---|---|
| a flash in the pan | half-baked | the pot calling the kettle black | watered down |
| take with a grain of salt | hard-boiled | single-serve coffee system | |

# 3: Eating  *also see #1 Food and #2 Cooking*

## Dishes and Utensils

carving knife
dessert dish
cup
fork
 dessert
 dinner
 salad

glass
goblet
gravy boat
knife
napkin
plate
platter

salad bowl
saucer
serving dish
spoon
soup bowl
soup spoon
tureen

## Meals

appetizer
breakfast
brunch
buffet

course
dessert
dinner
lunch

picnic
smorgasbord
snack
supper

## Verbs

bite
chew
diet
dine
drink

eat
gobble
graze
munch
nibble

ruin your appetite
sip
snack
swallow
taste

## Adjectives

bitter
coarse
delicious
dry
famished
full

hungry
moist
rich
sour
starved
succulent

sweet
tart
thick
thin
thirsty
tough

## Misc.

baker
chef
cook
gourmet

natural food
nutritious
organic
potluck

seconds
vegan
vegetarian
whole food

## Idioms

to eat like a bird
a picky eater
to eat like a pig

to pig out
to wolf down one's food
to eat for two

to bite off more than
 one can chew
have no appetite for

# 4: Housing/Housekeeping

## General

| | | | |
|---|---|---|---|
| building | gated community | quarter | town |
| city | ghetto | residence | town plan |
| community | home | rural | trailer park |
| country | house | sprawl | urban |
| development | housing development | subdivision | village |
| farm | neighborhood | suburb | zoning |

## Types

| | | | |
|---|---|---|---|
| adobe | high-rise | palace | tenement |
| A-frame | houseboat | ranch house | tent |
| apartment | hut | row house | tepee |
| cape | igloo | saltbox | town house |
| condominium, condo | log cabin | shack | trailer |
| chalet | manor | skyscraper | tree house |
| flat | mobile home | split-level | wigwam |

## Construction Materials

| | | | |
|---|---|---|---|
| brick | insulation | plywood | steel |
| cement | linoleum | roofing | stone |
| clapboard | log | sheetrock | tile |
| concrete | molding | shingles | vinyl |
| flooring | paneling | siding | wall board |
| glass | | | wood |

## Parts

| | | | |
|---|---|---|---|
| addition | door | fireplace | plumbing |
| bay | back | floor | rafters |
| breaker box | front | foundation | sill |
| breezeway | screen | frame | stairs |
| bulkhead | storm | fuse box | steps |
| ceiling | drive(way) | garage | walk |
| chimney | electric outlets | heating system | wall |
| chimney flue | ell | light switch | window |
| dormer | electrical outlet | picture window | wiring |

## Places

| | | | |
|---|---|---|---|
| attic, store room | den | lawn | porch, balcony, |
| basement | dining room | living room | deck, veranda |
| bath(room) | family room | mud room | study |
| bedroom | garage | nursery | sun room |
| breakfast room/nook | hall | pantry | toilet |
| cellar | kitchen | patio | utility room |
| closet | laundry room | play room | yard |

# Events and Activities

| | | | |
|---|---|---|---|
| babysitting | doing the laundry | house cleaning | TV watching |
| cooking | home improvement | light repair work | visitors |
| delivery person | house guests | mail carrier | yard work |

# Furnishings and Equipment

| | | | |
|---|---|---|---|
| ashtray | crib | hutch | shades |
| basin | cupboard | iron | shelf |
| bathtub | curtains | ironing board | sheets |
| bed | desk | kitchen table | shower |
|   double | dining room table | lamp | sideboard |
|   twin | dishwasher | laundry basket | sink |
|   bunk | draperies | light | sofa |
|   queen-size | dresser | linen | stereo |
|   king-size | dryer | linoleum | stove |
| blanket | DVD player | love seat | table |
| bookshelves/case | easy chair | mircrowave oven | television |
| cabinet | end table | oven | TV stand |
| carpet | electric outlet | plasma TV | toaster |
| CD player | entertainment center | radio | toilet bowl |
| chair | fireplace | record player | towel |
| coffee table | flat screen TV | refrigerator | vacuum cleaner |
| computer | freezer | rug | washing machine |
| cot | furnace | scanner | water heater |
| counter | | | |

# Activities

| | | | |
|---|---|---|---|
| change (the linen/ sheets) | do the ironing | straighten (up) | lease |
| | make the bed | sweep | let |
| clean (up) | paint | vacuum | mortgage |
| do the dishes | pick up | wash | move |
| do the laundry | polish | wax | own |
| dust | put away | buy | renovate |
| fix | repair | build | remodel |
| fold the laundry | scrub | furnish | rent |
| hang out the laundry | set the table | insure | sub-let |

# Idioms and Expressions

| | | |
|---|---|---|
| to hit home | to hit the sack | to make a clean sweep of |
| on the house | spick/spic and span | to ride a broomstick |
| to raise the roof | to whitewash | handwriting on the wall |
| wet blanket | to turn the tables on | to keep up with the Joneses |
| on the carpet | up/down one's alley | A new broom sweeps clean. |
| to pull up stakes | blind alley | A house is not a home. |

# 5: Lawn and Garden  also see #16 Plants & Trees

## Materials

| | | | |
|---|---|---|---|
| dirt | mud | potting soil | seed starter mix |
| earth | mulch | fertilizer | seedling |
| insecticide | compost | seed | soil |
| manure | | | weed killer |

## Tools and Equipment

| | | | |
|---|---|---|---|
| aerator | grafting tape | plant stand | shovel |
| bulb planter | greenhouse | plant stakes | spade |
| bushel basket | hedge clipper/trimmer | plant support ring/ | sprayer |
| clipper | hoe |   cage | spreader |
| compost bin | hose | posthole digger | sprinkler |
| compost heap | lawn mower | pot, flower pot | snow shovel |
| cultivator | lawn roller | pruner | snow blower |
| edger | leaf blower | pruning knife | tiller |
| garden cart | lopper | pruning saw | tractor |
| gardening glove | netting | rake | trimmer |
| gardening shears | pest control | rider mower | trowel |
| gardening scissors | pitchfork | rototiller/roto tiller | weeder |
| grafting knife | planter | seed tray | wheelbarrow |

## Procedures

| | | | |
|---|---|---|---|
| broadcasting seed | harvesting | planting | splitting |
| clearing | heading off | potting | shoveling |
| clipping | grafting | pruning | tilling |
| composting | mowing | raking | transplanting |
| culling | mulching | replanting | trimming |
| cultivating | picking | seeding | watering |
| fertilizing | pinching back/off | soil testing | weeding |

## Miscellaneous

| | | | |
|---|---|---|---|
| annual | fallow | gate | root |
| bouquet | fence | organic gardening | stem |
| branch | flower bed | overfeeding | trunk |
| brush | garden – types | over watering | perennial |
| bulb |   flower | plant – parts | raised bed |
| bush |   formal |   branch | row |
| crop |   herb |   bud | scarecrow |
| drought |   vegetable |   leaf | tree |

## Common Flowers

| | | | |
|---|---|---|---|
| bulb – types | iris | columbine | pansy |
|   bluebell | oriental lily | geranium | peony |
|   crocus |   snowdrops | hibiscus | petunia |
|   day lily | aster | impatiens | phlox |
|   daffodil | buttercup | marigold | poppy |
|   tulip | chrysanthemum | morning glory | rose |
|   hyacinth | | | zinnia |

# 6: Clothes
## General

bathing suit/trunks
bathrobe
belt
blazer
blouse
bow tie
boxer shorts
bra
briefs
buckle
cap
cape
cardigan
coat
cocktail dress
dinner jacket
dress
dungarees
earmuffs
garter
girdle
gloves
gown
hat
jacket

(blue)jeans
leotard
jumpsuit
mittens
muffler
nightgown
nylons
overalls
overcoat
pajamas
panties
pants
pantsuit
pantyhose/panty hose
parka
raincoat
running shorts
scarf
shirt
   dress
   sport
shorts
ski jacket
    pants
skirt

slacks
slicker
slip
snowsuit
sport coat/jacket
stole
suit
suspenders
sweater
sweat pants
sweat suit
sweatshirt
(neck)tie
tank top
tights
trench coat
trousers
T-shirt/tee shirt
turtleneck
tuxedo
underclothes
underpants/under shorts
undershirt
vest
wig

## Footwear

boots
   cowboy
   dress
   riding
clogs
flats
high heels

galoshes
gym shoes
moccasins
knee socks
overshoes
peds
rubbers

running shoes/walking shoes
shoes
shoelaces/strings
slippers
sneakers
socks
stockings

## Sewing and Parts

bobbin
button
buttonhole
cloth
collar
cuff
darn

elastic
fabric
fringe
knit
hem
hemline
hood

material
mend
nap
neckline
needle
notch
patch

## Sewing and Parts, continued

| | | |
|---|---|---|
| pattern | sewing machine | thread |
| pins | size | threader |
| pocket | sleeve | tack down |
| ruffle | snap | tape measure |
| scissors | stitch | tuck |
| seam | thimble | yarn |
| | | zipper |

## Adjectives

| | | |
|---|---|---|
| brand new | knit | second-hand |
| checkered | large (sized) | silk |
| corduroy | loose | small (sized) |
| cotton | machine washable | striped |
| dress | medium (sized) | tight |
| dry | nylon | torn |
| cleanable | permanent press | velvet |
| flannel | plaid | washable |
| frayed | polka dot | worn out |
| hand-me-down | polyester | wool |
| hand washable | rayon | woven |

## Verbs

| | | |
|---|---|---|
| baste | hem | take in |
| cut (out) | knit | take off |
| darn | pin up | take up |
| dress | put on | tear (out) |
| fit | rip (out) | thread |
| gather | sew (up) | trace |
| get dressed | stitch (up) | wear |
| grow out of (into) | tack | wear out |

## Idioms and Expressions

| | | |
|---|---|---|
| all dressed up | to handle with kid gloves | on pins and needles |
| to be in someone's shoes | to hit below the belt | the shoe's on the other foot |
| to burn a hole in one's pocket | If the shoe fits, wear it. | to spin a yarn |
| to buttonhole someone | to keep one's shirt on | spit and polish |
| to collar someone | to look for a needle in a haystack | stuffed shirt |
| clothes make the man | to lose one's shirt | tied to someone's apron strings |
| dolled up | on a shoestring | wear and tear |

# 7: Paraphernalia
## Nouns

address book
bag
barrette
beads
billfold
bobby pin
body jewelry (nose ring, etc.)
bracelet
briefcase
brooch
calling/business card case
calculator
cane
cell phone (mobile)
change purse
checkbook
chewing tobacco
choker
cigar
cigarette
coin
coin purse
comb
contact lens
credit card case
crutches
cufflinks
date book
dip
discman/diskman CD player
earring
(eye) glasses
   bifocal
   progressive/multifocal

sun
   reading
flash light
glasses case
hair pin
hair brush
hair pull
handbag
handheld PC
handkerchief
identification
ID bracelet
iPod/ mp3 player
jack knife
kerchief
key chain
key ring
keys
laptop computer
lighter
lipstick, lipgloss
locket
mace
marker
matches
nail clippers
nail file
necklace
notebook
overnight bag
pager
pen – ball point pen
   fountain pen
   rollerball

pencil - mechanical
   wooden
pencil eraser
pencil sharpener
penknife
pen light
pillbox
pin
pipe
playing cards
pocketbook
pocket calendar
pocketknife
pocket watch
purse
ring
   engagement
   school
   signet
   wedding
shopping bag
shoulder bag
smartphone/iPhone
snuff
tablet
tie clip
tie pin
tissues
tobacco pouch
token
umbrella
wallet
walking stick
wristwatch

## Idioms and Expressions

to flip a coin
to make heads or tails of
key to the city
little black book

to pick someone's pocket
pipe dream
purse snatcher
to put that in one's pipe and smoke it

rose colored glasses
up to snuff
well groomed

# 8: Family  also see Culture #31 Family Relationship Chart

adopted child
adoptive parent
aunt
baby brother/sister
big brother/sister
biological parent
bride
brother
cousin
dad
daddy
daughter
dependent
family dog
folks
father
fiance(e)
first husband/wife
foster parent
foster child
genealogy
godparents
gram

gramp
grandchild(ren)
granddaughter
grandfather
grandma
grandmother
grandpa
grandson
great aunt/uncle
great grandchild(ren)
groom
guardian
half-brother/sister
husband
in-laws
kin, kin folks
kindred
ma
maternal
middle child
mom
mommy

mother
(mother)-in-law
niece
nephew
orphan
pa
partner
paternal
pop
relative
sibling
sis
sister
son
spouse
step-brother
    -father
    -mother
    -sister
uncle
widow
widower
wife

## Idioms and Expressions

all in the family
absentee father
apples never fall
    far from the tree
better half
blended family
blood brother
blood is thicker than water
chip off the old block
civil union

close/distant relations
to come by it naturally
extended/nuclear family
kissing cousins
family feud
family tree
favorite son
like father, like son
one's old (man)

runs in the family
same-sex mariage
sibling rivalry
single parent
spitting image
to take after
son of a gun
wicked stepmother
wife (to be)

# 9: Human Relationships, Qualities, and Stages

## Nouns

| | | | | | | |
|---|---|---|---|---|---|---|
| admiration | antagonism | competition | envy | hatred | love | rivalry |
| affection | cooperation | friendship | hate | intimacy | marriage | sex |
| | | | | | | teamwork |

## Verbs

| | | | | | | |
|---|---|---|---|---|---|---|
| admire | cooperate | dislike | envy | have sex | like | make love |
| befriend | compete | distrust | hate | ignore | love | share |
| | | | | | | trust |

## People

| | | | | | | |
|---|---|---|---|---|---|---|
| acquaintance | colleague | crony | fiance/fiancee | guest | mistress | party |
| antagonist | companion | crowd | follower | host | mob | playmate |
| associate | company | date | friend | leader | newbie | relative |
| boyfriend | comrade | disciple | gang | lover | pal | roommate |
| buddy | counselor | enemy | girlfriend | mate | partner | team |
| | | | | | | teammate |

## Qualities

| | | | | | |
|---|---|---|---|---|---|
| aloof | cooperative | fresh | insane | pretty | sexy |
| artistic | courageous | friendly | intelligent | quiet | shy |
| attractive | courteous | funny | jealous | reserved | spiteful |
| bashful | cowardly | gorgeous | kind | romantic | stand-offish |
| beautiful | crazy | greedy | lazy | rude | strong |
| bold | cruel | gullible | loud | ruthless | stuck up |
| brave | dependable | handsome | lovely | sane | studious |
| brazen | determined | hard-working | lovable | self-conscious | stupid |
| cheerful | diligent | helpful | mean | selfish | trustworthy |
| conceited | disciplined | humorous | plain | sensitive | ugly |
| cold | dumb | ill-mannered | pleasant | sentimental | up-tight |
| complacent | foolish | impolite | polite | serious | well-mannered |

## Stages

| | | | | | |
|---|---|---|---|---|---|
| adolescent | child | immature | juvenile | old | teenager |
| adult | childhood | infant | mature | pre-teen | toddler |
| age | childish | infantile | middle-age | retired | young |
| aged | elderly | kid | newborn | senior citizen | young adult |
| baby | grownup | | | senile | youth |

## Idioms and Expressions

| | | | |
|---|---|---|---|
| to have an affair | fair sex | to hang it all out | to pull no punches |
| assisted living | fall-guy | to have a crush on | ringleader |
| blind date | to flip one's lid | living together | side-kick |
| to break up | to gang up on | live-in boyfriend | to sponge off |
| cruising | to go through the motions | old man (lady) | steady date |
| dating sites | to hang in there | playing the field | to take someone down a peg |
| | | | every Tom, Dick and Harry |

# 10: Travel

## Places

airport
auto rental agency
baggage check in
baggage claim area
baggage office
bed and breakfast
berth
bus station
camp site
car sharing/Zip car
Chamber of Commerce
check-in counter
club car
coach (car)
commuter train
cruise ship
customs
diner

dining room/car
garage
gas station/service station
gate
hotel
immigration
inn
information booth
intersection
interstate highway
junction
light rail
limousine
lobby
lounge
motel
parking garage
parking lot

parking place/space
passing lane
repair shop
resort
rest area
restaurant
round-about
security
shuttle bus
terminal
text stop/area
train station
ticket office
toll booth
tourist office
travel agency
valet parking
waiting room

## Some Events

arrival
auto accident
boarding
checking bags
checking flight times
checking in
checking out
take a cruise

delay
departure
eco-tour
flat tire
flight cancellation
going through security
hitch-hiking
hailing a cab

layover
making internet reservations
packing
parking ticket
passing
speeding ticket
tour
traffic violation

## Idioms and Expressions

to bump into
to car pool
to get a move on
to split
to take off

to hang around
to hit the road
to catch the (bus)
to take the (bus)
to travel light

to go through customs
life in the fast lane
jet lag
to hitch a ride
to bum a ride

# 11: Time

## Daily

| | | | |
|---|---|---|---|
| dawn | forenoon | p.m. | evening |
| sunrise | morning | sunset | night |
| sunup | noon | sundown | midnight |
| morning | midday | twilight | middle of the night |
| a.m. | afternoon | dusk | |

## Instruments

| | | | |
|---|---|---|---|
| alarm clock | chronometer | metronome | sun dial |
| almanac | clock | stop watch | watch |
| calendar | | | wristwatch |

## Measures

| | | | |
|---|---|---|---|
| second | day | month | decade |
| minute | week | year | century |
| half-hour | fortnight | leap year | millennium |
| hour | | | |

## General measures

| | | | |
|---|---|---|---|
| instant | era | every day | yearly |
| moment | eon | weekly | annually |
| period | split-second | bi-weekly | past |
| age | daily | monthly | present |
| epoch | | | future |

## Seasons

| | | | |
|---|---|---|---|
| spring | summer | fall | winter |
| | | autumn | |

## Idioms and Expressions

| | | | |
|---|---|---|---|
| all in a day's work | the time is right | from the first | ASAP - as soon as |
| behind the times | to lose time | in the beginning | possible |
| for the time being | behind the times | in the blink of an eye | PDQ - pretty darn |
| in the nick of time | it's high time | in the wink of an eye | (or damn) quick |
| in time | time zones | in a jiffy | B.C. - before Christ |
| timely | time-and-a-half | in a minute/second | A.D. - *anno Domini* |
| to kill time | the time of one's life | the crack of doom | in the year of our |
| to pass the time | time will tell | doomsday | Lord |
| on time | double time | to call it a day | CE - in the Common/ |
| once upon a time | to two-time | all the live long day | Current/Christian |
| overtime | at no time | fly-by-night | Era |
| to keep time | time out | to make a night of it | BCE - Before the CE |
| to make time | time-honored | to get along in years | |

# 12: Weather and Climate

## Nouns

air
air mass
blizzard
breeze
climate change
cloud
cumulus
cyclone
downpour
drift
drizzle
drought
el niño. la niña
fog
freezing point
front
frost
gale

global warming
gust
hail
high
humidity
hurricane
ice
low
lightning (bolt)
mist
ozone layer
pressure
rain
shower
sleet
smog
snow

squall
temperature
thunder
thunderstorm
thunderhead
tornado
tsunami
twister
velocity
wind
wind chill factor

barometer
hygrometer
thermometer
weather forecast
weather report

## Verbs

blow (up)
cloud up
drift
drizzle
freeze

hail
lift
mist
pour
rain

shine
sleet
snow
thaw
thunder

## Adjectives

breezy
chilly
cloudy
cold
dreary
dusty
dry
foggy
freezing
frigid
frosty

hazardous
hazy
hot
humid
icy
inclement
lowering
mild
overcast
partly (sunny/cloudy)
pleasant

polar
rainy
scorching
severe
slippery
smoggy
snowy
sunny
temperate
tropical
wet

## Idioms & Expressions

to blow over
bolt from the blue
to break the ice
castles in the air
cats and dogs
cold snap
come rain or shine
environmental activist

environmental change
Every cloud has a silver lining.
to be full of hot air
heat wave
to make hay while
   the sun shines
to rain on one's parade
to ride out the storm

to shoot the breeze
to take the wind out of
   one's sails
three sheets to the wind
up in the air
weather the storm
windbag
windfall

# 13: Geography

## Space

| | | | | |
|---|---|---|---|---|
| asteroid | falling star | moon | quasar | solar wind |
| black hole | galaxy | nebula | ring | star |
| comet | meteor | orbit | satellite | sun |
| constellation | meteorite | outer space | shooting star | sun spot |
| dark matter | meteor shower | planet | space | universe |

## Solar System: 8 Planets and the Dwarf Planet

| | | | | |
|---|---|---|---|---|
| The sun | Jupiter | Mercury | Saturn | Dwarf planet: |
| Planets: | Mars | Neptune | Uranus | Pluto |
| Earth | | | Venus | |

## Earth

| | | | | |
|---|---|---|---|---|
| Antarctic Circle | cliff | field | lake | plain | strait |
| Arctic Circle | coastline | fiord | lagoon | plateau | stream |
| area | continent | forest | latitude | pole | surf |
| atoll | crater | geyser | ledge | pond | swamp |
| bay | current | glacier | longitude | prairie | tide |
| beach | dam | globe | marsh | range | Tropic of Cancer |
| bog | dale | gorge | meadow | ravine | Tropic of Capricorn |
| brook | delta | gulf | mountain | reef | undertow |
| canal | desert | gully | north | reservoir | valley |
| canyon | ditch | hedge | NW passage | rift | volcano |
| cape | east | hill | ocean | river | wave |
| cascade | equator | icecap | peak | sea | waterfall |
| channel | estuary | island | peninsula | south | west |
| chasm | fault | isthmus | | | woods |

## Material

| | | | | |
|---|---|---|---|---|
| dirt | pebble | igneous | sod | stone |
| earth | rock – types: | metamorphic | soil | turf |
| mud | sedimentary | | | |

## Events

| | | | | |
|---|---|---|---|---|
| after shock | ebb | eruption | flood | tidal wave |
| avalanche | erosion | flow | landslide | tremor |
| earthquake | | | | tsumani |

## Idioms and Expressions

| | | |
|---|---|---|
| a stone's throw | East is East and West is West. | over the hill |
| babes in the woods | high and dry | to sell down the river |
| to bog down | to leave no stone unturned | to show true grit |
| dirt cheap | to make a mountain of a mole hill | spaced out |
| down-to-earth | once in a blue moon | to stem the tide |
| earthy | out of the woods | a stick in the mud |
| | out of this world | under the sun |
| | over hill and dale | to win by a landslide |

# 14: Natural Resources
## Ore and Minerals

| | | | | |
|---|---|---|---|---|
| aluminum | flint | lead | rock | stone |
| bauxite | gold | limestone | rock salt | sulphur |
| chromium | gravel | marble | sand | talc |
| clay | gypsum | nickle | salt | tin |
| cobalt | granite | phosphates | silicon | uranium |
| copper | iron | platinum | silver | zinc |

## Forest and Sea Products

| | | | | |
|---|---|---|---|---|
| bamboo | fertilizer | medicinal herbs | rubber | turpentine |
| bark | guano | mulch | sea salt | wood |
| coral | lumber | peat moss | seaweed | wood chips |
| chicle | maple syrup | reeds | sod | wood pulp |

## Energy-producing Products

| | | | | |
|---|---|---|---|---|
| carbon | gas | methane | petroleum | thermal energy |
| coal | hydrogen | natural gas | petrochemical | water |
| firewood | hydro power | oil | products | wind power |
| fuel | | | | |

## Gases

| | | | |
|---|---|---|---|
| helium | methane | neon | oxygen |
| hydrogen | natural gas | nitrogen | ozone |

## Gems

| | | | |
|---|---|---|---|
| agate | garnet | opal | sapphire |
| amethyst | heliotrope | pearl | topaz |
| aquamarine (beryl) | jade | quartz | tourmaline |
| carnelian | lapis lazuli | rhinestone | turquoise |
| diamond | malachite | ruby | zircon |
| emerald | | | |

## Idioms and Expressions

All that glitters is not gold.
as good as gold
Silence is golden.
between a rock and a hard place
diamond in the rough
A diamond is forever.
fire and brimstone
fracking

genetic diversity
a gold rush
heart of stone
feet of clay
pearls of wisdom
a pearl of great price
platinum blond

a real gem
renewable energy
rub salt in a wound
strip mining
silver threads among the gold
Every cloud has a silver lining.
You can't make bricks
    without straw.

# 15: Animals

## Domestic animals – common pets and farm animals

| | | | | |
|---|---|---|---|---|
| cat | elephant | guinea pig | mouse | pig |
| cow | ferret | hamster | mule | pony |
| dog | gerbil | horse | ox | sheep |
| donkey | goat | llama | parrot | rabbit |

## Wild Animals

| | | | | |
|---|---|---|---|---|
| armadillo | deer | manatee | otter | sea cow |
| badger | dolphin | mole | porcupine | seal |
| bear | dugong | moose | porpoise | skunk |
| beaver | elk | mountain goat | possum, opossum | squirrel |
| bobcat | fisher (cat) | mountain lion | prairie dog | whale |
| caribou | fox | mouse | rabbit | wildcat |
| chipmunk | groundhog | muskrat | raccoon | wolf |
| cougar | hare | narwhale | rat | wolverine |
| coyote | hedgehog | lynx | reindeer | woodchuck |

## Zoo Animals

| | | | | |
|---|---|---|---|---|
| alligator | cheetah | giraffe | leopard | panther |
| ape | chimpanzee | gorilla | lion | rhinoceros |
| bear | crocodile | hippopotamus | monkey | tiger |
| buffalo | elephant | hyena | orangutan | zebra |

## Reptiles and Amphibians

| | | | | |
|---|---|---|---|---|
| boa constrictor | gecko | newt | snake | tortoise |
| chameleon | iguana | python | tadpole | tree frog |
| frog | lizard | salamander | toad | turtle |

## Fish, Shellfish, Crustaceans. etc

| | | | | |
|---|---|---|---|---|
| bass | cod | lobster | salmon | snail |
| bluegill | eel | monk(fish) | scallop | starfish |
| carp | flounder | mussel | sea horse | sturgeon |
| catfish | goldfish | oyster | sea urchin | sunfish |
| clam | guppy | perch | shark | trout |
| crab | herring | pike | shrimp | tuna |

## Insects, etc

| | | | | |
|---|---|---|---|---|
| ant | caddis fly | fly, house fly | millipede | spider |
| aphid | caterpillar | fruit fly | mosquito | springtail |
| bedbug | centipede | gnat | moth | termite |
| bee /bumble bee | cockroach | grasshopper | no-see-um | thrip |
| beetle | cricket | hornet | praying mantis | tick |
| blackfly | daddy longlegs | lady bug | sandflea | wasp |
| blowfly | dragonfly | louse | scorpion | water strider |
| bug | earwig | maggot | silverfish | worm |
| butterfly | flea | mayfly | snowflea | yellowjacket |

# Body parts

| | | | | | |
|---|---|---|---|---|---|
| abdomen | fur | horns | paw | spot | trunk |
| antennae | hair | legs | scale | stripe | tusk |
| claw | head | muzzle | shell | tail | whiskers |
| fangs | hide | neck | snout | teeth | wings |
| feelers | hoof | nostril | spine | thorax | wool |

# Dwellings

| | | | | |
|---|---|---|---|---|
| aquarium | burrow | cave | nest | pen |
| barn | cage | hutch | pasture | tank |
| | | | | trap |

# Groupings

| | | | | |
|---|---|---|---|---|
| band (gorillas) | colony (ants) | herd (elephants) | pod (whales) | team (horses) |
| bed (clams) | flock (sheep) | herd (horses) | pride (lions) | tribe (goats) |
| brood (hens) | flock (birds) | nest (snakes) | school (fish) | troop (monkeys) |
| cloud (gnats) | gaggle (geese) | pack (dogs) | swarm (bees) | yoke (oxen) |

# Young Animals

| | | | |
|---|---|---|---|
| bunny - rabbit | cygnet - swan | fingerling - fish | kid - goat, man |
| calf - cattle, elephant, whale | duckling - duck | fledgling - birds | kitten - cat |
| chick - chicken, other fowl | eaglet - eagle | foal - horse, zebra | lamb - sheep |
| colt - horse (male) | fawn - deer | fry - fish | piglet - pig |
| cub - fox, bear, lion, whale | filly - horse (female) | gosling - goose | polliwog/tadpole - frog |
| | | | puppy- dog |

# Comparative Expressions

| | | | |
|---|---|---|---|
| big as a whale | fat as a pig | slippery as an eel | drinks like a fish |
| blind as a bat | fast as a jackrabbit | slow as a turtle | eats like a horse |
| brave as a lion | happy as a clam | sly as a fox | eats like a bird |
| busy as a bee | proud as a peacock | strong as an ox | runs like a deer |
| crazy as a loon | quiet as a mouse | stubborn as a mule | swims like a fish |
| dumb as an ox | silly as a goose | wise as an owl | climbs like a monkey |

# Idioms and Expressions

| | | |
|---|---|---|
| to back the wrong horse | to get one's goat | pig-headed |
| black sheep | to look a gift horse in the mouth | to play possum |
| bull session | to go to the dogs | road hog |
| bum steer | to hold one's horses | to shoot fish in a barrel |
| to let the cat out of the bag | to horse around | to smell a rat |
| cock and bull story | horse of another color | snake in the grass |
| copycat | in the doghouse | straight from the horse's mouth |
| crocodile tears | to make a beeline for | to take the bull by the horns |
| cry wolf | to make a monkey out of | to throw the bull |
| darkhorse | to monkey around with | white elephant |
| fish out of water | monkey business | wolf in sheep's clothing |

# 16: Birds

**Kinds:**

| | | | **Body parts:** |
|---|---|---|---|
| albatross | grackle | pheasant | beak |
| blackbird | grosbeak | phoebe | bill |
| bluebird | grouse | pigeon | breast |
| bobwhite | gull | puffin | claw |
| boobie | hawk | quail | crest |
| cardinal | heron | raven | egg |
| catbird | hummingbird | roadrunner | feather |
| chickadee | jay | robin | feet |
| chicken | kingbird | sandpiper | head |
| condor | kingfisher | snipe | leg |
| cormorant | kite | snowy owl | nest |
| cowbird | kiwi | sparrow | peck |
| crane | lark | starling | tail |
| crow | loon | stork | talon |
| cuckoo | magpie | swallow | wattle |
| duck | meadowlark | swan | wing |
| eagle | nighthawk | tern | |
| egret | nuthatch | thrasher | |
| emu | oriole | thrush | egg |
| falcon | osprey | titmouse | shell |
| finch | ostrich | turkey | white |
| flamingo | owl | vulture | yolk |
| flycatcher | parrot | warbler | |
| frigate bird | partridge | whippoorwill | **Nouns** |
| goldfinch | peacock | woodpecker | brood |
| goose | pelican | wren | flock |
| | penguin | | nest |

## Activities

| | | |
|---|---|---|
| brood | hatch | nest |
| flock | incubate | preen |
| fly | lay | |

## Idioms and Expressions

| | | |
|---|---|---|
| bird in the hand | early bird | swan song |
| birds of a feather flock together | to eat crow | to talk turkey |
| the bluebird of happiness | feather in one's cap | ugly duckling |
| chicken | to kill two birds with one stone | water off a duck's back |
| to cook one's goose | nest egg | wild goose chase |
| | pecking order | |

# 17: Plants and Trees also see #5 Lawn and Garden

## Types, etc.

| | | | | | |
|---|---|---|---|---|---|
| arbor | field | garden | hedge | park | wilderness |
| bush | forest | grove | orchard | swamp | woods |

## Trees

| | | | | | |
|---|---|---|---|---|---|
| ash | chestnut | elm | lilac | palm | redwood |
| beech | deciduous | evergreen | maple | pine | spruce |
| birch | dogwood | hemlock | oak | poplar | sumac |
| cedar | | | | | willow |

## Fruit trees

| | | | | | |
|---|---|---|---|---|---|
| apple | avocado | grapefruit | lemon | orange | pear |
| apricot | cherry | kiwi | lime | peach | plum |

## Tree parts

| | | | | | |
|---|---|---|---|---|---|
| acorn | bud | needle | ring | seed | stump |
| bark | flower | nut | root | seedling | thorn |
| branch | leaf | pine cone | sap | seed pod | trunk |
| graft | | | | | twig |

## Plants, Weeds, etc.

| | | | | | |
|---|---|---|---|---|---|
| berry bushes | crabgrass | grass | mushroom | reed | tumbleweed |
| burdock | fern | milkweed | poison ivy | toad stool | vine |
| cattail | | | | | water lily |

## Wildflowers, etc.

| | | | | |
|---|---|---|---|---|
| clover | daisy | goldenrod | Indian paintbrush | sunflower |
| columbine | dandelion | lady's slipper | Queen Anne's lace | violet |

## Garden flowers

| | | | | | |
|---|---|---|---|---|---|
| alyssum | daffodil | iris | lily of the valley | petunia | snapdragon |
| begonia | geranium | lily | marigold | poppy | sunflower |
| chrysanthemum | impatiens | | pansy | rose | tulip |
| crocus | | | | | zinnia |

## Flower parts

| | | | | | |
|---|---|---|---|---|---|
| anther | petal | pollen | seed | stamen | stigma |
| ovary | pistil | | | stem | style |

## Idioms and Expressions

| | | |
|---|---|---|
| Adam's apple | to hit the hay | to rest on one's laurels |
| against the grain | in a nutshell | to reap what one sows |
| to beat around the bush | that's just peachy | to sow wild oats |
| bed of roses | the last straw | to turn over a new leaf |
| grapevine | out on a limb | wallflower |

# 18: Language and Literature

also see Metalinguistic Aspect #1
*A Glossary of Grammatical Terms*

## Nouns

| | | | | |
|---|---|---|---|---|
| adjective | essay | lie | poetry | signature |
| adverb | etymology | linguistics | prayer | slang |
| article | exaggeration | literature | pronoun | speech |
| autograph | exclamation | meaning | pronunciation | spiel |
| comma | fiction | monologue | prose | statement |
| comprehension | grammar | narration | pun | stress |
| conversation | idiom | narrative | punctuation | style |
| definition | interview | noun | question | syntax |
| dialect | intonation | paragraph | quotation | title |
| dialogue | jargon | paraphrase | recitation | usage |
| diction | joke | period | semantics | verb |
| drama | journalism | phonology | sentence | verbiage |

## Verbs

| | | | | |
|---|---|---|---|---|
| abridge | discuss | lie | recite | symbolize |
| call | drawl | mean | relate | talk |
| censor | edit | mislead | report | tell |
| chat | elaborate | misspell | respond | title |
| communicate | encode | mutter | say | transcribe |
| comprehend | erase | narrate | scrawl | translate |
| converse | exaggerate | paraphrase | sign | transliterate |
| cry | explain | pray | speak | type |
| curse | explicate | print | spell | utter |
| debate | express | pronounce | sputter | vow |
| decode | gossip | punctuate | stammer | whisper |
| define | interpret | quote | stutter | write |
| dictate | interview | read | swear | |

## Idioms and Expressions

| | | |
|---|---|---|
| to call a spade a spade | double talk | neither rhyme nor reason |
| to call to order | gobbledygook | talk of the town |
| a close call | to read between the lines | tall story |
| far cry | to sign on the dotted line | |
| It's Greek to me. | to swear on a stack of Bibles | |

## Literary Terms

| | | | | |
|---|---|---|---|---|
| adventure story | | | | science fiction |
| autobiography | detective story | historical fiction | novella | story, plot |
| biography | drama, melodrama | lyric | play | subject matter |
| character | fantasy | memoir | poem | theater |
| children's books | fiction | meter, metrics | poetry | theme |
| classic | flash fiction | mystery | prose | title, subtitle |
| comedy | free verse | narrative | rhyme | tragedy |
| crime fiction | Gothic, horror story | non-fiction | romance | verse |
| criticism | graphic novel | novel | short story | young adult, adult |

# 19: Thinking

## Nouns

| | | | |
|---|---|---|---|
| analysis | decision | intention | reason |
| attitude | deduction | judgement | reflection |
| belief | deliberation | knowledge | speculation |
| brains | experience | logic | stupidity |
| certainty | fantasy | meditation | thinking |
| cogitation | feeling | mind | thought |
| comprehension | idea | notion | truth |
| conception | image | observation | understanding |
| conclusion | impression | perception | view |
| contemplation | intellect | rationale | wisdom |
| conviction | intelligence | realization | wit |

## Verbs

| | | | |
|---|---|---|---|
| analyze | distinguish | misconstrue | reflect |
| appreciate | doubt | misunderstand | remember |
| apprehend | experience | mull | reminisce |
| believe | fantasize | note | retain |
| brood | feel | notice | ruminate |
| cogitate | figure out | observe | see |
| comprehend | forget | perceive | sense |
| conceive | imagine | plan | speculate |
| conclude | judge | ponder | think |
| consider | know | question | trust |
| contemplate | learn | realize | understand |
| decide | meditate | recall | view |
| deliberate | memorize | reconstruct | wonder |

## Adjectives

| | | | |
|---|---|---|---|
| analytical | cognizant | intellectual | smart |
| appreciative | convinced | intelligent | stupid |
| aware | crafty | irrational | thoughtful |
| brainy | decisive | knowing | trusting |
| brilliant | deliberate | observant | truthful |
| certain | dull | perceptive | understanding |
| clever | experiential | pensive | vague |
| conclusive | imaginative | rational | wise |
| cognitive | indecisive | reasonable | witty |

## Idioms and Expressions

| | | |
|---|---|---|
| absent minded | level-headed | pipe dream |
| fat headed | literal minded | narrow minded |
| to know the ropes | to make neither head nor tail | neither rhyme nor reason |

# 20: Numbers and Math also see #22 Shapes

## Nouns

addition
algebra
analysis
angle
arithmetic
average
axis
axiom
calculation
calculator
calculus
cipher
circumference
computation
computer
constant
corollary
cube
curve
decimal
decimal point
denominator
difference
diagram
diameter
digit
dimension

division
equation
figure
formula
fraction
function
geometry
   plane
   solid
hypotenuse
infinity
integral
irrational number
logarithm
logic
long division
mathematics
mean
median
multiplication
numeral
percentage
pi
postulate
prime number
probability
problem

product
proof
quotient
radius
rate
ratio
rational number
relativity
remainder
root
set
sequence
solution
square root
statistics
straight line
subtraction
sum
term
theorem
theory
topology
trigonometry
value
variable
whole number

## Verbs

add
average
balance
calculate
compute
count
divide

double
equal
equate
figure
formulate
graph

multiply
reduce
round up/down
solve
square
subtract
triple

## Idioms and Expressions

double or nothing
face value
fifty-fifty
It doesn't add up.
lump sum

math facts
multiplication tables
to play by the numbers
to put two and two together
sewing circle

second-rate
to see double
sixes and sevens
to be square
Two's company; three's a crowd.

# 21: Colors

## Primary

| | | |
|---|---|---|
| red | yellow | blue |
| orange | green | indigo |
| | | violet/purple |

## Secondary

| | | |
|---|---|---|
| aquamarine | emerald | pink |
| beige | gold | rose |
| black | gray | ruby |
| bronze | ivory | silver |
| brown | khaki | slate |
| buff | lavender | tan |
| chestnut | maroon | teal |
| chocolate | off white | turquoise |
| coffee | olive | umber |
| copper | olive drab | white |

## Adjectives

| | | |
|---|---|---|
| bright | earth | metallic |
| brilliant | fluorescent | mottled |
| cool | glossy | pale |
| dark | hot | pied |
| dull | light | rich |
| flat | lurid | vivid |

## Miscellaneous

| | | |
|---|---|---|
| rainbow | spectrum | CMYK (cyan, magenta, |
| camouflage | RGB (red, green, and blue) | yellow, and black) |

## Paints, etc.

| | | |
|---|---|---|
| acrylic | crayons | oil |
| chalk | enamel | pastel |
| charcoal | finger | stain |
| colored marker | ink | tempera |
| colored pencil | latex | water colors |

## Idioms and Expressions

| | | |
|---|---|---|
| black and blue | in the black, in the red | red letter day |
| black hearted | in the pink | red tape |
| blue, the blues | to paint the town red | rose colored glasses |
| dyed in the wool | pink and blue | to be seeing red |
| greenhorn | red carpet | silver lining |
| green with envy | red cent | Silence is golden. |
| in black and white | red herring | yellow (cowardly) |

# 22: Shapes   also see #20 Numbers and Math

## Adjectives

angular
arched
blunt
circular
concave
concentric
congruent
conical
convex
curved
crooked
cylindrical
elliptical
elongated
flat

flattened
globular
heptagonal
hexagonal
horizontal
irregular
linear
long
narrow
octagonal
oval
parallel
pentagonal
perpendicular
pointed

polygon
ragged
round
rectangular
regular
sharp
slender
slim
square
smooth
straight
triangular
twisted
warped
wide

## Nouns

arc
arch
block
blob
circle
cone
cube
cylinder
diamond
disc
dome

globe
helix
heptagon
hexagon
horseshoe
mound
octagon
oval
parallelogram
peak
pentagon

point
polygon
pyramid
quadrangle
rectangle
sphere
spiral
square
surface
tip
triangle

## Idioms and Expressions

round peg in a square hole
domestic triangle
vicious circle
a crooked person

odds and ends
sharp as a tack
square
straight as an arrow

to run circles around someone
the Pentagon
point of an argument
tip of an iceberg

# 23: Substances and Materials

## Nouns

| | | |
|---|---|---|
| acid | flint | plastic |
| air | gas | plywood |
| aluminum | gasoline | powder |
| ashes | glue | rock |
| asphalt | goo | rubber |
| base | grease | sand |
| brass | gunk | sheet |
| bronze | kerosene | rock |
| cement | lubricant | smoke |
| cloth | moisture | soil |
| cloud | mud | steam |
| concrete | oil | steel |
| copper | ointment | stuff |
| dirt | paste | tar |
| dust | petroleum | water |
| earth | plaster | wood |

## Adjectives

| | | |
|---|---|---|
| abrasive | | slippery |
| corroded | impermeable | slimy |
| corrosive | invisible | soft |
| crumbly | liquid | solid |
| dull | metallic | soluble |
| durable | pliable | spongy |
| dusty | resilient | sticky |
| flammable | rough | strong |
| gaseous | rubbery | thick |
| gooey | rusty | thin |
| gritty | sharp | tough |
| hard | shiny | wet |
| | slick | |

## Idioms and Expressions

| | | |
|---|---|---|
| to blow off steam | to go up in smoke | to scratch the surface |
| brass tacks | to lay it on thick | to throw cold water on |
| a fly in the ointment | to take a powder | to knock on wood |
| slick operator | greaseball | powder keg |
| to grease the wheel | to grease one's palm | to cement a deal |
| to cast in concrete | to be plastered | dull as dishwater |

# 24: Containers

| | | | | |
|---|---|---|---|---|
| bag | canteen | dish | pack | snifter |
| barrel | carafe | file folder | package | thermos |
| basket | carton | flask | pail | tin |
| bottle | case | glass | pitcher | tray |
| bowl | container | jar | portfolio | tub |
| box | crate | jug | pot | tube |
| bucket | cup | keg | rack | vase |
| can | demitasse | mug | sack | vessel |
| canister | demijohn | | | |

## Idioms and Expressions

| | | |
|---|---|---|
| in the bag | boxed in | lock, stock and barrel |
| to have someone over a barrel | a drop in the bucket | soapbox |
| bottleneck | left holding the bag | windbag |
| barrel of monkeys | jug wine | ugly mug |
| bag lady | on the bottle | a real dish |

# 25: Manipulations

| | | | | |
|---|---|---|---|---|
| aim | fill | mold | screw | tip |
| arrange | flatten | move | scratch | trip |
| assemble | flex | open | seal | turn |
| attach | flick | pick up | set | turn off |
| bash | flip | pick out | set down | turn on |
| beat | flop | pick over | slam | turn over |
| bend | fold | pluck | spin | turn under |
| bolt | hammer | plug in | start | turn around |
| break | hang (up) | plug up | stop | twist |
| close | heat | pound | strike | undo |
| cool off, down | hook | press | strip | unfold |
| crack | ignite | pull | take apart | unhook |
| crumble | insert | punch | take out | unplug |
| crush | knead | push | take up | unlatch |
| cut | latch | put in | take down | unlock |
| deposit | level | reverse | tap | unscrew |
| depress | light | rap | tear | untie |
| disassemble | load | rip | thread | unzip |
| detach | lock | roll | throw | weave |
| drain | loop | rub | thrust | wipe |
| drive | maneuver | sand | tie | work |
| empty | mix | scrape | tilt | zip |

## Idioms and Expressions

| | | |
|---|---|---|
| flop house | to put the screws to someone | spin doctor |
| to pull a fast one | to put a spin on information | to strike while the iron's hot |

# 26: Emotions

## Nouns

| | | | | |
|---|---|---|---|---|
| affection | bravery | fatigue | joy | rage |
| aggravation | cheer | fear | joviality | regret |
| amusement an- | courage | feeling | laughter | restlessness |
| ger | craziness | fright | love | sadness |
| anguish | dejection | gladness | mood | sorrow |
| annoyance | delight | glee | nervousness | tears |
| anxiety | depression | greed | pain | temper |
| awe | disappointment | happiness | passion | terror |
| belligerence bit- | disgust | hope | pity | tiredness |
| terness | embarrassment | horror | pleasure | trouble |
| bliss | enthusiasm | indifference jeal- | prejudice | weariness |
| boredom | envy | ousy | pride | zest |

## Verbs

| | | | | |
|---|---|---|---|---|
| abhor | bother | disgust | hate | please |
| aggravate | burn up | embarrass | hope | rejoice |
| agitate | calm | envy | laugh | sadden |
| amuse | cheer up | excite | lament | shake up |
| anger | console | fatigue | like | sob |
| annoy | cry | fear | love | stir |
| antagonize | delight in | feel | moan | tire |
| bewilder | depress | frighten | mope | tremble |
| blush | detest | fume | mourn | trouble |
| bore | disappoint | gladden | pain | weep |

## Adjectives

| | | | | |
|---|---|---|---|---|
| abhorrent | bitter | disgusted | happy | painful |
| abject | blissful | embarrassed | hopeful | passionate |
| affectionate | bored | enthusiastic | insane | pleased |
| afraid | bothered | envious | irritated | restless |
| aggravated amo- | brave | excited | jealous | sad |
| rous | calm | fatigued | jolly | sexy |
| amused | cheerful | fearful | joyful | shy |
| angry | cheery | flustered | jovial | sorrowful |
| annoyed | crazy, crazed | forlorn | loving | tearful |
| anxious | dejected | frightened | melancholy | timid |
| apprehensive bel- | delighted | gay | merry | tired |
| ligerent | depressed | glad | moody | troubled |
| berserk | disappointed dis- | gleeful | mournful | upset |
| bewildered | consolate | grouchy | nervous | weary |

## Idioms and Expressions

| | | | |
|---|---|---|---|
| at wit's end | happy as a clam | method in one's madness | a heart breaker |
| to blow one's top | hot and bothered | love will find a way | tear jerker |
| fit to be tied | in a dither | out of sorts | troubled waters |
| to go to pieces | to make a scene | standoffish | at the end of one's rope |

# 27: The Body and its Functions

## External

| | | | | |
|---|---|---|---|---|
| abdomen | fist | hand | head | testes |
| ankle | foot | palm | hip | testicles |
| anus | heel | thumb | knee | thigh |
| arm | instep | finger | leg | shin |
| armpit | sole | index | neck | shoulders |
| breast | toe | middle | nipple | waist |
| buttocks | big toe | ring | penis | wrist |
| calf | little toe | little | foreskin | |
| chest | forearm hair | knuckle | stomach/ | |
| elbow | | fingernail | belly | |

## Face

| | | | | |
|---|---|---|---|---|
| chin | eyebrow | forehead | mouth | temple |
| cheek | eye | jaw | tongue | mustache |
| dimple | pupil | nose | tooth | beard |
| ear | white | nostril | gums | sideburns |
| eardrum | eyeball | bridge | lip | |
| earlobe | eyelash | | | |
| | eyelid | | | |

## Bones

| | | | | |
|---|---|---|---|---|
| backbone | kneecap | ribs | spine | thigh bone |
| collarbone | pelvis | skull | shoulder blade | skeleton |
| hipbone | | | | vertebrae |

## Insides

| | | | | |
|---|---|---|---|---|
| appendix | brain | larynx | vein | tonsils |
| artery | heart | liver | muscle | vagina |
| bladder | intestines | lung | nerves | rectum |
| blood | kidney | pancreas | throat | windpipe |

## Body products

| | | | | |
|---|---|---|---|---|
| urine | saliva/ | perspiration/ | tears | sperm |
| feces | spit | sweat | oil | eggs |

## Adjectives

| | | | | |
|---|---|---|---|---|
| athletic | lithe | pregnant | sick | tall |
| fat | loose | pudgy | skinny | thin |
| healthy | muscular | robust | strong | tight |
| ill | plump | short | supple | weak |

## Verbs

| | | | | |
|---|---|---|---|---|
| belch | cry | hear | run | stand |
| bend | defecate | hiccup | see | swallow |
| bite | digest | hop | sit | taste |
| burp | eat | jump | skip | titter |
| breathe | flex | laugh | smell | twist |
| chew | fornicate | leap | smile | urinate |
| choke | gasp | menstruate | spit | groan |
| copulate | giggle | moan | sniffle | scowl |
| creep | grin | nibble | sob | weep |

## Idioms and Expressions

after one's own heart
all ears
apple of one's eye
to give one's right arm
at arm's length
with open arms
to strong arm
bad blood
to beat one's brains out
to beat one's head against a
   stone wall
to bend over backwards
to bite off more than one
   can chew
in cold blood
brainstorm
to waste one's breath
to save one's breath
to take away one's breath
to breathe freely
cold feet
to cool one's heels
to cut off one's nose to
   spite one's face
to eat one's heart out
to eat one's words
to rub elbows with
elbow grease
to keep an eye on
to see eye to eye
to make eyes at
to keep a straight face
to keep one's fingers crossed
To put one's finger on it
first-hand

to foot the bill
to put one's foot down
to put one's best foot forward
to put one's foot in one's mouth
on all fours
funny bone
bone headed
to get on one's nerves
to get something off
   one's chest
guts
potbelly
to let down one's hair
to split hairs
hard-hearted
hard-headed
head and shoulders above
over one's head
heart-to-heart
by heart
to have a heart
a heel
to keep a stiff upper lip
to knock one's block off
lowbrow, highbrow
to make no bones about
by word of mouth
to shoot one's mouth off
foul-mouthed
narrow-minded
to neck
neck and neck
up to one's neck
nose is out of joint
nosey

to pay lip service to
to pay through the nose
to pick a bone with
to piss off
to pull one's leg
to pull the wool over
   one's eyes
to shake a leg
straight from the shoulder
a cold shoulder
a chip on one's shoulder
by the skin of one's teeth
to get under one's skin
a slap in the face
a pain in the neck
a slip of the tongue
sweet tooth
to take a load off one's feet
to set one's teeth on edge
under one's thumb
all thumbs
to toe the mark
to be on one's toes
tooth and nail
tongue in cheek
tongue tied
tongue twister
on the tip of one's tongue
to turn the other cheek
to turn up one's nose at
to turn one's back on
to turn a blind eye on
to watch one's step
to make one's mouth water
to wet one's whistle

There are many vulgar terms for body parts and functions. Some of these are available as supplementary web material: http://www.prolinguaassociates.com/The_ESL_Miscellany/index.

# 28: Automobiles and Motorcycles

## Auto Makes

Acura
Aston Martin
Audi
Bentley
BMW
Buick
Cadillac
Chevrolet
Chrysler

Citroen
Datsun
Dodge
Ferrari
Fiat
Ford
GMC
Honda
Hummer

Hyundai
Infiniti
Isuzu
Jaguar
Jeep
Kia
Lamborgini
Land Rover
Lexus

Lincoln
Lotus
Mserati
Mazda
Mercedes Benz
Mercury
Mini Cooper
Mitsubishi
Nissan

Rolls Royce
Scion
Smart Car
Subaru
Suzuki
Tesla
Toyota
Volkswagen/VW
Volvo

## Auto Types

ATV (all-terrain vehicle)
camper
compact
convertible

coupe (2-door)
crossover
economy
hatchback

hybrid
mid-size
minivan
pickup

RV (recreational vehicle)
sedan (4-door)
sports car

station wagon
stock car racer
SUV (sport utility vehicle)
van

## Motorcycle Makes

Aprilia
BMW
Ducati
Harley-Davidson

Honda
Indian
Kawasaki

KTM
Moto Guzzi
Polara

Suzuki
Triumph
Vespa

Victory
Yamaha
Zero

## Motorcycle Types

chopper
cruiser
dual-purpose

dirt bike
electric

off roadscooter
moped

scooter
sport

standard
touring
underbone

## Parts (external)

back-up light
blinker
brake light
bumper
fender
fog light
gas cap

grill
headlight
  high beam
  low beam
hood
hub cap
inspection sticker

license plate
luggage rack
lug nut
moonroof
rim
snow tire

spare tire
sunroof
tailgate
taillight
tire
trunk

turn signal
wheel
window
windshield
windshield washer
windshield wiper

## Parts (internal)

airbag
anti-lock brakes
brake pedal
catalytic converter
CD/iPod player
child seat
clutch
coin holder
console

cup holder
dome light
EZ Pass
  Transponder
gas pedal
gages:
  gas
  odometer

oil
tachometer
temperature
gearshift
glove compartment
GPS System
hand brake
ignition key

instrument panel
odometer
radio
rear view mirror
seat
seat belt
spare tire
speedometer

steering wheel
stick shift
tool kit:
  crowbar
  flare
  jack
  lug wrench
  snow/ice scraper
  visor

# Parts (engine and mechanical, etc.)

air filter/cleaner
alternator
battery
brake
carburetor
catalytic converter
cruise control
dip stick
drive belt
drive train
engine

exhaust pipe
exhaust manifold
fan belt
fluids
   antifreeze/coolant
   brake fluid
   oil
   washer fluid
   water
fuel pump
gas tank

gear shift
   automatic
   stick
generator
horn
muffler
piston
radiator
serpentine belt
shock absorber
spark plug

starter
suspension
transmission
   all-wheel drive
   automatic
   four-wheel drive
   front/back wheel
     drive
   standard
universal joint

# Verbs

back up
brake
break down
bump into
check the oil
coast
crash
dim (the lights)

drive
fill the tank
get/have a flat tire
honk the horn
lease
park
put on the brakes

rent
roll down the window
run out of gas
shift
signal ( a turn)
skid
slow down

speed (up)
stall
steer
swerve
tow
turn
turn around
to make a U-turn

# Places

back road
barrier
breakdown lane
bridge
car wash
clover leaf

construction
exit
fast lane
gas station
garage
Interstate highway

junk yard
median
off-ramp/on-ramp
overpass
shoulder
rest area/text area

roundabout
toll booth
toll road/bridge
traffic circle
travel lane
underpass

# People

backseat driver
car salesman

driver

mechanic

passenger
police officer

# Directions

Caution
Curves
Deer Crossing
Divided Highway
Exit Only
Junction

Keep Left/Right
Merge
Moose
No Passing
No Left/Right Turn

No U-Turn
Pedestrians
Reduce Speed
School Zone
Signal Ahead

Speed Limit
Stop Ahead
Traffic Turning and
   Entering
Two-Way Traffic

# Miscellaneous

AAA/America Auto-
   mobile Association
auto insurance
beater
car pool
clunker

demolition derby
DWI
emergency kit
fender bender
flare
four-by-four/4X4

Indy 500
junker
limo/limosine
NASCAR
parts car
to total a car

tow truck
road hazard
rolling coffin
rust bucket
winter beater
wreck

# 29: Transportation

## Land

| | | | |
|---|---|---|---|
| ATV | chariot | rickshaw | subway |
| (all-terrain vehicle) | coach | RV (recreational vehicle) | tanker |
| automobile, auto | convertible | scooter | tank |
| bus | el, elevated railway | sedan | truck |
| bicycle, | jeep | skateboard | taxicab, taxi, cab |
| bike | litter | skimobile/snowmobile | train |
| cable car | locomotive | sled | tricycle |
| camper | moped | sleigh | trolley |
| car | motorcycle | snowmobile | truck |
| carriage | pickup | sports car | van |
| cart | railroad, railway | stagecoach | wagon |

## Animals

| | | | |
|---|---|---|---|
| burro | dog (sled) | horse | pony |
| camel | donkey | llama | oxen |
| cow | elephant | mule | water buffalo |

## People

| | | | |
|---|---|---|---|
| bus driver | driver | taxi cab driver | copilot |
| chauffeur | engineer | teamster | flight attendant |
| coachman | guide | truck driver | pilot |
| conductor | mechanic | aviator | steward/stewardess |

## General

| | | | |
|---|---|---|---|
| alley | E-Z pass | rest area | timetable |
| bridge | gasoline | road | trail |
| burden | highway | schedule | tire |
| cargo | interstate | station | toll booth |
| coal | lane | steam | turnpike |
| diesel | oil | street | vehicle |
| engine | path | thruway | wheel |

## Air

| | | | |
|---|---|---|---|
| aircraft | concourse | jet | seat assignment |
| airliner | control tower | light plane | security |
| airplane | engine | luggage | spacecraft, ship |
| airport | gate | propeller | space shuttle |
| baggage check | glider | reservation | ticket |
| baggage claim area | hangar | rocket | ticket counter |
| blimp | helicopter | runway | window |
| boarding pass | hot air balloon | seat | wings |

# Water

| | | | |
|---|---|---|---|
| aircraft carrier | fleet | motorboat | sailboat |
| amphibian | freighter | motor launch | sea |
| ark | frigate | navy | shell |
| barge | galley | oar | ship |
| boat | gunboat | ocean | spar |
| bow | harbor | ocean liner | square rigger |
| buoy | helm | paddle | steamship/steamboat |
| canal | hovercraft | paddlewheel | steering wheel |
| canalboat | hull | pond | stern |
| canoe | jet ski | port | stream |
| catamaran | kayak | propeller | submarine |
| centerboard | keel | rapids | surfboard |
| channel | lake | river | trimaran |
| craft | landing craft | raft | tugboat/towboat |
| cruiser | lifeboat | rowboat | vessel |
| cruise ship | lighter | rudder | warship |
| dinghy | lighthouse | runabout | yacht |
| ferry/ferryboat | mast | sail | white water |

# Verbs

| | | | |
|---|---|---|---|
| arrive | fly | park | take off |
| check in | glide | ride | tour |
| depart | hitchhike | row | tow |
| disembark | land | sail | trek |
| drive | launch | soar | travel |
| embark | paddle | steer | walk |

# Idioms and Expressions

| | |
|---|---|
| to backfire | to miss the boat |
| to get on the bandwagon | to pave the way for |
| on the (water) wagon | water under the bridge/ over the dam |
| in the same boat | to fall asleep at the wheel |
| off the beaten track | to take a back seat to |
| to burn one's bridges behind one | to run around in circles |
| to be up a creek withot a paddle | to hit the road |
| to know the ropes | slow boat to China |
| to lose one's way | shipshape |
| to make way for someone or something | up the creek without a paddle |
| to meet someone halfway | backseat driver |

# 30: Community
## Places and Organizations

arts council
Boys and Girls Club
chamber of commerce
sidewalk
park
park bench
civic center
community center
public library

church
mosque
Jewish synagogue
Grange
VFW - Veterans of
    Foreign Wars
YMCA - the "Y"
Elks
Eagles

Knights of Columbus
Lions Club
Shriners
Masons
Boy/Girl Scouts
4-H Club
playground
FFA - Future Farmers
    of America

American Legion
PTA - Parent-Teachers
    Association
school board
senior center
town hall
garden club
union hall
university club

## Events

auction
band concert
beauty contest
bingo
church bazaar
church supper
county fair

demonstration
farmers' market
flea market
funeral
hoedown
memorial service

parade
picket line
political rally
rodeo
rummage sale
scouting jamboree

strike
tag, yard, lawn sale
Town Meeting
voting
wake
walk-a-thon
wedding reception

# 31: Hotels

airport limousine,
    limo
baggage
ball room
bar
bath
bed
bellhop
bill
bureau
bed and breakfast
boarding house
call (wake-up)
cashier
currency exchange
chair
chambermaid

coffee shop
convention desk
concierge
clerk
dining room
doorman
elevator
elevator operator fit-
    ness center
flop house
gardener
guest
guest house
health club
hospitality center
housekeeper
hostel

hotel
ice machine
information desk
inn, innkeeper
key/ room key
laundry
lobby
lounge
luggage
maid
manager
meeting
motel
operator
organization
party
reservation

residential hotel
resort
room
    single
    double
room clerk
room service
restaurant
safety deposit box
security guard
suite
table
tourist
tourist cabins
tourist court
tour guide
travel desk

## Verbs

call (room service)
check in

check out
disturb (do not)

pack
register

reserve
stay

## Idioms and Expressions

bag and baggage
room and board

It's the Ritz.
stop for the night

overnight guest
overnight stay

home away from home
weekend rates

# 32: Restaurants

## Nouns

| | | | |
|---|---|---|---|
| appetizer | cup | meal | refill (of coffee) |
| ashtray | dessert | menu | salad bar |
| bar | dish | mug | salt |
| bowl | fork | napkin | serving spoon |
| booth | glass | order | table |
| buffet | gourmet | plate | tablecloth |
| chair | gratuity | platter | tax |
| check | knife | reservation | tip |
| cocktail | main course | round (of drinks) | wine cellar |
| course | | | wine list |

## Verbs

| | | | |
|---|---|---|---|
| dine | order | prepare | tip |
| eat out | pay | reserve | take out |

## Types

| | | | |
|---|---|---|---|
| automat | deli(catessen) | fast-food | pizzeria |
| cafe | diner | gourmet | pizza parlor |
| cafeteria | drive-in | luncheonette | snack bar |
| coffee shop | drive thru | natural foods | soda fountain |
| | | | vending machine |

## Personnel

| | | | |
|---|---|---|---|
| baker | chef | headwaiter | pastry chef |
| barista | cook | host/hostess | prep cook |
| bartender | dishwasher | maitre d' | server |
| busboy | guest | manager | waiter |
| cashier | | | waitress |

## Adjectives

| | | | |
|---|---|---|---|
| a la carte | fresh | rare | succulent |
| baked | fried | raw | take-out |
| bland | grilled | salty | tasteless |
| boiled | hot | scrumptious | tasty |
| broiled | mashed | sliced | to go |
| cold | medium | spicy | vegan |
| delicious | overdone | steamed | vegetarian |
| dry | | | well-done |

## Idioms and Expressions

| | | | |
|---|---|---|---|
| to wine and dine | doggy bag | to go dutch | to foot the bill |
| bill of fare | dutch treat | pick up the check | dine and dance |
| bottomless cup | room and meals tax | to take the check | specials |
| | chief cook and bottle washer | | |

# 33: Stores and Shops

## General

browsing
chain store
department store
downtown

main street
mall
neighborhood

one-stop shopping
outlet center
specialty shops

shopping center
shopping district
window shopping
variety store

## Specific

antique shop
appliance store
art gallery
arts and crafts store
auto parts store
bakery
bookstore
cafeteria
camera shop
candy store
car dealership
carpets & flooring
cellphone store
clothing store
coffee shop
comic book/game store
computer store
convenience store

country store
delicatessen
department store
discount store
dollar store
drug store
electronics store
fabric/draperies store
farmers' market
fast-food chain
fix it shop
flea market
florist
furniture store
garden center
gift shop
grocery store
hardware store

health food store
hobby shop
jewelry store
liquor store
mail-order
minimart
music store
newsstand
office supply store
optician
outlet store
paint store
pawn shop
pet shop
pizza parlor
pharmacy
photography store
printing/copy center

restaurant
Salvation Army store
service center
sewing center
shoe store
snack bar
sporting goods store
stationery store
supermarket
telephone store
thrift shop
tobacconist/cigar store
toy store
TV-radio store
used book store
used clothing store
used furniture store
vegetable stand

# 34: Agencies and Services

advertising agency
animal shelter/SPCA
appliance repair
auto rental agency
auto repair shop
bank/savings and loan
barber shop
beauty parlor
business consultant
cable/satellite company office
carpenter shop
certified public
    accountant office
charities
copy center
counseling office
dance studio
day-care center
dry cleaners
electrician
employment agency

fire department
funeral parlor
gardener/lawn care
health center/club
homeless shelter
insurance agency/broker
Internal Revenue Service
laundry
laundromat
law firm
loan association
martial arts studio
medical clinic
military recruiting office
moving company
newspaper office
news stand
Planned Parenthood
plumber
police department
post office

radio-TV repair
real estate agency
shoe repair service
self-storage units
service station
storage warehouse
senior citizen's center
shipping center
social security office
soup kitchen
stockbroker
tailor
tanning salon
tax consultant
travel agency
telephone company
    business office
town/city hall/offices
welding shop
welfare office
Women's Crisis Center

# 35: Post Office/Delivery Services

## Personnel

carrier

clerk

delivery person

mail carrier

mail sorter

post office worker

postmaster/mistress

## Nouns and Adjectives

address

aerogram

airmail

booklet of stamps

book rate

box

bulk mail

cancellation

certified mail

C.O.D.

coil of stamps

commemorative stamp

customs form

dead letter

envelope

express mail

fee

first class/second, third.

forever stamp

franking privileges

general delivery

global priority mail

insured mail

international mail

junk mail

letter

lobby

magazine rate

mail box

media mail

money order

next day

newspaper

overnight

package

parcel post

philatelic window

postage

postage due

postage meter

postage stamp

post card

post office (P. O.) box

priority mail

registered mail

return address

return receipt

self-addressed envelope

self-adhesive stamp

service window

sheet of stamps

special delivery

special handling

stamp

stamp collecting

surface mail

tracking

U.S.P.S

weight

ZIP Code

    plus four

Zone (shipping)

## Verbs

address

cancel

certify

deliver

fill out

forward

insure

lick

mail

post

pick up

receive

register

return

seal

send

ship

sort

stamp

trace

track

## Other

courier service

delivery

    afternoon/p.m.

    morning/a.m.

    next-day

    overnight

    same-day

    two-day

    second-day

    three-day

handle with care

fragile

pick-up

snail mail

FedEx (Federal Express)

UPS (United Parcel Service)

DHL/Airborne Express

# 36: Banks and Money

## Verbs

| | | | |
|---|---|---|---|
| apply for | change | deposit | overdraw |
| authorize | charge | endorse | pay |
| balance | close out | insure | put in |
| borrow | convert | justify | save |
| cancel | count | loan | stop payment |
| call in a loan | credit | lend | take out |
| cash | debit | make change | withdraw |

## Nouns

| | | | |
|---|---|---|---|
| asset | coin | line of credit | safe |
| automatic payment | commercial loan | loan | safe deposit box |
| ATM - automatic | credit card | loan agreement | savings account |
| teller machine | currency | loan payment | savings bond |
| balance | debit card | money | second mortgage |
| bank | deposit | mortgage | secured loan |
| bank account | deposit slip | nickel | silver dollar |
| bank book | deposit receipt | on-line banking | statement |
| bill | dime | paycheck | transfer |
| cash | dollar | payment book | traveler's check |
| CD - certificate of | fixed rate (interest) | penny | total |
| deposit | half dollar, 50¢ piece | piggy bank | variable rate (interest) |
| check | home equity loan | principal | vault |
| checking account | interest | quarter | window |
| check register/book | invoice | receipt | wire transfer |
| check stub | frozen assets | record book | withdrawal |
| | | | withdrawal slip |

## Personnel

| | | | |
|---|---|---|---|
| drive-up teller | loan officer | president | secretary |
| executive officer | messenger | safe deposit clerk | security guard |
| | | | teller |

## Idioms and Expression

| | | |
|---|---|---|
| to bank on something | pretty penny | I.O.U. |
| a bear market/a bull market | to take a rain check | a man of means |
| to bounce a check | rubber check | a panhandler |
| bottom dollar | a run on the bank | penny wise and pound foolish |
| cash in your chips | bank holiday | queer as a three-dollar bill |
| cheapskate | flat broke | to nickel and dime to death |
| as good as gold | in the money | under the mattress |
| to get one's money's worth | to corner the market | under the table |
| greenback | to make or break | Waste not, want not. |
| layaway plan | to make a buck | A penny saved is a penny earned. |
| to pass the buck | to make both ends meet | A fool and his money are soon parted. |

134

# 37: Recreation

## Games (also see 38)

backgammon
board games
bridge
canasta
cards
charades
checkers
chess

Chinese checkers
cribbage
crossword puzzle
computer games
hearts
jig saw puzzle
mahjong
mankala

Monopoly
poker
role playing games
rummy
solitaire
Scrabble
twenty questions
video games

## Hobbies

aquariums/ tropical fish
butterfly collecting
coin collecting
collecting antiques, etc.
canning
ceramics
cooking
dolls/ doll houses

embroidery
flower arranging
gardening
gun collecting
house plants
miniatures
model building
model railroading

painting
pottery
rock collecting
sewing
terrariums
stamp collecting
Sports (see List 35)
Music (see List 36)

## Amusements & Shows

amusement park
carnival
circus
concert hall
dinner theater/ summer stock

disco
flash mob
ice show
magic show
movies

pool hall
night club
radio
television
theater
video game arcade

## Arts

ballet
concert
dance
drama

exhibition
martial arts
music
painting

photography
recital
sculpture
theater

## Crafts

batik
carpentry
crewel
crocheting

embroidery
knitting
model making
needlepoint

pottery
quilting
sewing
weaving

135

## Places

| | | |
|---|---|---|
| amusement park | country club | racquet/racket club |
| aquarium | discotheque | ski resort |
| bar | health club | social club |
| beach | historical site | sports stadium |
| botanical garden | marina | swimming pool |
| campground | movie theatre | teen center |
| circus | museum | tennis club |
| cocktail lounge | national park, forest | theatre |
| concert hall | nightclub | zoo |

## Activities

| | | |
|---|---|---|
| backpacking | golf | racquetball |
| badminton | gymnastics | reading |
| ballet | handball | roller blading |
| baseball | hiking | roller skating |
| basketball | hockey | sailing |
| bicycling/ cycling | horseback riding | sewing |
| birdwatching | horse race | skating |
| board game | hunting | skate boarding |
| body building | in-line skating | skiing |
| bowling | jogging | sky diving |
| bungee jumping | kite flying | soccer |
| camping | listening to radio, stereo | softball |
| canoeing | long-distance running | snowboarding |
| car race | making music | squash |
| concert | martial arts | surfing |
| croquet | minature golf | swimming |
| diving | motor boating | tennis |
| dog race | mountain climbing | track and field |
| extreme sports | opera | video games |
| fishing | painting | volleyball |
| flying | paragliding | water skiing |
| football | playing cards | watching TV |
| frisbee | pottery making | wind surfing |
| gourmet cooking | rally | weight lifting |
| gardening | | wrestling |

## Idioms and Expressions

| | | |
|---|---|---|
| to put one's cards on the table | drawing card | to steal the show |
| to put one's money on the line | to flip over something | up one's sleeve |
| to put up or shut up | go fly a kite | surfing the net |
| no dice | a flop | Do not pass Go. |
| dicey | to hit the jackpot | to win by a nose |
| an ace up one's sleeve | on the wrong track | nip and tuck |

136

# 38: Sports and Games

| | | | | |
|---|---|---|---|---|
| archery | curling | hiking | polo | speed skating |
| badminton | diving | hockey | racquetball | squash |
| baseball | extreme sports | horseback riding | roller blading | surfing |
| basketball | fencing | hunting | roller skating | swimming |
| billiards | figure skating | jogging | running | table tennis |
| bowling | fishing | lacrosse | skiing | tennis |
| boxing | football | marathon running | downhill | track |
| bicycling | golf | mountaineering | cross-country | volleyball |
| bronco busting | gymnastics | Ping-Pong | soccer | water polo |
| canoeing | handball | pool | softball | weight lifting |
| climbing | | | | wrestling |

## Equipment

| | | | | |
|---|---|---|---|---|
| arrow | fishing rod | mat | racket/racquet | soccerball |
| balance beam | flying rings | net | racquetball | softball |
| baseball bat | glove | paddle | reins | surf/snowboard |
| birdie | golf ball | parallel bars | saddle | target |
| bow | golf clubs | Ping-Pong ball | shuttlecock | tee |
| bicycle | hockey stick | pole | skates | tennis ball |
| canoe | horse | pool cue | ski pole | tennis racket |
| fishing lure | indian clubs | puck | skis | trampoline |

## Areas

| | | | | |
|---|---|---|---|---|
| arena | course | green | pool | roller drome |
| coliseum | court | gymnasium | ring | stadium |
| country club | field | lane | rink | track |
| | | | | trail |

## Verbs

| | | | | |
|---|---|---|---|---|
| aim | defend | kick | play | serve |
| attack | hike | lose | punt | tackle |
| catch | hit | participate | run | take part in |
| club | hurl | pitch | save | tie |
| coach | jog | place | score | throw |
| defeat | | | | win |

## Idioms and Expressions

| | | |
|---|---|---|
| all part of the game | hook, line, and sinker | last lap |
| batting average | to keep the ball rolling | for keeps |
| below par | to make a hit | long shot |
| behind the eight ball | in the rough | to be punchy |
| to break the record | to rate a ten | to pull one's punches |
| comeback | right off the bat | to know what the score is |
| doubleheader | to pinch hit | second wind |
| to get on the ball | rain check | to have a score to settle |
| to get to first base | free-for-all | seventh inning stretch |
| to go to bat for | hit or miss | a shot in the dark |
| to have a lot on the ball | to jump the gun | to win hands down |

137

# 39: Music

## Nouns

| | | | |
|---|---|---|---|
| album | composition | jazz | release |
| alto | concert | lyrics | rhythm |
| artist | conductor | measure | singer |
| ballad | concerto | melody | solo |
| band | disc | MP3 | sonata |
| bar | disc jockey (DJ) | note | song |
| bass | folk song | piece | soprano |
| beat | group | program | symphony |
| cassette | hit | recital | tape |
| chorus | hymn | record | tenor |
| compact disc (CD) | | | tune |

## Verbs

| | | | |
|---|---|---|---|
| accompany | harmonize | play | sing |
| compose | hum | pluck | strum |
| conduct | interpret | rap | toot |
| croon | jam | read (music) | whistle |
| finger | pick | record | write |

## Types

| | | | |
|---|---|---|---|
| acoustic | classical | jazz | popular, pop |
| background | contemporary | light classical | rap |
| band | country & western | modern | religious |
| baroque | dance | mood music | rock and roll, rock |
| bebop | electronic | musical | rhythm and blues |
| bluegrass | folk | new age | spirituals |
| chamber | hard rock | opera | soul |
| church | hip hop | operetta | symphonic |

## Instruments

| | | | |
|---|---|---|---|
| banjo | dulcimer | keyboard | strings |
| bass | electric guitar | oboe | synthesizer |
| bassoon | fiddle | organ | tambourine |
| cello | gospel | mandolin | trombone |
| clarinet | guitar | piano | trumpet |
| cornet | harp | punk | tuba |
| cymbals | horn | saxophone | viola |
| drums | | | violin |

## Idioms and Expressions

| | | | |
|---|---|---|---|
| to blow your own horn | golden oldies | to pipe down | to sing for one's supper |
| elevator music | to play second fiddle | song and dance | music to one's ears |
| to face the music | to soft-pedal | for a song | the blues |
| to fiddle around with | | | to beat the band |

# 40: Photography, Cinema, and Video

also see #55 *The Media*

## Photography

| | | | | |
|---|---|---|---|---|
| accessory | darkroom | frame | pixel | shutter |
| album | definition | F-stop | Photoshop | slide |
| aperture | depth of field | glossy | portrait | snapshot |
| automatic | developer | ISO | pose | speed |
| battery | digital | lens | positive | strap |
| black and white | dodge | lens flare | process | studio |
| blow up | double exposure | light meter | projector | take (a picture) |
| burn | double prints | load | print | telephoto |
| camera | duplicate | long exposure | red eye | time lapse |
| canister | enlarge | macro | reduce | tone |
| cartridge | enlargement | matte | rewind | tripod |
| cellphone photos | exposure | megapixel | roll (of film) | under-exposed |
| case | film | mug shot | rez, resolution | viewer |
| color | filter | negative | screen | viewfinder |
| come out | fisheye lens | out-of-focus | SD card | washed out |
| composition | flash | over-exposed | selfie | white balance |
| contrast | focal length | photo(graph) | setting | wide-angle lens |
| crop | focus | | | zoom lens |

## Cinema/ Movies

| | | | | |
|---|---|---|---|---|
| action | digitalization | green screen | rating | short subject |
| actor/actress | director | independent film | reel | show |
| adult | documentary | letter-box | release | sound track |
| adventure | drama | matinee | restricted | star |
| animation | dubbed | mature | reverse | sub-titled |
| blockbuster | entertainment | movie | romance | supporting actor |
| blue/green screen | epic | musical | running time | tear-jerker |
| cartoon | fantasy | mystery | score | thriller |
| CG/CGI/CA | feature | Oscar | sci-fi (science | ticket |
| (computer | film | pacing | fiction) | 3D (3 dimension) |
| graphics) | film festival | porno(graphy) | screen | trailer |
| classic | film studio | prequel | sequel | x-rated |
| comedy | flash animation | preview | SFX (special | videographer |
| composit | gaffer | producer | effects | western |
| critic | | | | wide-screen |

## Video

| | | | | |
|---|---|---|---|---|
| camcorder | fast forward | pan & scan | SmartPhone | video |
| cassette | format(ted) | playback | video | camera |
| closed captioned | freeze | Redbox | tracking | disc |
| DVD (digital | home video | rent | YouTube | game |
| video disc) | music video | rewind | VCR (video tape | player |
| download | Netflix | | player and | recorder |
| | | | recorder – | rental |
| | | | now obsolete) | streaming |

# 41: Medicine and Health

## Places and Areas

| | | | |
|---|---|---|---|
| admitting | emergency room | labor room | out-patient clinic |
| ambulance | hospital | laboratory | pediatric ward |
| assisted living | HMO (health | maternity ward | private room |
| birthing room | maintenance org.) | mental hospital | recovery room |
| clinic | insane asylum | nursing home | sanitarium |
| check in | intensive care unit | operating room | waiting room |
| delivery room | (ICU) | | ward |

## Equipment

| | | | |
|---|---|---|---|
| adhesive tape | crutches | sanitary | tongue |
| band-aid | gauze | napkins | depressor |
| bandage | heating pad | scalpel | toothpaste |
| bed | hot water bottle | stethoscope | tweezers |
| bed pan | operating table | thermometer | vaporizer |
| cane | oxygen tent | oral | walker |
| cast | Q-tip (swab) | rectal | wheelchair |
| | | | x-ray machine |

## People

| | | | |
|---|---|---|---|
| anesthetist | lab technician | pathologist | psychoanalyst |
| candy striper | neurologist | patient | psychologist |
| chiropractor | nurse | pediatrician | radiologist |
| dermatologist | nurse practitioner | pharmacist | receptionist |
| doctor (M.D.) | nursing assistant | physician | registered nurse (R.N.) |
| general practitioner | obstetrician | physician's assistant | specialist |
| (G.P.) | ophthalmologist | podiatrist | surgeon |
| gynecologist | orthopedic surgeon | practical nurse | undertaker |
| intern | out-patient | psychiatrist | urologist |

## Verbs

| | | | |
|---|---|---|---|
| ache | discharge | irritate | recuperate |
| admit | examine | nurse | relapse |
| bleed | faint | operate | set |
| cough | give birth | pain | swell |
| deliver | gargle | prescribe | throb |
| diagnose | hurt | recover | throw up |
| | | | vomit |

## Processes

| | | | |
|---|---|---|---|
| appendectomy | examination | MRI | surgery |
| blood pressure | heart beat | observation | temperature |
| Caesarean section | hysterectomy | prognosis | tonsillectomy |
| D&C | implant | pulse | transplant |
| delivery (of a baby) | injection | sample | vaccination |
| diagnosis | inoculation | shot | vasectomy |
| EKG | intensive care | specimen | x-ray |

## Medicine

| | | | | |
|---|---|---|---|---|
| antacid | aspirin | eyedrops | penicillin | sedative |
| antidote | capsules | laxative | pill | suppository |
| antihistamine | contraceptive | nasal spray | the Pill | tablet |
| antiseptic | decongestant | ointment | prescription | vitamins |

## Problems/Symptoms

| | | | | |
|---|---|---|---|---|
| abscess | a cold | exhaustion | injury | sprain |
| accident | constipation | fever | infection | stiff |
| ache | cough | the flu | inflammation | strain |
| allergy | cut | fracture | nausea | swollen |
| asthma | deaf | hemorrhoids | pain | virus |
| blind | diarrhea | (piles) | rash | vomit |
| burn | dislocation | hyperthermia | runny nose | wart |
| chills | dumb | indigestion | sore | wound |

## Diseases and Conditions

| | | | | |
|---|---|---|---|---|
| AIDS | Crohn's disease | herpes | multiple sclerosis | shingles |
| allergy | dementia | high blood pressure | mumps | skin cancer |
| alcoholism | diabetes | HIV positive | neurosis | smallpox |
| Alzheimer's | diarrhea | immunity | paranoia | stroke |
| angina | Down syndrome | influenza (flu) | pneumonia | syndrome |
| arteriosclerosis | drug addiction | leukemia | polio | syphilis |
| arthritis | dysentery | malaria | psychosis | tetanus |
| asthma | emphysema | measles | rheumatic fever | tuberculosis (T.B.) |
| autism | fetal alcohol | meningitis | rubella (German | tumor |
| bronchitis | syndrome | mental | measles) | typhoid fever |
| bursitis | gonorrhea | retardation | SARS | typhus |
| cancer | heart attack | mononucleosis | scarlet fever | ulcer |
| chicken pox | hepatitis | (mono) | schizophrenia | V.D. (venereal |
| cholera | hernia | | | disease) |

## Idioms and Expressions

| | | |
|---|---|---|
| on call | over the hill | a shiner |
| office hours | to kick the bucket | a black eye |
| Say "ah." | a new lease on life | a shot in the arm |
| Turn your head and cough. | to give someone a dose | a sight for sore eyes |
| born with a silver spoon | of their own medicine | to turn one's stomach |
| in one's mouth | to take one's medicine | under the weather |
| to cough up | nuts, nutty as a fruitcake | on the wagon |
| chain smoker | to go off the deep end | "break a leg" |
| dead as a doornail | a bitter pill to swallow | An apple a day |
| dead to the world | in the pink | keeps the doctor away. |
| over one's dead body | safe and sound | skin and bones |
| one foot in the grave | to have a screw loose | sick and tired of |
| to croak | hooked on drugs | to catch a cold |
| to give up the ghost | monkey on your back | to come down with |
| hard of hearing | horrors (withdrawal) | |

# 42: Dentistry

## Places

clinic　　　　　　　　office　　　　　　　　waiting room

## Equipment

| | | | |
|---|---|---|---|
| air compressor | dental floss | drill | toothbrush |
| cleaning tools | dentist's chair | mirror | toothpaste |
| | | | x-ray machine |

## People

| | | | |
|---|---|---|---|
| dentist | dental hygienist | oral surgeon | orthodontist |
| dental assistant | | | receptionist |

## Verbs

| | | | |
|---|---|---|---|
| ache | drill | hurt | seal |
| cap | extract | pull out | x-ray |
| clean | fill | repair | |

## Miscellaneous

| | | | |
|---|---|---|---|
| abscess | crown | false teeth | molar |
| bicuspid | canines | front tooth | nerve |
| braces | decay | filling | novocaine |
| bridge | dentures | gap toothed | pain |
| buck teeth | dog tooth | incisor | root |
| cavity | eye tooth | jaw | root canal |
| checkup | | | wisdom tooth |

## Idioms and Expressions

| | | |
|---|---|---|
| baby teeth | to cut one's teeth on | long in the tooth |
| one's bark is worse than one's bite | to give one's eye tooth for | toothy grin |
| to bite the hand that feeds one | to knock your teeth out | winning smile |
| to bite off more than one can chew | like pulling teeth | the tooth fairy |

# 43: Hygiene

## Nouns

| | | | |
|---|---|---|---|
| antibacterial soap | dishwasher | mouthwash | soap, hand and bath |
| bath bathtub | feminine hygiene | shampoo | sterile |
| deodorant | products | shower | toothbrush, toothpaste |
| detergent | hand washing | shower stall | washing machine |

## Verbs

| | | | |
|---|---|---|---|
| bathe | filter water | sanitize | sterilize |
| clean | do laundry | scrub | wash |
| clean up | purify | shower | wash up |

A page of vocabulary on Hygiene and Contaception is available as supplementary web material:
http://www.prolinguaassociates.com/The_ESL_Miscellany/index.

# 44: Barber and Beautician

## Nouns

| | | | |
|---|---|---|---|
| Afro | cream rinse | hair net | razor cut |
| appointment | crew-cut | hair oil | razor blade |
| bangs | curl | hairpiece | receding hairline |
| barber | curler | hairpins | redhead |
| barrette | dandruff | hair style | rollers |
| beard | depilatory | hair stylist | scissors |
| beautician | dreadlocks | handlebar moustache | shampoo |
| blond/blonde | drier | highlight | shave |
| bobby pin | dye | manicure | setting lotion |
| bowl cut | fashion | manicurist | sideburns |
| braid | flat top | Mohawk | split ends |
| brunette | goatee (beard) | mousse | streak |
| brush | hairbrush | moustache | tatoo |
| butch | haircut | page boy | tint |
| carrot top | hairdo | pedicure | towhead |
| clippers | hairdresser | permanent | toupee |
| comb | hair drier | pigtails | wave |
| conditioner | hair grease | ponytail | whiskers |
| cosmetics | hairline | razor | wig |

## Verbs

| | | | |
|---|---|---|---|
| bleach | curl | dye | shampoo |
| blow dry | cut | massage | shave |
| brush | design | rinse | tint |
| clip | dry | set | trim |
| comb | | | wave |

## Adjectives

| | | | |
|---|---|---|---|
| bald | dyed | long | short |
| bleached | frizzy | normal | straight |
| bushy | hairless | oily | thick |
| close | hairy | over the ear | thin |
| curly | kinky | scraggly (beard) | unisex |
| dry | | | wavy |

## Hair colors

| | | | |
|---|---|---|---|
| auburn | brown | honey blonde | gray |
| black | brunette | flaxen blond | red |
| blond, blonde | dishwater blonde | strawberry blond | white |

## Idioms and Expressions

| | | | |
|---|---|---|---|
| to get in one's hair | hairline crack | not a hair out of place | Handsome is as handsome |
| hairbreadth escape | long hair | one's hair stands on end | does. |
| hairpin turn | to put one's hair up | tall, dark, and handsome | Beauty is in the eye of the |
| let one's hair down | hairy | blonds have more fun | beholder. |

# 45: Cosmetics and Toiletries

## Nouns

after-shave lotion
baby shampoo
bath oil
bath salts
bath soap
beauty cream
beauty lotion
blush
body lotion
body cream
bubble bath
cold cream
cologne
comb
compact
cosmetic base
cotton balls
cotton swabs/ Q-tips
cuticle remover
deodorant
   roll-on
   soap

solid
spray
stick
dental floss
depilatory
emery board
eyebrow pencil
eye drops
eye-liner
eye-shadow
eye wash
facial cleanser
facial mask
facial soap
hand cream
hand cleanser
hand lotion
hand soap
hair brush
hair color
hair dye
hair remover

hair rinse
lip balm
lip gloss
lipstick
make up
mascara
moisturizer
mouth wash
mud pack
nail clippers
nail file
nail polish
nail polish remover
ointment
oral rinse
perfume
powder
razor
   disposable
   one-track
   safety
   two-track

razor blade
rouge
scent
septic stick
shampoo
shaver (electric)
shaving brush
shaving cream
shaving mug
shaving soap
skin cream
soap
sun block
sun screen
suntan lotion
tissues
toilet water
toothbrush
toothpaste
toothpaste gel
tooth powder
tweezers
witch hazel

## Verbs

apply
beautify
blend
brush
cleanse

clip
cut
dab
deodorize

manicure
moisten
perfume
put on

shave
trim
touch up

## Idioms and Common Sayings

Beauty is in the eye of the beholder.
Beauty is only skin deep.
B.O. (body odor)
Cleanliness is next to Godliness.
a close shave
five o'clock shadow
a greaser

the great unwashed
Handsome is as handsome does.
a little shaver
to look oily
a painted woman
to smell of trouble
to wash one's mouth out with soap

# 46: Jobs and Work

accountant
advertising agent
artist
assembly line worker
automotive engineer
babysitter
baggage handler
baker
banker
bank teller
barber
beautician
bookkeeper
building contractor
bureaucrat
bus driver
business consultant
businessman/woman
butcher
carpenter
car washer
cashier
chambermaid
chef
chiropractor
civil engineer
cleaningman/ woman
commercial artist
computer programmer
construction worker
cook
courier
cowboy/ cowgirl
crossing guard
delivery person
dental hygienist
dentist
detective
diplomat
dishwasher
doctor
dog walker
doorman/woman
editor
electrical engineer
electrician
employment officer
engineer

entertainer
factory worker
farmer
farm hand
field hand
file clerk
fireman, firefighter
fisherman
flight attendant
food handler
garbage collector
gardener
glazier
guard
groundskeeper
heating contractor
hotel/motel clerk
house detective
housekeeper
housewife/ -husband
insurance agent
insurance claims
   adjustor
insurance
   investigator
interpreter
illustrator
interior decorator
jack of all trades
janitor
jeweler
journalist
judge
junk dealer
lab technician
landscape architect
laundry worker
lawyer
legislator
librarian
life guard
lighting contractor
lobbyist
logger
longshoreman
machine operator
mail carrier
maintenance worker

manager
mason
masseur, masseuse
mechanic
merchant marine
messenger
meter reader
mover
musician
news reporter
nurse
office boy
ombudsman
optician
optometrist
painter (house)
parking lot attendant
pest exterminator
pharmacist
photographer
piano tuner
pilot
plumber
podiatrist
police officer
politician
pollster
post office clerk
potter
priest, minister,
   rabbi, evangelist
   nun, imam
press spokesperson
printer
psychiatrist
psychologist
publicist
publisher
receptionist
real estate agent
red cap
repairman/woman
reporter
research specialist
roustabout
rubbish collector
sailor
sales clerk

scientist
school administrator
secretary
security officer
service station
   attendant
shipping clerk
shoemaker
soldier
spy
stenographer
steward(ess)
store clerk
street cleaner
student
surgeon
surveyor
swimming pool
   contractor
tailor
tax consultant
taxidermist
taxi driver
teacher, professor
technician
telephone lineman
telephone operator
teller
translator
travel agent
traveling salesman
tree surgeon
trucker, truck driver
TV/radio repairman/
   woman
typesetter
typist
undertaker
upholsterer
veterinarian
volunteer
waiter, waitress
webmaster
weather forecaster
   meteorologist
window washer
writer
zoo keeper

# 47: Office

## Nouns

adding machine
appointment
business
calculator
carbon copy
computer
  hard disc
  hardware
  mainframe
  network
  personal (PC)
  program
  server
  software
conference
copier
department
desk
desk chair

dictation
disc storage
duplicate
envelope
equipment
FAX machine
file cabinet
files
information backup
intercom
letter
letterhead
mail
meeting
modem
paper clip
pencil sharpener
postage meter
postage scales

printer
records
router
scanner
shorthand
shredder
stapler
stationery
supplies
supply cabinet
switchboard
swivel chair
telephone
telephone answering machine
tape dispenser
typewriter
voice mail
word processor
work station

## Verbs

copy
dictate
input
fax

file
mail
manage
program

staple
take dictation
transmit
type

## Personnel

accountant
assistant
boss
board of directors
bookkeeper
bursar
chairman/woman
clerk
chief executive officer (CEO)

chief financial officer (CFO)
director
employee
employer
executive
executive secretary
IT/internet technology specialist
manager
office manager

officer
personnel officer
president
receptionist
secretary
supervisor
treasurer
typist
vice-president (VP)

## Idioms and Expressions

to take a letter
secretarial/typing pool

to be called on the carpet
right-hand man/woman

business is business
office politics

# 48: Business

## Nouns

account
accounting software
accounts payable
accounts receivable
advertisement,
 ad, advertising
annual report
asset
audit
bad debt
balance
balance sheet
benefit/benefits
 package
bid
bill
bill of lading
bond
books
bottom line
buy out
capital
capital gains
cash
cash flow
commercial
commission
common stock
computer

computer support
contract
corporate seal
corporate secretary
corporate officers
cost benefit analysis
cost of sales
credit
credit check
debit
debt
deduction
deficit
department
depletion
depreciation
Dow-Jones Average
(the) economy
equipment
equity
estimate
excise tax
expenditure
expense
expense account
fee
fiscal year
financial statement
fringe benefit

income
income tax
interest
inventory
investment
invoice
labor
labor union
labor contract
lease
ledger
leverage
liability
license
loss
maintenance
management
margin
(the) market
merger
mortgage
negotiations
offer
operations
overhead
payroll
petty cash
president
profit

pro forma invoice
purchase order
quotation (quote)
research and
 development (R&D)
receipt
rent
rental
retained earnings
royalty
sales
sales tax
securities
share (of stock)
social security
spread sheet
supplies
statement
stock
stock exchange
stock market
takeover
tax
value added tax
wage
wage scale
Wall Street
worksheet
write off

## People

accountant
administrative
 assistant
agent
analyst
bookkeeper
broker
certified public
 accountant (CPA)
chairman of the board
chief executive
 officer (CEO)
chief financial
 officer (CFO)

clerk
communications
 specialist
comptroller
consultant
coworker
dealer
department head
director
employee
employer
executive
executive secretary
filing clerk

foreman
investor
lawyer
legal counsel
mail room clerk
manager
market researcher
mentor
operator
owner
partner
part-time employee
proprietor
salesman/woman

secretary
shipping clerk
specialist
supervisor
stenographer
stockholder
telemarketer
temporary worker
trader
treasurer
trustee
typist
vice president
worker

# Types

| | | | |
|---|---|---|---|
| agency | dealership | monopoly | partnership |
| chain | franchise | non-profit | service |
| charity | holding company |    organization | single proprietorship |
| company | industry | non-governmental | subsidiary |
| conglomerate | limited liability |    organization (NGO) | trust |
| corporation |    corporation (LLC) | | |

# Verbs

| | | | |
|---|---|---|---|
| balance | fire | lease | sell |
| borrow | invest | loan | staff |
| buy | lend | merge | take over |
| finance | liquidate | restructure | tender an offer |

# Adjectives

| | | | |
|---|---|---|---|
| commercial | incorporated (Inc.) | net | private |
| fiscal | industrial | non-commercial | public |
| gross | limited (Ltd.) | not-for-profit | volunteer |

# Idioms and Expressions

| | | | |
|---|---|---|---|
| in the black | monkey business | "There's no business | employee relations |
| bullish | profit motive |    like show business." | employment benefits |
| in the red | good repute | funny business | industrial wasteland |
| bearish | "The business of | good morale | It's none of your |
| black market |    America is business." | customer relations |    business. |
| the bottom line | | | |

# Employment: Getting a Job

| | | | |
|---|---|---|---|
| apply for a job | work permit/ | workman's | competency testing |
| application |    Green Card |    compensation | work evaluation |
| employment forms | probationary period | benefit packages | performance review |
| employment record | wages, pay, salary | reimbursement | discrimination |
| former employer | hours, work week | vacation | affirmative action |
| interview | payroll deduction | child care | classified ads |
| reference | W-4 form | civic duties (jury, etc.) | help wanted ads |
| resume | W-2 form | union membership | employment office, |
| skills | I9 eligibility | union dues |    agency |
| training |    verification | drug screening | |

# 49: Agriculture

## Nouns

| | | | |
|---|---|---|---|
| acreage | farmer | kitchen garden | shepherd |
| agronomy | farmers' market | manure | sheep farm |
| aqua culture | feed | market | silage |
| baler | fence | milking equipment | silo |
| barn | field | milk | spreader |
| bulk tank | fish | processing plant | staple crops |
| combine | farm | mowing | subsidy |
| commodity | fodder | gardening | ranch |
| contour plowing | garden | orchard | thresher |
| crop | harrow | pasture | tiller |
| crop-dusting | harvest | pesticides | tractor |
| cultivation | herb garden | pitchfork | truck |
| cultivator | horticulture | plow | truck farming |
| dairy | horticulturist | produce | veterinarian (vet) |
| earth | hydroponics | product | wagon |
| fallow ground | insecticide | rotation | well |
| farm | irrigation | reaper | yield |
| | implements | seed | |

## Verbs

| | | | | |
|---|---|---|---|---|
| breed | graze | hoe | plant | thresh |
| clone | grow | inseminate | plow | water |
| cultivate | harvest | irrigate | raise | weed |
| fertilize | harrow | mow | reap | winnow |
| graft | hay | mulch | sow | |

## Livestock

| | | | | |
|---|---|---|---|---|
| bull | cow | goose | lamb | rabbits |
| calf | duck | hog | ox | sheep |
| cattle | goat | horse | pig | steer |
| chicken | | | poultry | turkey |

## Crops and Products

| | | | | |
|---|---|---|---|---|
| berries | dairy | grains | milk | sugar beets |
| citrus | eggs | legumes | organic produce | vegetables |
| cotton | fruit | livestock | silage | wool |

## Idioms and Expressions

| | | |
|---|---|---|
| cut and dried | 40 acres and a mule | one reaps what one sows |
| to farm something out | The grass is always greener on | to sow one's wild oats |
| to make hay while the | the other side of the fence. | to separate the wheat from the |
| sun shines | genetically altered | chaff |

# 50: Shops and Tools

## Names of tools

| | | |
|---|---|---|
| ax, axe | hatchet | square |
| bit | level | straight edge |
| blow torch | mallet | staple gun |
| brace | plane | tape measure |
| calipers | pliers | tin snips |
| chisel | router | vise |
| clamp | sander | wedge |
| drill | saw | wire cutters |
| hammer | screwdriver | wrench |

## Verbs

| | | |
|---|---|---|
| bolt | nail | scribe |
| build | paint | solder |
| clamp | plane | staple |
| cut | pound | turn |
| glue | sand | varnish |
| hammer | saw | weld |
| measure | screw | wire |

## Miscellaneous

| | | |
|---|---|---|
| apprentice | paint | stain |
| bolt | plumber | staple |
| brad | plywood | steel |
| carpenter | polyurethane | wool |
| coat (of paint) | primer | tack |
| electrician | sandpaper | tubing |
| helper | screw | varnish |
| nail | shellac | welder |
| nut | spike | wire |

## Idioms and Expressions

| | | |
|---|---|---|
| to get the axe | jack of all trades | handyman |
| to have an axe to grind | live wire | on the level |
| to hit the nail on the head | nuts and bolts | to measure up |
| many irons in the fire | | |

# 51: Law

## People

attorney
bailiff
clerk
coroner
counsel
court
court reporter
defendant
defense attorney
district attorney

expert witness
Grand Jury
investigating officer
judge
juror
jury
jury foreman
law office
lawyer

minor
offender
parole officer
plaintiff
probation officer
prosecutor
prosecuting attorney
public defender
state's attorney
witness

## Places and Things

bar
bench
civil trial
court
courthouse
Court of Appeals
courtroom

criminal trial
Family Court
Federal District Court
gavel
jury box
judge's chambers
legal aid service

probate court
public defender
session (of the court)
Small Claims Court
State District Court
Supreme Court
witness stand

## Adjectives

alleged
hanged (criminal)
hung (jury)
guilty

innocent
judicial
legal
liable

no contest; *nolo contendre*
(objection) over-ruled
(objection) sustained
pre-trial

## Verbs

accuse
acquit
allege
appeal
argue
award
call (a witness)
charge
charge the jury
commute
convict

defend
deliberate
dissent
enter a plea
find
hear a case
indict
instruct
jump bail
overturn
plead

post bail
prosecute
reverse a decision
sentence
serve a sentence
sue
swear
testify
throw out a case
try
uphold

## Events and Processes

| | | |
|---|---|---|
| accusation | deposition | opinion |
| aquittal | DNA | parole |
| alimony | evidence | perjury |
| allegation | exhibit | probation |
| appeal | findings | prosecution |
| bail | forensics | recess |
| case | fraud | retrial |
| charge | grievance | right(s) |
| claim | hearing | ruling |
| conviction | indictment | sentence |
| court order | injunction | sequester |
| crime | inquiry | settlement |
| crime scene investigation | inquest | suit |
| cross-examination | law | summons |
| damages | libel | testimony |
| death penalty | litigation | trial |
| decision | manslaughter | verdict |
| defense | mistrial | writ |

## Idioms and Expressions

| | | |
|---|---|---|
| to bail out | legalese | to take the law into one's |
| cop a plea | the letter of the law | own hands |
| death row | Miranda warning | to take the stand |
| to do time | of age | to take the fifth amendment |
| to get away with murder | open and shut case | third degree |
| jailbird | out-of-court settlement | to throw away the key |
| you be the judge | plead bargain | to throw the book at |
| to lay down the law | the question is mute | to throw out of court |
| | | under age |

# 52: Police, Crime, and Emergencies

## Good Guys

| | | | |
|---|---|---|---|
| chief of police | game warden | police officer | SWAT team |
| constable | investigator | private eye | traffic cop |
| cop | meter maid | private investigator | undercoverman/woman |
| detective | narcotics officer (narc) | riot police | U.S. Marshal |
| deputy | patrolman | sergeant | vice squad |
| F. B. I. | plainclothesman | sheriff | victim |
| fireman | policeman/woman | state trooper | warden |

## Bad Guys

| | | | |
|---|---|---|---|
| arsonist | gang | mob | second-story man |
| burglar | hit man | mobster | serial killer |
| call girl | hood | mole | street walker |
| child abuser/molester | inforcer | mugger | swindler |
| con artist | juvenile delinquent | petty thief | terrorist |
| con man | Ku Klux Klan (KKK) | pickpocket | thief |
| crook | killer | prostitute | thug |
| deadbeat dad/mom | loan shark | pusher | tough |
| drug dealer/trafficker | lynch mob | rapist | underworld |
| felon | madam | rioter | vandal |
| fence | Mafia | robber | whore |

## Crimes

| | | | |
|---|---|---|---|
| armed robbery | domestic violence | investment fraud | robbery |
| arson | drug trafficking | kickback | scam |
| assault (and battery) | drunk driving | kidnapping | sexual molestation |
| assassination | extortion | larceny | skimming profits |
| blackmail | holdup | laundering money | slavery |
| breaking and entering | homicide | libel | smuggling |
| break in | embezzlement | manslaughter | spousal abuse |
| bribery | extortion | mugging | speeding |
| burglary | forced labor | murder | stalking |
| carjacking | forgery | narcotics smuggling | statutory rape |
| child abuse/molestation | fraud | pornography | stealing |
| child pornography | gambling | premeditated murder | stick up |
| child labor | gun running | prostitution | swindling |
| computer fraud | harassment | protection racket | telemarketing fraud |
| con/confidence game | hijacking | purse snatching | terrorism |
| counterfeiting | identity theft | pushing dope | theft |
| cyberbullying | insider trading | road rage | treason |
| defamation of character | internet fraud | rape | vandalism |
| domestic assault | | | white collar crime |

## Places

| | | | |
|---|---|---|---|
| beat | jail | prison | station |
| betting parlor | lockup | precinct | sweatshop |
| cell | penitentiary | rounds | whorehouse |

153

# Events

| | | |
|---|---|---|
| apprehension | frame up | racial profiling |
| arraignment | get away | raid |
| arrest | investigation | reading one's rights |
| capture | line up | round up |
| chase | mug shot | speed trap |
| conviction | pay off | traffic violation |

# Emergencies

| | | |
|---|---|---|
| accident | emergency room | natural disaster |
| ambulance | emergency vehicle | neck brace |
| blood bank | evacuation | nuclear alert |
| civil defense | explosion | pharmacist |
| clinic | fire | pharmacy |
| CPR - cardiopulmonary | fire department | public alarm signal |
|   resuscitation | fire drill | rescue |
| dentist | fire engine | robbery |
| doctor | fire horn | shock |
| doctor's office | fireman | siren |
| drowning | flashing lights | stretcher |
| drug overdose | jaws of life | tourniquet |
| drug store | loud speaker | training |
| Emergency Broadcasting | megaphone | transfusion |
|   System | monitor | veterinarian's office |
| emergency entrance | mouth-to-mouth | 911 |

# Things

| | | |
|---|---|---|
| assault weapon | knife | police gazette |
| badge | mace | revolver |
| billy club | manacles | shackles |
| contraband | night stick | siren |
| finger print | paddy wagon | squad car |
| gun | pistol | tazer |
| handcuffs | | wanted posters |

# Idioms and Expressions

| | | |
|---|---|---|
| cement overshoes | fuzz | police protection |
| close the case | the godfather | the rackets |
| cops and robbers | by hook or by crook | to rub someone out |
| Cosa Nostra | inside job | Smoky the Bear |
| crime boss | in the name of the law | the syndicate |
| Crime doesn't pay. | the mob | ten most wanted |
| deadly weapon | organized crime | victimless crime |

# 53: Communication Technology

## Computer Hardware

| | | | | |
|---|---|---|---|---|
| back-up | desktop | games | laptop | router |
| blackberry | dial-up | gigabyte | megabyte | save |
| boot up/reboot | connection | GPU | memory | scanner, to scan |
| break in | disk | graphics card | minidisk | server |
| cable | DVD | hack | modem | tablet computer |
| CD-ROM | ethernet | hard disk | monitor | terabyte |
| chip | e-waste | hardware | mouse | thumb drive, |
| click on | external hard | input | network | USB flash |
| CPU | drive | iPod | optical drive | drive |
| crash | fire wall | keyboard | printer | touch screen |
| delete | freeze | kilobyte | printout | upgrade |

## Computer Software/Internet

| | | | |
|---|---|---|---|
| APP/ application | DSL (digital | menu | undo |
| banner advertising | subscripting line) | open | URL |
| band width | e-commerce | operating system | virus |
| broadband, | EFT (electronic | plug in | virus protection |
| high-speed | funds transfer) | podcast | webinar |
| internet service | email | program | web site |
| chat room | enable/disable | quit | wireless |
| the cloud | finder | screen saver | communication |
| close/close down | fire wire | search engine | WiFi |
| cookies | font | share | window |
| copy and paste | icon | shareware | word processor |
| cyberspace | internet | software | worm |
| display | ISP (internet | spam | WWW (world |
| distance learning | service provider) | surf | wide web) |
| double click | link | trash/to trash | YouTube |
| download/upload | linked in | Trojan | |
| drag and drop | malware | Twitter/tweet | |

## Telephone

| | | | |
|---|---|---|---|
| 800 line | dial | phonathon | speakerphone |
| answering | dial tone | phone bill | star |
| machine | extension | phone book | telemarketing |
| answering service | fund raising | phone booth | toll free |
| call | 3G/4/G | pound sign | text message |
| caller ID | hang up | prepaid phone card | touchtone |
| call forwarding | information | pulse | trace |
| call waiting | landline | redial | to transfer a call |
| car phone | local | reception | voice mail |
| cell phone/mobile | long distance | ringtone | yellow/white |
| collect | pay phone | smartphone | pages |
| conference call | | | |

## Internet Communication

| | | | |
|---|---|---|---|
| blog | post | Twitter | virtual game world |
| chat room | social media | user generated | virtual social world |
| Facebook | social media marketing |   content | Wikipedia |
| internet dating | social networks | virtual communities | YouTube |

## Other

| | | | |
|---|---|---|---|
| CB (citizen's band radio) | fax | internet cafe | sonar |
| | GPS/global positioning system | network | tower |
| communication tower | | pager | walkie-talkie |
| | intercom | radar | satellite |

## Idioms and Expressions

| | | |
|---|---|---|
| the computer is down. | Sorry, wrong number. | a hacker |
| computer freak, whiz, nerd | Your call cannot be completed as dialed. | to surf the net |
| to crash | | to troll |
| to cut and paste | Your call is important to us. | channel surfing |
| drag-down menu | Can you hear me now? | |
| to Google | a computer geek, nerd | |
| go viral | to fish | |

# 54: Politics and Government

*See topics on Government in the Cultural Aspect section.*

## People

| | | |
|---|---|---|
| aide | congressperson | representative |
| alderperson | delegate | secretary of state |
| assemblyperson | governor | selectperson |
| attorney general | incumbent | senator |
| candidate | mayor | sheriff |
| city council person | member of congress | speaker |
| columnist | pollster | vice president |
| commentator | president | voter |

## Places, etc.

| | | |
|---|---|---|
| apportionment | hearing | minority |
| bill | homeland security | negotiation |
| cabinet | inauguration | Pentagon |
| campaign | independent | petition |
| capitol | investigation | polling place |
| congress | INS (Immigration and | precinct |
| congressional district | Naturalization Service) | primary |
| Congressional Record | IRS (Internal Revenue | progressive |
| convention | Service) | Republican |
| district | legislation | State House |
| Democrat | majority | voter check list |
| election | | ward |

## Adjectives

| | | |
|---|---|---|
| city | judicial | national |
| conservative | legislative | populist |
| county | liberal | radical |
| executive | libertarian | state |
| federal | local | town |

## Verbs

| | | |
|---|---|---|
| campaign | govern | propose |
| debate | impeach | re-elect |
| elect | lobby | reform |
| enact | pass | veto |
| filibuster | preside | vote |

## Idioms, Expressions, and Issues

| | | |
|---|---|---|
| abortion rights | equal rights | minority representation |
| affirmative action | fiscal responsibility | minority rights |
| balanced budget | graft and corruption | one person, one vote |
| campaign contribution | international security | political action committee (PAC) |
| civil rights | lame-duck | pork barrel |
| discrimination | machine politics | rights and obligations |
| environmental protection | military expenditures | terrorism |
| equality before the law | military-industrial complex | undue influence |

# 55: The Media

## Print

| | | | |
|---|---|---|---|
| ad(vertisement) | front page | newsprint | review |
| by-line | headline | obituary | scandal sheet |
| classifieds | journal | op-ed | scoop |
| columnist | journalist | press | subscribe |
| copy editor | lead story | print | subscription |
| correspondent | magazine | publish | (newspaper) syndicate |
| daily | monthly | publisher | tabloid |
| edition | news | quarterly | wedding announcement |
| editor | news magazine | reader | weekly |
| editorial | newspaper | reporter | writer |

## Television/TV

*also see #40 Photography, Cinema, and Video and # 53 Communication Technology*

| | | | |
|---|---|---|---|
| ad (advertisement) | game show | pay-per-view | set |
| affiliate | HDTV (high definition | on-demand | show |
| anchorman/woman | television) | prime time | sit-com |
| antenna | host | premium channel | special |
| audience | interview | producer | sponsor |
| broadcast | live | program | studio |
| bulletin | mini-series | public access TV | syndication |
| cable | mute | public television | talk show |
| cameraman/woman | network | ratings | taped |
| channel | news | reality TV | televise |
| closed caption | newscaster | reception | TiVo |
| commercial | OVA (original video | remote | transmitter |
| coverage | animation) | satellite dish | viewer |
| digital television | paid programming | screen | weather channel |
| episode | panelist | series | |

## Radio

| | | |
|---|---|---|
| air wave | commercial | ham operator |
| AM (amplitude modulation) | dial | local broadcasting |
| antenna | DJ (disc jockey) | on-line/web radio |
| band | FM (frequency modulation) | NPR (National Public Radio) |
| broadcast | frequency | satellite radio |
| call letters | fund raising | short-wave |
| CB (Citizen's Band Radio) | | station |

## Idioms and Expressions

| | | |
|---|---|---|
| "All the news that's fit to print" | the cable, cable news | investigative reporting |
| No news is good news. | the comics/ funny papers | late breaking story |
| Stop the presses! | couch potato | late night programming |
| Don't touch that dial. | hard news | letter to the editor |
| We'll be right back. | headline news | entertainment section |
| Keeping them honest. | hot tip | top of the hour |
| | | top story |

# 56: Religion

*See the topic on Religion in the Cultural Aspect section.*

## Nouns

| | | |
|---|---|---|
| altar | hymnal | pew |
| baptismal font | meeting house | prayer book |
| belfry | mission | pulpit |
| cathedral | mosque | Star of David |
| chapel | nave | steeple |
| church | synagogue | temple |
| confessional | organ | transept |
| cross | parish | under croft |

## People

| | | |
|---|---|---|
| altar boy | congregation | missionary |
| alter guild | deacon | monk |
| acolyte | elder | nun |
| archbishop | evangelist | organist |
| bishop | fundamentalist | pastor |
| cantor | imam | Pope |
| cardinal | laity | priest |
| choir | lay brother/ sister/ man/ woman | rabbi |
| cleric/ clergy | minister | reader |
| crucifer | | usher |

## Sacraments, Rituals, and Scriptures

| | | |
|---|---|---|
| baptism | Gospel | psalm |
| Bible | Haj | pilgrimmage |
| bar mitzvah | hymn | Ramadan |
| call to prayer | Koran/Quran | ritual |
| catechism | last rites | scroll |
| christening | marriage | seder |
| circumcision | mass | sermon |
| communion | New Testament | Sunday school |
| confirmation | offering | Talmud |
| confession | Old Testament | Torah |
| cross | prayer | Veda |
| funeral | | vestments |

## Verbs

| | | |
|---|---|---|
| believe | meditate | proselytize |
| be saved, to save | persecute | shun |
| celebrate | pray | sing hymns |
| convert | preach | worship |

## Major Religions and Denominations

African, Asian, and American
  traditional religions and
  shamanism
Baha'i Faith
Baptist Churches
Brethren (German Baptist)
Buddhism
(Roman) Catholic Church
Churches of God
Congregationalist Churches
Christianity
Christian Science
Eastern Orthodox Churches
Episcopal Church

Greek Orthodox
Hinduism
Islam
Jehovah's Witnesses
Judaism
  Conservative
  Orthodox
  Reform
Lutheran Churches
Mennonite Churches
Methodist Churches
Mormon Churches (Church of

the Latter Day Saints)
Pentecostal Churches
Presbyterian
Protestant
Quaker (Society of Friends)
Russian Orthodox Seventh Day
Adventist
Shi'ah Islam
Sikhism
Shinto
Sufism (Islamic Mysticism)
Sunni Islam
Unitarian Universalist

## Adjectives

agnostic
atheist
Buddhist
Christian
conservative
fundamentalist
Hindu

holy
Jewish
kosher
liberal
low/high church
Muslim
orthodox

reformed
religious
reverend
reverent
sacred
spiritual
strict

## Important days

Ash Wednesday
Christmas
Easter Sunday
Eid
Good Friday

Hannukah
holy week
Kwanza
Lent

Palm Sunday
Passover
Ramadan
Rosh Hashana
Yom Kippur

## Idioms, Expressions, and Concepts

act of God
Amen!
apocalypse
between the devil and the deep
  blue sea
Bible belt
born again
call to prayer
charity
crucifixion
damnation,
to damn
diaspora
end of the world is at hand
epiphany
eye for an eye
faith

fire and brimstone
good heavens
goodness gracious
God bless you
God willing
go to hell
Hadj
Hallelujah!
heaven
heavens to Betsy
hell fire
Holy City
holy Moses!
holy roller
Jihad
judgment day

kismet
matter of faith
messiah
month of Sundays
next year in Jerusalem
paradise
pass the hat
pass the plate
redemption
reincarnation
resurrection
revelation
to raise Cain
salvation
seventh heaven
straight and narrow
vengeance

# 57: Elementary and Secondary Education

## Types of school

| preschool programs | primary school | secondary school | parochial school |
|---|---|---|---|
| day care | elementary school | high school | charter school |
| nursery school | grade school | senior high | magnet school |
| toddler program | day school | preparatory (prep) | specialized schools for: |
| head start program | **middle school** | school | the blind, the deaf |
| kindergarten | **junior high school** | public school | children with learning |
| | | private school | disabilities |
| | | | competitive athletes |

## Nouns

| | | | |
|---|---|---|---|
| assignment | desk | language lab | snow day |
| auditorium | detention | learning center | study hall |
| blackboard | exam | lunch room | teachers' room |
| bulletin board | grade | photocopier | test |
| bullying | grading period | playground | textbook |
| cafeteria | gymnasium, gym | quiz | vacation |
| chalk | high honor roll | recess | varsity |
| charter school | homework | report card | voucher |
| classroom | honor roll | school | workbook |
| computer center | science laboratory | semester | worksheets |

## People

| | | | |
|---|---|---|---|
| instructor | pupil | student | teacher |
| mentor | school board | substitute teacher | teacher's aide |
| principal | secretary | superintendent | tutor |

## Verbs

| | | | |
|---|---|---|---|
| cram | fail, flunk | learn | study |
| enroll | grade | pass | take a course |
| evaluate | graduate | register | teach |

## Subjects

| Elementary: | reading | Secondary, | foreign language |
|---|---|---|---|
| art | science | the elementary | history |
| arithmetic, math | social studies | subjects plus: | home economics |
| geography | spelling | chemistry | physics |
| music | writing | English | shop |

## Classroom Activities

| | | | |
|---|---|---|---|
| manipulating objects | using a voice recorder | taking attendance | pencil and paper work |
| moving furniture | using a computer | operating a language lab | cutting and pasting |
| operating equipment | taking dictation | body movements | map work |
| using the blackboard | spelling bee | games | |

## Idioms and Expressions

to play hooky    teacher's pet    apple polishing    tardy    SAT    HiSET    NCLB    CORE Standards

# 58: College Education

## Types of schools

business school
divinity school
college
community college

graduate school
junior college
law school
medical school

on-line, distance learning
trade schools
training schools
university

## Places

administration building
assembly hall
auditorium
boat house
book store
cafeteria
campus police
class room
chapel
computer center

dining hall
dormitory
field house
fraternity house
gym
housing office
lab
language lab
lecture hall
library

locker room
mail room
playing field
science lab
seminar room
sorority house
stadium
student union/center
study carrol
theater

## Offices

academic dean
academic departments
accounting
admissions
athletic department
bursar
campus dean

carreer counseling
chancellor
counseling
dean
foreign student adviser
health

housing
physical education
president
registrar
R.O.T.C. headquarters
student activities
treasurer

## Events

baccalaureate
convocation
drop period
examination
exam week
faculty
faculty tea
faculty meeting
fellowship
field trip
fraternity/sorority rush

games
  home
  away
  championship
graduation
hell week
homecoming
open house
orientation
party
prom

registration
reunion
semester
spring break
summer school
term
  fall
  winter
  spring
trimester
vacation

## People

assistant professor
counselor
chaplain
coach
dean

department head/chair
dorm head
instructor
intern
librarian

professor
psychologist
school nurse
teaching assistant
tutor

## Academic activities

| | | |
|---|---|---|
| academic paper | final exams | semester/study abroad |
| all nighter | GRE (Graduate Records Exam) | seminar |
| aural exam | grades | standardized test |
| hand in | Law Boards | study group |
| lecture | quiz | switch courses |
| lab | research | test |
| class discussion | research paper | thesis |
| comprehensive exams | SAT (Scholastic Achievement | TOEFL |
| essay | Test) | workshop |
| field work | scheduling | written exam |

## Miscellaneous

| | | |
|---|---|---|
| academia | humanities | major |
| academic credit | sciences | marking period |
| academic freedom | social sciences | minor |
| academic gown | interdisciplinary programs | mortar board |
| application | excuse | online courses |
| campus newspaper | expulsion | pass-fail grading |
| campus radio station | extracurricular | plagiarism |
| certificate | grade | pre-med |
| cheerleader | grading periods | schedule |
| co-education | grind | school newspaper |
| co-ed | humor magazine | social life |
| deadline | homecoming queen | suspension |
| degree | institute | student political organizations |
| diploma | late | tardy |
| disciplinary action | liberal arts | transcript |
| distance learning | literary magazine | undergraduate |
| division | | year book |

## Academic Departments

| | | |
|---|---|---|
| African America/Black Studies | Education | International Studies |
| Anthropology | Engineering Sciences | Linguistics, Cognitive Science |
| Archaeology | English | Mathematics |
| Art/Studio Art, Art History | English as a Second Language | Music |
| Asian Studies | Environmental Science | Native American Studies |
| Biological Sciences | Film and Television Studies | Philosophy |
| Chemistry | Foreign Language, Literature | Physics and Astronomy |
| Classics | Asian and Middle-Eastern, | Political Science. Government |
| Comparative Literature | French, German, Italian, | Religion |
| Creative Writing | Russian, Spanish | Sociology |
| Earth Sciences, Geology | Geography | Theater |
| Economics | History | Women's and Gender Studies |

## Idioms and Expressions

| | | |
|---|---|---|
| to bone up on | to cram | to hit the books |
| to burn the midnight oil | to flunk | sheepskin |

# 59: History

## Periods

| | | | |
|---|---|---|---|
| AD | CE | era | prehistoric |
| age | episode | geological time | Stone Age |
| BC | epoch | millennium | time |
| century | eon | period | |

## People

| | | | |
|---|---|---|---|
| admiral | emperor | peasant | scout |
| adventurer | explorer | peon | seer |
| anthropologist | founder | philosopher | serf |
| archaeologist | frontiersman | political boss | scholar |
| artist | general | politician | secret agent |
| assassin | geographer | pope | senator |
| barbarian | hero | president | slave |
| bishop | high priest | prime minister | spy |
| builder | historian | prince | statesman |
| businessman | innovator | princess | teacher |
| captive | inventor | promoter | terrorist |
| chief | judge | prophet | trader |
| common man | king | queen | tradesman |
| counselor | knight | rabble rouser | traitor |
| creative genius | labor leader | rebel | tycoon |
| dictator | leader | representative | usurper |
| duke | orator | saint | warlord |
| engineer | | | warrior |

## Events

| | | | |
|---|---|---|---|
| assassination | defeat | famine | natural disasters |
| coronation | depression | genocide | overthrow |
| coup d'etat | discovery | holocaust | plague |
| battle | election | inflation | rebellion |
| breakthrough | epidemic | invention | revolution |
| Crusades | exploration | massacre | war |

## Miscellaneous

| | | | |
|---|---|---|---|
| agreement | constitution | historical research | social unrest |
| alliance | economic growth | mob | social upheaval |
| biography | enemy | pact | starvation |
| chronicle | historical novel | saga | treaty |

## Idioms and Expressions

| | | |
|---|---|---|
| chronicle of events | history is bunk | milestone of history |
| history is yesterday's news | lessons of history | since the dawn of time |

Those who ignore history are condemned to repeat it.

# 60: Disasters

## Nouns

accidents
aftershock
airplane crash
ambulance
atomic/nuclear disaster
avalanche
blizzard
bomb
carnage
catastrophe
civil war
collision
conflagration
cyclone
death
deforestation
desertification
devastation
disaster relief
drought
earthquake
emergency
environmental destruction

epidemic
eruption
evacuation
explosion
ethnic cleansing
famine
fatality
fire
fire storm
first aid
flash flood
flood
genocide
global warming
hurricane
injury
loss of life
mud slide
nuclear meltdown
oil slick
oil spill
pestilence
plague

plane crash
pollution
Richter scale
relief
rescue
riot
shelter
shipwreck
sinking
starvation
state of emergency
storm
terrorism
tidal wave
tornado
tropical storm
tsunami
twister
typhoon
victim
war
wild fire
wreckage

## Verbs

blow up
blow down
burn
bury
collapse
collide
crash
crush

damage
destroy
devastate
drown
evacuate
explode
flatten
flood

freeze
injure
massacre
rescue
ruin
smash
starve
suffocate

## Idioms and Expressions

an act of God
any port in a storm

better safe than sorry
calm before the storm

death toll
loss of life

165

# 61: The Military and War

## Nouns

aircraft carrier
air force
airplane
air defense
air raid
alliance
allies
armed forces
armor
armored division
armory
army
artillery
attack
battle
battleship
base
biological weapon
blackout
bomber
bomb
bomb blast
boot camp
briefing
brigade
bullet
bunker
cannon
casualty
cease fire
chain of command
chemical warfare
civil defence
cluster bomb
coalition
coast guard
collateral damage
command
cruiser
defeat
defense
depot
destroyer
disinformation
division

DMZ (demilitarized zone)
draft
drone
field of battle
field command
field hospital
field promotion
fighter
fire storm
fleet
foot soldier
foxhole
germ warfare
grenade
guided missile
gun
headquarters
helicopter
humvee
IED (improvised explosive
   device)
infantry
intelligence
jeep
jet
logistical support
land mine
map room
marines
materiel
morale
mine
mine sweeper
missile
national alert
national guard
navy
Navy SEAL
offense
offensive
officer
peace
peacekeeper
personnel
planning session

platoon
poison gas
propaganda
promotion
Post-traumatic Stress Disorder
   (PTSD)
reconnaissance
radioactive cloud
recruit
regiment
reserves
retreat
rocket
seabees (CB - Construction
   Battalion)
shell
smart bomb
special operations
squad
staff
stealth bomber
strategy
submarine
suicide bomber
superior officer
surrender
tactics
tank
target
target practice
terrorist cell
torpedo
training camp
transport
trench
victory
volunteer
volunteer army
warfare
war games
weapon
weaponry
WMD
   (weapon of mass destruction)

# People

| | | | |
|---|---|---|---|
| admiral | deserter | lieutenant | private |
| bombardier | draft dodger | liaison | pilot |
| canine officer | foot soldier | major | sailor |
| captain | general | marine | sergeant |
| cavalry | G.I. (government | military adviser | sharpshooter |
| chaplain | issue) | military police (MP) | sniper |
| chief of staff | guerrilla | navigator | soldier |
| colonel | gunner | officer | suicide bomber |
| corporal | hostage | petty officer | terrorist |

# Events and actions

| | | | |
|---|---|---|---|
| advance | cut off | make war | sink |
| ambush | defeat | offensive | sortie |
| battle | deploy | order | skirmish |
| break through | dissent | overrun | surround |
| bombardment | infiltrate | retreat | strafe |
| casualty | interrogation | shell(ing) | torpedo |
| court-martial | invasion | shoot | wound |

# Peace

| | | | |
|---|---|---|---|
| appeasement | defeat | peace conference | peace treaty |
| armistice | disengagement | peace initiative | reconciliation |
| cease fire | make peace | peacekeeping force | surrender |
| concessions | mediation | peacemaker | truce |
| conciliation | negotiation | peace settlement | United Nations |
| conscientious objector | pacification | peace talks | victory |

# Idioms and Expressions

| | | |
|---|---|---|
| All's fair in love and war. | MIA (missing in action) | to turn tail |
| An army lives on its stomach. | mutual assured destruction | under the gun |
| AWOL (absent without leave) | Nobel Peace Prize | USO |
| balance of power | peace at any cost | War and Peace |
| balance or terror | "peace in our time" | war criminal |
| battle hardened | peace with honor | the war to end all war |
| to bear arms | PTSD (post traumatic | win the war but lose the peace |
| camp follower | stress disorder) | world war |
| concentration camp | POW (prisoner of war) | yeoman service |
| Cowards die twice. | to pull rank | Symbols: |
| deterrence | point blank | flags |
| Geneva Convention | on the warpath | flags flown at half mast |
| isolationist | R and R (rest and recreation) | flags in a graveyard |
| 4F | scorched earth policy | hands raised over the head |
| a just and lasting peace | shell shock | white flag |
| a just war | to stick to one's guns | red cross |
| make love, not war | TBI (traumatic brain injury) | red poppy |
| marked man | turncoat | yellow ribbon |

167

# 62: Energy and Environment

## Nouns

acid rain
atomic wastes
barrel of oil
battery
biodiesel
carbon emissions
carbon tax
catalytic converter
climate change
coal
combustion
compost
conservation
consumable resources
consumption
dam
deforestation
depletion
diesel fuel
diesel engine
drilling rig
electricity
endangered species
energy costs
energy efficiency
energy (in)dependence
energy loss
energy grid
energy taxes
engine

environmentalist
environmental cleanup
environmental law
environmental policy
environmental science
erosion
ethanol
e-waste
extinction
filter
fire
fission
fossil fuel
fracking (hydralic
   fracturing)
fuel
fuel efficiency
fusion
gas pump
gasoline, gas
gasoline taxes
generator
global warming
heat
hexane
hydroelectric power
hydrogen power
insulation
kinetic

land fill
light
mass transit
methane
motor
natural gas
nuclear power
nuclear reactor
octane
oil
oil drilling
oil field
oil production
oil slick
oil spill
oil well
ozone
particulates
petroleum
pipeline
polar vortex
pollution
power
propane
radioactive waste
reactor
recycling
refinery
regulations

renewable energy
   sources
resources
scrubbers
sea level rise
sea surface
   temperature
shale gas
smog
smoke
solar power
solar cell
source
steam
super conductors
Superfund site
superstorm
tidal
tidal power
transformer
transmission lines
turbine
utilities
waste management
water power
wildcat operator
wind farm
windmill
wind power

## Adjectives

active
chemical
electric(al)
extinct

geothermal
hydro-
mechanical
nuclear

offshore
petro-
passive
post-petroleum

radioactive
solar
wood-burning

## Idioms and Expressions

to burn the candle at both ends
to carry coals to Newcastle
energy czar
environmental catastrophe
environmental impact statement
gas guzzler

greenhouse effect
to hold a candle to
IPCC (intergovernmental
   Panel on Climate Change)
limits to growth
population bomb

sustainable growth
OPEC
R factor
unbridled consumption
Where there's smoke there's fire.

# 63: Death

## Nouns

ashes
asphyxiation
autopsy
(the) bereaved
bereavement
body
burial
cadaver
capital
  punishment
casket
catacomb
cemetery
churchyard
coffin
coroner

corpse
cremation
crematorium
crypt
(the) deceased
(the) dead
death
demise
dissection
doctor-assisted
  suicide
effigy
elegy
epitaph
eulogy
euphemism

euthanasia
fatal illness
funeral
funeral director
funeral home
funeral parlor
funeral
  procession
grave
grave digger
graveside
gravestone
graveyard
hospice care
inscription
lamentation

last rites
last words
mausoleum
medical examiner
memorial
memorial
  contribution
memorial service
mercy killing
moaning
monument
morgue
mortician
mortuary
mourner
mourning

murder
necropolis
obituary
pall bearer
pit
plot
(the) remains
sepulcher
suicide
tomb
undertaker
urn
vault
wake
widow
widower

## Verbs

bereave
bury

cremate
die

elegize
eulogize

expire
grieve

inter
mourn

## Idioms and Expressions

ashes to ashes, dust to dust
to cash in one's chips
cause of death
deader than a door nail
dearly departed

to give up the ghost
in deep mourning
Irish wake
to kick the bucket
to pass away

open-casket funeral
living will
right to die
to wake the dead
RIP (rest in peace)

## Of the Living Dead

ashen
apparition
to appall
banshee
bat
body snatcher
black magic
cadaverous
to conjure
demon
devil, Satan
dreadful

evil spirit
fiend
frightful
gallows
ghastly
ghost
ghost story
ghoul
gibbet
glimmer
gloom
goblin

gore
grave robber
grisly
hangman
to haunt
hell fire
hideous
horrible
horror story
loathsome
mummy
murmuring

necromancer
night walker
pact with the
  devil
pallid
phantom
resurrectionist
revolting
sorcery
seance
shade
specter

spell
spider web
spirit
spook
spooky
terrifying
undead
vampire
voodoo
werewolf
wolfman
wraith
zombie

# Communicative Functions

The sub-aspect of Communicative Functions is similar to a notional-functional syllabus. However, we have used the term communicative function to focus on the how and why of the communicative exchange. To relate this sub-aspect to the Situations and Topics, we can say that the Situation is concerned with the "where" of the exchange, the Topic the "what" and the Function the "how" and "why."

To organize the various communicative functions in some useful way, we have presented them as a kind of syllabus/check list. We have used as a sequential basis, four levels of language sophistication. These levels represent a transition from beginning language student to fully functioning bilingual person. These four levels are:

❑ Level 1 **Surviving** (Beginner)     171
❑ Level 2 **Adjusting; Settling In** (Advanced beginner)     172
❑ Level 3 **Participating** (Intermediate)     173
❑ Level 4 **Integrating** (Advanced)     174

Within each level we have organized the functions into general types as described below:

A. **Basic Needs.** Using the language to satisfy basic physical requirements of food, shelter, and clothing.

B. **Socializing.** Using the language to make social links with native speakers. At its lowest level it satisfies basic emotional needs.

C. **Metalinguistic.** Using the language to deal with the language. This includes certain fundamental linguistic labels (noun, etc.) and tactics and strategies for managing communication (paraphrasing, interrupting, clarifying, etc.).

D. **Professional.** Using the language to make a living.

E. **Cultural.** Using the language to deal with the social and cultural milieu.

# Level 1: Surviving

*(Beginner)*

## A. Basic Needs

❑ 1. Respond physically to simple instructions such as **give, take, stand, sit, open, close, pick up, put down, put on, take off**, etc.

❑ 2. Give another person simple instructions to perform the actions above.

❑ 3. Give and understand basic warnings such as **Look out! Stop! Freeze!**

❑ 4. State basic wants and needs.

❑ 5. Request and comprehend simple information.

❑ 6. Ask for and respond to simple street directions and give simpe directions to a taxi driver.

❑ 7. Ask for assistance.

❑ 8. Get someone's attention and also use appropriate gestures.

❑ 9. Buy a small item.

❑ 10. Use a menu and order something to eat and drink.

## B. Socializing

❑ 1. Greet others.

❑ 2. Take leave of another person or a group of people.

❑ 3. Arrange to meet someone.

❑ 4. Introduce yourself.

❑ 5. Identify yourself. (**I'm a ___**)

❑ 6. Use ritual apologies.

❑ 7. Reject unwanted attention firmly and simply.

❑ 8. Agree.

❑ 9. Express thanks.

❑ 10. State and comprehend simple biographical and family information.

## C. Metalinguistic

❑ 1. Use and identify basic numbers.

❑ 2. Ask and tell time.

❑ 3. Use simple time expressions such as **today, yesterday, tomorrow morning, noon.**

❑ 4. Use and comprehend days of the week, months, and ways of expressing dates.

❑ 5. Control a conversation with simple phrases such as **speak slowly, please,** or **please repeat that.**

❑ 6. Identify and label the environment. (**What's that? It's a ___**)

❑ 7. Decipher simple signs and notices.

❑ 8. Use appropriate basic gestures.

# Level 2: Adjusting; Settling In
*(Advanced Beginner)*

## A. Basic Needs

❏ 1. State plans for the future.

❏ 2. Ask to borrow something.

❏ 3. Respond to a loan request.

❏ 4. Complain mildly.

❏ 5. Ask about the purpose of something.

❏ 6. Purchase household objects, equipment and clothing.

❏ 7. Make travel arrangements.

❏ 8. Describe a physical health problem.

❏ 9. Carry out a limited financial transaction such as cashing a check.

❏ 10. Fill out life forms such as a credit card application, a work permit, a school registration.

## B. Socializing

❏ 1. Introduce another person.

❏ 2. Make small talk.

❏ 3. Share simple likes and dislikes.

❏ 4. Issue an invitation.

❏ 5. Decline an invitation.

❏ 6. Visit.

❏ 7. Entertain a visitor.

❏ 8. Play simple games/sports.

❏ 9. Recount past events.

❏ 10. Express basic emotions.

❏ 11. Apologize for a specific error.

❏ 12. Request and give permission to do something.

❏ 13. Compliment another person.

❏ 14. Accept a compliment.

❏ 15. Explain personal plans.

❏ 16. Express a personal opinion.

❏ 17. Express doubt.

❏ 18. Express irritation.

❏ 19. Express disappointment.

## C. Metalinguistic

❏ 1. Clarify misunderstandings.

❏ 2. Use simple interjections.

❏ 3. Make a basic phone call.

❏ 4. Perform arithmetic operations aloud.

❏ 5. Spell words aloud.

❏ 6. Comprehend ads and announcements on radio and TV.

❏ 7. Read advertisements.

❏ 8. Read short notices, time tables, menus, etc.

❏ 9. Take simple dictation.

❏ 10. Write short informational notes.

## D. Professional

❏ 1. Describe one's job.

❏ 2. Describe one's profession in general terms.

❏ 3. Explain professional objectives.

❏ 4. Express a basic professional opinion..

## E. Cultural

❏ 1. Follow or sing-along with popular songs and/or folk songs.

❏ 2. Identify folk tale characters and national heroes.

❏ 3. Make general cultural comparisons in these areas:

❏ etiquette

❏ mealtimes

❏ kinship terms

❏ housing

❏ cooking

❏ gift-giving

❏ holidays and festivals

172

# Level 3: Participating

*(Intermediate)*

## A. Basic Needs

☐ 1. Ask for favors.
☐ 2. Grant favors.
☐ 3. Sell a personal possession.
☐ 4. Make arrangements with household help.
☐ 5. Arrange for repairs and service (household; automotive).

☐ 6. Make substantial purchases such as a TV or refrigerator.
☐ 7. Apply for specific status (insurance, citizenship, etc.)
☐ 8. Retrieve a borrowed item.
☐ 9. Dispute a bill.

## B. Socializing

☐ 1. Plan a social event.
☐ 2. Attend a recreational event.
☐ 3. Discuss current events.
☐ 4. Comment on sports events.
☐ 5. Avoid commitments.
☐ 6. Sympathize.
☐ 7. Share personal hopes and dreams.

☐ 8. Tell an anecdote.
☐ 9. Understand jokes.
☐ 10. Give personal advice.
☐ 11. Disagree tactfully.
☐ 12. Ask for forgiveness.
☐ 13. Make an excuse.
☐ 14. Use social media.

## C. Metalinguistic

☐ 1. Understand radio and TV news.
☐ 2. Break social contact with appropriate mannerisms,
☐ 3. Summarize.
☐ 4. Ask for definitions.
☐ 5. Make a complicated telephone call.
☐ 6. Translate for a new-comer.
☐ 7. Swear.

☐ 8. Use verbal gestures such as **uh-uh, hm, well, huh?**
☐ 9. Read newspapers.
☐ 10. Read professional material.
☐ 11. Read magazine articles.
☐ 12. Write social notes and letters.
☐ 13. Write professional reports.

## D. Professional

☐ 1. Allow or not allow another's requests.
☐ 2. Give professional advice.
☐ 3. Give detailed instructions and explanations.

☐ 4. Evaluate.
☐ 5. Give short talks/speeches on professional matters.

## E. Cultural

☐ 1. Explain institutions of native country.
☐ 2. Compare major cultural differences.
☐ 3. Discuss major aspects of host culture, including:

☐ courtship
☐ marriage
☐ sex
☐ family
☐ racial and ethnic groups

☐ government
☐ religion
☐ death
☐ mourning
☐ funerals

☐ education
☐ superstitions
☐ folklore
☐ hospitality
☐ humor

173

# Level 4: Integrating
## (Advanced)

### A. Basic Needs

❑ 1. Act in emergencies.

### B. Socializing

❑ 1. Share secrets.
❑ 2. Flirt.
❑ 3. Speak of personal accomplishments.
❑ 4. Tease.
❑ 5. Break off a relationship.
❑ 6. Counsel.
❑ 7. Praise.
❑ 8. Flatter.

❑ 9. Insult.
❑ 10. Plead.
❑ 11. Soften the truth.
❑ 12. Chastise another person.
❑ 13. Threaten.
❑ 14. Tell jokes.
❑ 15. Blog.

### C. Metalinguistic

❑ 1. Interpret and translate.
❑ 2. Paraphrase.
❑ 3. Play word games such as crossword puzzles.

❑ 4. Use source materials such as the Oxford English Dictionary.
❑ 5. Read books.
❑ 6. Write letters to the editor.

### D. Professional

❑ 1. Debate ideas.
❑ 2. Negotiate.

❑ 3. Give professional direction.
❑ 4. Exercise leadership.

### E. Cultural

❑ 1. Take and defend a stand on a current national issue.

❑ 2. Discuss, study, and critique the following aspects of the culture:
❑ arts
❑ law
❑ attitudes toward animals and nature
❑ community organization
❑ residence rules
❑ property rights
❑ status differentiation
❑ social mobility
❑ ethics

*Crystal goblet, American cut glass*

# The
# Cultural
# Aspect

Language and culture are intertwined. In the previous section on the communicative aspect, North American culture makes its presence felt, especially in the lists of communicative situations and topics. To a lesser extent, communicative functions are also modified by culture. Ways of expressing thanks or extending invitations can be quite different in the English typical of Toronto, Los Angeles, Boston, or Bombay.

Because we have already listed communicative situations, topics, and functions in Part II, we will not repeat those lists here. Instead we will present cultural information that does not fit under these categories.

In other, paralinguistic ways, notably in body language and gestures, culture also impinges on communication, but we will deal with that in Part V.

And then there are all the cultural practices (customs) that can only be hinted at in a book such as this. Rather than attempt to describe North American cultural practices, we will instead present a list of Cultural Common Denominators. This list can be used as a checklist by both teacher and student to see if these areas have been adequately explored in class.

In this part of The ESL Miscellany, we will attempt to deal with the huge body of information that is commonly known by most contemporary Americans and Canadians. For example, the foreigner, unaware that the New York Yankees is a baseball team, could easily be mystified by overhearing one American ask another, "How did the Yankees do last night?" or, even more mystified when they are invited to go watch the Blue Jays play.

Obviously, it takes years to learn everything there is to know about North American culture; it is even possible that some native speakers do not know who Babe Ruth was. The capsule summaries of selected areas of North American culture contained in this section are at best a starting point for discussion, research, explanation, and study. Once again our lists should be considered only guidelines.

# Cultural Common Denominators*

Every culture has customs, traditions, practices, and beliefs associated with the following cultural items. Each item in the list represents an essay, if not an entire book, but we will do no more here than suggest that the list can be used as a guideline for an orientation to North American culture. Incidentally, the list can also serve as a checklist for a series of fascinating discussions of a cross-cultural nature.

❏ numerals
❏ calendar
❏ personal names
❏ greetings
❏ gestures
❏ etiquette
❏ mealtimes
❏ kinship nomenclature
❏ age-grading
❏ athletic sports
❏ games
❏ leisure activities
❏ music
❏ dancing
❏ feasting
❏ bodily adornment
❏ folklore
❏ luck superstitions
❏ cooking
❏ food and food taboos
❏ family
❏ marriage
❏ kin-groups
❏ housing
❏ hospitality
❏ visiting

❏ gift-giving
❏ friendship customs
❏ courting
❏ joking
❏ sexual restrictions
❏ incest
❏ taboos
❏ modesty in natural functions
❏ funeral rites
❏ mourning
❏ medicine
❏ education
❏ law
❏ land-use policies
❏ attitude toward animals
❏ community organization
❏ residence rules
❏ property rights
❏ status differentiation
❏ racial and ethnic groups
❏ mobility
❏ trade
❏ government
❏ patriotism
❏ religious practices

*Adapted from George P. Murdock, "The Common Denominators of Culture," in *The Science of Man in the World Crisis,* ed Ralph Linton, N.Y: Columbia University Press, 1945.

# 1: Immigration Statistics

## 15 Largest Ancestries in U.S.

| | | *Percentage of population* | | | | *Percentage of population* |
|---|---|---|---|---|---|---|
| 1 | German | 15.2 | 9 | French | | 3.0 |
| 2 | Irish | 10.8 | 10 | American Indian | | 2.8 |
| 3 | African | 8.8 | 11 | Scottish | | 1.7 |
| 4 | English | 8.7 | 12 | Dutch | | 1.6 |
| 5 | American | 7.2 | 13 | Norwegian | | 1.6 |
| 6 | Mexican | 6.5 | 14 | Scotch-Irish | | 1.5 |
| 7 | Italian | 5.6 | 15 | Chinese | | 1.4 |
| 8 | Polish | 3.2 | | | | |

## *Immigration – Top 20 Countries 1986-2012*

| | | |
|---|---|---|
| 1. | Mexico | 5,551,757 |
| 2. | Philippines | 1,480,946 |
| 3. | China | 1,399,667 |
| 4. | India | 1,323,011 |
| 5. | Vietnam | 955,967 |
| 6. | Dominican Republic | 904,721 |
| 7. | El Salvador | 676,776 |
| 8. | Cuba | 666,657 |
| 9. | Korea | 609,321 |
| 10. | Haiti | 536,657 |
| 11. | Jamaica | 507,741 |
| 12. | Colombia | 498,551 |
| 13. | Russia | 476,306 |
| 14. | Canada | 394,790 |
| 15. | United Kingdom | 383,037 |
| 16. | Poland | 360,669 |
| 17. | Iran | 358,586 |
| 18. | Peru | 320,611 |
| 19. | Taiwan | 269,873 |
| 20. | Ecuador | 243,217 |

# 2. Native Americans of North America
## Largest Tribes in the United States (2010 census)

| | | | | | |
|---|---|---|---|---|---|
| Navajo | 286,231 | AZ, UT, NM | Chickasaw | 27,973 | OK |
| Cherokee | 284,247 | OK | Pima | 22,040 | AZ |
| Mexican | | | Yaqui | 21,679 | AZ |
|   American Indian | 121,221 | Southwest | South American Indian | 20, 901 | US |
| Chippewa | 112,757 | MN, WI, MI | Potawatomi | 21,412 | MI, WI, OK, |
| Sioux | 112,176 | MT, ND, SD, | | | Ontario |
| | | MN, Man, Sas | Tohono O'Odham | 19,522 | AZ |
| Choctaw | 103,910 | OK | Central American Indian | 15,882 | US |
| Alaska Native tribes | 98,892 | AK | Puget Sound Salish | 14,320 | WA |
| Apache | 63,193 | AZ, NM, OK | Seminole | 14,080 | FL |
| Lumbee | 62,306 | NC | Spanish American Indian | 13,460 | US |
| Pueblo | 49,695 | NM | Hopi | 12,580 | AZ |
| Creek (Muscogee) | 48,352 | OK, AL, | Comanche | 12,284 | OK |
| | | GA, FL | Cheyenne | 11,375 | MT |
| Iroquois | 40,570 | NY, Canada | Crow | 10,322 | MT |
| Blackfeet | 27,279 | MT, Alberta | | | |

## First Nations People in Canada

First Nations people are descendants of the original inhabitants of Canada who lived here for many thousands of years before explorers arrived from Europe.

According to the Indian Register there are 901,053 Registered Indians living in Canada. This population lives in a variety of types of communities. Almost half (47.4%) of these First Nations people live off reserve; the others (52.6%) live on reserve and in communities on Crown land.

There are 617 First Nation communities in Canada. Here are the numbers of First Nations in each province and territory:

| | | | |
|---|---|---|---|
| Newfoundland | 4 | Manitoba | 63 |
| Nova Scotia | 13 | Saskatchewan | 70 |
| Prince Edward Island | 2 | Alberta | 45 |
| New Brunswick | 15 | British Columbia | 198 |
| Quebec | 39 | Yukon | 16 |
| Ontario | 126 | Northwest Territories | 26 |
| | | **Total** | **617** |

# 3: Population by Ethnic Identity

## Racial and National Origin for the U.S. in 2000

| Origin | 2000 Census | 2010 Census |
|---|---|---|
| Total U.S. population | 281,421,906 | 308,745,538 |
| White | 216,930,975 (77.1%) | 31,040,398 (74.8%) |
| Black | 36,419,434 (12.9%) | 42,020,743 (13.6%) |
| America Indian and Alaska Native | 4,119,301 (1.5%) | 5,220,579 (1.7%) |
| Asian | 11,898,828 (4.2%) | 17,320,856 (5.6%) |
| Native Hawaiian and other Pacific Islander | 874,414 (0.3%) | 1,225,195 (0.4%) |
| Other | 18,521,486 (6.6%) | 21,748,084 (7.0%) |

| Black Population by State (rounded to 100) | | | Hispanic/Latino Population by State (rounded to 100) | | |
|---|---|---|---|---|---|
| | Total | Percent | | Total | Percent |
| New York | 3,334,600 | 17.2 | California | 14,013,700 | 37.6 |
| Florida | 3,200,700 | 17.0 | Texas | 9,461,000 | 37.6 |
| Texas | 3,168,500 | 12.6 | New York | 3,417,000 | 17.6 |
| Georgia | 3,054,100 | 31.5 | Illinois | 2,027,600 | 15.8 |
| California | 2,683,900 | 7.2 | Arizona | 1,895,100 | 29.6 |
| North Carolina | 2,151,500 | 22.6 | New Jersey | 1,555,100 | 17,7 |
| Illinois | 1,974,100 | 15.4 | Colorado | 1,038,700 | 20.7 |
| Maryland | 1,783,900 | 17.0 | New Mexico | 953,400 | 46.3 |
| Virginia | 1,653,600 | 20.7 | Georgia | 853,700 | 8.8 |
| Ohio | 1,541,800 | 12.3 | North Carolina | 800,100 | 8.4 |
| Pennsylvania | 1,508,000 | 11.9 | Washington | 755,800 | 11.2 |
| Michigan | 1,505,500 | 15.2 | Pennsylvania | 719,700 | 5.7 |
| Louisiana | 1,486,900 | 32.8 | Nevada | 716,500 | 26.5 |
| South Carolina | 1,332,200 | 28.8 | Virginia | 631,800 | 7.9 |
| New Jersey | 1,300,400 | 14.8 | Massachusetts | 627,700 | 9.6 |
| Alabama | 1,281,100 | 26.8 | Connecticut | 479,100 | 13.4 |
| Mississippi | 1,115,800 | 37.6 | Maryland | 470,600 | 4.4 |
| Tennessee | 1,107,200 | 17.4 | Oregon | 450,100 | 11.7 |
| | | | Michigan | 436,400 | 4.4 |

# 4: Major U.S. Cities

| Rank 2012 | Rank 2000 | City | Population 2012 (estimated) |
|---|---|---|---|
| 1 | 1 | New York | 8,336,700 |
| 2 | 2 | Los Angeles | 3,857,800 |
| 3 | 3 | Chicago | 2,714,900 |
| 4 | 4 | Houston | 2,160,800 |
| 5 | 5 | Philadelphia | 1,547,600 |
| 6 | 6 | Phoenix | 1,488,800 |
| 7 | 9 | San Antonio | 1,383,000 |
| 8 | 7 | San Diego | 1,338,300 |
| 9 | 8 | Dallas | 1,241,200 |
| 10 | 11 | San Jose | 982,800 |
| 11 | 16 | Austin | 842,600 |
| 12 | 14 | Jacksonville | 836,500 |
| 13 | 12 | Indianapolis | 834,900 |
| 14 | 13 | San Francisco | 825,900 |
| 15 | 15 | Columbus | 809,800 |
| 16 | 27 | Fort Worth | 778,000 |
| 17 | 26 | Charlotte | 775,200 |
| 18 | 10 | Detroit | 701,500 |
| 19 | 23 | El Paso | 672,500 |
| 20 | 18 | Memphis | 655,200 |
| 21 | 20 | Boston | 636,500 |
| 22 | 24 | Seattle | 634,500 |
| 23 | 25 | Denver | 634,300 |
| 24 | 21 | Washington | 632,300 |
| 25 | 22 | Nashville | 624,500 |
| 26 | 17 | Baltimore | 621,300 |
| 27 | 67 | Louisville | 605,100 |
| 28 | 28 | Portland, OR | 603,100 |
| 29 | 29 | Oklahoma City | 599,200 |
| 30 | 19 | Milwaukee | 598,900 |
| 31 | 32 | Las Vegas | 596,400 |
| 32 | 35 | Albuquerque | 555,400 |
| 33 | 32 | Tucson | 524,300 |
| 34 | 37 | Fresno | 505,900 |
| 35 | 40 | Sacramento | 475,500 |
| 36 | 34 | Long Beach | 467,900 |
| 37 | 36 | Kansas City | 464,300 |
| 38 | 42 | Mesa | 452,100 |
| 39 | 38 | Virginia Beach | 447,000 |
| 40 | 39 | Atlanta | 443,800 |
| 41 | 48 | Colorado Springs | 431,800 |
| 42 | -- | Raleigh | 423,200 |
| 43 | 44 | Omaha | 421,600 |
| 44 | 47 | Miami | 413,900 |
| 45 | 41 | Oakland | 400,700 |
| 46 | 43 | Tulsa | 394,000 |
| 47 | 45 | Minneapolis | 392,900 |
| 48 | 33 | Cleveland | 391,000 |
| 49 | 50 | Wichita | 385,600 |
| 50 | 54 | Arlington TX | 375,600 |

**Source:** U.S. Census estimate, 2012

# 5: States of the United States

| Date Entered the Union | State | Capital | | | |
|---|---|---|---|---|---|
| 1787 | Delaware | Dover | 1837 | Michigan | Lansing |
| 1787 | Pennsylvania | Harrisburg | 1845 | Florida | Tallahassee |
| 1787 | New Jersey | Trenton | 1845 | Texas | Austin |
| 1788 | Georgia | Atlanta | 1846 | Iowa | Des Moines |
| 1788 | Connecticut | Hartford | 1848 | Wisconsin | Madison |
| 1788 | Massachusetts | Boston | 1850 | California | Sacramento |
| 1788 | Maryland | Annapolis | 1858 | Minnesota | St. Paul |
| 1788 | South Carolina | Columbia | 1859 | Oregon | Salem |
| 1788 | New Hampshire | Concord | 1861 | Kansas | Topeka |
| 1788 | Virginia | Richmond | 1863 | West Virginia | Charleston |
| 1788 | New York | Albany | 1864 | Nevada | Carson City |
| 1789 | North Carolina | Raleigh | 1867 | Nebraska | Lincoln |
| 1790 | Rhode Island | Providence | 1876 | Colorado | Denver |
| 1791 | Vermont | Montpelier | 1889 | North Dakota | Bismarck |
| 1792 | Kentucky | Frankfort | 1889 | South Dakota | Pierre |
| 1796 | Tennessee | Nashville | 1889 | Montana | Helena |
| 1803 | Ohio | Columbus | 1889 | Washington | Olympia |
| 1812 | Louisiana | Baton Rouge | 1890 | Idaho | Boise |
| 1816 | Indiana | Indianapolis | 1890 | Wyoming | Cheyenne |
| 1817 | Mississippi | Jackson | 1896 | Utah | Salt Lake City |
| 1818 | Illinois | Springfield | 1907 | Oklahoma | Oklahoma City |
| 1819 | Alabama | Montgomery | 1912 | New Mexico | Santa Fe |
| 1820 | Maine | Augusta | 1912 | Arizona | Phoenix |
| 1821 | Missouri | Jefferson City | 1959 | Alaska | Juneau |
| 1836 | Arkansas | Little Rock | 1959 | Hawaii | Honolulu |

## The Thirteen Original States

| | | |
|---|---|---|
| Connecticut | New Hampshire | Pennsylvania |
| Delaware | New Jersey | Rhode Island |
| Georgia | New York | South Carolina |
| Maryland | North Carolina | Virginia |
| Massachusetts | | |

These states were the original 13 British colonies that established the United States of America starting with the Declaration of Independence in 1776. The dates given for entering the union are the dates they ratified the constitution between 1787 and 1790. They were the only states until the independent Republic of Vermont joined the union as the fourteenth state in 1791.

## State and Territory Ranking by Population, US House Representatives, and Electoral Votes

| State/Territory | Population Estimate July 2013 | Seats in U.S. House | Electoral votes | State/Territory | Population Estimate July 2013 | Seats in U.S. House | Electoral votes |
|---|---|---|---|---|---|---|---|
| California | 38,332,500 | 53 | 55 | Connecticut | 3,596,100 | 5 | 7 |
| Texas | 26,448,200 | 36 | 38 | Iowa | 3,090,400 | 4 | 6 |
| New York | 19,651,100 | 27 | 29 | Mississippi | 2,991,200 | 4 | 6 |
| Florida | 19,552,900 | 27 | 29 | Arkansas | 2,959,400 | 4 | 6 |
| Illinois | 12,882,100 | 18 | 20 | Utah | 2,900,900 | 4 | 6 |
| Pennsylvania | 12,773,800 | 18 | 20 | Kansas | 2,894,000 | 4 | 6 |
| Ohio | 11,570,800 | 16 | 18 | Nevada | 2,790,100 | 4 | 6 |
| Georgia | 9,992,200 | 14 | 16 | New Mexico | 2,085,300 | 3 | 5 |
| Michigan | 9,895,600 | 14 | 16 | Nebraska | 1,868,500 | 3 | 5 |
| North Carolina | 9,848,100 | 13 | 15 | West Virginia | 1,854,300 | 3 | 5 |
| New Jersey | 8,899,300 | 12 | 14 | Idaho | 1,612,100 | 2 | 4 |
| Virginia | 8,260,400 | 11 | 13 | Hawaii | 1,404,100 | 2 | 4 |
| Washington | 6,971,400 | 10 | 12 | Maine | 1,328,300 | 2 | 4 |
| Massachusetts | 6,692,800 | 9 | 11 | New Hampshire | 1.323,500 | 2 | 4 |
| Arizona | 6,626,600 | 9 | 11 | Rhode Island | 1,051,500 | 2 | 4 |
| Indiana | 6,570,900 | 9 | 11 | Montana | 1, 015,200 | 1 | 3 |
| Tennessee | 6,496,000 | 9 | 11 | Delaware | 925,700 | 1 | 3 |
| Missouri | 6,044,200 | 8 | 10 | South Dakota | 844,900 | 1 | 3 |
| Maryland | 5,928,800 | 8 | 10 | Alaska | 735,100 | 1 | 3 |
| Wisconsin | 5,742,700 | 8 | 10 | North Dakota | 723,400 | 1 | 3 |
| Minnesota | 5,304,000 | 8 | 10 | District of Columbia | 646,400 | (1) | 3 |
| Colorado | 5,268,400 | 7 | 9 | Vermont | 626,600 | 1 | 3 |
| Alabama | 4,833,700 | 7 | 9 | Wyoming | 582,700 | 1 | 3 |
| South Carolina | 4,774,800 | 7 | 9 | Guam | 159,400 | (1) | 0 |
| Louisiana | 4,625,500 | 6 | 8 | U.S. Virgin Islands | 106,405 | (1) | 0 |
| Kentucky | 4,395,300 | 6 | 8 | American Samoa | 55,500 | (1) | 0 |
| Oregon | 3,930,100 | 5 | 7 | Northern Mariana Islands | 53,900 | (1) | 0 |
| Oklahoma | 3,850,600 | 5 | 7 | | | | |
| Puerto Rico | 3,615,100 | (1) | 0 | ( 1) = non-voting | | | |

182

# 6: Provinces and Major Cities of Canada
## Provinces and Territories by Population (2011 Census)

| | Population | Percent of total | House of Commons Seats | Capital |
|---|---|---|---|---|
| Ontario | 12,851,800 | 38.4 | 106 | Toronto |
| Quebec | 7,903,000 | 23.6 | 75 | Quebec City |
| British Columbia | 4,400,100 | 13.1 | 36 | Victoria |
| Alberta | 3,645,300 | 10.9 | 28 | Edmonton |
| Manitoba | 1,208,300 | 3.6 | 14 | Winnipeg |
| Saskatchewan | 1,033,400 | 3.1 | 14 | Regina |
| Nova Scotia | 921,700 | 2.8 | 11 | Halifax |
| New Brunswick | 751,200 | 2.2 | 10 | Fredericton |
| Newfoundland and Labrador | 514,500 | 1.5 | 7 | St. John's |
| Prince Edward Island | 140,200 | 0.4 | 4 | Charlottetown |
| Northwest Territories | 41,500 | 0.1 | 1 | Yellowknife |
| Yukon | 33,900 | 0.1 | 1 | Whitehorse |
| Nunavut | 31,900 | 0.1 | 1 | Iqalit |
| **Canada total** | 33,476,700 | | | |

## Major Cities of Canada (2011 census)

| | |
|---|---|
| Toronto, Ontario | 2,615,100 |
| Montreal. Quebec | 1,649,500 |
| Calgary, Alberta | 1,096,800 |
| Ottawa, Ontario | 883,400 |
| Edmonton, Alberta | 812,200 |
| Mississauga, Ontario | 713,400 |
| Winnipeg, Manitoba | 663,600 |
| Vancouver, British Columbia | 603,500 |
| Brampton, Ontario | 523,900 |
| Hamilton, Ontario | 520,000 |
| Quebec City, Quebec | 516,600 |
| Surrey, British Columbia | 468,300 |
| Laval, Quebec | 401,600 |
| Halifax, Nova Scotia | 390,100 |
| London, Ontario | 366,200 |

# 7: Government Structure of the U.S.

also see #41 Constitution

There are three basic levels of government: local, state, and federal (national). At each level, there are three, independent branches: the legislative, the executive, and the judicial. Because each branch is independent, it can check and balance (control) the authority of the other branches. This is called the balance of powers.

The United States is a democracy; it is controlled by its citizens. As Abraham Lincoln said, it is a "government of the people, by the people, and for the people." The United States is also a republic, to be specific, a democratic republic. This means that its laws are made and administered by representatives elected by the people. (In this sense, the President, senators, and even local mayors are representatives.)

The only governments in the U.S. run directly by the people (pure democracies) are those of small towns, like those in New England, which make all basic decisions in Town Meetings, and even in those towns elected volunteers (selectpersons) run the town between Town Meetings.

## Federal Government

The structure and function of the federal government are established and limited by the Constitution of the United States and its twenty-six amendments. The responsibilities of the federal government are for the common defense and the general welfare of the citizens, for the regulation of interstate commerce, and for relations with other countries and between the states. All powers not specifically given to the federal government by the Constitution or prohibited by the Bill of Rights (the first ten amendments) are left to the states.

**How laws are made and used:** The executive branch can suggest laws to the congress (the legislative branch) or the congress can originate laws. Laws authorizing the government to tax or spend money are written by the House of Representatives. All laws must be passed by both houses of congress and signed by the President. If the President will not sign (vetoes) a law, the congress can vote to override the veto.

The executive branch uses the laws made by congress; it spends the government's money and runs most of the functions of government following the instructions (laws) passed by congress, and it makes the people obey the law (enforces the law).

When people or the government are accused of breaking the law, the courts (the judiciary branch) judge whether the law has been broken and what the government should do if it has been. The courts interpret the laws made by congress, but they also base their decisions on previous decisions made by the courts. Under this system (called "common law"), the courts make decisions which function as new laws.

## Legislative Branch

The Congress of the U.S. has two houses (a bicameral structure). The congress makes laws, advises the President, and must consent (agree with) his appointments and certain of his decisions such as treaties with other countries and declarations of war.

**U.S. Senate:** There are 100 senators, two from each state, elected directly by popular vote to serve six-year terms. Each senator has their own office and staff.

*Officers:* President of the Senate (the Vice President of the U.S.), President Pro Tempore, Majority Leader and Whip, Minority Leader and Whip.
*Annual salary of a senator:* $174,000.

**U.S. House of Representatives:** There are 435 Representatives, apportioned to the states based on the size of each state's population, elected directly by popular vote to serve two-year terms. Each representative has their own office and staff.
Officers: Speaker of the House, Majority Leader and Whip, Minority Leader and Whip.
*Annual salary of a representative:* $174,000

**Major Offices of the Congress:**
• General Accounting Office
• Government Printing Office
• Office of Technology Assessment
• Congressional Budget Office
• Library of Congress

# Executive Branch

**President**: The President is the Chief Executive Officer of the federal government and Commander-in-Chief of the Armed Forces. He or she serves a four-year term. No president can be elected for more than two, four-year terms.

*Annual salary of the President:* $400,000 plus expenses.

The President is the head of the administration. The administration runs the government. The White House staff and the President's Cabinet work directly for the President. They are all political appointees; most of these appointments are then sent to the congress for its advice and consent (approval). The staff advises the President and does his planning and office work. The cabinet advises the President and runs the many departments and agencies of the federal government.

**Election of the President:** People who want to become President usually try to become the nominees of one of the two major political parties. They run in the primary elections held in some of the states. In these primaries, delegates to each party's national convention are elected by direct popular vote. In some states, the parties choose their delegates in political caucuses. At the national conventions, the delegates elect the man or woman who will be the nominee of their party.

During the presidential campaign, the two major party candidates and sometimes candidates representing minor, third parties or independent candidates try to win the support of the majority of voters in each state. No third party has won the presidency since the new Republican Party won its first election under Abraham Lincoln in 1860.

In the general election in November, the voters in each state elect electors to represent their state in the electoral college; these electors vote for the candidate who won the election in their state. Each state has as many electors (the electoral vote) as it has senators and representatives, which gives smaller states some extra influence. The candidate who wins the greatest number of electoral votes becomes president; this is not necessarily the candidate who gets the greatest number of popular votes nationwide. The winner of the popular vote has failed to become president four times, in 1824, 1876, 1888, and 2000

**Order of presidential succession:** When a President dies or leaves office for any reason during his or her term, he or she is succeeded by the Vice President, Speaker of the House, President Pro Tempore of the Senate, Secretary of State.

The President (or Vice President) can be removed from office only by being impeached by the House of Representatives and convicted by the Senate presided over by the Chief Justice of the Supreme Court. The congress also has the power to impeach, convict, and remove from office federal judges and other civil officers.

**Vice President:** The Vice President is the successor to the President if he or she leaves office, a member of the President's Cabinet, and the President of the Senate. Recently, he has also been an adviser on most of the President's decisions.

*Annual salary of the Vice President:* $230,000 plus expenses.

**Election of the Vice President:** After he or she is elected by the national convention of his or her party, each presidential candidate chooses a running mate, a nominee for Vice President. After he or she is elected by the convention, the candidate joins the presidential ticket for the election campaign. The President and Vice President win the election together.

**Other parts of the executive branch:**

*The Civil Service:* Most employees of the federal government are not political appointees but civil servants who stay in the government from one administration to the next.

*The Diplomatic Corps:* The ambassador and delegation to the United Nations, other ambassadors, their staffs, and the rest of the diplomatic service are directed by the Secretary and Department of State.

*Legal Services:* All the departments and agencies of the federal government have lawyers. The Department of Justice under the Attorney General reviews and coordinates all laws proposed to the congress, enforces the law, and represents the executive branch in the courts. The FBI (Federal Bureau of Investigation) is part of this department.

*The Military:* The Army, the Navy and Marines, and the Air Force are under the direct command of the President through the Secretary of Defense and then the Chairman of the Joint Chiefs of Staff, who is the nation's top military officer.

185

# Judicial Branch

**General:** The legal system in the U.S. is Common Law rather than Civil Law. Laws are written and enacted by the legislatures of the states and by congress, but the decisions of the courts in interpreting these laws are based on precedents (earlier court decisions). Court decisions function as new laws; the courts have a powerful influence on all levels of government.

Some judges at the state and local levels are elected for specific terms in some states. Federal judges are appointed by the President and confirmed with the advice and consent of the Senate. They all serve for life or until they choose to resign; this protects them from political influence.

**Criminal Law:** All people accused of breaking criminal law before the state or federal courts have the right to be tried by a jury of either six or twelve citizens who will decide if they are guilty or innocent. They are indicted (formally accused) by the government, sometimes by a grand jury of citizens. In court they are prosecuted by a government prosecutor and defended by their own lawyer or a public defender. If they are found guilty, they can appeal the decision of the jury or the judge to a higher court, a court of appeals. If the verdict is innocent, the government cannot appeal. The constitution says nobody can be tried twice for the same crime.

If a defendant does not appeal a guilty verdict, punishment is decided on by the judge following the penal code (penalty law). Sometimes the judge is advised by the jury; sometimes his or her choice of judgments is limited by a uniform sentencing law enacted by the legislature. The punishment is then administered by the justice department of the executive branch (the police and prison system). Punishments may be appealed to the Supreme Court if they may be cruel or unusual because such punishments are forbidden by the Constitution's Bill of Rights.

**Civil Law:** All forms of business and relations between people, companies, and states are regulated (ruled) by either criminal or civil law. Conflicts between people, etc., which do not involve criminal activity, are resolved by the courts using civil law. Juries are used in some cases; others are decided by a judge or a panel of judges.

**Federal and State Jurisdictions:** The federal courts have authority (jurisdiction) in all criminal and civil cases involving the federal government or law, federal officers, and other countries, their officers or their citizens. The federal courts also have authority in cases between states, between any state and a citizen of another state, or between citizens of different states. This includes most cases involving big businesses. All other cases are tried in the state courts.

**The U.S. District Courts:** These courts are the lowest level of the federal court system. Most cases involving federal law, both civil and criminal, begin at this level.

There are 91 district courts, at least one and sometimes several in each state and in the territories of Guam, Puerto Rico, and the Virgin Islands.

**The U.S. Courts of Appeals:** There are eleven Circuit Courts, each covering a multistate region, plus two special courts, one for the District of Columbia and one for temporary emergencies. Each court holds court in several places which make up a circuit. These Circuit Courts hear appeals brought to them from the lower district courts and cases involving federal regulatory agencies.

**The U.S. Supreme Court:** There are nine justices of the Supreme Court (one Chief Justice and eight Associate Justices). They are appointed by the President and confirmed with the advice and consent of the Senate. The justices serve for life unless they choose to retire or they are impeached by the House and convicted by the Senate.

*Annual salary of the Chief Justice: $255,500;*
*Annual salary of the Associates Justices: $244,400.*

The Supreme Court is the highest court of appeals; its main function is to decide whether decisions of the lower courts and laws passed by the states or federal government are constitutional (in accord or agreement with the Constitution and the Bill of Rights.) The Supreme Court also decides cases when there is a conflict between the laws of one state and another or the federal government. It chooses the cases it will hear from among cases appealed to it from the lower courts and cases involving challenges to state and federal laws.

Because the Supreme Court interprets the Constitution and either cancels or defines the meaning of laws based on its interpretations of the Constitution, it has a great influence on the way the laws of the country are used. From the beginning of U.S. history, the Supreme Court has often used its power to change the political and social development of the country.

## State Governments

There are 50 states in the U.S. and 15 associated states and possessions in the Caribbean and Pacific. Each has its own government. Although their structures vary in many ways, each of these governments has three branches like the federal government. The following descriptions are generally true for most states.

**LEGISLATIVE BRANCH:** The legislative branch of each state has a bicameral (two-house) structure like the federal government. There is an upper house called the senate and a lower house called the house or assembly of representatives. The state legislatures make both civil and criminal laws for their states.

**EXECUTIVE BRANCH:** Each state has a governor and a lieutenant governor, who are elected by the people of the state. The structure and functions of the executive branch differ from state to state. Most states have a secretary of state, a treasurer, a comptroller, and an attorney general.

**JUDICLAL BRANCH:** The highest court is called the appellate court, the court of appeals, or the supreme court. Below it are the superior and inferior courts, which in some states include all local and municipal courts.

## Local Governments

There are many variations in the structures of local governments. The smallest government structures are villages. Towns are generally larger, and cities are larger still. The whole state is divided into counties. In some states, each county is divided into several townships, each containing several towns and villages. In other states, each county is divided into towns, which may have several villages, town centers, or hamlets in them. The open (unincorporated) countryside between villages is governed by the township (town) or the county.

**LEGISLATIVE BRANCH:** Villages, towns, and cities (municipalities) always have some form of legislative board, which is directly elected by the local citizens. In cities and large towns it is called the town or city council or the board of alderpersons. In smaller towns and villages, the town council is sometimes called the board of selectpersons. The local legislatures make regulations and spend local tax money. To help them plan for changes, they often appoint local zoning and planning boards.

In most municipalities, the school system is run by a local school board, which is also directly elected by the people. Sometimes there is a township school board.

**EXECUTIVE BRANCH:** The smallest towns are run by the selectpersons with the help of an elected town clerk or manager. In larger towns and cities there is always an independent town or city manager or mayor.

**JUDICIAL BRANCH:** Villages and small towns have elected justices of the peace or local town magistrates. Larger towns and cities have municipal courts. In some states, these are part of the state court system; in others, they are independent.

## Other Organizations

There are other organizations which govern life in the United States, usually through political and financial influence.

**POLITICAL PARTIES:** There are two major political parties, the Democratic Party and the Republican Party. There are also many minor, special interest, and regional and local parties including the Progressive Party, Libertarian Party, Socialist Party, Socialist Labor Party, Communist Party, and Socialist Workers Party. Individuals may also run for political office as independents (without party support).

**Other Groups With Political Influence:**
- Business and trade associations
- Chambers of commerce
- Professional organizations
- Labor unions
- Public service boards
- School boards
- Political action committees
- Veteran's and Fraternal organizations
- Alumni associations
- Consumer and public interest groups
- Churches
- Other special interest groups

# 8: U.S. Departments and Agencies

## Departments and The Cabinet

**Note:** Each department is headed by a member of the president's Cabinet, who is given the title of secretary, with the exception of the Department of Justice, which is headed by the attorney general. The vice president is also a member of the Cabinet.

Department of Agriculture
Department of Commerce
Department of Defense
Department of Education
Department of Energy
Department of Health and Human Services
Department of Housing and Urban Development
Department of Homeland Security
Department of Justice
Department of Labor
Department of State
Department of the Interior
Department of the Treasury
Department of Transportation
Department of Veterans' Affairs

## White House Staff

Chief of Staff
Assistant to the President/Deputy Chief of Staff
Assistants to the president:
  Cabinet Secretary
  Communications
  Counsel to the President
  Deputy Counsel to the President
  Counselor to the President
  Special Counsel
  Domestic Policy Council
  Intergovernmental Affairs
  Legislative Affairs
  Management and Administration
  National AIDS Policy
  National Economic Policy
  National Security
  Presidential Personnel
  Press Secretary
  Political Affairs
  Public Liaison
  Staff Secretary
  Director of Scheduling
  Director of Speechwriting
  Chief of Staff to the First Lady
  Special Projects

## Executive Agencies

Council of Economic Advisers (CEA)
Council on Environmental Quality
National Security Council (NSC)
Office of Administration
Office of Management and Budget (OMB)
Office of National Drug Control Policy
Office of Science and Technology Policy
U.S. Trade Representative

## Major Independent Agencies

Central Intelligence Agency (CIA)
Commission on Civil Rights
Commodity Futures Trading Commission
Consumer Product Safety Commission
Corporation for National and Community Service
Environmental Protection Agency (EPA)
Equal Employment Opportunity Commission (EEOC)
Export-Import Bank of the U.S.
Farm Credit Administration
Federal Communications Commission (FCC)
Federal Deposit Insurance Commission (FDIC)
Federal Election Commission
Federal Maritime Commission
Federal Mediation and Conciliation Service (FMCS)
Federal Reserve System
Federal Trade Commission (FTC)
Foundation on the Arts and the Humanities
General Services Administration (GSA)
Inter-American Foundation
National Aeronautics and Space Administration (NASA)
National Archives and Records Administration
National Labor Relations Board (NLRB)
National Railroad Passenger Corporation (AMTRAK)
National Science Foundation
National Transportation Safety Board
Nuclear Regulatory Commission
Occupational Safety and Health Review Commission
Office of Personnel Management
Peace Corps
Securities and Exchange Commission (SEC)
Selective Service System (SSS)
Small Business Administration (SBA)
Social Security Administration (SSA)
Tennessee Valley Authority (TVA)
Trade and Development Agency
U.S. International Trade Commission
U.S. Postal Service (USPS)

# 9: Government Structure of Canada

There are three basic levels of government: local, state, and federal (national). Although the legislative, the executive, and the judicial functions are done at all levels, under a parliamentary system like Canada's the executive function is dependent on the legislature.

Canada is a democracy, controlled by its citizens. On the national level, it is a federation of provinces and territories. There are ten provinces: Alberta, British Columbia, Manitoba, New Brunswick, Newfoundland (including Labrador), Nova Scotia, Ontario, Prince Edward Island, Quebec, and Saskatchewan. There are three territories: the Northwest Territories, Nuvavut, and the Yukon.

On a less formal but politically very important basis, Canada is a federation of two peoples, one English speaking and the other French. The history of the union of these two peoples has been one of political strain. The nation as a whole is officially bilingual. Although the distinct French character of Quebec culture and society have always been recognized in Canada, the increasing population, prosperity, and political power of English speaking Canada have stimulated a seperatist movement in Quebec that has been a major political factor throughout the 1970s, '80s, and '90s.

On another level, Canada is a monarchy. This is important historically and today many Canadians are loyal to Elizabeth II as Queen of Canada, as well as Great Britain. She is officially Head of State. The Queen's representative in Canada is the Governor General.

Canada gained functional independence from Great Britain with the British North America Act of 1867. The Constitution Act of 1982 formally ended the colonial control of Canada by the British Parliament. The government of Canada was transferred under the Constitution to the Canadian people.

## Federal Government

The Head of State is the Queen, represented by the Governor General. This is a ceremonial and advisory position. The real leader of the country is the Prime Minister, who is the leader of the majority party in the House of Commons. The Prime Minister and his cabinet are members of the Commons. They serve as the executive branch, advising the Governor General and running the civil service. The capital city of Canada is Ottawa, Ontario.

There are two houses of parliament, the Commons with 301 members and the Senate with 104. Members of the Commons are elected by the people in elections every five years or when the Prime Minister and his government are voted down in the Commons and they decide to call for an election. The Senators are appointed for terms ending with their 75th birthdays. Laws must be passed by both houses of the legislature and signed by the Governor General in the Queen's name.

## Provincial Government

Each of the ten provincial governments is officially headed by a Lieutenant Governor, appointed by the federal government. This is a largely formal, symbolic position, like that of the Governor General on the federal level. The real executive head of each province is the Premier, the leader of the majority party in the provincial legislature.

These are single-house legislative bodies elected every four years . In eight of the provinces, the legislature is called the Legislative Assembly. In Newfoundland, which became a province in 1949, it is traditionally called the House of Assemblies, and in Quebec it is significantly called the National Assembly.

# 10: U.S. Presidents
*Official Whitehouse Portraits*

1. **George Washington**
   (1732-1799)
   Party: Federalist
   Term: 1789-1797
   Birthplace: Virginia

2. **John Adams**
   (1735-1826)
   Party: Federalist
   Term: 1797-1801
   Birthplace: Massachusetts

3. **Thomas Jefferson**
   (1743-1826)
   Party: Democratic-Republican
   Term: 1801-1809
   Birthplace: Virginia

4. **James Madison**
   (1751-1836)
   Party: Democratic-Republican
   Term: 1809-1817
   Birthplace: Virginia

5. **James Monroe**
   (1758-1831)
   Party: Democratic-Republican
   Term: 1817-1825
   Birthplace: Virginia

6. **John Quincy Adams**
   (1767-1848)
   Party: Democratic-Republican
   Term: 1825-1829
   Birthplace: Massachusetts

7. **Andrew Jackson**
   (1767-1845)
   Party: Democratic
   Term: 1829-1837
   Birthplace: South Carolina

8. **Martin Van Buren**
   (1782-1862)
   Party: Democratic
   Term: 1837-1841
   Birthplace: New York

**9. William Harrison**
(1773-1841)
Party: Whig
Term: 1841 *
Birthplace: Virginia

**10. John Tyler**
(1790-1862)
Party: Whig
Term: 1841-1845
Birthplace: Virginia

**11. James Polk**
(1795-1849)
Party: Democratic
Term: 1845-1849
Birthplace: North Carolina

**12. Zachary Taylor**
(1784-1850)
Party: Whig
Term: 1849-1850 *
Birthplace: Virginia

**13. Millard Fillmore**
(1800-1874)
Party: Whig
Term: 1850-1853
Birthplace: New York

**14. Franklin Pierce**
(1804-1869)
Party: Democratic
Term: 1853-1857
Birthplace: New Hampshire

**15. James Buchanan**
(1791-1868)
Party: Democratic
Term: 1857-1861
Birthplace: Pennsylvania

**16. Abraham Lincoln**
(1809-1865)
Party: Republican
Term: 1861-1865 **
Birthplace: Kentucky

*\* Died in office*
*\*\* Assassinated in office*
*§ Resigned from office*

191

**17. Andrew Johnson**
(1808-1875)
Party: Union
Term: 1865-1869
Birthplace: North Carolina

**18. Ulysses S. Grant**
(1822-1885)
Party: Republican
Term: 1869-1877
Birthplace: Ohio

**19. Rutherford B. Hayes**
(1822-1893)
Party: Republican
Term: 1877-1881
Birthplace: Ohio

**20. James Garfield**
(1831-1881)
Party: Republican
Term: 1881 **
Birthplace: Ohio

**21. Chester Arthur**
(1829-1886)
Party: Republican
Term: 1881-1885
Birthplace: Vermont

**22. Grover Cleveland**
(1837-1908)
Party: Democratic
Term: 1885-1889
Birthplace: New Jersey

**23. Benjamin Harrison**
(1833-1901)
Party: Republican
Term: 1889-1893
Birthplace: Ohio

**24. Grover Cleveland**
(second nonconsecutive term)
Term: 1893-1897

**25. William McKinley**
(1843-1901)
Party: Republican
Term: 1897-1901 **
Birthplace: Ohio

**26. Theodore Roosevelt**
(1858-1919)
Party: Republican
Term: 1901-1909
Birthplace: New York

**27. William Taft**
(1857-1930)
Party: Republican
Term: 1909-1913
Birthplace: Ohio

**28. Woodrow Wilson**
(1856-1924)
Party: Democratic
Term: 1913-1921
Birthplace: Virginia

**29. Warren Harding**
(1865-1923)
Party: Republican
Term: 1921-1923 *
Birthplace: Ohio

**30. Calvin Coolidge**
(1872-1933)
Party: Republican
Term: 1923-1929
Birthplace: Vermont

**31. Herbert Hoover**
(1874-1964)
Party: Republican
Term: 1929-1933
Birthplace: Iowa

**32. Franklin D. Roosevelt**
(1882-1945)
Party: Democratic
Term: 1933-1945 *
Birthplace: New York

*\* Died in office*
*\*\* Assassinated in office*
*§ Resigned from office*

**33. Harry S. Truman**
(1884-1972)
Party: Democratic
Term: 1945-1953
Birthplace: Missouri

**34. Dwight D. Eisenhower**
(1890- 1969)
Party: Republican
Term: 1953-1961
Birthplace: Texas

**35. John F. Kennedy**
(1917-1963)
Party: Democratic
Term: 1961-1963 **
Birthplace: Massachusetts

**36. Lyndon B. Johnson**
(1908-1973)
Party: Democratic
Term: 1963-1969
Birthplace: Texas

**37. Richard Nixon**
(1913- 1994)
Party: Republican
Term: 1969-1974 §
Birthplace: California

**38. Gerald Ford**
(1913-2006)
Party: Republican
Term: 1974-1977
Birthplace: Nebraska

**39. Jimmy Carter**
(1924- )
Party: Democratic
Term: 1977-1981
Birthplace: Georgia

**40. Ronald Reagan**
(1911-2004)
Party: Republican
Term: 1981-1989
Birthplace: Illinois

**41. George Bush**
(1924- )
Party: Republican
Term: 1989 - 1993
Birthplace: Massachusetts

**42.  Bill Clinton**
(1946- )
Party: Democrat
Term: 1993 - 2001
Birthplace: Arkansas

**43.  George W. Bush**
(1946- )
Party: Republican
Term: 2001-2009
Birthplace: Connecticut

**44.  Barack Obama**
(1961- )
Party: Democrat
Term: 2009-2017
Birthplace: Hawaii

*The White House*

# 11: Canadian Governors General, Prime Ministers

| Term | Governor General | Term | Prime Minister, Party |
|------|------------------|------|-----------------------|
| 1867-1868 | Viscount Monck | 1867-1873 | Sir John A. Macdonald, Conservative |
| 1869-1872 | Baron Lisgar | 1873-1878 | Alexander Mackenzie, Liberal |
| 1872-1878 | Earl of Dufferin | 1878-1891 | Sir John A. Macdonald, Conservative |
| 1878-1883 | Marquess of Lome | 1891-1892 | Sir John J. C. Abbott, Conservative |
| 1883-1888 | Marquess of Lansdowne | 1892-1894 | Sir John S. D. Thompson, Conservative |
| 188-1893 | Baron Stanley of Preston | 1894-1896 | Sir Mackenzie Bowell, Conservative |
| 1893-1898 | Earl of Aberdeen | 1896 | Sir Charles Tupper, Conservative |
| 1898-1904 | Earl of Minto | 1896-1911 | Sir Wilfrid Laurier, Liberal |
| 1904-1911 | Earl Grey | 1911-1917 | Sir Robert Borden, Conservative |
| 1911-1916 | Duke of Connaught | 1917-1920 | Sir Robert Borden, Unionist |
| 1916-1921 | Duke of Devonshire | 1920-1921 | Arthur Meighen, Unionist |
| 1921-1926 | Baron Byng of Vimy | 1921-1926 | W. L. Mackenzie King, Liberal |
| 1926-1931 | Viscount Willingdon | 1926 | Arthur Meighen, Conservative |
| 1931-1935 | Earl of Bessborough | 1926-1930 | W. L. Mackenzie King, Liberal |
| 1935-1940 | Baron Tweedsmuir | 1930-1935 | Richard B. Bennett, Conservative |
| 1940-1948 | Earl of Athlone | 1935-1948 | W. L. Mackenzie King, Liberal |
| 1948-1952 | Viscount Alexander | 1948-1957 | Louis S. St. Laurent, Liberal |
| 1952-1959 | Viscount Massey | 1957-1963 | John G. Diefenbaker, Conservative |
| 1959-1967 | Georges P. Vanier | 1963-1968 | Lester B. Pearson, Liberal |
| 1967-1973 | Roland Michener | 1968-1979 | Pierre Elliott Trudeau, Liberal |
| 1974-1979 | Jules Léger | 1979-1980 | Charles Joseph Clark, Conservative |
| 1979-1984 | Edward R. Schreyer | 1980-1984 | Pierre Elliott Trudeau, Liberal |
| 1984-1990 | Jeanne Sauvé | 1984 | John Turner, Liberal |
| 1990-1995 | Raymond John Hnatyshyn | 1984-1993 | Brian Mulroney, Conservative |
| 1995-1999 | Roméo LeBlanc | 1993 | Kim Campbell, Conservative |
| 1999-2005 | Adrienne Clarkson | 1993-2003 | Jean Chrétien, Liberal |
| 2005-2010 | Michäelle Jean | 2003-2006 | Paul Martin, Liberal |
| 2010- | David Lloyd Jahnston | 2006- | Stephen Harper, Conservative |

# 12: World Industries

## World's Largest Companies by Revenue 2014

| Rank | Company | Industry | Revenue in Billions | Headquarters |
|---|---|---|---|---|
| 1. | Walmart | Retail | $476 | USA |
| 2. | Royal Dutch Shell | Oil and Gas | 451 | Netherlands, UK |
| 3. | Exxon Mobil | Oil and Gas | 420 | USA |
| 4. | China National Petroleum | Oil and Gas | 425 | China |
| 5. | Sinopec Group | Oil and Gas | 411 | China |
| 6. | BP | Oil and Gas | 379 | UK |
| 7. | Aramco | Oil and Gas | 311 | Saudi Arabia |
| 8. | Vitol | Commodities | 303 | Netherlands, Switzerland |
| 9. | State Grid Corp of China | Electric Utility | 290 | China |
| 10. | Samsung | Conglomerate | 268 | Korea |
| 11. | Volkswagen | Automotive | 254 | Germany |
| 12. | Total | Oil and Gas | 240 | France |
| 13. | Toyota | Automotive | 222 | Japan |
| 14. | Chevron | Oil and Gas | 220 | USA |
| 15. | Glencore Xstrata | Commodities | 214 | Switzerland |
| 16. | E.ON | Electric Utility | 174 | Germany |
| 17. | Phillips 66 | Oil and Gas | 171 | USA |
| 18. | Apple | Electronics | 170 | USA |
| 19. | Japan Post Holdings | Conglomerate | 168 | Japan |
| 20. | Eni | Oil and Gas | 167 | Italy |
| 21. | Gazprom | Oil and Gas | 164 | Russia |
| 22. | Berkshire Hathaway | Conglomerate | 162 | USA |
| 23. | General Motors | Automotive | 156 | USA |
| 24. | Daimler | Automotive | 150 | Germany |
| 25. | LG Corp | Conglomerate | 148 | Korea |

## Top US Franchises 2014

| | | | |
|---|---|---|---|
| 1. Subway | Fast Food (sandwiches) | 13. Circle K | Convenience Store |
| 2. McDonald's | Fast Food (burgers) | 14. InterContinental Hotels | Hotels |
| 3. KFC | Fast Food (chicken) | 15. Hertz | Car Rental |
| 4. Burger King | Fast Food (burgers) | 16. Baskin-Robbins | Ice Cream |
| 5. 7-Eleven | Convenience Store | 17. Jani-King | Commercial Cleaning |
| 6. Pizza Hut | Fast Food (pizza) | 18. Liberty Tax Service | Tax Preparation |
| 7. GNC Live Well | Wellness products and services | 19. Snap-on Tools | Tools |
| | | 20. Taco Bell | Fast Food (Mexican) |
| 8. Wyndham Group | Hotels | 21. Choice Hotels | Hotels |
| 9. Dunkin' Donuts | Bakery and Coffee Shop | 22. Anytime Fitness | Gyms |
| 10. RE/MAX | Real Estate | 23. JAN-PRO | Commercial Cleaning |
| 11. Domino's Pizza | Fast Food (pizza) | 24. Chem-Dry | Carpet Cleaning |
| 12. Ace Hardware | Home Improvement | 25. Marriott International | Hotels |

# 13: Some Famous Americans

## Before 1812

| | | |
|---|---|---|
| Adams, Samuel | (1722-1803) | Patriot, Boston Tea Party firebrand |
| Allen, Ethan | (1738-1789) | Leader of the Green Mountain Boys |
| Arnold, Benedict | (1741 -1801) | Treasonous Revolutionary War general |
| Attucks, Crispus | (c.1723-1770) | Led group that began the Boston Massacre in 1770 |
| Boone, Daniel | (1734-1820) | Frontiersman |
| Clark, William | (1770-1838) | Explored the northwest with Lewis in 1804 |
| Crockett, Davy | (1786-1836) | Frontiersman, died at the Alamo |
| Franklin, Benjamin | (1706-1790) | Writer, statesman, scientist |
| Hale, Nathan | (1755-1776) | Revolutionary War officer |
| Hamilton, Alexander | (1755-1894) | Statesman, author, first secretary of the treasury |
| Hancock, John | (1737-1793) | Statesman, Declaration of Independence signer |
| Henry, Patrick | (1736-1799) | Revolutionary war figure, orator |
| Jones, John Paul | (1747-1792) | Naval hero |
| LaSalle, Sieur de (R.C.) | (1643-1687) | Explored and claimed Mississippi Basin for France |
| Lewis, Meriwether | (1774-1809) | Explored the northwest with Clark in 1804 |
| Pilgrims | | Founded Plymouth Plantation Colony in 1720 |
| Pocahontas | (c. 1595-1617) | Indian princess, saved explorer John Smith's life |
| Revere, Paul | (1735-1818) | Silversmith, hero of famous ride in 1775 |
| Ross, Betsy | (1752-1836) | Designed and sewed first American flag |
| Sacagawea | (1784-1884) | Guided Lewis and Clark |
| Smith, Capt. John | (c. 1580-1631) | Led first colony (1607-9) in Jamestown, Virginia |
| Thomas Paine | (1737-1809) | Political philosopher |
| Turnbull, John | (1756-1843) | Historical themes painter |
| Whitney, Eli | (1765-1825) | Invented cotton gin and manufacture |

## 1812-1865

| | | |
|---|---|---|
| Audubon, John James | (1785-1851) | Artist, ornithologist |
| Brown, John | (1800-1859) | Abolitionist |
| Carson, Kit | (1809-1868) | Scout |
| Clay, Henry | (1777-1852) | Political leader |
| Custer, George | (1839-1876) | Union general in Civil War, killed by Indians |
| Davis, Jefferson | (1808-1889) | President of the Confederacy |
| Douglass, Frederick | (1817-1895) | Author, diplomat, abolitionist |
| Emerson, Ralph Waldo | (1803-1882) | Philosopher, author, lecturer |
| Geronimo | (1829-1909) | Apache chieftain |
| Jackson, Thomas (Stonewall) | (1824-1863) | Confederate general in Civil War |
| Key, Francis Scott | (1779-1843) | Author of national anthem |
| Lee, Robert E. | (1807-1870) | Confederate general in Civil War |
| Sherman, William T. | (1820-1891) | Union general in Civil War |
| Sitting Bull | (1835-1890) | Dakota chief |
| Thoreau, Henry David | (1817-1862) | Philosopher, author, naturalist |
| Truth, Sojourner | (1797-1883) | Suffragette, abolitionist |
| Tubman, Harriet | (1820-1913) | Abolitionist, liberator |
| Webster, Daniel | (1782-1852) | Statesman |
| Webster, Noah | (1759-1843) | Lexicographer |
| Young, Brigham | (1801-1877) | Mormon leader, colonized Utah |

## 1866-1916

| | | |
|---|---|---|
| Anthony, Susan B. | (1820-1906) | Suffragette |
| Barton, Clara | (1821 -1906) | Organizer of American Red Cross |
| Bell, Alexander Graham | (1847-1922) | Inventor of telephone, teacher of deaf |
| Buffalo Bill (William Cody) | (1846-1917) | Scout, showman |
| Carver, George Washington | (1861-1943) | Educator, botanist |
| Cassatt, Mary | (1845-1926) | Impressionist painter |
| Crazy Horse | (1849-1877) | Dakota war chief victorious at Little Bighorn |
| DuBois, W. E. B. | (1868-1963) | Historian, sociologist, founded NAACP |
| Edison, Thomas | (1847-1931) | Inventor of lightbulb, practical electric power |
| Ford, Henry | (1863-1947) | Industrialist, built first assembly-line cars |
| Homer, Winslow | (1836-1910) | Painter of marine themes |
| Liliuokalani, Lydia Kamekeha | (1838-1917) | Last monarch of Hawaii |
| Long, Huey | (1893-1935) | Politician |
| Peary, Adm. Robert E. | (1856-1920) | Explorer, first to reach North Pole 1909 |
| Rockefeller, John D. | (1839-1937) | Established Standard Oil, philanthropist |
| Sargent, John Singer | (1856-1925) | Portrait artist |
| Washington, Booker T. | (1856-1915) | Educator |
| Wright, Orville | (1871 -1948) | Built first powered airplane with brother Wilbur |

## 1917-1970

| | | |
|---|---|---|
| Bethune, Mary McLeod | (1875-1955) | Educator |
| Copland, Aaron | (1900-1990) | Composer |
| Cronkite, Walter | (1916-2009) | Television journalist |
| Disney, Walt | (1901-1966) | Film animator and producer |
| Earhart, Amelia | (1898-1937) | Aviatrix |
| Friedan, Betty | (1921-2006) | Feminist, author |
| Goddard, Robert | (1882-1945) | Physicist, father of modern rocketry |
| Hearst, William Randolph | (1863-1951) | Publisher |
| Hopper, Edward | (1882-1967) | Painter of realistic urban scenes |
| Keller, Helen | (1880-1968) | Educator and writer |
| King Jr., The Rev. Dr. Martin Luther | (1929-1968) | Civil rights leader |
| MacArthur, Douglas | (1880-1964) | General in WW II, Korean War |
| Malcolm X | (1925-1965) | Civil rights leader |
| Marshall, Thurgood | (1908-1993) | Supreme Court justice, appointed 1967 |
| McCarthy, Joseph | (1908-1957) | Anti-communist, politician |
| Moses, Grandma | (1860-1961) | Folk painter |
| O'Keeffe, Georgia | (1887-1986) | Painter of southwestern motifs |
| Oppenheimer, J. Robert | (1904-1967) | Physicist, father of atomic bomb |
| Patton, George S. | (1885-1945) | General in WW II |
| Pollock, Jackson | (1912-1956) | Abstract expressionist painter |
| Rockwell, Norman | (1894-1978) | Illustrator |
| Roosevelt, Eleanor | (1884-1962) | Humanitarian, UN delegate |
| Spock, Benjamin | (1903-1998) | Pediatrician |
| Steinem, Gloria | (1934- ) | Feminist, author |
| Stevenson, Adlai | (1900-1965) | Statesman |
| Warhol, Andy | (1928-1989) | Pop artist |
| Wright, Frank Lloyd | (1867-1959) | Architect |

## 1970-2000

| | | |
|---|---|---|
| Armstrong, Neil | (1930-2012) | Astronaut, 1st on Moon |
| Brokaw, Tom | (1940-    ) | Television news anchor |
| Brothers, Joyce | (1928-2013) | Psychologist |
| Brown, Helen Gurley | (1922-2012) | Publisher |
| Cesar Chavez | (1927-1993) | Union/civil rights activist |
| Child, Julia | (1912-2004) | Chef |
| Chung, Connie | (1946-    ) | Television journalist, anchor |
| Donaldson, Sam | (1934-    ) | Television journalist |
| Eisner, Michael | (1942-    ) | Chairman of Walt Disney |
| Falwell, Jerry | (1933-2007) | Televangelist |
| Glenn, John | (1921-    ) | Senator, astronaut |
| Graham, Billy | (1918-    ) | Evangelist, author |
| Graham, Katharine | (1917-2001) | Publisher of *Washington Post* |
| Hefner, Hugh | (1926-    ) | Publisher of *Playboy* |
| Iacocca, Lee | (1924-    ) | Chairman of Chrysler |
| Jackson, The Rev. Jesse | (1941-    ) | Civil Rights leader, politician |
| Kennedy, Edward | (1938-2005) | Senator |
| Klein, Calvin | (1942-    ) | Fashion designer |
| Landers, Ann | (1918-2002) | Advice columnist |
| Lauren, Ralph | (1939-    ) | Fashion designer |
| Nader, Ralph | (1934-    ) | Consumer advocate |
| O'Connor, Sandra Day | (1930-    ) | Supreme Court justice |
| Onassis, Jacqueline | (1929-1998) | Widow of John F. Kennedy |
| Pei, I.M. | (1917-    ) | Architect |
| Quinn, Jane Bryant | (1939-    ) | Economist |
| Rather, Dan | (1931-    ) | Television anchor |
| Ride, Sally K. | (1952-2012) | Astronaut |
| Sagan, Carl | (1934-1996) | Astronomer, author |
| Steinbrenner, George | (1930-2010) | Owner of the New York Yankees |
| Van Buren, Abigail | (1918-2013) | Advice columnist |
| Westheimer, Ruth | (1928-    ) | Sex therapist |

## 2001-present

| | | |
|---|---|---|
| Albright, Madeline | (1937-    ) | Secretary of State |
| Cheney, Dick | (1925-    ) | Vice-President |
| Chomsky, Noam | (1928-    ) | Linguist, political activist |
| Clinton, Bill | (1946-    ) | President |
| Clinton, Hillary Rodham | (1947-    ) | Senator, Secretary of State |
| Cosby, Bill | (1937-    ) | Comedian, author, educator |
| Eastwood, Clint | (1930-    ) | Actor, filmmaker |
| Gates, Bill | (1955-    ) | Microsoft Chairman |
| Gore, Al | (1948-    ) | Vice-President, environmentalist |
| Jobs, Steve | (1955-    ) | Inventor, Apple co-founder |
| Jordan, Michael | (1963-    ) | Basketball player, entrepreneur |
| Kissinger, Henry | (1923-    ) | Statesman |
| Limbaugh, Rush | (1951-    ) | Radio talk show host |
| McCain, John | (1936-    ) | Senator |
| Mohammed Ali | (1942-    ) | Boxer |
| Obama, Barack | (1961-    ) | President |
| Powell, Colin | (1937-    ) | General, Secretary of State |
| Rice, Condoleeza | (1954-    ) | Writer, TV host, Secretary of State |

## 2001-present, continued

| | | |
|---|---|---|
| Spielberg, Steven | (1946- ) | Filmmaker |
| Stewart. Martha | (1941- ) | Business woman, writer, TV personality |
| Turner, Ted | (1938- ) | TV executive |
| Williams, Jody | (1950- ) | Nobel Prize winner |
| Winfrey, Oprah | (1954- ) | Actress, media innovator |
| Woods, Tiger | (1975- ) | Golfer |

## Famous People in Canadian History

| | | |
|---|---|---|
| Baffin, William | ( -1622) | Arctic explorer |
| Big Bear (Misto-a-ha-Musqua) | (1825-1888) | 1st Nation Plains Cree leader, NW Rebellion |
| La Bolduc, Mary Travis | (1894-1941) | 1st Quebecoise singer, songwriter in 1930s |
| Brant, Joseph | (1743-1807) | Mohawk/Iroquois League leader, British loyalist |
| Brant, Molly | (1736-1796) | Mohawk/Iroquois League leader, British loyalist |
| Brûlé, Étienne | (1592-1633) | 1st explorer beyond St. Lawrence, lived with Hurons |
| de Champlain, Samuel | (1574-1635) | Explorer, founded Quebec 1608 |
| Chomedey de Maisonneuve | (1612-1676) | Soldier, founded Montreal 1642 |
| Cunard, Samuel | (1787-1865) | Businessman, founded Cunard Line shipping |
| Edenshaw, Charles | (1839-1920) | Hockey player |
| Fessenden, Reginald | (1866-1932) | Inventor - radio transmission, sonar |
| Frobisher, Martin | (1535-1594) | Arctic explorer |
| Jolliet, Louis | (1645-1700) | Discovered Chicago, explored Upper Mississippi |
| Kane, Paul | (1908-2002) | Artist of Canadian West and 1st Nations |
| Karsch, Yousuf | (1810-1871) | Portrait Photographer |
| Labatt, John Kinder | (1803-1860) | Brewer |
| de LaSalle, Robert | (1643-1687) | Explorer of Great Lakes, Mississippi, Gulf of Mexico |
| Marquette, Pére Jacques | (1637-1675) | Founded Sault Ste. Marie, explored Upper Mississippi |
| McLuhan, Marshall | (1911-1980) | Philosopher developed media theory |
| Montgomery, Lucy Maud | (1874-1942) | Author of Anne of Green Gables |
| Naismith, James | (1861-1939) | Invented Basketball |
| Perry, Sir William | (1790-1855) | Explorer of the Canadian Arctic |
| Service, Robert W | (1874-1958) | Poet, "Bard of the Yukon" |

## Famous Canadians: 2001-present

| | | |
|---|---|---|
| Anka, Paul | (1941- ) | Singer, songwriter |
| Aykroyd, Dan | (1952- ) | Actor, comedian, screenwriter |
| Bieber, Justin | (1994- ) | Singer, songwriter, dancer |
| Carrey, Jim | (1962- ) | Actor, comedian, filmmaker |
| Cohen, Leonard | (1934- ) | Singer, songwriter, poet, writer |
| Dion, Celine | (1968- ) | Singer |
| Ferguson, Maynard | (1928-2006) | Jazz trumpter |
| Fox, Michael J. | (1961- ) | Actor. author |
| Gilliam, Terry | (1940- ) | Monty Python creator |
| Jennings, Peter | (1938-2005) | ABC news anchor |
| Jewison, Norman | (1926- ) | Filmmaker |
| Lang, K.D. | (1961- ) | Singer, songwriter |
| Mowat, Farley | (1921-2014) | Author, environmentalist |
| Orr, Bobby | (1948- ) | Hockey player |
| Plummer, Chrisopher | (1929- ) | Actor |
| Reeves, Keanu | (1964- ) | Actor |
| Shatner, William | (1931- ) | Actor |
| Young, Neil | (1945- ) | Singer, songwriter |

# 14: Entertainers

| Name | Occupation | Dates |
|------|------------|-------|
| Affleck, Ben | Actor | (1972-    ) |
| Allen, Woody | Actor, director, screenwriter | (1935-    ) |
| Andrews, Julie | Actress | (1935-    ) |
| Armstrong, Louis | Jazz musician | (1900-1971) |
| Astaire, Fred | Actor, dancer | (1904-1983) |
| Baez, Joan | Singer | (1941-    ) |
| Balanchine, George | Choreographer | (1904-1983) |
| Ball, Lucille | Actress, comedienne | (1911-1989) |
| Barnum, P. T. | Circus master | (1810-1891) |
| Baryshnikov, Mikhail | Dancer, actor | (1948-    ) |
| Belafonte. Harry | Singer, actor | (1927-    ) |
| Bernstein, Leonard | Conductor, composer | (1918-1990) |
| Bogart, Humphrey | Actor | (1899-1957) |
| Brando, Marlon | Actor | (1924-2004) |
| Cage, Nicolas | Actor | (1964-    ) |
| Capra, Frank | Director | (1897-1991) |
| Carey, Mariah | Singer | (1970-    ) |
| Carson, Johnny | Comedian, TV entertainer | (1925-2005) |
| Cash, Johnny | Country musician | (1932-2003) |
| Charles, Ray | Blues & rock musician | (1930-2004) |
| Cher | Actress | (1946-    ) |
| Clark, Dick | TV entertainer | (1929-2012) |
| Close, Glenn | Actress | (1947-    ) |
| Cody, Buffalo Bill | Creator of wild west show | (1846-1917) |
| Como, Perry | Singer | (1912-2001) |
| Connery, Sean | Actor | (1930-    ) |
| Coppola, Francis Ford | Director | (1939-    ) |
| Cosby, Bill | Actor, comedian | (1937-    ) |
| Costner, Kevin | Actor, director | (1955-    ) |
| Crosby, Bing | Actor, singer | (1904-1977) |
| Cruise, Tom | Actor | (1962-    ) |
| Davis, Bette | Actress | (1908-1990) |
| Davis, Sammy Jr. | Actor, singer | (1925-1990) |
| De Niro, Robert | Actor | (1943-    ) |
| Denver, John | Singer | (1943-1997) |
| Dietrich, Marlene | Actress | (1901-1992) |
| Dillon, Matt | Actor | (1964-    ) |
| Disney, Walt | Director, cartoonist | (1901-1966) |
| Domino, Fats | Musician | (1928-    ) |
| Donahue, Phil | Talk show host | (1935-    ) |
| Douglas, Michael | Actor | (1944-    ) |
| Dunaway, Faye | Actress | (1941-    ) |
| Duvall, Robert | Actor | (1931-    ) |
| Dylan, Bob | Rock musician | (1941-    ) |
| Eastwood, Clint | Actor, director | (1930-    ) |
| Ellington, Duke | Composer, pianist, band leader | (1899-1974) |
| Feliciano, Jose | Singer, guitarist, song writer | (1945-    ) |
| Fiedler, Arthur | Conductor | (1894-1979) |

| | | |
|---|---|---|
| Fields, W. C. | Actor, comedian | (1880-1946) |
| Fitzgerald, Ella | Jazz musician | (1918-1996) |
| Flynn, Errol | Actor | (1909-1959) |
| Fonda, Henry | Actor | (1905-1982) |
| Fonda, Jane | Actress | (1937-    ) |
| Fontaine, Joan | Actress | (1917-2013) |
| Ford, Harrison | Actor | (1942-    ) |
| Fosse, Bob | Director | (1927-1987) |
| Foster, Jodie | Actress | (1962-    ) |
| Franklin, Aretha | Soul and Gospel singer | (1942-    ) |
| Gable, Clark | Actor | (1901-1960) |
| Gabor, Zsa Zsa | Actress | (1917-    ) |
| Garbo, Greta | Actress | (1905-1990) |
| Garland, Judy | Actress | (1922-1969) |
| Gershwin, George | Composer | (1898-1937) |
| Gish, Lillian | Actress | (1896-1993) |
| Goldberg, Whoopi | Actress, commedienne | (1949-    ) |
| Griffin, Merv | Producer | (1925-    ) |
| Griffith, Andy | Actor | (1926-2012) |
| Guthrie, Woody | Folk singer | (1912-1967) |
| Hanks, Tom | Actor | (1956-    ) |
| Hayworth, Rita | Actress | (1918-1987) |
| Hendrix, Jimi | Rock musician | (1942-1970) |
| Henie, Sonja | Actress, skater | (1910-1969) |
| Hepburn, Audrey | Actress | (1929-1993) |
| Hepburn, Katharine | Actress | (1909-2003) |
| Heston, Charlton | Actor | (1923-2008) |
| Hines, Gregory | Actor, tap dancer | (1946-2003) |
| Hitchcock, Alfred | Director | (1899-1980) |
| Ho, Don | Singer | (1930-2007) |
| Hoffman, Dustin | Actor | (1937-    ) |
| Holiday, Billie | Blues singer | (1915-1959) |
| Hope, Bob | Comedian | (1903-2003) |
| Horne, Lena | Singer | (1917-2010) |
| Houdini, Harry | Magician | (1874-1926) |
| Huston, John | Director | (1906-1987) |
| Iglesias, Julio | Singer | (1943-    ) |
| Ives, Burl | Folk singer | (1909-1995) |
| Jackson, Michael | Rock musician | (1958-2009) |
| Jagger, Mick | Rock musician | (1943-    ) |
| John, Elton | Rock musician | (1947-    ) |
| Jolie, Angelina | Movie actress, model | (1975-    ) |
| Jones, James Earl | Actor | (1931-    ) |
| Joplin, Scott | Composer, pianist | (1868-1917) |
| Keaton, Diane | Actress | (1946-    ) |
| Keillor, Garrison | Writer, comedian, radio host | (1942-    ) |
| Kelly, Grace | Actress | (1929-1982) |
| King, B.B. | Blues musician | (1925-    ) |
| Lancaster, Burt | Actor | (1913-1994) |
| Landon, Michael | Actor | (1936-1991) |
| Lansbury, Angela | Actress | (1925-    ) |
| Lee, Spike | Director | (1957-    ) |
| Lennon, John | Rock musician, composer | (1940-1980) |
| Leno, Jay | Talk show host | (1950-    ) |
| Letterman, David | Talk show host | (1947-    ) |
| Lewis, Jerry | Comedian, Actor | (1935-    ) |

| | | |
|---|---|---|
| Liberace | Pianist | (1919-1987) |
| Lloyd-Webber, Andrew | Composer | (1948- ) |
| MacLaine, Shirley | Actress | (1934- ) |
| Madonna | Rock singer, actress | (1958- ) |
| Martin, Steve | Actor, comedian | (1945- ) |
| Marx, Groucho | Actor, comedian | (1890-1977) |
| McEntire, Reba | Country musician | (1955- ) |
| Miller, Glenn | Band leader | (1904-1944) |
| Monroe, Marilyn | Actress | (1926-1962) |
| Morrison, Jim | Rock singer | (1943-1971) |
| Murphy, Eddie | Actor, comedian | (1961- ) |
| Nelson, Willie | Country singer | (1933- ) |
| Newman, Paul | Actor | (1925-2008) |
| Nicholson, Jack | Actor | (1937- ) |
| Nimoy, Leonard | Director, actor | (1931- ) |
| Oakley, Annie | Sharp shooter | (1860-1926) |
| Orbison, Roy | Rock musician | (1936-1988) |
| Ozawa, Seiji | Conductor | (1935- ) |
| Parton, Dolly | Actress, country singer | (1946- ) |
| Peck, Gregory | Actor | (1916-2003) |
| Pitt, Brad | Actor | (1963- ) |
| Poitier, Sidney | Actor | (1927- ) |
| Porter, Cole | Composer | (1893-1964) |
| Presley, Elvis | Actor, rock singer | (1935-1977) |
| Quinn, Anthony | Actor | (1915-2001) |
| Redford, Robert | Actor | (1937- ) |
| Roberts, Julia | Actress | (1967- ) |
| Rogers, Ginger | Actress, dancer, singer | (1911-1995) |
| Schwarzenegger, Arnold | Actor, weigh lifter, governor | (1947- ) |
| Scorsese, Martin | Director | (1942- ) |
| Scott, George C. | Actor | (1927- ) |
| Selznick, David O. | Producer | (1902-1965) |
| Shepard, Sam | Actor, playwright | (1943- ) |
| Simon, Paul | Singer, musician | (1942- ) |
| Sinatra, Frank | Singer | (1915-1998) |
| Sousa, John Philip | Composer | (1854-1932) |
| Spielberg, Steven | Director | (1947- ) |
| Springsteen, Bruce | Rock musician | (1949- ) |
| Stallone, Sylvester | Actor | (1946- ) |
| Stewart, James | Actor | (1908-1997) |
| Stone, Oliver | Director | (1946- ) |
| Stravinsky, Igor | Composer | (1882-1971) |
| Streep, Meryl | Actress | (1949- ) |
| Streisand, Barbra | Singer, actress | (1942- ) |
| Sullivan, Ed | Variety show host | (1901-1974) |
| Taylor, Elizabeth | Actress | (1932-2011) |
| Temple, Shirley | Actress | (1928-2012) |
| Tracy, Spencer | Actor | (1900-1967) |
| Turner, Tina | Rock musician, actress | (1939- ) |
| Waller, Fats | Composer | (1904-1943) |
| Wayne, John | Actor | (1907-1979) |
| Welk, Lawrence | Band leader | (1903-1992) |
| Welles, Orson | Director | (1915-1985) |
| West, Mae | Actress | (1893-1980) |
| Williams, Hank | Country musician | (1923-1953) |
| Winfrey, Oprah | Talk show host, actress | (1954- ) |

# 15: Heroes

## Folk Heroes and Cultural Icons

Horatio Alger
Muhammad Ali
Johnny Appleseed
Billy the Kid
Bonnie and Clyde
Buffalo Bill
Daniel Boone
John Brown
Paul Bunyan
Al Capone
Kit Carson
Cesar Chavez
Davy Crockett
James Dean
Amelia Earhart
Wyatt Earp
Thomas Edison
Benjamin Franklin

Barbara Fritchie
John Henry
Wild Bill Hickock
Jesse James
Casey Jones
Martin Luther King, Jr.
Charles Lindbergh
Malcolm X
Marilyn Monroe
Mickey Mouse
John Muir
Annie Oakley
Jessie Owens
Rosa Parks
Pecos Bill
Molly Pitcher
Pocahontas
Elvis Presley

Paul Revere
Jackie Robinson
Betsy Ross
Babe Ruth
Tom Swift
Uncle Sam
Rip Van Winkle
Sergeant York

## Presidential Icons

George Washington
Thomas Jefferson
Andrew Jackson

Abraham Lincoln
Teddy Roosevelt
Franklin Roosevelt

## Comic Book/Cartoon/Action & Anime Movie Stars and Superheroes

Aquaman
Bart & Homer Simpson
Batman and Robin
Ben Ten
Betty Boop
Black Panther
Bugs Bunny
Calvin and Hobbes
Captain America
Captain Marvel
Catwoman
Charlie Brown
CyclopsDaffy Duck
Dagwood and Blondie
Dexter, Boy Genius
Donald Duck
Elmer Fudd

the Flash
Fred Flintstone
Garfield
Cats and Casco
Gene Gray
George Jetson
Green Arrow
Green Goblin
Green Lantern
the Incredible Hulk
the Inhumans Iron
Man
the Joker
Little Orphan Annie
Lex Luthor
Loki
Magneto

Mickey Mouse
Mike Doonesbury
Motoko Kusanagi
   & Batou
Mystique
Dr. Octopus
Doctor Strange
Peter Griffon
Penguin
Pikachu
Poison Ivy
Popeye
Princess Nausica
Professor X
Samurai Jack
Scooby Doo
Snoopy

Spiderman
Spike and Jet
Sponge-Bob
   Square Pants
Superman
Sylvester and Tweety
Teenage Mutant Ninja
   Turtles
Tesuo, Kanedo, & Akira
Thor
Tintin and Snowy
Vash the Stampede
Wile E. Coyote
   and the Roadrunner
Wolverine
Wonder Woman
Woody Woodpecker

# 16: Recent Nobel Peace Prize Winners

*2014* **Kailash Satyarthi and Malala Yousafzai** for their struggle against oppression of young people and children and for children's right to educaton. "The Nobel Committee regards it as an important point for a Hindu and a Muslim, an Indian and a Pakistani, to join in a common struggle for education and against extremism."

*2013* **Organization for the Prohibition of Chemical Weapons**, international,  for its extensive efforts to eliminate chemical weapons.

*2012* **European Union** , Europe, for having over six decades contributed to the advancement of peace and reconciliation, democracy, and human rights in Europe.

*2011* **Ellen Johnson Sirleaf** and **Leymath Gbowee**, Liberia, for their non-violent struggle for the safety of women and for women's rights to full participation in peace-building work.

*2010* **Liu Xiaobo**, China, for his long and non-violent struggle for fundamental human rights in China.

*2009* **Barak Obama**, President of the United States, for his extraordinary efforts to strengthen international diplomacy and cooperation among peoples.

*2008* **Martti Ahtisaari**, Finland, for his efforts, on several continents and over more than three decades, to resolve international conflicts.

*2007* **Intergovernmental Panel on Climate Change**, United Nations, **and Al Gore**, United States, for their efforts to build up and disseminate greater knowledge about man-made climate change, and to lay the foundations for the measures that are needed to counteract such change.

*2006* **Muhammad Yunus** and **the Grameen Bank**, Bangladesh, for advancing economic and social oportunities for the poor, especially women, through pioneering microcredit work.

*2005* **International Atomic Energy Agency**, United Nations, and **Mohamed ElBaradei**, Egypt, for their efforts to prevent nuclear energy from being used for military purposes and to ensure that nuclear energy for peaceful purposes is used in the safest possible way.

*2004* **Wangari Maathai** , Kenya, for her contribution to sustainable development, democracy, and peace,

*2003* **Shirin Ebadi**, Iran, for her efforts for democracy and human rights.

*2002* **Jimmy Carter, Jr.**, former President of the United States of America, for his decades of untiring effort to find peaceful solutions to international conflicts, to advance democracy and human rights, and to promote economic and social development

*2001* **The United Nations** and **Kofi Annan,** United Nations Secretary General

*2000* **Kim Dae Jung** for his work for democracy and human rights in South Korea and in East Asia in general, and for peace and reconciliation with North Korea in particular.

*1999* **Doctors without Borders (Médecins sans Frontiéres),** Brussels, Belgium.

*1998* **John Hume** and **David Trimble** for their efforts to find a peaceful solution to the conflict in Northern Ireland.

*1997* **The International Campaign to Ban Landmines (ICBL)** and **Jody Williams** for their work for the banning and clearing of anti-personnel mines.

*1996* **Carlos Felipe Ximenes Belo** and **Jose Ramos-Horta** for their work towards a just and peaceful solution to the conflict in East Timor.

*1995* **Joseph Rotblat** and **the Pugwash Conferences on Science and World Affairs** for their efforts to diminish the part played by nuclear arms in international politics and in the longer run to eliminate such arms.

*1994* **Yasser Arafat**, Chairman of the Executive Committee of the PLO, President of the Palestinian National Authority, **Shimon Peres** , Foreign Minister of Israel, and **Yitzhak Rabin,** Prime Minister of Israel, for their efforts to create peace in the Middle East.

*1993* **Nelson Mandela,** Leader of the African National Congress, and **Fredrick Willem de Klerk,** President of the Republic of South Africa.

*1992* **Rigoberta Menchu Tum,** Guatemala. Campaigner for human rights, especially for indigenous peoples.

*1991* **Aung San Suu Kyi**, Burma. Oppositional leader, human rights advocate.

*1990* **Mikhail Sergeyevich Gorbachev,** President of the USSR, helped to bring the Cold War to an end.

*1989* **The 14th Dalai Lama (Tenzin Gyatso)**, Tibet. Religious and political leader of the Tibetan people.

*1988* **The United Nations Peace-Keeping Forces.**

*1987* **Oscar Arias Sanchez,** Costa Rica, President of Costa Rica, initiator of peace negotiations in Central America.

*1986* **Elie Wiesel,** U.S.A., Chairman of *The President's Commission on the Holocaust.* Author, humanitarian.

*1985* **International Physicians for the Prevention of Nuclear War,** Boston, MA, U.S.A.

*1984* **Desmond Mpilo Tutu**, South Africa, Bishop of Johannesburg, former Secretary General South African Council of Churches (S.A.C.C.). for his work against apartheid.

*1983* **Lech Walesa,** Poland. Founder of Solidarity, campaigner for human rights.

*1982* **Alva Myrdal**, former Cabinet Minister, diplomat, delegate to United Nations General Assembly on Disarmament, writer, and **Alfonso García Robles**, diplomat, delegate to the United Nations General Assembly on Disarmament, former Secretary for Foreign Affairs .

*1981* **Office of the United Nations High Commissioner for Refugees,**Geneva, Switzerland.

## Other Nobel Prizes

Literature
Economics
Physiology and Medicine
Physics
Chemistry

Information from The Nobel Prize Internet Archive http://almaz.com/nobel/nobel.html

# 17: Points of Interest

| United States | Site |
|---|---|
| Alabama | First capital of the Confederacy in Montgomery |
| Alaska | Denali National Park, wildlife sanctuary surrounding Mt. McKinley |
| Arizona | Taliesin West in Scottsdale, home of Frank Lloyd Wright |
| Arkansas | Eureka Springs, resort since 1880s |
| California | Disneyland in Anaheim |
| Colorado | Mesa Verde National Park, cliff-dwelling Indians' cities |
| Connecticut | Mark Twain House in Hartford |
| Delaware | John Dickinson home in Dover, residence of "Penman of the Revolution" |
| Florida | Cape Kennedy, NASA Space Center |
|  | Saint Augustine, oldest city in U.S., est. by Spanish in 1565 |
| Georgia | Chickamauga Battlefield Park, site of decisive 1863 victory for South in Civil War |
| Hawaii | Iolani Palace in Honolulu, last residence of Hawaiian royalty |
| Idaho | Hell's Canyon, deepest gorge in North America |
| Illinois | Lincoln shrines in Springfield, New Salem and Sangamon |
| Indiana | Fort Vincennes, one of the first white settlements west of the Appalachians |
| Iowa | Herbert Hoover birthplace and library in West Branch |
| Kansas | Dodge City, frontier town on Santa Fe Trail |
| Kentucky | Churchill Downs in Louisville, home of Kentucky Derby since 1875 |
| Louisiana | Mardi Gras in New Orleans |
| Maine | Seacoast, Acadia National Park |
| Maryland | U.S. Naval Academy in Annapolis |
| Massachusetts | Plymouth Plantation, pilgrims' first colony |
|  | Old North Church in Boston, beginning of Paul Revere's ride |
|  | Witch trials in Salem in 1692 |
| Michigan | Sault Ste. Marie, French settlement est. 1668 |
| Minnesota | Minnehaha Falls in Minneapolis, inspiration for Longfellow's "Hiawatha" |
| Mississippi | Vicksburg National Military Park and Cemetery |
| Missouri | Pony Express Museum in St. Joseph |
| Montana | Custer Battlefield National Cemetery at Little Bighorn River |
| Nebraska | Buffalo Bill Ranch State Historical Park in Nebraska City |
| Nevada | Legalized gambling casinos in Las Vegas, Reno and Tahoe |
| New Hampshire | Strawbery Banke in Portsmouth, historical buildings dating to 17th century |
| New Jersey | Miss America Pageant and casinos in Atlantic City |
| New Mexico | Carlsbad Caverns, a national park with caverns on three levels and the largest natural cave in the world |
| New York | Ellis Island, immigration station for East Coast |
| North Carolina | Kitty Hawk, Wright brothers' first flight |
|  | Roanoke Island, first English colony in America |
| North Dakota | Theodore Roosevelt National Park in Badlands, contains the president's Elkhorn Ranch |
| Ohio | Mound City National Monuments, group of 24 prehistoric Indian burial mounds |

## States                    ## Site

| States | Site |
|---|---|
| Oklahoma | National Cowboy Hall of Fame, Oklahoma City |
| Oregon | Columbia River Gorge |
| Pennsylvania | Valley Forge, encampment grounds for Gen. Washington and troops in 1777, Gettysburg, site of Civil War battle, turning point in war for Union |
| Rhode Island | John Brown House in Providence, residence of 18th century merchant |
| South Carolina | Fort Sumter National Monument, Union troops were overrun by Confederate soldiers to start the Civil War in 1861 |
| South Dakota | Black Hills |
| Tennessee | Graceland in Memphis, home of Elvis Presley |
|  | The Grand Ole Opry in Nashville, country music show est. 1925 |
| Texas | The Alamo in San Antonio, fort was overrun by Santa Anna in1836 |
| Utah | Temple Square in Salt Lake City, Mormon Church headquarters |
| Vermont | Bennington Battle Museum |
| Virginia | Monticello in Charlottesville, Jefferson's home, Mount Vernon, Washington home |
|  | Appomattox, site of surrender of Gen. Lee and Confederacy in 1865 |
|  | Lexington, birthplace and tomb of Gen. Lee |
|  | Mount St. Helens, volcanic eruption in 1989 |
| Washington | Harper's Ferry, John Brown led slave uprising in 1859 |
| West Virginia | Heritage Hill in Green Bay, museum of historical buildings and artifacts |
| Wisconsin | Yellowstone National Park |
| Wyoming | Washington Monument, Lincoln Memorial, Jefferson Memorial, National Archives |
| District of Columbia | Franklin Delano Roosevelt Memorial, U, S. Capitol, White House, World War II, Korean War Memorial, Vietnam War Memorial, Smithsonian Institution, museums |

## Canadian Provinces

| Province | Points of Interest |
|---|---|
| Alberta | Lake Louise, Banff, wildlife, Canadian Rockies |
| British Columbia | Kelowna, Okanagan Valley, Vancouver, Victoria and Vancouver Island, Vancouver to Banff train ride |
| Ontario | Ottawa (Capital of Canada), Parliament Hill, changing of the guard, Niagara Falls |
| Manitoba | Winnipeg, Assiniboine Park, Riding Mountain Park, Eskimo Museum |
| New Brunswick | Churchill, polar bears, beluga whales, aurora borealis/northern lights |
| New Foundland | Bay of Fundy, St. John Reversing Falls, King's Landing and Arcadian Historic Sites |
| Northwest Territories | Yellow Knife, Old Town, Visitors Centers: Northern Heritage, Northern Frontier, Frame Lake Trail, Twin Falls and Nahanni Parks, Mackenzie River |
| Prince Edward I | beaches and red cliffs, Confederation Bridge, mussels, light house, Green Gables |
| Nova Scotia | Halifax, Bay of Fundy, beaches, Truro Victoria Park, lighthouses, Cape Breton |
| Nunavut | Arctic outdoor and nature/wildlife adventures, Inuit culture, Unikkaarvik Centre |
| Quebec | Chateau Frontenac, Old Quebec on the St. Lawrence River, Montreal |
| Saskatchewan | Cultural museums and events, dinosaur exhibits, outdoor adventure |
| Yukon | Whitehorse, Yukon River, Kluane Park, Klondike Highway Gold Rush route |

# 18: National Parks

| Name | Location | Est. | Features |
|------|----------|------|----------|
| Acadia | Maine | 1916 | Mt. Desert Island and adjacent mainland |
| Arches | Utah | 1929 | Stone arches and pedestals caused by erosion |
| Badlands | South Dakota | 1929 | Arid land inhabited by bison, antelope, deer |
| Big Bend | Texas | 1935 | Mountains and desert bordering Rio Grande |
| Biscayne | Florida | 1968 | Coral reef south of Miami |
| Black Canyon | Colorado | 1999 | Deep, narrow canyon of the Gunnison |
| Bryce Canyon | Utah | 1923 | Brilliantly colored eroded rocks |
| Canyonlands | Utah | 1964 | Red-rock canyons, spires and arches |
| Capitol Reef | Utah | 1937 | Sedimentary rock formations in high narrow gorges |
| Carlsbad Caverns | New Mexico | 1923 | World's largest known caves |
| Channel Islands | California | 1938 | Marine mammals, endangered species, archaeology |
| Congaree | South Carolina | 2003 | Largest old-growth flood plain, hardwood forest in N. America |
| Crater Lake | Oregon | 1902 | Lake in the heart of an inactive volcano |
| Cuyahoga Valley | Ohio | 2000 | Meandering river valley, old forests, farmland, rail journeys |
| Death Valley | California, Nevada | 1994 | Large desert: lowest point in the hemisphere |
| Denali | Alaska | 1917 | North America's highest mountain, Mt. McKinley, 20,320 ft. |
| Dry Tortugas | Florida | 1992 | Offshore islands; marine life |
| Everglades | Florida | 1934 | Subtropical swamp |
| Gates of the Arctic | Alaska | 1978 | Diverse wilderness, part of the Brooks Range |
| Glacier | Montana | 1910 | Rocky Mountains |
| Glacier Bay | Alaska | 1925 | Whales, glaciers |
| Grand Canyon | Arizona | 1908 | Mile-deep gorge, 4-18 miles wide, 217 miles long |
| Grand Teton | Wyoming | 1929 | High mountain range |
| Great Basin | Nevada | 1922 | Biological and geological attractions |
| Great Smoky Mts. | NC, TN | 1926 | Highest mountain range east of Black Hills |
| Guadalupe Mts. | Texas | 1966 | Highest peak in Texas (8,751 ft.) |
| Haleakala | Hawaii | 1916 | Dormant Haleakala volcano (10,023 ft.) |
| Hawaii Volcanoes | Hawaii | 1916 | Volcanoes, luxuriant vegetation at lower levels |
| Hot Springs | Arkansas | 1832 | 47 hot springs |
| Isle Royale | Michigan | 1931 | Largest wilderness island in Lake Superior |
| Joshua Tree | California | 1994 | Desert region |
| Katmai | Alaska | 1918 | Dormant volcano, bears |
| Kenai Fjords | Alaska | 1978 | Mountain goats, marine mammals, birdlife |
| Kings Canyon | California | 1890 | Huge canyons, high mountains, giant sequoias |
| Kobuk Valley | Alaska | 1978 | Native culture and anthropology center |
| Lake Clark | Alaska | 1978 | Across Cook Inlet from Anchorage |
| Lassen Volcanic | California | 1907 | Impressive volcanic phenomena |
| Mammoth Cave | Kentucky | 1926 | Limestone labyrinth with underground river |
| Mesa Verde | Colorado | 1906 | Best-preserved prehistoric cliff dwellings in U.S. |
| Mount Rainier | Washington | 1899 | Single peak glacial system, dense forest |
| North Cascades | Washington | 1968 | Alpine landscape, glaciers, mountain lakes |
| Olympic | Washington | 1909 | Finest Pacific Northwest rainforest |
| Petrified Forest | Arizona | 1906 | Extensive natural exhibit of petrified wood |
| Redwood | California | 1968 | Coastal redwood forests, world's tallest known tree |
| Rocky Mountain | Colorado | 1915 | 107 named Rocky Mountain peaks over 10,000 ft. |
| Saguaro | Arizona | 1994 | Giant cactus |
| Samoa | American Samoa | 1988 | Two rainforest preserves and a coral reef |
| Sequoia | California | 1890 | World's largest trees |
| Shenandoah | Virginia | 1926 | Scenic Skyline Drive |
| Theodore Roosevelt | North Dakota | 1947 | Roosevelt Ranch, valley of the Little Missouri River |
| Virgin Islands | U.S. Virgin Islands | 1956 | Prehistoric Caribbean Indian relics, beaches |
| Voyageurs | Minnesota | 1971 | Wildlife, canoeing, fishing, hiking |
| Wind Cave | South Dakota | 1903 | Limestone caverns in the Black Hills, buffalo herd |
| Wolf Trap Farm | Virginia | 2003 | First park for the performing arts |
| Wrangell-St. Elias | Alaska | 1978 | Second highest peak in U.S. (Mt. Elias) |
| Yellowstone | WY, MT, ID | 1872 | World's greatest geyser area, falls and canyons |
| Yosemite | California | 1890 | Giant sequoias, enormous gorges and waterfalls |
| Zion | Utah | 1909 | Multicolored gorge in southwestern Utah desert |

# 19: Natural Features

## United States

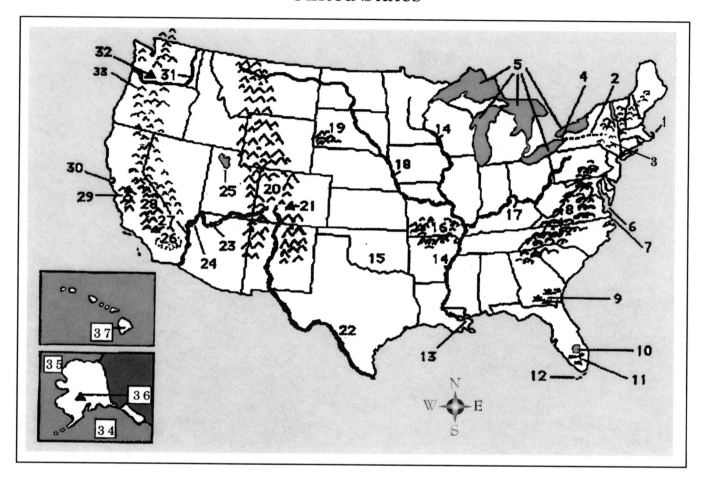

1. Cape Cod
2. Erie Canal
3. Catskill Mountains
4. Niagara Falls
5. Great Lakes
6. Chesapeake Bay
7. Cape Hatteras
8. Appalachian Mountains
9. Okefenokee Swamp
10. Lake Okeechobee
11. Everglades Swamp
12. Key West (islands)
13. Mississippi Delta

14. Mississippi River
15. Arkansas River
16. Ozark Mountains
17. Ohio River
18. Missouri River
19. Black Hills
20. Rocky Mountains
21. Pike's Peak
22. Rio Grande
23. Grand Canyon
24. Colorado River
25. Great Salt Lake

26. Death Valley
27. Mt. Whitney
28. Sierra Nevada Mountains
29. Big Sur Coastline
30. San Francisco Bay
31. Columbia River
32. Mt. St. Helens
33. Cascade Range
34. Aleutian Islands
35. Bering Strait
36. Denali (Mt. McKinley)
37. Kilauea Volcano

# Natural Features of Canada

| | |
|---|---|
| 1. Hudson Bay | 11. St. Lawrence River |
| 2. Jasper and Banff National Parks | 12. Gulf of St. Lawrence |
| 3. Great Slave Lake | 13. Bay of Fundy |
| 4. Great Bear Lake | 14. Labrador Sea |
| 5. Athabasca Lake | 15. Baffin Island |
| 6. Reindeer Lake | 16. Baffin Bay |
| 7. Lake Winnipeg | 17. Victoria Island |
| 8. Coast Range | 18. Bank Island |
| 9. North Rocky Mountains | 19. Queen Elizabeth Islands |
| 10. Maritime Provinces | 20. Ellesmere Island |

# 20: Important Days and Holidays

| US Holidays | Date | *Federal legal holidays in the U.S.* |
|---|---|---|
| * New Year's Day | January 1 | |
| *Martin Luther King Day | Third Monday in January | |
| Chinese New Year | First new moon after the sun enters Aquarius | |
| Groundhog Day | February 2 | |
| Boy Scouts' Day | February 8 | |
| Lincoln's Birthday | February 12 | |
| Saint Valentine's Day | February 14 | |
| Susan B. Anthony Day | February 15 | |
| *Presidents' Day | Third Monday in February | |
| Washington's Birthday | February 22 | |
| Leap Year Day | February 29 | |
| Johnny Appleseed Day | March 11 | |
| Girl Scouts' Day | March 12 | |
| St. Patrick's Day | March 17 | |
| April Fool's Day | April 1 | |
| World Health Day | April 7 | |
| Jefferson's Birthday | April 13 | |
| Income taxes due | April 15 | |
| Patriots' Day | April 19 | |
| National Secretaries' Day | April 23 | |
| Arbor Day | Last Tuesday in April | |
| May Day | May 1 | |
| Law Day | May 1 | |
| Lei Day (Hawaii) | May 1 | |
| Cinco de Mayo | May 5 | |
| Mother's Day | Second Sunday in May | |
| *Memorial Day | Last Monday in May | |
| Children's Day | June 8 | |
| Flag Day | June 14 | |
| Emancipation Day | June 19 | |
| Fathers' Day | Third Sunday in June | |
| *Independence Day | July 4 | |
| *Labor Day | First Monday in September | |
| Grandparents' Day | September 7 | |
| Citizenship Day | September 17 | |
| World Peace Day | September 21 | |
| Native American Day | September 26 | |
| Leif Erikson Day | October 9 | |
| *Columbus Day | Second Monday in October | |
| Halloween | October 31 | |
| Election Day | First Tuesday after the first Monday in November | |
| *Veterans' Day | November 11 | |
| *Thanksgiving | Fourth Thursday in November | |
| Human Rights Day | December 10 | |
| Bill of Rights Day | December 15 | |
| *Christmas | December 25 | |
| Kwanzaa | December 26 - January 1 | |

## Canadian Federal Holidays

| | | | |
|---|---|---|---|
| Victoria Day | Penultimate Monday in May | Thanksgiving Day | 2nd Monday in October |
| Canada Day | July 1 | Remembrance Day | November 11 |
| Labour Day | 1st Monday in September | Boxing Day | December 26 |

## Major Jewish and Christian Holidays

| Holiday | Religion | Date |
|---|---|---|
| Epiphany | Christian | January 6 |
| Three King's Day | Christian | January 6 |
| Eastern Orthodox Christmas | Christian | January 7 |
| Shrove Tuesday (Mardi Gras) | Christian | Day before Ash Wednesday |
| Ash Wednesday | Christian | 40 days (excluding Sundays) before Easter |
| World Day of Prayer | Inter-faith | March 7 |
| Saint Patrick's Day | Christian | March 17 |
| Palm Sunday | Christian | Sunday before Easter |
| Purim (Feast of Lots) | Jewish | 14th or 15th of Hebrew month of Adar |
| Good Friday | Christian | Friday before Easter Sunday |
| Easter Sunday | Christian | The first Sunday after the full moon occurring on or after March 21 |
| Passover (Pesach) | Jewish | 15-22 of Hebrew month of Nisan |
| Ascension Day | Christian | Ten days before Pentecost |
| Pentecost | Christian | 50 days after Easter |
| Trinity Sunday | Christian | Sunday after Pentecost |
| Shavuot (Feast of Weeks) | Jewish | 6th or 7th of Hebrew month of Sivan |
| Rosh Hashanah (New Year) | Jewish | First day of Hebrew month of Tishri |
| Yom Kippur (Day of Atonement) | Jewish | 10th day of Tishri |
| Sukkot (Tabernacles) | Jewish | 15-21 Tishri |
| All Saint's Day | Christian | November 1 |
| Advent | Christian | Four-week period before Christmas |
| Baha'U'Llah Birthday | Baha'i | November 12 |
| Saint Lucia's Day | Christian | December 13 |
| Christmas | Christian | December 25 |
| Hanukkah | Jewish | 25th of Hebrew month of Kislev |

## Major Islamic Holidays

**Note:** Because the Muslim calendar, containing only 354 days, is shorter than the Gregorian calendar Islamic holidays do not always fall on the same days of the Gregorian calendar and so are listed seperately.

| Holiday | Date |
|---|---|
| Islamic New Year | First day of Islamic month of Muharram |
| Mawlid an-Nabi (Muhammad's Birthday) | 12th of Islamic month of Rabi |
| Fast of Ramadan | 9th month of Islamic calendar |
| Id al-Fitr (Festival of Fast Breaking) | 29th or 30th of Ramadan to 3rd of following month of Shawwal |
| Beiram (The first day of spring) | 10th of Islamic month of Zu'lhijjah |
| Id al-Adhh (The Great Festival) | 10th to 13th of the Islamic month of Zu'lhijjah |

# 21: Major Religions

## Major Religious Groups in the U.S.
### *(Pew Forum on Religion and Public Life)*

Christians    78.4%
    Protestant    51.3%
        Evangelical churches    26.3%
        Mainline churches    18.1%
        Historically Black    6.9%
    Roman Catholic    23.9%
    Mormon    1.7%
    Jehovah's Witnesses    0.7%
    Orthodox    0.6%
        Greek    0.3%
        Russian    0.3%
        Other    0.3%
    Other Christian    0.3%
Other Religions    4.7%
    Jewish    1.7%
        Reform    0.7%
        Conservative        0.5%
        Orthodox    0.3%
        Other    0.3%
    Buddhist    0.7%
        Zen Buddhist    0.3%
        Theravada Buddhist    0.3%
        Tibetan Buddhist    0.3%
        Other    0.3%
    Muslim    0.6%
        Sunni    0.3%
        Shia    0.3%
        Other    0.3%
    Hindu    0.4%
    Other World Religions    0.3%
    Other Faiths            1.2%
        Unitarians and other    0.7%
        liberal faiths
        New Age    0.4%
        Native American    0.3%
Unaffiliated    16.1%
    Atheist    1.6%
    Agnostic    2.4%
    Nothing in Particular    12.1%
Don't Know/Refused    0.8%

# Other Survey Highlights from the Pew Survey

Men are significantly more likely than women to claim no religious affiliation. Nearly one-in-five men say they have no formal religious affiliation, compared with roughly 13% of women.

Among people who are married, nearly four-in-ten (37%) are married to a spouse with a different religious affiliation. (This figure includes Protestants who are married to another Protestant from a different denominational family, such as a Baptist who is married to a Methodist.) Hindus and Mormons are the most likely to be married (78% and 71%, respectively) and to be married to someone of the same religion (90% and 83%, respectively).

Mormons and Muslims are the groups with the largest families; more than one-in-five Mormon adults and 15% of Muslim adults in the U.S. have three or more children living at home.

The Midwest most closely resembles the religious makeup of the overall population. The South, by a wide margin, has the heaviest concentration of members of evangelical Protestant churches. The Northeast has the greatest concentration of Catholics, and the West has the largest proportion of unaffiliated people, including the largest proportion of atheists and agnostics.

Of all the major racial and ethnic groups in the United States, black Americans are the most likely to report a formal religious affiliation. Even among those blacks who are unaffiliated, three-in-four belong to the "religious unaffiliated" category (that is, they say that religion is either somewhat or very important in their lives), compared with slightly more than one-third of the unaffiliated population overall.

Nearly half of Hindus in the U.S., one-third of Jews and a quarter of Buddhists have obtained post-graduate education, compared with only about one-in-ten of the adult population overall. Hindus and Jews are also much more likely than other groups to report high income levels.

People not affiliated with any particular religion stand out for their relative youth compared with other religious traditions. Among the unaffiliated, 31% are under age 30 and 71% are under age 50. Comparable numbers for the overall adult population are 20% and 59%, respectively.

By contrast, members of mainline Protestant churches and Jews are older, on average, than members of other groups. Roughly half of Jews and members of mainline churches are age 50 and older, compared with approximately four-in-ten American adults overall.

In sharp contrast to Islam and Hinduism, Buddhism in the U.S. is primarily made up of native-born adherents, whites and converts. Only one-in-three American Buddhists describe their race as Asian, while nearly three-in-four Buddhists say they are converts to Buddhism.

Jehovah's Witnesses have the lowest retention rate of any religious tradition. Only 37% of all those who say they were raised as Jehovah's Witnesses still identify themselves as Jehovah's Witnesses.

Members of Baptist churches account for one-third of all Protestants and close to one-fifth of the total U.S. adult population. Baptists also account for nearly two-thirds of members of historically black Protestant churches.

## Major Religious Groups in Canada (2011)

Christians    67.3%
　　　Protestant    23.9%
　　　Roman Catholic     38.7%
　　　Orthodox    1.7%
　　　Other Christian     3%
Other Religions    8.1%
　　　Jewish    1.0%
　　　Buddhist    1.1%
　　　Sikhism    1,4%
　　　Muslim    2.3%
　　　Hindu    1.5%
　　　Other Faiths  .6%
Non-religious    23.9% Atheist, Agnostic, Nothing in Particular

## Major World  Religions *(source: www.adherents.com)*

### *Religions found concentrated in only one country are indicated with the country name.*

| | | |
|---|---|---|
| Christianity | 2.1 billion | 33% |
| Islam | 1.5 billion | 21% |
| Secular/Non-religious | 1.1 billion | 16% |
| Hindu | 900 million | 14% |
| Chinese Traditional | 394 million | 6.1% |
| Buddhism | 376 million | 5.85% |
| Primal-Indigenous | 300 million | 4.7% |
| African Traditional & Diasporic | 100 million | 1.6% |
| Sikhism | 23 million | .36% |
| Juche (North Korea) | 19 million | .3% |
| Spiritism | 15 million | .25% |
| Judaism | 14 million | .22% |
| Baha'i | 7 million | .11% |
| Jainism (India) | 4.2 million | .063% |
| Shinto (Japan) | 4 million | .06% |
| Cao Dai (Vietnam) | 4 million | .06% |
| Zoroastrianism | 2.6 million | .039% |
| Tenrikyo (Japan) | 2 million | .03% |
| Neo-Paganism | 1 million | .015% |
| Unitarian-Universalist | 800 thousand | .012% |
| Rastafarianism | 600 thousand | .009% |
| Scientology | 500 thousand | .0075% |

# 22: A Brief History of the U.S.

| | |
|---|---|
| c. 1000 | Leif Erikson explores North America. |
| 1492- 1502 | Columbus explores the Caribbean for Spain in four voyages and publicizes the New World. |
| 1497 | John Cabot explores the Northeast American coast to Delaware. |
| 1513 | Juan Ponce de Leon explores Florida, searches for the Fountain of Youth. |
| 1519 | Cortes conquers Mexico. |
| 1539 | Hernando de Soto explores Florida, travels past the Mississippi River. |
| 1540 | Coronado and other Spanish explorers explore Northern Mexico, the Southwest U.S. and California. |
| 1607 | English found Jamestown. |
| 1609 | Henry Hudson explores New York Harbor and the Hudson River; Samuel de Champlain explores Lake Champlain; Santa Fe, New Mexico, founded. |
| 1619 | First black laborers brought to Jamestown as indentured servants. Slavery legalized in 1650. |
| 1620 | Plymouth Plantation, Massachusetts, founded by the Pilgrims, who came on the *Mayflower*. |
| 1626 | Peter Minuet buys Manhattan Island for the Dutch; pays the Indians $24 in trinkets. |
| 1634 | Frenchman Jean Nicolet explores the Great Lakes to Lake Michigan. |
| 1636 | First college, Harvard, founded. Roger Williams founds Rhode Island with democratic rule and religious toleration. |
| 1654 | First Jewish settlers come to New Amsterdam (later New York). |
| 1664 | British seize Dutch colony of New Netherland and rename it New York. |
| 1673 | Father Jacques Marquette and Louis Jolliet explore the upper Mississippi, claiming it for France. |
| 1682 | Sieur de La Salle explores the Mississippi south to the Gulf of Mexico. |
| 1692 | Witchcraft trials in Salem, Massachusetts. |
| 1704 | First regular newspaper, *Boston News Letter,* founded. |
| 1741 | Capt. Vitus Bering discovers Alaska for Russia. |
| 1744-1763 | French lose Canada and Ohio Valley to British after 20 years of war. Indians fight on both sides |

| | |
|---|---|
| 1754-1776 | British attempts to tax and control the colonies cause resentment and rebellion. |
| 1773 | Boston Tea Party. |
| 1775 | Battles of Lexington and Concord—"The shot heard 'round the world." Capture of Fort Ticonderoga, New York, and the Battle of Bunker Hill in Massachusetts are colonial victories. Gen. George Washington takes charge of the colonial army in Boston. |
| 1776 | Colonies declare independence from Britain on July 4. |
| 1777 | First constitution (Articles of the Confederation) adopted. |
| 1781 | British lose Revolutionary War |
| 1784 | Peace treaty signed with British. |
| 1787 | New constitution written and adopted. |
| 1791 | Bill of Rights enacted. |
| 1793 | Eli Whitney's invention of the cotton gin makes slavery profitable for the Southern states. |
| 1797 | Navy started with three ships. |
| 1803 | U.S. under President Thomas Jefferson buys Louisiana from Napoleon. |
| 1804-1806 | Lewis and Clark, with Sacagawea, an Indian woman guide, explore the Louisiana Purchase. |
| 1808 | Slave importation outlawed. Illegal imports continue until 1860. |
| 1812 | War with Britain. |
| 1814 | In Washington, D.C., the new Capitol and White House are burned by British. Peace treaty of Ghent. |
| 1815 | British are defeated in Battle of New Orleans. |
| 1818 | Troops under Gen. Andrew Jackson invade Florida to attack the Seminole Indians and weaken the Spanish government. |
| 1819 | Spain, whose American empire from Chile and Argentina in the south to Mexico and Florida in the north is collapsing, gives Florida to the U.S. |
| 1823 | Monroe Doctrine opposes any new colonies or any European intervention in the Americas. |
| 1825 | The Erie Canal, stretching from the Great Lakes to the Hudson River, is completed. The settlement of the MiddleWest and the growth of its towns and industries is stimulated. New York, New York, the largest city in the U.S. since 1790, expands rapidly. |

1828    "Jacksonian Revolution." The new Democratic Party under Andrew Jackson wins the presidency and takes power in Washington. This first major political change, staged without violence, proves the stability of the government.

1836    Mexican-U.S. struggle for Texas. Mexican Gen. Santa Anna takes the Alamo in San Antonio and is then captured by Sam Houston at San Jacinto.
First wagon train of settlers travels from Missouri to California.

1848    Gold discovered in California. Development of the West is accelerated.

1853    Commodore Matthew C. Perry opens trade with Japan for U.S. ships.

1860    Abraham Lincoln elected.

1861    Seven Southern states withdraw from the U.S., set up the Confederate States of America and start the Civil War.

1863    Lincoln legally frees the slaves. Battle of Gettysburg. Lincoln's Gettysburg address.

1865    Civil War ends with Northern victory. Lincoln is re-elected and then assassinated. Thirteenth Amendment abolishes slavery.

1866    Reconstruction of the South. Ku Klux Klan formed secretly.

1867    U.S. buys Alaska from Russia.

1869    Transcontinental railroad completed. Knights of Labor founded.

1871    Fire burns the center of Chicago.

1872    Amnesty Act restores civil rights to the South.

1876    U.S. Centennial celebrated. Gen. Custer's last stand: 265 soldiers killed by Dakota Indians. Reconstruction ended in the South.

1886    Haymarket riot and other labor unrest. (AFL) American Federation of Labor formed.

1890    "Battle" of Wounded Knee; 200 Indian men, women, and children, and 29 U.S. soldiers killed in last major conflict of the Indian wars. Sherman Antitrust Act begins to curb big business monopolies.

1898    U.S. begins to take an aggressive interest in international affairs. Spanish-American War fought to aid independence of Cuba. U.S. annexes Hawaii.

1899    U.S. attempts to save Chinese independence and make China an international market by declaring the Open Door Policy.

1903    U. S. fosters Panama's independence from Colombia to get treaty to build Panama Canal. Wright brothers fly first airplane at Kitty Hawk.

1906    San Francisco earthquake. Pure Food and Drug and Meat Inspection acts.

1911    Supreme Court breaks up Rockefeller's Standard Oil Co. monopoly.

1914    Henry Ford raises pay of his workers from $2.40 for a nine-hour day to $5 for an eight-hour day so they can afford to buy a car. The sales of Ford cars booms.

1915    The Great War starts in Europe. U.S. remains neutral. Clayton Antitrust Act spurs anti-monopoly suits by federal government. U.S. frees Haiti to make it a "protectorate." U.S. actively supports various factions in Mexican Revolution of 1913-1916. U.S. hegemony expands in Caribbean.

1917    U.S. declares war on Germany. Prohibition amendment submitted; enacted 1919-1933.

1918    World War I ends November 11.

1919    First transatlantic flight.

1920    U.S. refuses to join the League of Nations.

1921    Congress curbs immigration and sets national quotas. Ku Klux Klan revives terror against blacks and Jewish Americans.

1924    Indians are made U.S. citizens.

1925    Scopes Monkey Trial dramatizes the changing understanding of evolution, science versus religion, and education in the U.S.

1926    Robert Goddard fires first fuel rocket.

1927    Marines are sent into China to protect U.S. interests during civil war. Charles Lindbergh crosses Atlantic solo.

1929    St. Valentine's Day Massacre dramatizes the power and violence of gangsters. Stock market crash begins the Great Depression.

1932    Roosevelt initiates new federalist approach to solving the crisis in the economy. To give Americans a "New Deal" and try to end the Depression, Roosevelt rapidly increases the size and spending of the federal government over the next eight years.

1935    Committee for Industrial Organization (CIO) forms, promoting stronger unions in auto, steel and other heavy industry. Congress passes the Social Security Act.

1939    World War II begins in Europe. U.S. remains neutral but rearms and supports Britain more and more actively through 1941.

1941    Japan attacks Pearl Harbor December 7. U.S. declares war on Axis Powers (Japan, Germany and Italy).

1945    Germany surrenders May 7. First atomic bomb dropped on Hiroshima August 6. Second atomic bomb destroys Nagasaki August 9. Japan surrenders August 15. United Nations founded.

| | |
|---|---|
| 1946 | Philippines given independence by U.S. on July 4. |
| 1947 | Truman Doctrine combats communism. The Marshall Plan aids reconstruction in Europe. Congress passes the Taft-Hartley Labor Relations Act over President Truman's veto to curb strikes. |
| 1948 | U.S.S.R. blockades West Berlin. British and U.S. break blockade with a massive airlift. Organization of American States founded. |
| 1949 | NATO founded for mutual protection of West Europe, Canada and U.S. People's Republic of China established under Mao Tse-tung; U.S. refuses recognition and maintains relations with the Nationalist government in exile in Taiwan (Formosa). |
| 1950 | Korean War begins; UN (including U.S.) sides with South Korea against Communist China-backed North Korea. U.S. agrees to give economic and military support to South Vietnam. |
| 1951 | Senate investigations, led by Estes Kefauver, expose the power of the Mafia and organized crime. Popular Gen. Douglas MacArthur is fired from his command in Korea. |
| 1953 | Peace is declared in Korea. U.S. supports anti-communists with massive aid in Indochina War. |
| 1954 | Anti-communist investigations by Senator Joseph McCarthy end in his condemnation by Senate. |
| 1955 | AFL-CIO formed. Rosa Parks refuses to give up her bus seat, beginning a citywide boycott in Birmingham, Alabama, led by Martin Luther King, Jr. Federal court overturns bus segregation law. Civil Rights movement gains strength. |
| 1956 | Supreme Court requires schools to desegregate. |
| 1957 | Congress passes the first civil rights bill on voting rights since Reconstruction. |
| 1958 | U.S.S.R.'s successful launch of the first man-made satellite, *Sputnik,* spurs U.S. scientific efforts and the space race. U.S. *Explorer I* launched. |
| 1959 | Alaska and Hawaii become states. St. Lawrence Seaway opens. |
| 1960 | Congress passes a stronger voting rights bill. |
| 1961 | Cuban exiles, with help from the CIA, invade Cuba at the Bay of Pigs; they fail to inspire a revolt and withdraw against Fidel Castro. |
| 1962 | Military advisors sent to Vietnam are permitted to "fire if fired upon." John Glenn is the first American in space. |
| 1963 | President John F. Kennedy is assassinated. |
| 1964 | Major civil rights legislation is proposed. President Johnson and Congress begin a great increase in government spending on social welfare programs to create Johnson's "Great Society." |
| 1965 | President Johnson orders continuous bombing in South Vietnam and sends 184,300 troops. Riots in Watts section of Los Angeles, California. |
| 1966 | U.S. fights in North Vietnam and Cambodia. |
| 1967 | Riots in Newark, New Jersey, and Detroit, Michigan. 475,000 troops in Vietnam. |
| 1968 | Vietnam War peace talks begin in Paris. Martin Luther King, Jr., and Robert Kennedy are assassinated. |
| 1969 | President Nixon expands the peace talks and begins phased withdrawal of U.S. troops from Vietnam. Neil Armstrong walks on the moon. |
| 1970 | U.S. and South Vietnamese fight in Cambodia. |
| 1972 | President Nixon reopens relations with China. |
| 1973 | Vietnamese peace pacts signed. |
| 1974 | President Nixon resigns when threatened with impeachment for covering up evidence on the 1972 break-in at the Democratic National Committee offices in Watergate in Washington. |
| 1975 | South Vietnam, without U.S. military support, falls to North Vietnam. |
| 1978 | The U.S. agrees to hand the Panama Canal over to Panama in 1999. |
| 1979 | 90 hostages are taken in Iran as the Shah's U.S.-backed government falls in a popular uprising. The crisis continues for 444 days. |
| 1981 | President Reagan's tax cuts are passed by Congress. The economy grows for nine years, but so does the national debt. |
| 1982 | The Equal Rights Amendment, guaranteeing women and others equal rights, fails to be ratified by enough states to change the Constitution. The Space Shuttle *Columbia* successfully returns from space. |
| 1983 | 281 U.S. and French military personnel serving in a UN peacekeeping force in Lebanon are killed by terrorist bombs. President Reagan and six Caribbean nations send troops into Grenada to restore democratic government. |
| 1984 | Marines are withdrawn from Lebanon; civil war continues. |
| 1985 | President Reagan and Soviet leader Mikhail Gorbachev hold their first summit. Congress passes Gramm-Rudman bill to try to reduce government spending. |

1986    Space Shuttle *Challenger* explodes while the world watches on TV. U.S. war planes attack Libya in response to terrorism. AIDS is acknowledged as an international health emergency.

1989    President Bush sends troops into Panama and ousts Gen. Manuel Noriega. U.S., U.S.S.R. and their allies declare the end of the Cold War.

1990    U.S. sends troops to Saudi Arabia to protect Middle East allies after Iraqi leader Saddam Hussein seizes Kuwait.

1991    U.S. and other UN forces bomb Iraq and reclaim Kuwait.

1992    Bill Clinton elected president. U.S. with U.N. enters Somalia.

1993    World Trade Center bombed. Great flood in the Midwest. Brady Bill (gun law) signed. Clinton attacks Iraq with missiles for alleged assassination attempt against ex-President Bush. 18 U.S. soldiers killed in ambush in Somalia; U.S. withdraws.

1994    NAFTA takes effect. Earthquake in L.A. Republican party gains control of congress.

1995    U.S. with the U.N. enters Haiti. Truck bomb destroys federal building in Oklahoma City. Diplomatic relations with Vietnam re-established. War ends in Bosnia; U.S. sends peacekeepers. Partial government shutdown as Clinton forces Congress to cut budget.

1996    TWA flight 800 crashes. Bomb explodes at the Olympics in Atlanta. Clinton reelected.

1997    Madeline Albright becomes 1st woman Secretary of State. Tobacco companies agree to settlements in antismoking suits.

1998    Clinton sex scandal erupts. House votes to impeach Clinton. Senate does not remove Clinton from office. Terrorists bomb embassies in Kenya and Tanzania. U.S. retaliates with missiles against terrorists in Sudan and Afghanistan. U.S./British air strikes against weapon sites in Iraq.

1999    Computer system disruption, "Y2K bug," and millennium terrorist attacks, expected at the New Year, don't occur. Violence in several schools around the country. U.S. economic expansion, prosperity, and budget discipline reduce national debt. Explosive growth in the use of the internet, 3rd-world population, and AIDS continue.

2000    The presidential election between Al Gore (Democratic Vice President) and Texas Governor George W. Bush, son of President George Bush, was a virtual tie. Gore won the popular vote, but the final decision on who would get Florida's electors was delayed for weeks while Florida recounted votes. The Supreme Court stopped the recount; Bush was given Florida, the majority of the Electoral College, and the presidency.

2001    Some of Bush's more conservative cabinet appointments caused controversy. The new President's budget provided a $1.35 trillion tax cut over ten years to stimulate the U.S. economy. The economy, particularly technology stocks, continued a drop begun in 2000. Projected budget surpluses changed to deficits. On 9/11 terrorists destroyed the World Trade Towers in New York City and one side of the Pentagon using three full commercial airliners, about 3000 people were killed. In retaliation, the U.S. and U.K. attacked Afghanistan where the Taliban government was sheltering the al-Qaeda terrorists. The Taliban government fell in November. In December Enron, an energy company, filed for the largest bankruptcy in U.S. history.

2002    The war continued in Afghanistan. A U.S. Department of Homeland Security was organized. The stock market hit a new five-year low. Several priests of the Catholic Church were accused of pedophilia.

2003    The Bush and British administrations failed to pressure the U.N. to invade Iraq. They attacked in a "preemptive strike," claiming the Saddam Hussein was working with al-Qaeda and readying weapons of mass destruction (chemical, biological, and nuclear) for use by terrorists. The Iraq regime fell. Bush declared an end of major action; but a guerrilla war continued and no weapons of mass destruction were not found. The U.S. was accused of giving misleading information before the war. The space shuttle Columbia, disintegrated re-entering the atmosphere. The U.S. faced the largest budget deficit in history. Bush signs a $350 billion tax cut. In December Saddam Hussein was captured.

2004    The budget deficit reached $412 billion. The cost of energy, health care, and education increased. In Iraq terrorism, partisan violence, and casualties increased. U.S. Contractors working in Iraq were accused of corruption. In the presidential campaign, Senator John Kerry failed to convince the majority of voters that the Bush administration had mismanaged the economy, the wars in Iraq and Afghanistan, and the "war on terrorism." The Republicans focused on Kerry's personality and on "moral values" and won the presidency by a narrow margin.

2005   President Bush claimed electoral support for his policies, but his popularity declined as the public learned of the administration's use of domestic wiretapping, torture of military prisoners, and "signing statements" by which the President signed a law saying he would not obey it. Secretary of State Colin Powell resigned, and later admitting he had been misled by the administration into supporting the war. Insisting that he should "stay the course" on tax-cut economics and Iraq, Bush ignored evidence of global warming and political scandals. Then the administration ignored warnings that Hurricane Katrina might hit and flood New Orleans. It did. The government at all levels was unprepared and responded slowly. In Iraq, Hussein was tried in a special Iraqi court. The political and military situation in the Middle East continued to decline.

2006   The death toll from government suppression of the people of Darfur, Sudan, reached 200,000, with 2.5 million refugees. North Korea tested an atomic bomb. Iran planed to enrich uranium for atomic power, ignoring U.N. mandates. The anti-Israel Hamas won Palestinian elections, taking over the government. Hezbollah guerillas attacked Israel from Lebanon, and Israel was badly hurt in stopping them. The Taliban regained strength in Afghanistan. In Iraq civil war deepened. Saddam was found guilty and hanged. Al-Qaeda leaders continued to plan and execute terrorist strikes worldwide from safe headquarters in Pakistan. In the "off-year" elections, the Democrats won both houses of Congress. Corruption and a perceived lack of effective domestic and foreign policy seem to have been the cause. A bipartisan presidential commission was set up and suggested policy changes.

2007   President Bush, after considering the advice and consulting widely, decided not to take much of the advice involving finding a diplomatic solution in Iraq. Instead he decided to escalate the military effort by sending 20,000 more troops to secure Baghdad. The New York Stock Market reaches a new, all-time high. In December, the economy officially went into recession with the collapse of the mortgage-backed securities market. The 2008 Presidential campaign began.

2008   Arkansas, Kentucky, Tennessee, and Alabama suffer $1 billion in tornado damage on Super Tuesday in February. In September Hurricane Ike did $31 billion in damage and killed 100 on the Texas coast. Oil prices soared to $147 per barrel. The Global financial crisis began in 2007 and grew worse through 2008. The U.S. stock market crashed, investment bank Lehman Brothers became the largest bankruptcy in U.S. history. In November, Barack Obama was elected the first African-American President.

2009   President Obama signed a $787 billion economic stimulus bill. Conservative activists, called the Tea Party, protested the expense and Congressional conservatives blocked other administration initiatives and court and administration nominations, particularly in the Senate using the threat of filabuster. Ignoring clear documentation, other anti-Obama politicians claimed he was born in Kenya, not in Hawaii, and thus could not legally be President. The economy continued to decline with growing unemployment, two wars, and increasing political and ideological tension in the U.S. and abroad.

2010   President Obama signed a national health care bill, called by critics Obamacare, and established a Consumer Financial Protection Bureau. In April, oil rig Deepwater Horizon exploded in the Gulf of Mexico causing the largest marine oil spill in history. After several domestic shootings, gun control pressure built. Conservatives organized, and in the November mid-term elections, the House was won by the Republicans. The Democrats kept the Senate majority by only one vote. Before the conservatives took over, during what is called a "lame-duck session," Congress passed an extension of the Bush tax cuts to avoid hurting businesses, and it repealed "Don't ask, don't tell," helping gays serve openly in the military, A new START (arms reduction) treaty was ratified by the Senate.

2011   The new Congress having a Repubican majority in the House continued obstructing legistation and nominations. The 2012 Presidential campaign began early, further hampering new legislation; there were many Republican candidates. Obama began to reduce deficit spending. The U.S. recovery was weak, unemployment remained high. The global economy continued to decline. Gun violence in the U.S. continued to gain public attention through mass shootings and the dramatic attempted assassination of Representative Gabrielle Giffords and a federal judge. Congress blocked reforms. Public concern over environmental change increased as huge forest fires broke out across the West with increasing drought starting in 2010 and building to the present. And major storms continued: tornados in Alabama, Mississippi River floods, a tornado in Missouri, and Hurricane Irene with $13 billion damage from N. Carolina to Maine and Vermont. Congress blocked action on the environment. In December, the last U.S. troops were withdrawn from Iraq. Starting in 2010 and building early in 2011, protests and rebellion spread in much of the Islamic world. The "Arab Spring" forced several leaders to resign. Gaddafi fought the rebellion in Lybia. The U.S., working with allies, supported the rebels without sending in troups; Gaddafi was killed in October. Rebellion spread to Egypt and Syria. The U.S. under President Obama and Secretary of State Hilary Clinton worked with allies and avoided direct involvement. Osama bin Laden was killed in Pakistan May.

2012 There were mass shootings in Colorado and Connectict. Hurricane (Superstorm) Sandy, the second most costly hurricane in U.S. history, did major damage to the East Coast, particularly NYC and NJ. Drought and fire continued in the West. War spread in Africa. The presidential campaign ended with the re-election of Obama.

2013 Terrorists attacked the Boston Marathon. Economic recovery contined, but slowly. The stock market reached new highs. War spread in Africa and Syria. John Kerry became Secretary of State. Edward Snowden breached National Security Council files and leaked them to the world press. Storms, drought, and fires dramatized the environmental crisis, but Congress took no action. The Supreme Court ruled on voting rights, same-sex marriage, and women in combat. Congress blocked legislation and nominations proposed by the administration. It then shut down the government rather than raise the national debt ceiling, It then made a temporary deal with the President to reopen it.

2014 Edward Snowden, given asylum in Russia continued to release classified data on U.S. surveillance of communications both globally and in the U.S., causing political problems for the administration. Much of

the Affordable Care Act, called "Obamacare" by the Republicans, went into effect and was generally popular. To get around Congressional obstruction, Obama changed governmental regulations on several issues. The Democratic majority in the Senate changed Senate rules to make filibusters less effective. More and more states accepted same-sex marriage; Federal Courts upheld these state laws. A scandal in the Veteran's Administration over the health care of veterans caused the VA Secretary to resign. A bi-partisan bill improving the regulaton of the VA was passed. The income gap between the richest Amaricans and the rest of the public contined to grow dramatically. Obama raised the minimum wage for government workers in an attempt to get Congress and big business to do the same for everyone. Although polls showed that the great majority of Congress and of the public wanted immigration reform, Congress was unable to act; thousands of children crossed into the U.S. alone without adults, fleeing poverty and violence in Central America. The administration tried to slow the flood of children and to find ways to care for those who came. The gap between Republican conservatives and Democratic progressives continued to increase, stopping legistative action of any kind in Congress and many states. Both parties predicted gains in the mid-term election in November. In international affairs, turmoil continued in various parts of the world – between Ukraine and Russia and in Africa where ebola broke out killing thousands in many countries. In the Middle East, Secretary of State John Kerry worked with allies on an Israeli-Palestinian peace agreement, but a war betreen the parities broke out in Gaza. Then a new Egypt goverment brought the Palistinians and Israelis together in talks. Civil war continued in Syria, and a radical fundamentalist group called ISIS (Islamic State in Syria) sent troups from Syria to seize much of norther Iraq, This brought down the Iraqi govenment, which in turn allowed an international initiative to attack by air and slow down ISIS, giving Iraq time to form a new government. In December the U.S. and allies plan to withdraw troops and end their involvement in the 13-year Afghan war.

# 23: Brief Highlights of Canadian History

**c. 50,000 years ago** Archeological and genetic evidence shows Aboriginal Americans entering Canada from 50,000 to 16,000 years ago.

**16,000 or more years ago** Varied peoples began to move south from Northwest Canada and possibly from the Arctic northeast as hunter gatherers and then settlng first Canada and then the rest of the Americas. They developed into several distinct cultural groups

**c. 1000 BC** Leif Erikson and other Norse Vikings sailed to the Atlantic Coast of Canada from Greenland, made temporary settlements, and were driven away by the "Skraelings," the indigenous Inuit inhabitants.

**1497** John Cabot, sailing for the English king, explored the coast of Newfoundland looking for a northwest passage to the Orient.

**1534** Jacques Cartier discovered the St. Lawrence River and the Great Lakes.

**1576-1578** Martin Frobisher explored the Canadian Artic (Baffin Island and Froisher Bay) on three voyages seeking the Northwest Passage.

**1603-1608** Samuel de Champlain followed Cartier and founded Port Royal, first successful French colony, and then Quebec in 1608.

**1608-1633** Étienne Brûlé, aide and interpeter for Champlain, lived with the Algonquins and Hurons and learned their languages and cultures. He explored Georgian Bay and the Great Lakes, perhaps including Lake Michigan.

**1642** Chomedey de Maisonneuve founded Montreal (Ville Maie)

**1670** The Hudson's Bay Company was established to foster the fur trade

**1672-1674** Louis Jolliet and Pére Jacques Marquette explored the Upper Mississippi to within 435 miles of the Gulf of Mexico and then discovered and wintered over at the site of Chicago.

**1672-1698** Louis de Frontenac, Governor of New France expanded the colony, building forts and battling the English and the Iroquois, expanding the fur trade.

**1758** Fort Louisburg on Cape Breton fell to the British

**1759** The Battle of Quebec on the Plains of Abraham was the climax of the Seven Years' War (French and Indian War). Both British General Wolf and French General Montcalm died. The British took over Quebec and eventually with the Treaty of Paris all of Canada.

**1763**
**1778** Captain James Cook explored the Pacifc coast of Canada.

**1791** The British Constitutional Act 1791 reformed and divided Canada into Upper Canada (with British law and customs and many Loyalists from the American Revolution) and Lower Canada (with French language, law, and customs).

**1812** A U.S. invasion of Canada to free it from the British during the British War of 1812 invasion of the U.S.ended with a British victory in Canada. They also defeated Napoleon in Russia, but were defeated in the U.S.

**1840** The Act of Union united Upper and Lower Canada into the Province of Canada. There were significant constitutional changes at that time.

**1867** The Dominion of Canada was established. Self-government was granted to Ontario (Upper Canada), Quebec (Lower Canada), New Brunswick, and Nova Scotia.

**1873** The Mounties (NW Mounted Police) were established.

**1885** The Canadian Pacific Railway was finished, tying the nation together.

**1898** The Gold Rush in the Klondike transformed the Yukon, Canadian West, and the economy.

**1899-1945** Canada played a vital role as ally and partner in North American and British Commonwealth history from the Boer War, through World War I, the Great Depression, and World War II.

**1960** The Quebec Separation movement was strenghtened by The Quiet Revolution.

**1970** The 1914 War Measures Act giving the government extra powers during WWI and WWII was used in the October Crisis to weaken the Quebec Separatists.

**1982** The present Canadian Costitution was adopted. Under it, Quebec has been allowed to vote for independence. It has voted to hold Canada together.

# 24: Folk Songs

## Places
The Banks of the Ohio
Dixie
Down in the Valley
The Eyes of Texas
Home on the Range
My Old Kentucky Home
Red River Valley
The Sidewalks of New York
The Streets of Laredo

## Traveling
Five Hundred Miles
Freight Train
The Golden Vanity
Sloop John B.
The Wabash Cannonball

## Work
Blow the Man Down
Drill, Ye Tarriers, Drill
The Erie Canal
Git Along Little Dogies
Goodbye, Old Paint
I've Been Working on the Railroad

## Children's Songs
Bingo
Hush Little Baby
This Old Man
Pop Goes the Weasel
Rock-a-Bye Baby
Row, Row, Row Your Boat
Skip to My Lou
Old MacDonald
Three Blind Mice

## People
Barbara Allen
Casey Jones
Clementine
Dan Tucker
Go Tell Aunt Rhodie
Jeanie with the Light Brown Hair
John Henry
Oh, Susanna
She'll Be Coming 'Round the Mountain
Sweet Betsy from Pike
Tom Dooley

## Love
Black Is the Color of My True Love's Hair
Goodnight Irene
House of the Rising Sun
In the Good Old Summertime
My Bonnie Lies over the Ocean
On Top of Old Smokey

## Animals
Blue Tail Fly
The Fox
Froggie Went A-Courtin'
The Old Gray Mare

## Play
A Bicycle Built for Two
Camptown Races
For He's a Jolly Good Fellow
Happy Birthday
Mountain Dew
Turkey in the Straw

## Spirituals
Amazing Grace
Joshua Fought the Battle of Jericho
Kum Bay Yah
Nobody Knows the Trouble I've Seen
Old Folks at Home
Rock of Ages
Rock-a My Soul
Swing Low, Sweet Chariot
When the Saints Go Marching In

## Patriotism
The Battle Hymn of the Republic
When Johnny Comes Marching Home Again
Yankee Doodle

## Modern
Blowin' in the Wind
Brother, Can You Spare a Dime?
City of New Orleans
If I Had a Hammer
Old Man River
This Land is Your Land
We Shall Overcome

# 25: Nursery Rhymes

## Common Nursery Rhymes

**Humpty Dumpty**
Humpty Dumpty sat on a wall,
Humpty Dumpty had a great fall.
All the king's horses and all the king's men
Couldn't put Humpty together again.

**There Was an Old Woman**
There was an old woman
Who lived in a shoe,
She had so many children
She didn't know what to do.
She gave them some broth,
Without any bread,
Whipped them all soundly,
And sent them to bed.

**The Cat and the Fiddle**
Hey diddle diddle,
The cat and the fiddle,
The cow jumped over the moon.
The little dog laughed to see such sport,
And the dish ran away with the spoon.

**Old Mother Hubbard**
Old Mother Hubbard went to the cupboard
To get her poor dog a bone.
But when she got there, the cupboard was bare,
And so the poor dog had none.

**Jack and Jill**
Jack and Jill went up the hill
To fetch a pail of water.
Jack fell down and broke his crown
And Jill came tumbling after.

**Baa, Baa, Black Sheep**
Baa, baa, black sheep, have you any wool?
Yes, sir, yes, sir, three bags full.
One for my master and one for my dame
And one for the little boy who lives down the lane
Baa, baa, black sheep, have you any wool?
Yes, sir, yes, sir, three bags full.

**Hickory Dickory Dock**
Hickory dickory dock,
The mouse ran up the clock
The clock struck one,
The mouse ran down,
Hickory dickory dock.

**Mary Had a Little Lamb**
Mary had a little lamb,
Little lamb, little lamb,
Mary had a little lamb
Its fleece was white as snow.
And everywhere that Mary went,
Mary went, Mary went,
Everywhere that Mary went
The lamb was sure to go.

**Old King Cole**
Old King Cole was a merry old soul,
And a merry old soul was he.
He called for his pipe
And he called for his bowl
And he called for his fiddlers three.
Every fiddler had a very fine fiddle
And a very fine fiddle had he.
Oh, there's none so rare as can compare
With King Cole and his fiddlers three.

**Rain, Rain, Go Away**
Rain, rain, go away,
Come again some other day.

**Rock-a-bye Baby**
Rock-a-bye, baby, on the treetop
When the wind blows the cradle will rock.
When the bough breaks, the cradle will fall,
And down will come baby, cradle and all.

**Thirty Days**
Thirty days hath September,
April, June and November.
All the rest have thirty-one,
Save February which alone
Has twenty-eight and one day more
When Leap Year comes one year in four.

**Solomon Grundy**
Solomon Grundy,
Born on Monday,
Christened on Tuesday,
Married on Wednesday,
Sick on Thursday,
Worse on Friday,
Died on Saturday,
Buried on Sunday.
That was the end
Of Solomon Grundy.

One, two, buckle my shoe,
Three, four, shut the door,
Five, six, pick up sticks,
Seven, eight, lay them straight.
Nine, ten, a big fat hen,
Eleven, twelve, dig and delve,
Thirteen, fourteen, maids a-courting,
Fifteen, sixteen, maids a-stitching,
Seventeen, eighteen, maids a-waiting,
Nineteen, twenty, food's a-plenty,
My plate is empty.

There was an old woman lived under a hill,
And if she's not gone, she's living there still.

If wishes were horses, beggers would ride;
if turnips were watches, I'd wear one by my side.

Three wise men from Gotham went to sea in a bowl.
If the bowl had been stronger, my song 'd been longer.

One misty, moisty morning,
When cloudy was the weather,
I chanced to meet an old man
Clothed all in leather.
He began to compliment
And I began to grin.
How do you do? And how do you do?
And how do you do, again?

A,b,c,d,e,f,g,
H,i,j,k,l,m,n,o,p,
Q,r,s,t,u,v,
W and x, y, z.
Now I know my ABCs,
Next time won't you sing with me?

## Others

Barber, Barber, Shave a Pig
Birds of a Feather Flock Together
Bow, Wow, Wow,
    Whose Dog Art Thou?
Bye, Baby Bunting
Cock-a-doodle Doo
Cock Robin
Diddle, Diddle, Dumpling,
    My Son John
Ding dong bell. Doctor Foster
Went to Gloucester
Georgie Porgie
Goosey Goosey Gander
Hark, Hark, the Dogs Do Bark
Here We Go Round
    the Mulberry Bush
Hot Cross Buns
It's Raining, It's Pouring

Jack Be Nimble
Jack Sprat
Little Bo Peep
Little Boy Blue
Little Jack Horner
Little Miss Muffet
Mistress Mary, Quite Contrary
Now I Lay Me Down to Sleep
Old Mother Goose
Pat-a-cake, Pat-a-cake,
    Baker's Man
Pease Porridge Hot
Peter, Peter, Pumpkin Eater
Pussy Cat, Pussy Cat
The Queen of Hearts
Ride a Cock Horse
Ring around the Roses
Simple Simon

Sing a Song of Sixpence
The Man in the Moon
The Queen of Hearts
There Was a Crooked Man
There Was a Little Girl
This is the House that Jack Built
Three Blind Mice
Three Little Kittens
Tom, Tom, the Piper's Son
To Market, to Market,
    to Buy a Fat Pig
Tweedle Dumb and Tweedle Dee
Twinkle, Twinkle, Little Star
Wee Willie Winkie
Willy Boy, Willy Boy,
    Where Are You Going
Will You Walk Into My Parlor?
What Are Little Boys Made of?

## Tongue Twisters

Peter Piper picked a peck of pickled peppers,
A peck of pickled peppers, Peter Piper picked.
If Peter Piper picked a peck of pickled peppers,
Where's the peck of pickled peppers
    Peter Piper picked?

She sells sea shells by the seashore.
The shells she sells are seashore shells.

Rubber baby buggy bumpers

The sixth sheik's sixth sheep's sick.

A tutor who tooted a flute
Tried to teach two tooters to toot.
Said the two to the tutor,
"Is it harder to toot or
To tutor two tooters to toot?"

*For a more complete collection of rhymes, visit the supplemental **ESL Miscellany** material at **ProLinguaAssociates.com***

# 26: Light Verse

## Light Verse

### The Owl and the Pussy-cat

The Owl and the Pussy-cat went to sea
    In a beautiful pea-green boat.
They took some honey, and plenty of money,
    Wrapped up in a five-pound note.
The Owl looked up to the stars above,
    And sang to a small guitar,
"O lovely Pussy! O Pussy, my love,
    What a beautiful Pussy you are,
      You are,
      You are!
    What a beautiful Pussy you are!

Pussy said to Owl, "You elegant fowl!
    How charmingly sweet you sing!
O let us be married! too long we have tarried:
    But what shall we do for a ring?"
They sailed away, for a year and a day,
    To the land where the Bong-tree grows
And there in a wood a Piggy-wig stood
    With a ring at the end of his nose,
      His nose,
      His nose,
    With a ring at the end of his nose.

"Dear Pig, are you willing to sell for one shilling
    Your ring?" Said the Piggy, "I will."
So they took it away, and were married next day
    By the Turkey who lives on the hill.
They dined on mince, and slices of quince,
    Which they ate with a runcible spoon;
And hand in hand, on the edge of the sand,
    They danced by the light of the moon,
      The moon,
      The moon,
    They danced by the light of the moon.
—*Edward Lear, 1851*

### Wynken, Blynken, and Nod

Wynken, Blynken, and Nod one night
    Sailed off in a wooden shoe,—
Sailed on a river of crystal light
    into a sea of dew.
"Where are you going, and what do you wish?"
    The old moon asked the three.

"We have come to fish for the herring-fish
    That live in this beautiful sea;
Nets of silver and gold have we,"
    Said Wynken,
      Blynken,
        And Nod.

The old moon laughed and sang a song,
    As they rocked in the wooden shoe;
And the wind that sped them all night long
    Ruffled the waves of dew;
The little stars were the herring-fish
    That lived in the beautiful sea.
"Now cast your nets wherever you wish,—
    Never afraid are we!"
So cried the stars to the fishermen three,
    Wynken,
      Blynken,
        And Nod.

All night long their nets they threw
    To the stars in the twinkling foam,—
Then down from the skies came the wooden shoe,
    Bringing the fishermen home:
'Twas all so pretty a sail, it seemed
    As if it could not be;
And some folk thought 'twas a dream they'd dreamed
    Of sailing that beautiful sea;
But I shall name you the fishermen three:
    Wynken,
      Blynken,
        And Nod.

Wynken and Blynken are two little eyes,
    And Nod is a little head,
And the wooden shoe that sailed the skies
    Is a wee one's trundle-bed;
So shut your eyes while Mother sings
    Of wonderful sights that be,
And you shall see the beautiful things
    As you rock in the misty sea
Where the old shoe rocked the fishermen three:—
    Wynken,
      Blynken,
        And Nod.
      —*Eugene Field*

## As I Was Going to Saint Ives

As I was going to Saint Ives
I met a man with seven wives.
Every wife had seven sacks,
Every sack had seven cats,
Every cat had seven kits.
Kits, cats, sacks and wives,
How many were going to Saint Ives?

## Paul Revere's Ride

Listen my children, and you shall hear
Of the midnight ride of Paul Revere,
On the eighteenth of April in Seventy-five;
Hardly a man is now alive
Who remembers that famous day and year . . .
*—Henry Wadsworth Longfellow*

# Nonsense Verse

## Jabberwocky

'Twas brillig, and the slithy toves
    Did gyre and gimble in the wabe;
All mimsy were the borogroves,
    And the mome raths outgrabe.

"Beware the Jabberwock, my son!
    The jaws that bite, the claws that catch!
Beware the Jubjub bird, and shun
    The frumious Bandersnatch!"

He took his vorpal sword in hand;
    Long time the manxome foe he sought—
So rested he by the Tumtum tree,
    And stood awhile in thought.

And, as in uffish thought he stood,
    The Jabberwock, with eyes of flame,
Came whiffling through the tulgey wood,
    And burbled as it came!

One, two! One, two! And through and through
    The vorpal blade went snicker-snack!
He left it dead, and with its head,
    He went galumphing back.

"And hast thou slain the Jabberwock?
    Come to my arms, my beamish boy!
O frabjous day! Callooh! Callay!"
    He chortled in his joy.

'Twas brillig, and the slithy toves
    Did gyre and gimble in the wabe;
All mimsy were the borogroves,
    And the mome raths outgrabe.
*—Lewis Carroll, 1871*

# As I was going up the stair

As I was going up the stair,
    I met a man who wasn't there.
He wasn't there again today –
    I wish that he would go away!

*—Anonymous*

## The Jumblies

They went to sea in a sieve, they did;
    In a sieve they went to sea;
In spite of all their friends could say,
On a winter's morn, on a stormy day,
    In a sieve they went to sea.

And when the sieve turned round and round,
    And everyone cried, "You'll be drowned!"
They called aloud, "Our seive ain't big,
But we don't care a button, we don't care a fig—
    In a seive we'll go to sea!"

Far and few, far and few,
    Are the lands where the Jumblies live.
Their heads are green, and their hands are blue;
    And they went to sea in a sieve.
*—Edward Lear, 1871*

## The Crocodile

How doth the little crocodile
    Improve his shining tail,
And pour the waters of the Nile
    On every golden scale!

How cheerfully he seems to grin,
    How neatly spreads his claws,
And welcomes little fishes in,
    With gently smiling jaws.
*—Lewis Carroll, 1871*

## The Common Cormorant

The common cormorant or shag
    Lays eggs inside a paper bag.
The reason you will see no doubt
    It is to keep the lightning out.
But what these unobservant birds
    Have never noticed is that herds
Of wandering bears may come with buns
    And steal the bags to hold the crumbs.
*—Anonymous*

# 27: American Literature and Cinema

## 1776-1830

| | | |
|---|---|---|
| Cooper, James Fenimore | (1789-1851) | The Last of the Mohicans |
| Franklin, Benjamin | (1706-1790) | Poor Richard's Almanack |
| Irving, Washington | (1783-1859) | "Rip Van Winkle," "Legend of Sleepy Hollow" |
| Paine, Thomas | (1737-1809) | Common Sense, The Crisis |

## 19th Century Literature (1830-1900)

| | | |
|---|---|---|
| Alcott, Louisa May | (1832-1888) | Little Women |
| Crane, Stephen | (1871-1900) | The Red Badge of Courage |
| Emerson, Ralph Waldo | (1803-1882) | Essays, Nature |
| Fuller, Margaret | (1810-1850) | Woman in the Nineteenth Century |
| Hawthorne, Nathaniel | (1804-1864) | The Scarlet Letter |
| Melville, Herman | (1819-1891) | Moby Dick, Billy Budd |
| Poe, Edgar Allen | (1809-1849) | The Fall of the House of Usher |
| Stowe, Harriet Beecher | (1811-1896) | Uncle Tom's Cabin |
| Thoreau, Henry David | (1817-1862) | Walden |

## 20th Century Literature (1900-2000)

| | | |
|---|---|---|
| Ambrose, Stephen | (1936-2002) | Undaunted Courage, D-Day, Citizen Soldiers |
| Angelou, Maya | (1928-2014) | I Know Why the Caged Bird Sings |
| Anderson, Sherwood | (1876-1941) | Winesburg, Ohio |
| Baldwin, James | (1924-1987) | The Fire Next Time |
| Bellow, Saul | (1915-2005) | Herzog |
| Bradbury, Ray | (1920-2012) | Ferenheit 451 |
| Capote, Truman | (1924-1984) | In Cold Blood |
| Cather, Willa | (1876-1947) | Death Comes for the Archbishop |
| Chopin, Kate | (1851-1904) | The Awakening |
| Cheever, John | (1912-1982) | The Wapshot Chronicle |
| Dreiser, Theodore | (1871-1945) | Sister Carrie |
| Ellison, Ralph | (1914-1994) | The Invisible Man |
| Faulkner, William | (1897-1962) | The Sound and the Fury |
| Fitzgerald, F. Scott | (1896-1940) | The Great Gatsby |
| Gould, Stephen Jay | (1941-2002) | This View of Life, The Panda's Thumb |
| Heller, Joseph | (1923-1999) | Catch-22 |
| Hemingway, Ernest | (1899-1961) | The Sun Also Rises |
| Henry, O. | (1862-1910) | The Gift of the Magi |
| Hersey, John | (1914-1993) | A Bell for Adano |
| James, Henry | (1843-1916) | Portrait of a Lady, The Bostonians |
| Ketchum, Richard | (1922-2012) | Saratoga, Divided Loyalties, The Borrowed Years |
| Kosinski, Jerzy | (1933-1991) | The Painted Bird, Steps, Being There |
| Lewis, Sinclair | (1885-1951) | Babbit, Main Street, Arrowsmith |
| London, Jack | (1876-1916) | The Call of the Wild, Sea Wolf |
| Mailer, Norman | (1923-2007) | The Naked and the Dead |
| Malamud, Bernard | (1914-1986) | The Fixer, The Natural |
| Matthiessen, Peter | (1927-2014) | The Snow Leopard, At Play in the Fields of the Lord |
| McCullers, Carson | (1917-1967) | The Heart is a Lonely Hunter |
| Mitchell, Margaret | (1900-1949) | Gone with the Wind |

| | | |
|---|---|---|
| Michener, James | (1905-1970) | Tales of the South Pacific, Hawaii, Centenial |
| O'Hara, John | (1907-1998) | Ten North Frederick |
| Porter, Katherine Ann | (1890-1980) | Flowering Judas; Pale Horse, Pale Rider |
| Rand, Ayn | (1905-1982) | Atlas Shrugged |
| Salinger, J. D. | (1919-2010) | Catcher in the Rye |
| Schlesinger, Arthur | (1917-2007) | A Thousand Days, The Age of Jackson, The Vital Center |
| Sinclair, Upton | (1878-1968) | The Jungle |
| Stein, Gertrude | (1874-1946) | Three Lives |
| Steinbeck, John | (1902-1968) | The Grapes of Wrath |
| Tarkington, Booth | (1869-1946) | Seventeen, Penrod |
| Tuchman, Barbara | (1912-1989) | The Guns of August, Stilwell, A Distant Mirror |
| Twain, Mark | (1835-1910) | Huckleberry Finn, Tom Sawyer, Innocents Abroad |
| Updike, John | (1932-2009) | Rabbit, Run |
| Vonnegut, Kurt | (1922-2007) | Slaughterhouse Five, Jailbird |
| Warren, Robert Penn | (1905-1989) | All the King's Men |
| Welty, Eudora | (1909-2001) | The Optimist's Daughter |
| Wharton, Edith | (1862-1937) | Ethan Frome, The Age of Innocence |
| Williams, William Carlos | (1883-1963) | Tempers |
| Wodehouse, P.G. | (1881-1975) | Anything Goes |
| Wolfe, Thomas | (1900-1938) | You Can't Go Home Again |
| Wright, Richard | (1908-1960) | Native Son, Black Boy |

## Contemporary Literature (2000-present)

| | | |
|---|---|---|
| Bryson, Bill | (1951-     ) | A Walk in the Woods, A Short History of Nearly Everything |
| DeLillo, Don | (1936-     ) | White Noise, The Angel Esmeralda |
| Doctorow, E. L. | (1931-     ) | Ragtime |
| Frazier, Charles | (1950)-     ) | Cold Mountain, Thirteen Moons |
| Goodwin, Doris Kearns | (1943-     ) | Presidential studies: Roosevelt, Kennedy, Johnson, Lincoln |
| Guterson, David | (1956-     ) | Snow Falling on Cedars, East of the Mountains |
| Hosseini, Khaled | (1965-     ) | The Kite Runner, And the Mountains Echoed |
| Irving, John | (1942-     ) | The Cider House Rules, The World According to Garp |
| Kidder, Tracy | (1945-     ) | Among School Children, The Soul of a New Machine |
| Lee, Harper | (1926-     ) | To Kill a Mockingbird |
| McCann, Colum | (1965-     ) | Let the Great World Spin, TransAtlantic |
| McCarthy, Cormac | (1933-     ) | The Road, All the Pretty Horses, No Country for Old Men |
| McCullough, David | (1933-     ) | Mornings on Horseback, 1776, Truman |
| McMurtry, Larry | (1936-     ) | Lonesome Dove, Leaving Cheyenne |
| Monro, Alice (Canada) | (1931-     ) | Dance of the Happy Shades, Dear Life, Friend of My Youth |
| Morrison, Toni | (1931-     ) | Tar Baby, Beloved |
| Oates, Joyce Carol | (1938-     ) | Do with Me What You Will |
| Pinker, Steven | (1954-     ) | The Stuff of Thought, The Better Angels of Our Nature |
| Proulx, E. Annie | (1935-     ) | The Shipping News |
| Pynchon, Thomas | (1937-     ) | Gravity's Rainbow |
| Roth, Philip | (1933-     ) | Portnoy's Complaint, Zuckerman Unbound, The Humbling |
| Tan, Amy | (1952-     ) | The Joy Luck Club |
| Theroux, Paul | (1941-     ) | The Great Railway Bazaar, Dark Star Safari |
| Walker, Alice | (1944-     ) | The Color Purple |

## Poets

| | | |
|---|---|---|
| Auden, W. H. | (1907-1973) | The Sheild of Achilles, As I Walked Out One Evening |
| Benet, Stephen Vincent | (1898-1943) | John Brown's Body |
| Bradstreet, Anne | (c.1612-1672) | The Tenth Muse Lately Sprung up in America |
| Brooks, Gwendolyn | (1917-    ) | The Bean Eaters, "Malcolm X" |
| Carruth, Hayden | (1921-2008) | Scrambled Eggs and Whiskey |
| Collins, Billy | (1941-    ) | Aimless Love |
| cummings, e. e. | (1894-1962) | Tulips and Chimneys |
| Dickinson, Emily | (1830-1886) | There's a Certain Slant of Light |
| Eliot, T. S. | (1888-1965) | The Waste Land," "Four Quartets |
| Frost, Robert | (1874-1963) | Birches, Mending Wall |
| Ginsberg, Allen | (1926-1998) | Howl |
| Haas, Robert | (1941-    ) | Time and Marterials |
| Hughes, Langston | (1902-1967) | The Weary Blues, The Negro Speaks of Rivers |
| Jeffers, Robinson | (1887-1966) | Shine Perishing Republic, Hurt Hawks |
| Longfellow, Henry W. | (1807-1882) | Evangeline, Hiawatha |
| Merwin, W.S | (1927-    ) | Migration, The Shadow of Silino |
| Nash, Ogden | (1902-1971) | I'm a Stranger Here Myself |
| Oliver, Mary | (1935-    ) | Dog Stories, The Truro Bear |
| Parker, Dorothy | (1893-1967) | Laments for the Living |
| Plath, Sylvia | (1932-1963) | The Colossus |
| Poe, Edgar Allen | (1809-1849) | The Raven |
| Pound, Ezra | (1885-1972) | The Cantos |
| Riley, James Whitcomb | (1849-1916) | When the Frost is on the Pumpkin |
| Robinson, Edward | (1869-1935) | Richard Cory |
| Sandberg, Carl | (1878-1967) | Chicago Poems |
| Stevens, Wallace | (1879-1955) | The Auroras of Autumn |
| Teasdale, Sara | (1884-1933) | Helen of Troy |
| Millay, Edna St. Vincent | (1892-1950) | A Few Figs from Thistles |
| Warren, Robert Penn | (1905-1989) | Brother to Dragons |
| Whitman, Walt | (1819-1892) | Song of Myself |

## Playwrights

| | | |
|---|---|---|
| Albee, Edward | (1928-    ) | Who's Afraid of Virginia Woolf? |
| Baraka, Imamu Amiri | (1934-2014) | Dutchman, The Slave |
| Hart, Moss | (1904-1961) | Once in a Lifetime |
| Hellman, Lillian | (1904-1984) | The Little Foxes |
| Hughes, Langston | (1902-1967) | Shakespeare in Harlem |
| Mamet, David | (1947-    ) | American Buffalo, Speed the Plow |
| Miller, Arthur | (1915-2005) | Death of a Salesman, All My Sons, The Crucible |
| Odets, Clifford | (1906-1963) | Waiting for Lefty, The Golden Boy |
| O'Neill, Eugene | (1888-1953) | Long Day's Journey into Night |
| Saroyan, William | (1980-1981) | The Human Comedy |
| Shepard, Sam | (1943-    ) | True West, Buried Child, A Lie of the Mind, Fool for Love |
| Sherwood, Robert | (1896-1955) | The Petrified Forest |
| Simon, Neil | (1927-    ) | Barefoot in the Park, The Odd Couple, The Goodbye Girl |
| Wilder, Thornton | (1897-1975) | Our Town |
| Williams, Tennessee | (1911-1983) | A Streetcar Named Desire, The Glass Menagerie |

# Academy Awards (Oscars) - Best Films

| | | | |
|---|---|---|---|
| 1960 | The Apartment | 1988 | Rainman |
| 1961 | West Side Story | 1989 | Driving Miss Daisy |
| 1962 | Lawrence of Arabia | 1990 | Dances with Wolves |
| 1963 | Tom Jones | 1991 | The Silence of the Lambs |
| 1964 | My Fair Lady | 1992 | Unforgiven |
| 1965 | The Sound of Music | 1993 | Schindler's List |
| 1966 | A Man for All Seasons | 1994 | Forrest Gump |
| 1967 | In the Heat of the Night | 1995 | Braveheart |
| 1968 | Oliver! | 1996 | The English Patient |
| 1969 | Midnight Cowboy | 1997 | Titanic |
| 1970 | Patton | 1998 | Shakespeare in Love |
| 1971 | The French Connection | 1999 | American Beauty |
| 1972 | The Godfather | 2000 | Gladiator |
| 1973 | The Sting | 2001 | A Beautiful Mind |
| 1974 | The Godfather, Part II | 2002 | Chicago |
| 1975 | One Flew Over the Cuckoo's Nest | 2003 | The Lord of the Rings: The Return of the King |
| 1976 | Rocky | 2004 | Million Dollar Baby |
| 1977 | Annie Hall | 2005 | Crash |
| 1978 | The Deer Hunter | 2006 | The Departed |
| 1979 | Kramer vs. Kramer | 2007 | No Country for Old Men |
| 1980 | Ordinary People | 2008 | Slumdog Millionaire |
| 1981 | Chariots of Fire | 2009 | The Hurt Locker |
| 1982 | Gandhi | 2010 | The King's Speech |
| 1983 | Terms of Endearment | 2011 | The Artist |
| 1984 | Amadeus | 2012 | Argo |
| 1985 | Out of Africa | 2013 | 12 Years a Slave |
| 1986 | Platoon | 2014 | Birdman |
| 1987 | The Last Emperor | | |

# 28: A Few Famous Quotations

Early to bed and early to rise, makes a man healthy, wealthy and wise.

Nothing is certain but death and taxes.

There never was a good war or a bad peace.

**Benjamin Franklin, *Poor Richard's Almanack,* 1732-1757**

Taxation without representation is tyranny.                        **James Otis, 1761**

By uniting we stand, by dividing we fall.                        **John Dickinson, 1775**

Give me liberty or give me death.                        **Patrick Henry, 1775**

Don't one of you fire until you see the whites of their eyes.                        **William Prescott, 1775**

We must all hang together, else we shall all hang seperately.                        **Benjamin Franklin, 1776**

I only regret that I have but one life to give for my country.                        **Nathan Hale, 1776**

I have just begun to fight.                        **John Paul Jones, 1779**

These are the times that try men's souls.                        **Thomas Paine, 1785**

To be prepared for war is one of the most effectual means of preserving peace.   **George Washington, 1790**

There is always room at the top.                        **Daniel Webster**

Be sure you are right, then go ahead.                        **Davy Crockett, 1812**

Don't give up the ship.                        **Capt. James Lawrence, 1813**

Go West, young man.                        **John L. B. Soule, 1851**

The mass of men lead lives of quiet desperation.                        **Henry David Thoreau, 1854**

It is well that war is so terrible—we would grow too fond of it.                        **Robert E. Lee, 1862**

You can fool all of the people some of the time and some of the people all of the time,
but you can't fool all of the people all of the time.                        **Abraham Lincoln, 1863**

The true republic—men, their rights and nothing more; women, their rights and nothing less.
                        **Susan B. Anthony, 1868**

There's a sucker born every minute.                        **P.T. Barnum**

Politics makes strange bedfellows.                        **Charles Dudley Warner, 1871**

There's many a boy here today who looks on war as all glory, but, boys, it is all hell.
                        **Gen. William T. Sherman, 1888**

Everybody talks about the weather, but nobody does anything about it.                        **Charles Warner, 1890**

## Some Famous Quotations (Continued)

| | |
|---|---|
| The report of my death was an exaggeration. | **Mark Twain, 1897** |
| Speak softly and carry a big stick; you will go far. | **Theodore Roosevelt, 1901** |
| Win one for the Gipper. | **Knute Rockne, 1921** |
| You are all a lost generation. | **Gertrude Stein, 1926** |
| What this country really needs is a good five-cent cigar. | **Thomas Riley Marshall** |
| Never give a sucker an even break. | **W. C. Fields** |
| I tell you, folks, all politics is apple sauce. | **Will Rogers, 1932** |
| I never forget a face, but in your case I'll make an exception. | **Groucho Marx** |
| The only thing we have to fear is fear itself. | **Franklin D. Roosevelt, 1933** |
| A radical is a man with both feet firmly in the air. | **Franklin D. Roosevelt, 1939** |
| Here's looking at you, kid. Play it again, Sam. | **Humphrey Bogart, *Casablanca*, 1943** |
| You can never be too rich or too thin. | **Wallis Simpson, Duchess of Windsor** |
| The world is run by C students. The buck stops here. | **Harry S. Truman, 1945** |
| Fasten your seat belts; it's going to be a bumpy night. | **Bette Davis, *All About Eve*, 1950** |
| Ask not what your country can do for you; ask what you can do for your country. | **John F. Kennedy, 1961** |
| You win some, you lose some, and some get rained out. | **C. E. Wood** |
| One small step for a man, one giant step for mankind. | **Neil Armstrong, 1969** |
| I cried all the way to the bank. | **Liberace, 1973** |
| Nice guys finish last. | **Leo Durocher, 1975** |
| Sometimes when I look at my children, I say to myself, "Lillian, you should have stayed a virgin." | **Lillian Carter, 1980** |
| How do I know why there were Nazis? I don't even know how to work the can opener. | **Woody Allen, *Hannah and Her Sisters*, 1986** |

**Sources:** The Harper Book of American Quotations, Gordon Carruth and Eugene Ehrlich, eds. Harper & Row, New York , 1988
Wit and Wisdom of Famous American Women, Evelyn Beilenson and Ann Tenenbaum, eds. Peter Pauper Press, Inc., White Plains, 1986

# 29: Proverbs

Note: The list of proverbs has been correlated with the list of Topics (pp. 55-135); not all the topics are covered.  The assignment of a proverb to a particular semantic category can be done according to several different criteria. We have assigned the proverbs mostly on the basis of their literal, rather than figurative, meaning.

## Food
Half a loaf is better than none.
Variety is the spice of life.
The bread is buttered on both sides.

## Cooking
Too many cooks spoil the broth.
The pot calls the kettle black.
Out of the frying pan and into the fire.

## Eating
Don't bite the hand that feeds you.
You can't have your cake and eat it too.
First come, first served.

## Housing/Housekeeping
There's no place like home.
People in glass houses shouldn't throw stones.
Walls have ears.

## Clothing
Too big for their britches.
If the shoe fits, wear it.
A stitch in time saves nine.

## Relationships
Every man for himself.
A friend in need is a friend indeed.
Familiarity breeds contempt.
Live and let live.
It takes one to know one.
Two is company, three is a crowd.
Spare the rod and spoil the child.

## Human Qualities
He who hesitates is lost.
Honesty is the best policy.
Haste makes waste.
Where there's a will, there's a way.
Beauty is only skin deep.
Beggars can't be choosers.

## Human Stages
A sucker is born every minute.
Don't throw out the baby with the bath water.
Boys will be boys.
Never say die.
Dead men tell no tales.

## Time
Time heals all wounds.
Never put off 'til tomorrow what you can do today.
Rome was not built in a day.
Better late than never.
Here today, gone tomorrow.
Last but not least.

## Weather
Save it for a rainy day.
Make hay while the sun shines.
It never rains but it pours.
Red sky at morning, sailors take warning;
   Red sky at night, sailor's delight.

## Animals
You can't make a silk purse out of a sow's ear.
Don't throw pearls before swine.
His bark is worse than his bite.
Let sleeping dogs lie.
You can't teach an old dog new tricks.
Curiosity killed the cat.
Let the cat out of the bag.
There are many ways to skin a cat.
When the cat's away the mice will play.
You can lead a horse to water but you can't
   make it drink.
Don't look a gift horse in the mouth.

## Birds
The early bird catches the worm.
Kill two birds with one stone.
 A bird in the hand is worth two in the bush.
Birds of a feather flock together.
Don't count your chickens before they hatch.

## Language
Easier said than done.
No sooner said than done.
Ask me no questions and I'll tell you no lies.
Actions speak louder than words.

## Thinking
Seeing is believing.
Out of sight, out of mind.
Necessity is the mother of invention.
Let your conscience be your guide.
Two heads are better than one.

## Numbers/ Measures
Six of one and half-dozen of another.
Give them an inch and they'll take a mile.
One picture is worth a thousand words.

## Substances and Materials
A rolling stone gathers no moss.
All that glitters is not gold.
Good riddance to bad rubbish.
Every little bit helps.

## Containers
Don't put all your eggs in one basket.
One rotten apple spoils the barrel.

## Emotions
Love makes the world go 'round.
Absence makes the heart grow fonder.
It's no use crying over spilled milk.
Better safe than sorry.
Misery loves company.
Once bitten, twice shy.
He who laughs last, laughs best.

## The Body
In one ear and out the other.
Don't cut off your nose to spite your face.
Blood is thicker than water.
Look before you leap.

## Transportation
Don't put the cart before the horse.
Like carrying coals to Newcastle.
Time and tide wait for no man.

## Money
Money doesn't grow on trees.
Money talks.
Money is the root of all evil.
A fool and his money are soon parted.
A penny saved is a penny earned.
The best things in life are free.
Easy come, easy go.

## Recreation
All work and no play makes Jack a dull boy.
The more the merrier.
Thank God it's Friday.
All work and no play makes Jack a dull boy.

## Sports and Games
Slow and steady wins the race.
Sink or swim.
It's not whether you win or lose,
    but how you play the game.
If you can't beat 'em, join 'em.
Practice makes perfect.

## Medicine and health
An apple a day keeps the doctor away.
An ounce of prevention is worth a pound of cure.
One man's food is another man's poison.
What's good for the goose is good for the gander.

## Business
Nothing ventured, nothing gained.
Everyone has their price.
Business before pleasure.
The customer is always right.

## Shops and Tools
Jack of all trades, master of none.
Hit the nail on the head.
Give me the right tool, I will move the world.

## Law
Truth will out.
Two wrongs don't make a right.
The end justifies the means.

## Media
Bad news travels fast.
No news is good news.
The pen is mightier than the sword.
Don't judge a book by its cover.

## Education
Practice what you preach.
Do as I say, not as I do.

## War
Don't give up the ship.
All is fair in love and war.
War is hell.

## Energy
Where there's smoke, there's fire.
Burn the candle at both ends.
Fight fire with fire.

**Source:** The Dictionary of American Proverbs, David Kin, ed. Philosophical Library.

# 30: Bumper Stickers

*These sayings were collected off of bumpers around the United States in 2005 and 2006.*
*This is a kind of folk wisdom and humor, but we will gladly acknowledge the authors if contacted.*

Kids in sports stay out of courts.

Happy childhoods last a lifetime –
Prevent child abuse.

It's never OK to hit a child.

School's open. Drive carefully.

"Failure is impossible" – *Susan B. Anthony*

If you can read this, you're too damned close.

"It is not our differences that divide us,
it's our inability to recognize, accept, and
celebrate those differences." – *Andre Lorde*

Fight TV addiction.

Ignore your rights, and they'll go away.

Darwin lives.

Defunding education is defeating the future.

Remember you're UNIQUE, like everyone else.

Don't treat your soil like dirt.

I owe, I owe, It's off to work I go.

If only closed minds came with closed mouths.

War is costly. Peace is priceless.

Keep your temper. No one else wants it.

Real women drive trucks.

Politicians and diapers need to be changed –
often for the same reason.

The best way to predict the future
is to help create it,

Do not meddle in the affairs of dragons
for you are crunchy and good with ketchup.

Not all who wander are lost.

I started with nothing and
I have most of it left.

Better to build school rooms for boys
than prisons for men.

Those who are truly educated
never graduate.

I'm for the separation of church and hate.

Commit random acts of kindness
and senseless beauty.

Live simply that others may simply live.

Good planets are hard to find.

Minds are like parachutes.
They only function when open.

Urban Sprawl: Where they tear out the trees
and name streets after them.

Lord help me to be the man
my dog thinks I am.

Humans are not the only creatures on Earth.
We just act like it.

One people, one planet, one future.

Sow justice / Reap peace.

Your kids are watching.

Allow prejudice to grow
and violence will follow.

The problems we face will not be solved
by the minds that created them.

Answer my prayer: steal this car.

Never trust a skinny cook.

"What is a weed? A plant whose virtue is yet
to be discovered." – Emerson

War doesn't decide who's right, only who's left.

It's easier to make a baby than raise a child.

Well behaved women rarely make history.

# 31: Superstitions

The **ace of spades** is a sign of death.

Getting out of **bed** on the wrong side means you will have a bad day.

Letting a **black cat** cross your path brings bad luck.

The **bride** should not see the **husband** on the morning before the wedding.

**Cattle** lying down indicate rain.

A four-leaf **clover** brings good luck.

A **cricket** in the house is good luck.

Hanging a **horseshoe** over the door, points up, brings good luck.

Passing under a **ladder** brings bad luck.

Killing a **ladybug** beetle brings bad luck.

**Lightning** never strikes twice in the same place.

Lighting three cigarettes from one **match** brings bad luck or pregnancy to the third person.

Breaking a **mirror** brings seven years of bad luck.

Finding a **penny** brings good luck ("see a penny, pick it up, all day long you'll have good luck").

Carrying a **rabbit's foot** brings good luck.

Spilling **salt** brings bad luck, but a pinch of the spilled salt thrown over your right shoulder will keep away evil spirits.

Killing a **spider** brings rain.

If you make a wish on a falling **star,** your wish will come true.

The number **thirteen** brings bad luck.

Opening an **umbrella** in the house brings bad luck.

# 32: Family Relationships Chart

also see Communicative Aspect *#8 Family*

great great grandmother = great great grandfather*

great great aunt/uncle – great gandmother = great grandfather - great great uncle/aunt

great aunt/uncle – grandmother = grandfather - great aunt/uncle

aunt – uncle – mother = father – uncle – aunt

*big (older)* sister – *big* brother – **YOU**– *little (younger)* brother – *little* sister

YOU = husband** or wife** (*or* partner)          **spouse

son-in-law = daughter          son = daughter-in-law          *(your)* children

granddaugher/son          grandchildren

great granddaughter/son          **great grandchildren**

great great granddaughter/son          **great great grandchildren**

*(your)* brother = sister-in-law          *(your)* sister = brother-in-law

niece          nephew

great niece/nephew

*(your)* uncle = aunt

*(your)* first cousin = cousin

*(your child's)* second cousin *or (your)* first cousin once removed

*(your)* mother-in-law = father-in-law (*informally* in-laws)

*(your)* husband *or* wife

godparents  or  godmother, godfather

*(your)* late or ex-wife or husband ≠*** YOU = wife *(your children's* stepmother) ≠ ex-husband

*(your)* children          *(your children's)* step-brothers/sisters

***no longer married: death or divorce

*(you have)*
**2 parents –
mother = father
4 grandparents
8 great
grandparents
16 great great
grandparents**
*(2 of each are shown
on the chart)*

# 33: Names

## Most Common First Names (2013) Wikipedia

| US Female | | Canada Female | | US Male | | Canada Male | |
|---|---|---|---|---|---|---|---|
| Sophia | Mia | Maya/Mia | Chloe/Khloe | Noah | Ethan | William | Ethan |
| Emma | Emily | Sofia/Sophia | Ava | Liam | Michael | Jacob | Lucas/Lukas |
| Olivia | Abigail | Olivia | Isabella | Jacob | Alexander | Liam | Benjamin |
| Isabella | Madison | Emma | Sara/Sarah | Mason | Jayden | Nathan | Samuel |
| Ava | Elizabeth | Emily/Emilie | Lea/Leah | William | Daniel | Noah | Logan |

## Other Common Female Names (U.S. 2013) SS Administation

| | | | | | | | |
|---|---|---|---|---|---|---|---|
| Mary | Linda | Jennifer | Margaret | Nancy | Helen | Donna | Ruth |
| Patricia | Barbara | Maria | Dorothy | Karen | Sandra | Carol | Sharon |
| | | Susan | Lisa | Betty | | | |

## Other Common Male Names (U.S. 2013) SS Administation

| | | | | | | | |
|---|---|---|---|---|---|---|---|
| James | Robert | Richard | Thomas | Donald | George | Kenneth | Edward |
| John | David | Joseph | Christopher | Anthony | Mark | Andrew | Joshua |
| | | Charles | Matthew | Paul | Steven | | |

## Most Common Surnames (U.S. 2013) Wikipedia

| | | | | | | | |
|---|---|---|---|---|---|---|---|
| Smith | Garcia | Hernandez | Gonzalez | Young | Adams | Phillips | Stewart |
| Johnson | Rodriguez | Moore | Harris | Allen | Nelson | Evans | Flores |
| Williams | Wilson | Martin | Clark | Sanchez | Hill | Turner | Morris |
| Brown | Martinez | Jackson | Lewis | Wright | Ramirez | Torres | Nguyen |
| Jones | Anderson | Thompson | Robinson | King | Campbell | Parker | Murphy |
| Miller | Taylor | White | Walker | Scott | Mitchell | Collins | Rivera |
| Davis | Thomas | Lopez | Perez | Green | Roberts | Edwards | Cook |
| | | Lee | Hall | Baker | Carter | | |

## Common Irregular Nicknames

Nicknames in English are typically abbreviations of the full form of the name.
Thus, Benjamin becomes Ben, Samuel > Sam, Andrew > Andy, Christine > Chris, Patricia > Pat/Patty, and
Victoria > Vicky, Vickie, or Vicki

| | | | |
|---|---|---|---|
| Becky (Rebecca) | Jim (James) | Sally (Sarah) | Dusty |
| Bess, Beth, Betsy, | Kate, Kathy (Katherine) | Ted (Theodore) | Junior |
|   Betty, (Elizabeth) | Kit (Christopher) | Tom, Tommy (Thomas) | Lefty |
| Bill, Billy (William) | Kit, Kitty, Tina (Christine) | Tony (Anthony) | Mack |
| Cathy (Catherine) | Larry (Lawrence) | Trish (Patricia) | Missy |
| Bob, Bobby (Robert) | Lex (Alexander) | Babe | Red, Rusty |
| Chuck (Charles) | Liz, Lizzy (Elizabeth) | Bud, Buddy | Shorty, Slim |
| Dick, Rick (Richard) | Mandy (Amanda) | Buba | Sis, Sissy |
| Hank (Henry) | Maggie, Meg (Margaret) | Buck, Bucky | Sonny |
| Harry (Harold) | Micky, Mike (Michael) | Butch | Tex |
| Jack (John) | Marjie (Marjorie) | Chip | Tiger |
| | Peg (Margaret) | Doc | |

(Source for the information above: Social Security Administration)

# 34: Place Names

## Common Place Names

| | | | |
|---|---|---|---|
| Washington | Brookfield | Elkton | New Haven |
| Jefferson | Deerfield | Evanston | Riverdale |
| Madison | Fairfield | Hampton | Troy |
| Monroe | Greenfield | Lexington | Hanover |
| Jackson | Springfield | Princeton | Salem |
| Lincoln | Longmeadow | Wheaton | Richmond |
| Franklin | Edgewood | Guilford | London |
| Lafayette | Elmwood | Stratford | Dover |
| Leesburg | Pleasantville | Portland | Plymouth |
| Libertyville | Summerville | Columbia | Highland Park |
| Independence | Bloomington | Lebanon | Newport |
| | Canton | | |

## English Elements of Common Place Names in the U.S. and Canada

**Note:** In both Canada and the United States, Indian and French place names are common; Spanish place names are very common in the Western and Southern United States. Some examples are: Indian – Saskatchewan, Ottawa, Massachusetts, Mississippi, Illinois; French – Montreal, New Orleans, Vermont, Louisiana; Spanish – Santa Fe, San Francisco, Florida, Nevada. Many places in Canada and the U.S. are also named after places in England: Boston, MA; London, ON. However, one of the most common ways of creating North American place names has been the practice of building the names from standard elements prefixed and/or suffixed to family names or animal names. This is typically English, and done mostly with English names. For example, using the family name Hart, East Hartford Junction. Using an animal, Little Deerfield Falls.

| | | |
|---|---|---|
| North- | - town | - City |
| East- | - ton | - Village |
| South- | - ville | - Park |
| West- | - apolis | - Valley |
| New- | - burg | - Junction |
| Old- | - bury | - Hills |
| Great- | - boro(ugh) | - Heights |
| Big- | - minster | - Mills |
| Little- | - stead | - Locks |
| Fort- | - sex | - Lake |
| Port- | - ford | - Beach |
| Brook- | - land | - Point |
| River- | - wood | - Haven |
| Glen- | - forest | - Harbor |
| Mount- | - field | - Shores |
| Saint- | - vale | - Bay |
| Oak- | - dale | - Rock |
| Elm- | - crest | - Bluffs |
| Pine- | - port | - Falls |
| Maple- | - side | - Creek |
| Cedar- | - view | - Crossing |
| Belle- | - bridge | - Rapids |
| Green- | - ham | - Springs |
| Winter- | | - Ferry |

# 35: Sports Teams in the U.S. and Canada
## Major League Baseball

### American League

| Eastern Division | Central Division | Western Division |
|---|---|---|
| Baltimore Orioles | Chicago White Sox | Los Angeles Angels |
| Boston Red Sox | Cleveland Indians | Oakland Athletics |
| New York Yankees | Detroit Tigers | Seattle Mariners |
| Tampa Bay Rays | Kansas City Royals | Texas Rangers |
| Toronto Blue Jays | Minnesota Twins | Houston Astros |

### National League

| Eastern Division | Central Division | Western Division |
|---|---|---|
| Atlanta Braves | Chicago Cubs | Arizona Diamondbacks |
| Miami Marlins | Cincinnati Reds | Colorado Rockies |
| New York Mets | Milwaukee Brewers | Los Angeles Dodgers |
| Philadelphia Phillies | Pittsburgh Pirates | San Diego Padres |
| Washington Nationals | St. Louis Cardinals | San Francisco Giants |

## National Hockey League

### Eastern Conference

| Atlantic Division | Metropolian Division |
|---|---|
| Boston Bruins | Carolina Hurricanes |
| Buffalo Sabres | Columbus Blue Jackets |
| Detroit Red Wings | New Jersey Devils |
| Florida Panthers | New York Islanders |
| Montreal Canadiens | New York Rangers |
| Ottawa Senators | Philadelphia Flyers |
| Tampa Bay Lightning | Pittsburgh Penguins |
| Toronto Maple Leafs | Washington Capitals |

### Western Conference

| Pacific Division | Central Division |
|---|---|
| Anaheim Ducks | Chicago Black Hawks |
| Calgary Flames | Colorado Avalanche |
| Edmonton Oilers | Dallas Stars |
| Los Angeles Kings | Minnesota Wild |
| Phoenix Coyotes | Nashville Predators |
| San Jose Sharks | St. Louis Blues |
| Vancouver Canucks | Winnipeg Jets |

## Major League Soccer

### Eastern Conference

| | |
|---|---|
| Chicago Fire | New England Revolution |
| Columbus Crew | New York Red Bulls |
| D.C. United | Philadelphia Union |
| Houston Dynamo | Sporting Kansas City |
| Montreal Impact | Toronto FC |

### Western Conference

| | |
|---|---|
| Chivas USA | Real Salt Lake |
| Colorado Rapids | San Jose Earthquakes |
| FC Dallas | Seattle Sounders FC |
| LA Galaxy | Vancouver Whitecaps |
| Portland Timbers | |

# National Football League
## National Conference

| <u>North</u> | <u>South</u> | <u>East</u> | <u>West</u> |
|---|---|---|---|
| Chicago Bears | Atlanta Falcons | Dallas Cowboys | Arizona Cardinals |
| Detroit Lions | Carolina Panthers | New York Giants | San Francisco 49ers |
| Green Bay Packers | New Orleans Saints | Philadelphia Eagles | Seattle Seahawks |
| Minnesota Vikings | Tampa Bay Buccaneers | Washington Redskins | St Louis Rams |

## American Conference

| <u>North</u> | <u>South</u> | <u>East</u> | <u>West</u> |
|---|---|---|---|
| Baltimore Ravens | Houston Texans | Buffalo Bills | Denver Broncos |
| Cincinnati Bengals | Indianapolis Colts | Miami Dolphins | Kansas City Chiefs |
| Cleveland Browns | Jacksonville Jaguars | New England Patriots | Oakland Raiders |
| Pittsburgh Steelers | Tennessee Titans | New York Jets | San Diego Chargers |

# National Basketball Association
## Eastern Conference

| **Atlantic Division** | **Southeastern Division** | **Central Division** |
|---|---|---|
| Boston Celtics | Atlanta Hawks | Chicago Bulls |
| Brooklyn Nets | Charlotte Bobcats | Cleveland Cavaliers |
| New York Knicks | Miami Heat | Detroit Pistons |
| Philadelphia 76ers | Orland Magic | Indiana Pacers |
| Toronto Raptors | Washington Wizards | Milwaukee Bucks |

## Western Conference

| **Southwest Division** | **Northwest Division** | **Pacific Division** |
|---|---|---|
| Dallas Mavericks | Denver Nuggets | Golden State Warriors |
| Houston Rockets | Minnesota Timberwolves | Los Angeles Clippers |
| Memphis Grizzlies | Oklahoma City Thunder | Los Angeles Lakers |
| New Orleans Pelicans | Portland Trail Blazers | Phoenix Suns |
| San Antonio Spurs | Seattle Supersonics | Sacramento Kings |
| | Utah Jazz | |

# Women's National Basketball Associaton

| **Eastern Conference** | | **Western Association** | |
|---|---|---|---|
| Atlanta Dream | Indiana Fever | Los Angeles Sparks | San Antonio Stars |
| Chicago Sky | New York Liberty | Minnesota Lynx | Seattle Storm |
| Connecticut Sun | Washington Mystic | Phoenix Mercury | Tulsa Shock |

244

# 36: Sports Legends

Hank **Aaron** (baseball) 1934-
Kareem **Abdul-Jabbar** (basketball) 1947-
Andre **Agassi** (tennis) 1970-
Muhammad **Ali** (boxing) 1942-
Mario **Andretti** (auto racing) 1940-
Eddie **Arcaro** (horse racing) 1916-97
Arthur **Ashe** (tennis) 1943-1993
Ernie **Banks** (baseball) 1931-
Charles **Barkley** (basketball) 1963-
Elgin **Baylor** (basketball) 1934-
David **Beckham** (soccer) 1975-
Patty **Berg** (golf) 1918-2006
Yogi **Berra** (baseball) 1925-
Larry **Bird** (basketball) 1956-
Bonnie **Blair** (speed skating) 1964-
Ray **Bourque** (ice hockey) 1960-
Jim **Brown** (football) 1936-
Dick **Button** (ice skating) 1929-
Paul "Bear" **Bryant** (football) 1913-1983
Roy **Campanella** (baseball) 1921-1993
Wilt **Chamberlain** (basketball) 1936-1999
Roger **Clemens** (baseball) 1962-
Roberto **Clemente** (baseball) 1934-1972
Ty **Cobb** (baseball) 1896-1991
Nadia **Comaneci** (gymnastics) 1961-
Bob **Cousy** (basketball) 1928-
Buster **Crabbe** (swimming) 1908-1983
Oscar **De La Hoya** (boxing) 1973-
Jack **Dempsey** (boxing) 1895-1983
Joe **Dimaggio** (baseball) 1914-1999
Dale **Earnhardt** (auto racing) 1951-2001
Julius **Erving** (basketball) 1950-
Phil **Esposito** (ice hockey) 1942-
Chris **Evert** (tennis) 1954-
Patrick **Ewing** (basketball) 1962-
Marshall **Faulk** (football) 1973-
Brett **Favre** (football) 1969-
Bob **Feller** (baseball) 1918-2010
Peggy **Fleming** (ice skating) 1948-
Nomar **Garciaparra** (baseball) 1973-

Lou **Gehrig** (baseball) 1903-1941
Althea **Gibson** (tennis) 1927-2003
Pancho **Gonzalez** (tennis) 1928-1995
Evonne **Goolagong** (tennis) 1951-
Steffi **Graf** (tennis) 1969-
Red **Grange** (football) 1904-1991
Ken **Griffey**, Jr. (baseball) 1969-
Wayne **Gretzky** (ice hockey) 1961-
Lefty **Grove** (baseball) 1900-1975
Dorothy **Hamill** (ice skating) 1956-
Scot **Hamilton** (ice skating) 1958-
Mia **Hamm** (soccer) 1972-
Eric **Heiden** (speed skating) 1958-
Sonja **Henie** (ice skating) 1912-1969
Ben **Hogan** (golf) 1912-1997
Gordon **Howe** (ice hockey) 1928-
Bobby **Hull** (ice hockey) 1939-
Reggie **Jackson** (baseball) 1946-
Derek **Jeter** (baseball) 1974-
Earvin "Magic" **Johnson** (basketball) 1959-
Randy **Johnson** (baseball) 1963-
Michael **Jordan** (basketball) 1963-
Florence **Joyner** (track) 1959-1998
Jackie **Joyner-Kersee** (track) 1962-
Duke **Kahanamoku** (swimming, surfing) 1890-1968
Jean-Claude **Killy** (skiing) 1943-
Billie-Jean **King** (tennis) 1943-
Olga **Korbut** (gymnastics) 1955-
Sandy **Koufax** (baseball) 1935-
Anna **Kournikova** (tennis) 1981-
Michelle **Kwan** (ice skating) 1980-
Guy **LaFleur** (ice hockey) 1951-
Rod **Laver** (tennis) 1938-
Mario **Lemieux** (ice hockey) 1965-
Sugar Ray **Leonard** (boxing) 1956-
Carl **Lewis** (track & field) 1961-
Vince **Lombardi** (football) 1913-1970
Nancy **Lopez** (golf) 1957-
Joe **Louis** (boxing) 1914-1981

Tara **Lupinski** (*ice skating*)1982-
Karl **Malone** (*basketball*) 1963-
Mickey **Mantle** (*baseball*) 1931-1995
Diego **Maradona** (*soccer*) 1960-
Rocky **Marciano** (*boxing*) 1923-1969
Dan **Marino** (*football*) 1961-
Pedro **Martinez** (*baseball*) 1971-
Willie **Mays** (*baseball*) 1931-
Yao **Ming** (*basketball*) 1980-
John **McEnroe** (*tennis*) 1959-
Joe **Montana** (*football*) 1956-
Stan **Musial** (*baseball*) 1920-2013
Joe **Namath** (*football*) 1943-
Ilie **Nastase** (*tennis*) 1946-
Jack **Nicklaus** (*golf*) 1940-
Hakeem **Olajuwon** (*basketball*) 1963-
Shaquille **O'Neal** (*basketball*) 1972-
Bobby **Orr** (*ice hockey*) 1948-
Jesse **Owens** (*track & field*) 1913-1980
Satchel **Paige** (*baseball*)1906-1982
Arnold **Palmer** (*golf*) 1929-
Walter **Payton** (*football*) 1954-1999)
**Pele** (*soccer*) 1940-
Maurice **Richard** (*ice hockey*) 1921-2000
Jim **Rice** 1953-
Cal **Ripken** (*baseball*) 1960-
Mariano **Rivera** (*baseball*) 1969-

Frank **Robinson** (*baseball*) 1935-
Jackie **Robinson** (*baseball*) 1919-1972
Knute **Rockne** (*football*) 1988-1931
Wilma **Rudolph** (*track & field*) 1940-1994
Bill **Russell** (*basketball*) 1934-
Babe **Ruth** (*baseball*) 1895-1948
Nolan **Ryan** (*baseball*) 1947-
Tom **Seaver** (*baseball*) 1949-
Emmit **Smith** (*football*) 1969-
Sam **Snead** (*golf*) 1912-2002
Annika **Sorenstam** (*golf*) 1970-
Warren **Spahn** (*baseball*) 1921-2003
Mark **Spitz** (*swimming*) 1950-
Bart **Starr** (*football*) 1934-
Casey **Stengel** (*baseball*) 1991-1975
Lynn **Swann** (*football*) 1952-
Joe **Theisman** (*football*) 1946-
Frank **Thomas** (*baseball*) 1968-
Jim **Thorpe** (*track & field, football, baseball*) 1888-1953
Lee **Trevino** (*golf*) 1939-
John **Unitas** (*football*) 1933-2002
Jersey Joe **Walcott** (*boxing*) 1914-1994
Tom **Watson** (*golf*) 1949-
Ted **Williams** (*baseball*) 1918-2002
Katarina **Witt** (*ice skating*) 1965-
Babe **Zaharias** (*golf*) 1911-1956

# Contemporary Sports Heroes

Tom **Brady** (*football*)
Kobe **Bryant** (*basketball*)
Reggie **Bush** (*football*)
Madison **Bumgarner** (baseball)
Tim **Duncan** (*basketball*)
Ernie **Els** (*golf*)
Roger **Federer** (*tennis*)
Martina **Hingis** (*tennis*)
**Ichiro** Suzuki (*baseball*)
LeBron **James** (*basketball*)
Eli **Manning** (*football*)
Peyton **Manning** (*football*)
Rory **Mcilroy** (*golf*)
Phil **Mickelson** (*golf*)

Maya Moore (*basketball*)
Rafael **Nadal** (*tennis*)
David **Ortiz** (*baseball*)
Albert **Pujols** (*baseball*)
Andy **Roddick** (*tennis*)
Maria **Sharapova** (*tennis*)
Vijay **Singh** (*golf*)
Diana **Taurasi** (*basketball*)
Joe **Thornton** (*ice hockey*)
Mike **Trout** (*baseball*)
Serena **Williams** (*tennis*)
Venus **Williams** (*tennis*)
Michelle **Wie** (*golf*)
Tiger **Woods** (*golf*)

# 37: U.S. School System Chart

| Name of School | Grade | Age of Students | Subjects |
|---|---|---|---|
| **Nursery School** | | 3-5 | Games, songs, creative play |
| **Kindergarten** | K | 4-6 | Games, drawing, crafts, beginning reading, writing |
| **Elementary School** 1-5 or 1-6 | 1 2 3 | 5-7 6-8 7-9 | Reading, writing, spelling, adding, drawing, music Language arts, subtraction, spelling, drawing, music Language arts, social studies, multiplication, music |
| **Middle School** 5-9 or 6-9 | 4 5 6 | 8-10 9-11 10-12 | Language arts, social studies, division Language arts, social studies, fractions Language arts, social studies, decimals, science |
| **Junior High School** | 7 8 | 11-13 12-14 | Language arts, social studies, math, science, foreign language Language arts, social studies, math, science, foreign language |
| **High School** Freshman | 9 | 13-15 | **Core Courses:** English, algebra, civics, biology, foreign language **Electives:** Music, art, typing, bookkeeping, economics, technical education, home economics |
| Sophmore | 10 | 14-16 | **Core Courses:** English, geometry, history, chemistry, foreign language **Electives:** Music, art, bookkeeping, economics, consumer education, computer applications |
| Junior | 11 | 15-17 | **Core Courses:** English, advanced math, history, physics, foreign language **Electives:** Music, art, bookkeeping, economics, consumer education, computer applications |
| Senior | 12 | 16-18 | **Core Courses:** English, calculus, history, foreign language **Electives:** Music, art, bookkeeping, economics, consumer education, computer programming |

## College and University

| | Age | Degree | Length of time required |
|---|---|---|---|
| *Undergraduate College* | | | |
| Junior College | 17- | AA | 2 years |
| Four-Year College | 18- | BA, BS | 4-5 years |
| *University Graduate School* | 21- | MA, MS | 2-3 years plus thesis |
| Graduate school | | PhD, LHD, Litt. D., DCL | 3 years plus thesis |
| Medical school | | MD, DDS | 2 years plus residency |
| Law school | | JS | 3 years |

# 38. Currencies: U. S. Coins and Bills

| 1 cent/penny | 5 cents/nickel | 10 cents/dime | 25 cents/quarter | 50 cents/half dollar | 1 dollar |
|---|---|---|---|---|---|

(1¢) Lincoln    (5¢) Jefferson    (10¢) Roosevelt  (25¢) Washington    (50¢) Kennedy    ($1) Presidents

$1.00 Washington
The dollar bill
A "buck"

$10.00 Hamilton
Ten dollar bill
A "sawbuck" or
"ten spot."

U. S. Treasury
Building

$50.00 Grant
Fifty dollar bill

U. S. Capitol
Building

$2.00 Jefferson
Two dollar bill
*(rare)*

*Signing of the
Declaration of
Independence*

$20.00 Jackson
Twenty dollar bill

The White
House

$100.00 Franklin
One hundred
    dollar bill

Independence
Hall,
Philadelphia

$5.00 Lincoln
Five dollar bill
A "fiver" or "fin"

Lincoln
Memorial

Federal Reserve notes are printed and issued in denominations of $1, $2, $5, $10, $20, $50, and $100. The $500, $1,000, $5,000, and $10,000 denominations have not been printed since 1946.

Between 1999 and 2008 the Federal Reserve is issuing 5 new quarters each year, each commemorating one of the 50 states. The coins are being released in the order in which the states joined the Union beginning with Delaware and ending with Hawaii.

*See page 95:
Banks and Money.*
U.S. 25¢ coin is called "two bits."
Older U.S. $1 coins were called "silver dollars."

U.S. bills are called paper money and "green backs."

## Canadian Coins and Bills

| 1¢/penny | 5¢/nickel | 10¢/dime | 25¢/quarter | 50¢/half dollar | $1/Loonie | $2/Toonie | $2/Vootie/Noonie | Face |
|---|---|---|---|---|---|---|---|---|

Maple Leaf   Beaver    Schooner      Caribou      Coat of Arms      Loon      Polar Bear      Nunavut        Elizabeth II
                        Bluenose                                                                 Inuit Drummer     *on all coins*

$5.00
Sir Wilfred Laurier
*Back:*
Children at Play

$20.00
Queen Elizabeth II
*Back:*
Common Loon

$100.00
Sir Robert L. Borden
*Back:* Exploration
and Innovation

$10.00
Sir John Macdonald
*Back:*
Rememberance Day
and Peace Keeping

$50.00
William L. M. King
*Back:*
Snowy Owl

$1000.00
Queen Elizabeth II
*Back:*
Pine Grosbeak
*(rare)*

# 39: Television

## Traditional Programming

Morning      Game shows
Daytime talk shows
Cartoons (weekends)
News programs/weather
Religious programs (Sunday)
Children's/educational programs

Afternoon      Movies
Game shows
Daytime talk shows
Afternoon soap operas
Sports events (weekends)
News programs/weather/sports
Children's/educational programs

Evenings      Movies
Documentaries
Special reports
Drama programs
Situation comedies (Sitcoms)
Evening soap operas
News programs/weather/sports

Late night      Movies
Talk shows
News programs

## Television Sets

**Total TV Households:**      **Percent of households:** 96.7%

**Homes with:**

| | |
|---|---|
| Color TV sets | 100% |
| 2 or more sets | 81% |
| Basic cable/satellite | 86% |
| Remote control | 98% |

# Favorite TV Shows

**1960s**
Bonanza
The Red Skelton Show
The Andy Griffith Show
The Beverly Hillbillies
The Ed Sullivan Show
The Lucy Show/Here's Lucy
The Jackie Gleason Show
Bewitched
Gomer Pyle
Candid Camera
The Dick Van Dyke Show
The Danny Thomas Show
Family Affair
Laugh-in
Rawhide

**1970s**
All in the Family
M*A*S*H
Hawaii Five-O
Happy Days
The Waltons
The Mary Tyler Moore Show
Sanford & Son
One Day at a Time
Three's Company
60 Minutes
Maude
Gunsmoke
Charlie's Angels
The Jeffersons
Laverne & Shirley

**1980s**
Bill Cosby Show
Cheers
Dallas
Roseanne
A Different World
America's Funniest Home
Videos

Golden Girls
Wonder Years
Empty Nest
60 Minutes
Dynasty
Roseanne
Unsolved Mysteries
L.A. Law
Who's the Boss?
Grand
Murder, She Wrote
NBC Sunday Night Movie

**1990s**
Cheers
60 Minutes
Home Improvement
Seinfeld
E.R.
Oprah Winfrey
Veronica's Chest
Touched by an Angel
Friends
NYPD Blue
The Simpsons
Everybody Loves Raymond

**2000s**
Friends
The Daily Show
The Simpsons
The O.C.
American Idol
House
Charmed
Sex and the City
Desperate Housewives
CSI: Miami
Arrested Development
The West Wing
Dancing with the Stars
Grey's Anatomy

The Good Wife
The Vampire Diaries
The Big Bang Theory
The Supranos
Supernatural
Mad Men
How I Met Your Mother
NCIS

**2010s**
Futurama
The Colbert Report
Masterpiece Mystery
Arrested Development
Luther
The Americans
Battlestar Galactica
Sherlock
Justified
Hannibal
Boardwalk Empire
The Fall
Criminal Minds
Bones
Fargo
True Detective
American Horror Story
The Mentalist
30 Rock
Orange is the New Black
House of Cards
True Detective
Cosmos
Game of Thrones
Fargo
Firefly
The Wire
Breaking Bad
Modern Family
Lost
The Tutors
Vikings
John Adams
Homeland

# 40: U.S. Publications
## U.S. Magazines Circulation

**Rank Magazine, Circulation**

*http://www.psaresearch.com/images/TOPMAGAZINES.pdf*

| | | | | |
|---|---|---|---|---|
| 1 | *AARP The Magazine,* 23,721,626 | | 26 | *Parenting,* 2,229,253 |
| 2 | *AARP Bulletin,* 23,574,328 | | 27 | *Redbook,* 2,226,356 |
| 3 | *The Costco Connection,* 8,196,081 | | 28 | *Parents,* 2,202,324 |
| 4 | *Better Homes And Gardens,* 7,644,011 | | 29 | *FamilyFun,* 2,117,635 |
| 5 | *Reader's Digest,* 6,112,811 | | 30 | *TV Guide,* 2,093,124 |
| 6 | *National Geographic,* 4,493,110 | | 31 | *ESPN The Magazine,* 2,073,813 |
| 7 | *Good Housekeeping,* 4,427,964 | | 32 | *AAA World,* 2,072,502 |
| 8 | *Game Informer,* 4,364,170 | | 33 | *Martha Stewart Living,* 2,057,960 |
| 9 | *Woman's Day,* 3,919,488 | | 34 | *Smithsonian,* 2,054,696 |
| 10 | *Family Circle,* 3,849,673 | | 35 | *Seventeen,* 2,048,781 |
| 11 | *Ladies' Home Journal,* 3,831,072 | | 36 | *Guideposts,* 2,026,433 |
| 12 | *People,* 3,553,420 | | 37 | *Real Simple,* 2,014,781 |
| 13 | *Time,* 3,312,484 | | 38 | *Us Weekly,* 1,952,885 |
| 14 | *Taste of Home,* 3,257,200 | | 39 | *Money,* 1,928,179 |
| 15 | *Sports Illustrated,* 3,212,278 | | 40 | *Men's Health,* 1,917,411 |
| 16 | *Cosmopolitan,* 3,046,229 | | 41 | *Entertainment Weekly,* 1,798,643 |
| 17 | *Prevention,* 2,927,638 | | 42 | *American Rifleman,* 1, 794,633 |
| 18 | *Southern Living,* 2,841,894 | | 43 | *Cooking Light,* 1,783,139 |
| 19 | *Via,* 2,740,176 | | 44 | *InStyle,* 1,760,365 |
| 20 | *Maxim,* 2,549,893 | | 45 | *Every Day with Rachael Ray,* 1,709,636 |
| 21 | *Remedy/Remedy MD,* 2,517,659 | | 46 | *Golf Digest,* 1,676,792 |
| 22 | *AAA Living,* 2,460,455 | | 47 | *Birds & Blooms,* 1,655,052 |
| 23 | *O, The Oprah Magazine,* 2,415,336 | | 48 | *Shape,* 1,650,752 |
| 24 | *The American Legion Magazine,* 2,346,264 | | 49 | *Playboy,* 1,628,567 |
| 25 | *Glamour,* 2,320,325 | | 50 | *Country Living,* 1,614,398 |

# Top 25 U.S. and Canada News Sites
(www.alyoucanread.com)

| U.S. | | Canada | |
|---|---|---|---|
| 1 | CNN | 1 | CBC |
| 2 | ESPN | 2 | Canoe.ca |
| 3 | Fox Sports | 3 | The Globe and Mail |
| 4 | Fox News | 4 | TSN |
| 5 | New York Times | 5 | La Presse |
| 6 | ABC News | 6 | The Loop |
| 7 | USA Today | 7 | Toronto Star |
| 8 | People | 8 | Radio Canada |
| 9 | Washington P{ost | 9 | National Post |
| 10 | TMZ.com | 10 | Canada.com |
| 11 | Los Angeles Times | 11 | Toronto Sun |
| 12 | Yardbarker.com | 12 | Vancouver Sun |
| 13 | Wall Street Journal | 13 | TVA Nouvelles |
| 14 | Forbes | 14 | RDS |
| 15 | Bleacher Report | 15 | Huffington Post |
| 16 | ThePostGame | 16 | Le Journal de Montreal |
| 17 | CBS News | 17 | Montreal Gazette |
| 18 | Reuters | 18 | CTV News |
| 19 | NewsMax.com | 19 | Envedette |
| 20 | SI.com | 20 | Calgary Herald |
| 21 | New York Daily News | 21 | Winnipeg Free Pres |
| 22 | Sporting News | 22 | Celebedge.ca |
| 23 | Bloomberg | 23 | Argent |
| 24 | CNBC | 24 | Ottawa Citizen |
| 25 | Examiner.com | 25 | Edmonton Journal |

# 41. U.S. National Documents

## The U.S. National Anthem
### The Star-Spangled Banner
*Francis Scott Key, 1814*

O say, can you see, by the dawn's early light,
What so proudly we hail'd at the twilight's last gleaming?
Whose broad stripes and bright stars, thro' the perilous fight,
O'er the ramparts we watch'd, were so gallantly streaming?
And the rockets' red glare, the bombs bursting in air,
Gave proof thro' the night that our flag was still there,
O say, does that star-spangled banner yet wave
O'er the land of the free and the home of the brave?

## Declaration of Independence
### *Thomas Jefferson, 1776*

When in the Course of human Events, it becomes necessary for one People to dissolve the Political Bands which have connected them with another, and to assume among the Powers of the Earth, the separate and equal Station to which the Laws of Nature and of Nature's God entitle them, a decent Respect to the Opinions of Mankind requires that they should declare the causes which impel them to the Separation.

We hold these Truths to be self-evident, that all Men are created equal, that they are endowed by their Creator with certain unalienable Rights, that among these are Life, Liberty and the Pursuit of Happiness — That to secure these Rights, Governments are instituted among Men, deriving their just Powers from the Consent of the Governed, that whenever any Form of Government becomes destructive of these Ends, it is the Right of the People to alter or to abolish it, and to institute new Government, laying its Foundation on such Principles, and organizing its Powers in such Form, as to them shall seem most likely to affect their Safety and Happiness. Prudence, indeed, will dictate that Governments long established should not be changed for light and transient Causes; and accordingly all Experience hath shewn, that Mankind are more disposed to suffer while Evils are sufferable, than to right themselves by abolishing the Forms to which they are accustomed. But when a long Train of Abuses and Usurpations, pursuing invariably the same Object, evinces a Design to reduce them under absolute Despotism, it is their Right, it is their Duty, to throw off such Government, and to provide new Guards for their future Security.

## The Preamble of the Constitution, 1787

We the People of the United States, in order to form a more perfect Union, establish Justice, insure domestic Tranquility, provide for the common Defense, promote the general Welfare, and secure the Blessings of Liberty to ourselves and our Posterity, do ordain and establish this Constitution for the United States of America.

# U.S. Constitution: A Brief Summay

*as amended*     also see #7 *Government Structure of the U.S.*

## Article I – The Legislature

1. All laws are made by Congress: the Senate and the House of Representatives.
2. A representative must be 25 years old, a U.S. citizen for 7 years, and a resident of the state he or she represents. Representatives serve for 2 years. The rest of Section 2 and the amendments related to it explain how many representatives each state gets. The House chooses its own officers and has the sole power of impeachment.
3. A senator must be 30 years old, a U.S. citizen for 9 years, and a resident of the state he or she represents. Each state gets two senators and they serve for 6 years.
The Vice President is President of the Senate, but only votes to break a tie vote. The other officers of the Senate are chosen by the Senate. The Senate tries officials impeached by the House and can remove them from office.
4. Congress shall meet once a year.
5. Each house of Congress judges the election and qualifications of its members and sets its own rules. Members can be expelled by a 2/3 vote of that house.
6. Members of Congress are paid by the U.S. Treasury. They are not allowed to have any other government job. They cannot be arrested during their term in office except for treason, a felony, or a breach of the peace. They can only be questioned about what they say in Congress while they are in Congress.
7. All bills raising money originate in the House. The Senate may amend the bill. It then goes to the President. If he signs it, or holds it for 10 days without signing it, the bill becomes law. If he vetoes it, the bill goes back to the Congress. They can rewrite it, or if they vote on it again and it passes by a 2/3 majority, it becomes law.
8. Congress has the power to tax and set other duties, but all taxes and duties must be the same in all the states. It can borrow money, regulate trade with other countries and among the states, make laws regulating naturalization and bankruptcy, coin money, set its value, and set standards of weights and measures. It can set punishment for counterfeiting, set up a post office, and set up rules for patents and copyright. It can set up courts below the Supreme Court. It can define and punish piracy and felony at sea and offenses against international law. Only Congress can declare war or raise and support and make rules for regulating an army and navy. To enforce its laws, suppress insurrections, and repel invasions, Congress can also call up, organize, arm, and discipline a militia, although each state trains its militia and appoints its officers. Congress has authority over Washington, D.C., and all government property.
9. The writ of Habeas Corpus shall not be suspended except in cases of rebellion or invasion. Congress cannot favor one state over another in matters of taxes or duties. No money can be spent by the government unless Congress provides it. The government shall not grant titles of nobility, nor shall anyone working for the government accept anything of value from another country.
10. States cannot have treaties with other states or countries nor make laws or collect taxes which conflict with the rights of the federal government, without permission of Congress.

## Article II – The Executive

1. Section 1 describes the 4-year term of the President, the way he or she is elected, and how he or she is paid. It explains that the Vice President takes over if the Presidency is vacant. It gives the oath of office: *I do solemnly swear (or affirm) that I will faithfully execute the Office of President of the United States and will to the best of my ability, preserve, protect, and defend the Constitution of the United States.*
2. The President is the Commander-in-Chief of the Armed Forces, including the Malitia when it is serving the Federal Government. He also runs the executive departments, and he or she has the right to grant pardons, except in cases of impeachment.
With the advice and consent of the Senate, if 2/3 of the Senate agrees, the President can make treaties with other countries and appoint ambassadors, judges of the Supreme Court, and all other officers of the government

not mentioned in the Constitution, Congress may by law give the President the right to make these appointments or give that right to the courts or department heads. If offices need to be filled when the Senate is not in session, the President may appoint someone to serve until the end of that session of Congress.

3. From time to time the President must give Congress information on the State of the Union and recommend actions for their consideration. He or she can call either or both houses of Congress into a special session, and if they cannot decide when to adjourn, he may adjourn them until a date of his choice. The President receives ambassadors and other public ministers, commissions officers of the United States, and runs the country under law.

4. The President, Vice President, and all civil officers of the U.S. shall be removed from office only if they are impeached for and convicted of treason, bribery, or "other high crimes and misdemeanors."

### Article III – The Courts

1. The judicial power is vested in one Supreme Court and other courts set up by Congress. Judges hold their appointments for life as long as they are not removed by Congress for bad behavior. Their pay cannot be cut.

2. The federal courts decide all national and international cases, in law and equity, relating to the Constitution and treaties, involving the government and other nations or maritime law, or controversies between the states or between individuals and states other than their own, or between individuals in different states or involving property in different states. Cases involving any state or officers of other countries start in the Supreme Court. All other cases, unless Congress makes exceptions, go to lower courts but can be appealed to the Supreme Court. Trials of crimes are held in the state where the crime was committed, and they are jury trials. When a crime is not committed in a state, the site of the trial is set by the Congressional law.

3. The only crime considered to be treason is participation in a war against the U.S. or giving aid and comfort to its enemies. At least two witnesses of an overt act are necessary to prove treason. Congress can punish a traitor physically and financially, but only while living.

### Article IV – The States

1. The laws, records, and legal decisions of each state must be accepted by the others. Conflicts must be settled by laws passed by Congress.

2. Citizens of every state have the privileges and are protected by the laws of the U.S.

3. Persons charged with treason, felonies, or other crimes, when caught in another state, shall be returned to the state with jurisdiction over the crime, if that state requests it.

4. Congress can make new states, but if the new state includes territory of other states, the legislatures of those states must consent. Congress makes the rules and regulations for all territories and other properties of the U.S.

5. The U.S. guarantees a Republican form of government for every state and must protect every state from invasion or domestic violence.

### Article V – Amendments

A convention may be called to amend this Constitution if either 2/3 of both houses of Congress or 2/3 of the states vote that it is necessary. Once called, though the Congress or the states may have proposed specific amendments, the convention can propose any amendments to the Constitution. However, these amendments must then be ratified by the legislatures of or conventions in 3/4 of the states, the choice of legislatures or conventions being a Congressional decision. No amendment can deprive any state of its equal representation in the Senate without its consent, not shall the legislative power of the Congress nor the rights of individuals and states given in Article 1, section 9, be changed in any way before 1808.

### Article VI – The Constitution

All agreements and debts made by the U.S. under the old Articles of Confederation are valid under this Constitution.

This Constitution and all laws and treaties made under it shall be the supreme law of the land, overruling any laws or judges in the states. All officers of the U.S. and the states must be bound to support the Constitution, and no religious test may ever be required as qualification for such U.S. or state offices.

### Article VI – Ratification

9 states were needed to ratify the Constitution. The Constitutional Convention passed it on 17 September, 1787. It was ratified by all 13 states.

# The Bill of Rights
*The Ten Original Constitutional Amendments, 1791*

### First Amendment
Congress shall make no law respecting an establishment of religion, or prohibiting the free excercise thereof; or abridging the freedom of speech, or of the press; or the right of the people peaceably to assemble, and to petition the Government for a redress of grievances.

### Second Amendment
A well-regulated militia, being necessary to the security of a free State, the right of the people to keep and bear arms, shall not be infringed.

### Third Amendment
No soldier shall, in time of peace be quartered in any house, without the consent of the owner, nor in time of war, but in a manner to be prescribed by law.

### Fourth Amendment
The right of the people to be secure in their persons, houses, papers, and effects, against unreasonable searches and seizures, shall not be violated, and no warrants shall issue, but upon probable cause, supported by oath or affirmation, and particularly describing the place to be searched, and the persons or things to be seized.

### Fifth Amendment
No person shall be held to answer for a capital, or otherwise infamous crime, unless on a presentment or indictment of a Grand Jury, except in cases arising in the land or naval forces, or in the militia, when in actual service in time of war or public danger; nor shall any person be subject for the same offense to be twice put in jeopardy of life or limb; nor shall be compelled in any criminal case to be a witness against himself, nor be deprived of life, liberty, or property, without due process of law; nor shall private property be taken for public use without just compensation.

### Sixth Amendment
In all criminal prosecutions, the accused shall enjoy the right to a speedy and public trial, by an impartial jury of the State and district wherein the crime shall have been committed, which district shall have been previously ascertained by law, and to be informed of the nature and cause of the accusation; to be confronted with the witnesses against him; to have compulsory process for obtaining witnesses in his favor, and to have the assistance of counsel for his defense.

### Seventh Amendment
In suits at common law, where the value in controversy shall exceed twenty dollars, the right of trial by jury shall be preserved, and no fact tried by a jury shall be otherwise reexamined in a court of the United States, than according to the rules of the common law.

### Eighth Amendment
Excessive bail shall not be required, nor excessive fines imposed, nor cruel and unusual punishments inflicted.

### Ninth Amendment
The enumeration in the Constitution, of certain rights, shall not be construed to deny or disparage others retained by the people.

### Tenth Amendment
The powers not delegated to the United States by the Constitution, nor prohibited by it to the States, are reserved to the States respectively, or to the people.

# The Gettysburg Address
### *Abraham Lincoln, 1863*

Fourscore and seven years ago our fathers brought forth on this continent a new nation, conceived in liberty and dedicated to the proposition that all men are created equal.

Now we are engaged in a great civil war, testing whether that nation or any nation so conceived and so dedicated can long endure. We are met on a great battlefield of that war. We have come to dedicate a portion of that field, as a final resting place for those who here gave their lives that that nation might live. It is altogether fitting and proper that we should do this.

But, in a larger sense, we cannot dedicate—we cannot consecrate—we cannot hallow—this ground. The brave men, living and dead, who struggled here, have consecrated it, far above our poor power to add or detract. The world will little note, nor long remember, what we say here, but it can never forget what they did here. It is for us the living, rather, to be here dedicated to the great task remaining before us—that from these honored dead we take increased devotion to that cause for which they gave the last full measure of devotion—that we here highly resolve that these dead shall not have died in vain—that this nation, under God, shall have a new birth of freedom— and that government of the people, by the people, for the people, shall not perish from the earth.

## Statue of Liberty Inscription
### The New Colossus
### *Emma Lazarus*

Not like the brazen giant of Greek fame,
With conquering limbs astride from land to land;
Here at our sea-washed, sunset gates shall stand
A mighty woman with a torch, whose flame
Is the imprisoned lightning, and her name
Mother of Exiles. From her beacon-hand
Glows world-wide welcome; her mild eyes command
The air-bridged harbor that twin cities frame.
"Keep ancient lands, your storied pomp!" cries she
With silent lips. "Give me your tired, your poor,
Your huddled masses yearning to breathe free,
The wretched refuse of your teeming shore.
Send these, the homeless, tempest-tost to me,
I lift my lamp beside the golden door!"

## America the Beautiful
### *Katherine Lee Bates, 1893*

O beautiful for spacious skies,
For amber waves of grain,
For purple mountain's majesties
Above the fruited plain.
America! America!
God shed his grace on thee,
And crown thy good with brotherhood
From sea to shining sea.

## "I Have a Dream"
### *Martin Luther King, 1963*

Five score years ago, a great American, in whose symbolic shadow we stand, signed the Emancipation Proclamation. This momentous decree came as a great beacon of hope to millions of Negro slaves who had been seared in the flames of withering injustice. It came as a joyous daybreak to end the long night of captivity.

But one hundred years later, we must face the tragic fact that the Negro is still not free.

I say to you today, my friends, that in spite of difficulties and frustrations of the moments, I still have a dream. It is a dream deeply rooted in the American dream.

I have a dream that one day this nation will rise up and live out the true meaning of its creed: "We hold these truths to be self evident; that all men are created equal."

I have a dream that one day on the red hills of Georgia the sons of former slaves and the sons of former slave owners will be able to sit down together at the table of brotherhood.

I have a dream that one day even the state of Mississippi, a desert state sweltering with the heat of injustice and oppression, will be transformed into an oasis of freedom and justice.

I have a dream that my four little children will one day live in a nation where they will not be judged by the color of their skin but by the content of their character.

I have a dream today.

I have a dream that one day the state of Alabama, whose governor's lips are presently dripping with the words of interposition and nullification, will be transformed into a situation where little black boys and girls will be able to join hands with little white boys and white girls and walk together as sisters and brothers.

I have a dream today.

I have a dream that one day every valley shall be exalted, every hill and mountain shall be made low, the rough places will be made plain, and the crooked places will be made straight, and the glory of the Lord shall be revealed, and all flesh shall see it together.

This is our hope. This is the faith with which I return to the South. With this faith we will be able to hew out of the mountain of despair a stone of hope. With this faith we will be able to transform the jangling discords of our nation into a beautiful symphony of brotherhood. With this faith we will be able to work together, to pray together, to struggle together, to go to jail together, to stand up for freedom together, knowing that we will be free one day.

This will be the day when all God's children will be able to sing with new meaning:

> My country, 'tis of thee,
> Sweet land of liberty,
> Of thee I sing:
> Land where my fathers died,
> Land of the pilgrims' pride,
> From every mountain side
> Let freedom ring.

And if America is to be a great nation, this must become true. So let freedom ring from the prodigious hilltops of New Hampshire. Let freedom ring from the mighty mountains of New York. Let freedom ring from the heightening Alleghenies of Pennsylvania. Let freedom ring from the snow capped Rockies of Colorado. Let freedom ring from the curvaceous peaks of California. But not only that; let freedom ring from Stone Mountain of Georgia. Let freedom ring from Lookout Mountain of Tennessee. Let freedom ring from every hill and molehill of Mississippi. From every mountainside, let freedom ring.

When we let freedom ring, when we let it ring from every village and every hamlet, from every state and every city, we will be able to speed up that day when all of God's children, black men and white men, Jews and Gentiles, Protestants and Catholics, will be able to join hands and sing in the words of the old Negro spiritual, "Free at last, free at last, thank God almighty, we are free at last!"

## Pledge of Allegiance

I pledge allegiance to the flag of
the United States of America and
to the republic for which it stands,
one nation under God, indivisible,
with liberty and justice for all.

# 41. Canadian National Anthem

## Official Lyrics in English

O Canada! Our home and native land!
True patriot love in all thy sons command.
With glowing hearts we see thee rise,
The True North strong and free
From far and wide, O Canada,
We stand on guard for thee.
*Chorus.*
God keep our land glorious and free!
O Canada, we stand on guard for thee.
O Canada, we stand on guard for thee.

## Official Lyrics in French

O Canada! Terre de nos aïeux,
Ton front est ceint de fleurons glorieux.
Car ton bras sait porter l'épée,
Il sait porter la croix!
Ton histoire est une épopée
Des plus brillants exploits.
*Chorus.*
Et ta valeur, de foi trempée!
Protègera nos foyers et nos droits.
Protègera nos foyers et nos droits.

## English Translation of the Official French Lyrics

O Canada! Land of our forefathers,
Thy brow is wreathed with a glorious garland of flowers.
As is thy arm ready to wield the sword,
So also is it ready to carry the cross!
Thy history is an epic
Of the most brilliant exploits.
*Chorus.*
And thy valour steeped in faith!
Will protect our homes and our rights.
Will protect our homes and our rights.

**Note:** This material is from the Canadian National website: www.pch.gc.ca/ceremonial-symb/english/emb_anthem.html. There are many variations of both the French and English versions. The original French poem was by Sir Adolphe-Basile Routhier. It was first sung in 1880, and the first widely known translation was written by R. Stanley Weir in 1908.

# The
# Metalinguistic
# Aspect
# and
# Miscellaneous
# Materials

## Contents

# 1: Glossary of Grammatical Terms

**Absolute construction**

A word or phrase which modifies the sentence as a whole, not any single element in it.

*The **game over,** the players left the field.*
*The **cattle having been branded,** the cowboys saddled up and rode off.*

**Active**

See Voice

**Adjective**

A word which modifies a noun or a pronoun.

*The **old** man walked across the **narrow** street.*

**Adjective clause**

A dependent clause serving an adjective function. See **Relative clause.**

*The woman **who performed** lives next door to me.*

**Adjective phrase**

A word or group of words that functions as an adjective.

***dull, exceedingly dull, so very dull***

**Adverb**

A word which modifies a verb, an adjective, or another adverb.

*The car moved **slowly** in very heavy traffic.*

**Adverbial**

A word or group of words which functions as an adverb.

*He works **in a large university.***
*It rained **very hard.***
*He was happy **when his friend arrived.***

**Adverbial clause**

A dependent clause serving an adverbial function, Common adverbial clauses include:

**Comparison** (as...as, as...than)

*I can't run **as fast as I used to.***

**Concession** (though, although, even if)

***Although I had a good time,** I was happy to leave.*

**Condition - See Conditional sentences.**

**Reason** (because, as, since)

*They turned on the lights **because it was too dark.***

**Result** (so...that, such ...that)

*He spoke **so fast that no one understood a thing.***

**Time** (when, as, while, until, as soon as)

***As soon as he lit his cigar,** people began to leave the room.*

**Agreement**

Correspondence between grammatically related elements. Agreement in number and person between a subject and its verb.

*The **children play.** The **child plays.***

Agreement in gender, number, and person between a pronoun and its antecedent.

*The girl washed **her face.***

**Antecedent**

The word to which a pronoun refers.

***Aunt Mary** fainted when **she** heard the news.*

**Appositive**

A word, phrase, or clause used as a noun and placed next to another noun to modify it.

*George Washington, **the president,** slept here.*

**Article**

*A* and *an* are indefinite articles. *The* is the definite article.

**Auxiliary**

Function words which help other verbs indicate tense, mood, or voice (be, do, have). Modal auxiliaries *(can, may, might, must, should, etc.)* serve also as structural signals and have a meaning of their own *(ability, obligation, possibility).*

**Case**

English has the remnants of three cases: *subjective, possessive,* and *objective.* Nouns are inflected for case in the possessive *(John's).* Some pronouns and the relative pronoun *who* are inflected.

**subjective:** *I, he, she, we, they, who.*
**possessive:** *my (mine), your (yours), his, her (hers), its, our (ours), their (theirs), whose.*
**objective**: *me, him, her, us, them, whom.*

**Clause**

A group of words containing a subject and a predicate. See Independent clause and Dependent clause.

**Collective noun**

A noun singular in appearance which indicates a class or group of persons or things.

*a **committee** of citizens, an **army***

262

**Comparative**

The form of adjectives and adverbs which is used to indicate relative superiority.

| | | |
|---|---|---|
| *tall* | **taller** | **less tall** |
| *important* | **more important** | **less important** |
| *slowly* | **more slowly** | **less slowly** |

**Complement**

A word or group of words that follow the verb and complete the sentence.

> *She is **in the kitchen.***
> *I know **where she is.***

**Compound sentence**

A sentence which combines two or more independent clauses.

> *He whistled, and she worked.*

**Complex sentence**

A sentence which contains one or more dependent clauses.

> *He whistled while she worked.*

**Compound complex sentence**

A sentence which contains two or more independent clauses and one or more dependent clauses.

> *He whistled and she worked until they both got tired.*

**Conditional sentences**

Conditional sentences have two parts, the conditional clause and the main clause. There are three types:

1. Real condition:

> *If you bother the cat, it will scratch you.*

2. Unreal, contrary-to-fact condition (present):

> *If I were you, I would keep the money.*
> *If you took a trip, where would you go?*

3. Unreal, contrary-to-fact condition (past):

> *If I had known you were coming, I would have baked you a cake.*
> *If I had been Lincoln, I wouldn't have gone to the theater that night.*

**Conjunction**

A word used to connect sentences or sentence parts. See also **Coordinating conjunctions, Subordinating conjunctions.**

**Connective**

See **Conjunction.**

**Conjunctive adverbs**

Adverbs used to relate two independent clauses separated by a semicolon:

> *then, consequently, however, moreover, therefore, etc.*

**Coordinating Conjunctions**

The simple conjunction that connect sentences and sentence parts of equal rank:

> *and, but, or, nor, for, yet, so.*

**Correlative conjunctions**

Pairs of conjunctions which join sentence parts:

> *either. . .or, neither. . . nor,*
> *not only...but also, but...and.*

**Count noun**

A noun that can be made plural, usually by adding -s.

**Demonstrative adjectives and pronouns**

Words used to point out someone or something:

> *this, that, these, those.*

Also called demonstrative determiners.

**Dependent (subordinate clause)**

A group of words which contains both a subject and a predicate but which does not stand alone as a sentence. A dependent clause always serves a noun, adverb, or adjective function. See **Noun clause, Adjective clause, Adverbial clause, Relative clause.**

**Determiners**

A class of modifiers which includes articles *(a, an, the)*, possessives *(my, John's, his)*, demonstratives *(this, that)*, quantifiers *(some, any, two, each)*.

**Diphthong**

Two vowel sounds joined in one syllable to form one speech sound:

> *out, oil, I.*

**Direct object**

A noun, pronoun, or other substantive which receives the action of the verb.

> *Jack climbed the **bean stalk** into the sky.*

**Direct speech**

Repeats the speaker's exact words, enclosing them in quotation marks.

> *He said, **"I've lost my umbrella."***

**Elliptical clause**

A clause in which one or more words necessary for the full subject-predicate structure are omitted but "understood."

> *The manager admired no one else as much as **(he admired—**"understood"**)** her.*

**Expletive**

The *it* or *there* which serves to fill the subject slot in *it is, there is,* and *there are* sentences.

> ***It** is easy to understand.*
> ***There is** a fly in my soup.*

**Finite verb**

A verb in the present or past form, e.g., the finite forms of the verb *be* are *is, am, are, was,* and *were.* The non-finite forms are *be, being,* and *been.*

**Function words**

Words which establish grammatical relationships within a sentence: articles, auxiliaries, conjunctions, prepositions, pronouns, determiners, intensifiers, and interjections.

**Future**

*I will work, I shall work, I am going to work, I work tomorrow,* etc.

**Gender**

The quality of nouns and pronouns that determines the choice between masculine, female, or neuter *(he, she, it.)*

**Gerund**

See **Verbal**.

**Idiom**

An expression that does not conform to general grammatical patterns but is established through usage as the way of conveying a given meaning. *hold up, hold down, be beside oneself, kick the bucket.*

**Indefinite pronouns**

Pronouns not pointing out a particular person, thing, or definite quantity. *Some, any, each, every, everyone, everybody, nobody, anyone, anybody, one, neither* are among the most common.

**Independent clause**

A group of words which contains a subject and a predicate and which can stand alone as a sentence.

**Indirect object**

A word which indirectly receives the action of the verb.
*The witch gave **the pretty girl** a poisoned apple.*

**Indirect speech**

Paraphrases of the speaker's words.
*He said he had lost his umbrella.*

**Infinitive**

See **Verbal.**

**Inflection**

Changes in the form of words to reflect changes in grammatical relationships:
*the cabins; he walks; she's talking; quickest.*

**Intensifier**

Words that modify adjectives or adverbs and express degree: ***very** beautiful,* ***quite** young,* ***rather** old.*

**Intensive pronoun**

A reflexive pronoun ending in *-self -selves,* and used for emphasis.
*I'd rather do it **myself***

**Interjection**

A word used to exclaim or to express emotion: *ah, oh, ouch.*

**Interrogative pronouns**

*Who, whose, whom, what, which,* when used in questions.

**Intonation**

The rising and falling of the pitch of the voice in speech.

**Intransitive verb**

A verb which has no direct object
*The tide **turned** at noon.*

**Linking verb**

A verb which does not express action but links the subject to another word which names or describes it. *Be, become, seem, appear,* and *look* are common linking verbs.

**Mass noun (Non-count noun)**

A noun that refers to a quantity and cannot be preceded by a cardinal number, such as *three: sugar, milk, hunger.*

**Modal verb**

An auxiliary verb that adds meaning to the main verb: *can, may, might.*

**Modifier**

A word, phrase, or clause which limits or describes other sentence elements or the sentence as a whole.

**Mood**

The classification of verb forms as
**indicative** (plain or factual):
*I am ready;*
**imperative** (request or command):
*Be ready at six;* and
**subjunctive** (hypothetical or contrary-to-fact):
*I wish you were ready.*

**Nominal**

Any structure that functions as a noun.

**Nominative case**

See Case.

264

**Non-restrictive relative clause**
A clause which provides further information not essential to identification of the subject or complement and is set off usually with commas.
*John Jones, **who spends a lot of money,** has many friends.*

**Noun**
A word which names and classifies people, animals, things, ideas.
*Thomas Jefferson, lemon, religion, alligator, Paris, worm, justice, school, committee.*

**Noun clause**
A dependent clause serving a nominal function.
*Everyone agrees **that the play was a success.***

**Noun phrase**
The element in the sentence which functions as subject, object, or complement.
***The pretty girl** is **Julia.***
***She** is **my younger sister.***

**Number**
Forms that indicate singular or plural.

**Object of a preposition**
Completes the idea of time, position, direction, etc., begun by a preposition.
*at his desk, towards the door*

**Objective complement**
A complement after the direct object that provides another name for the object or otherwise amplifies it.
*They elected him president.*
*The war made many women widows.*
*Everyone believed him crazy.*

**Participle**
See **Verbal.**

**Parts of speech**
Noun, pronoun, adjective, adverb, conjunction, interjection, preposition, article.

**Past**
*I worked, etc.*

**Perfect**
*I have worked, I had worked, I will have worked.*

**Person**
Forms that express the person speaking, spoken to, or spoken about.
**first person:** I, *we*
**second person:** *you*
**third person:** *he, she, it, they*

**Phoneme**
A basic unit of sound in a language. (/i/, /p/, /iy/)

**Phrasal verbs**
A combination of a verb and a preposition or an adverb which forms a new vocabulary item. Phrasal verbs are classified as *intransitive, separable,* and *non-separable.*
**intransitive:** *John **got up** early this morning.*
**separable:** *John **calls up** his wife from the office.*
*John **calls** his wife **up** from the office.*
*John **calls** her **up** from the office.*
**non-separable:**
*Everybody **picks on** fat people.*

**Possessive adjectives**
*My, your, his, her, its, our, their.*

**Predicate adjective**
An adjective following a linking verb and describing the subject.
*The flowers look artificial.*

**Predicate nominative**
A word or group of words which follows a linking verb and identifies the subject.
*The book is a bestselling science-fiction novel.*

**Preposition**
A connective which joins a noun or a pronoun to the rest of the sentence. A prepositional phrase may serve either an adverb or an adjective function.
**adverb:** *The guide led us into the forest.*
**adjective:** *Jack is a master of many trades.*

**Present**
*I work, she/he works, etc.*

**Progressive (Continuous)**
*I am working, I was working, I have been working.*

**Pronouns**
Words which stand for nouns, classified as:
**personal:** (I, you, *he*)
**possessive:** *(mine, yours, his, hers)*
**reflexive/intensive:** *(myself, himself, ourselves)*
**demonstrative:** *(this, that, those)*
**relative:** *(who, which, what, that, whose)*
**interrogative:** *(who, which, what)*
**indefinite:** *(one, anyone, everyone)*

**Quantifiers**
Words denoting how much *(some, any, most, few, one, two, three)*

**Reciprocal pronouns**
*Each other, one another.*

**Relative clause**

A dependent clause that is related to the main clause by a relative pronoun.

*The book **that he recommended** is on sale.*

Restrictive relative clause: A clause that contributes to the identification of the noun it modifies, not separated by a comma from the noun. See Non-restrictive relative clause.

*The man who called me up was a complete stranger.*

**Sentence**

A grammatically complete unit of thought or expression, containing at least a subject and a predicate.

**Simple sentence**

A sentence consisting of only one independent clause.

**Stress**

Pronouncing a syllable or a word in such a way that it makes it more prominent in a word or sentence respectivley.

*conductor, Let's go.*

**Substantive**

See **Nominal.**

**Subject**

A word or group of words about which the sentence or clause makes a statement.

*The dog jumped into the car.*

**Subject complement**

See **Predicate nominative; Predicate adjective**

**Subjunctive**

See **Mood.**

**Subordinating conjunctions**

Conjunctions which join sentence parts of unequal rank. Usually they begin dependent clauses. Some of the most common ones are:

*because, since, though, although, if, when, while, before, after, as, until, so that, as long as, whereas, in order that.*

**Superlative**

The form of adjectives and adverbs used to express absolute superiority.

| ***the tallest*** | ***the least tall*** |
| *the most important* | *the least important* |
| *the most slowly* | *the least slowly* |

**Syntax**

The rules of sentence formation.

**Tag questions**

Short *yes / no* questions added to statements.

*It's a beautiful day, **isn't it?***
*You haven't seen the film, **have you?***

**Tense**

The system of verb forms expressing primarily different relationships in time.

**Transitive verb**

A verb which normally requires an object.

*Monkeys **love** bananas.*

**Verb**

A word or group of words expressing action, being, or state of being.

*I **swallowed** a fly.*
*What **is** man?*
*She **seems** happy.*

**Verbal**

A word or phrase derived from a verb and used as a noun, an adjective, or an adverb. Verbals consist of infinitives, gerunds, or participles.

**infinitive:** begins with to (sometimes understood) and is used as a noun, an adverb,or an adjective.

**noun:** ***To do such a thing*** *would be disastrous.*

**adverb:** *Many people jog **to keep physically fit.***

**adjective:** *I'm ready **to testify,** your Honor.*

**gerund:** ends in -ing and is used as a noun.

***Playing with matches*** *is a favorite passtime among children.*

**participle:** ends in *-ing, -ed,* and is used as an adjective.

*I can't live without **running** water.*
***Accompanied** by his faithful dog, Daniel roamed the woods.*

**Verb phrase**

Consists of the main verb and one or more auxiliaries.

*It **is beginning** to rain.*
*It **has been raining** for a long time.*

Modern grammarians use the term **verb phrase** to indicate the verb and all that goes with it (predicate) or the verb and its modifiers.

*The old man and the boy **had quietly taken the book from the library.***

**Voice**

A distinction in verb forms between *active* (the subject is acting) and passive (the subject is acted upon).

**active:** *Elmer **fed** the chickens.*

**passive:** *The chickens **were fed** by Elmer.*

266

# 2: A Comparison of Three Phonetic Alphabets

## Consonants

Sounds            Representations

| | I.P.A.* | PLA** | Dict.*** |
|---|---|---|---|
| **m**ay | m | M | m |
| **b**ay | b | B | b |
| **p**ay | p | P | p |
| **w**ay | w | W | w |
| **w**hey | hw | HW | hw |
| **v**ee | v | V | v |
| **f**ee | f | F | f |
| **th**ee | ð | TH | th |
| **th**igh | θ | th | *th* |
| **n**ew | n | N | n |
| **d**ew | d | D | d |
| **t**oo | t | T | t |
| **L**ou | l | L | l |
| **z**oo | z | Z | z |
| **S**ue | s | S | s |
| **y**ou | j | Y | y |
| **r**ue | r | R | r |
| mea**s**ure | ʒ | ZH | zh |
| **sh**ow | ʃ | SH | sh |
| **j**oke | dʒ | J | j |
| **ch**oo | tʃ | CH | ch |
| ba**ng** | ŋ | NG | ng |
| ba**g** | g | G | g |
| ba**ck** | k | K | k |
| **h**i | h | H | h |

*International Phonetic Alphabet
**Pro Lingua Associates System
***American Heritage dictionary

# Vowels

| Sounds | | I.P.A.* | PLA** | Dict.*** |
|--------|---|---------|-------|----------|
| beat | | i | EE | ē |
| bit | | ɪ | I | ĭ |
| bait | | e | AI | ā |
| bet | | ɛ | E | ĕ |
| bat | | æ | A | ă |
| | | | | |
| bird | | ər | Er | ûr |
| but | | ʌ | UH | ŭ |
| alone | | ə | uh | ə |
| | | | | |
| boot | | u | OO | ōō |
| put | | ʊ | U | o͝o |
| boat | | o | O | ō |
| bought | | ɔ | AW | ô |
| pot | | ɑ | AH | ŏ |
| | | | | |
| how | | aʊ | OU | ou |
| I | | aɪ | AY | ī |
| boy | | ɔɪ | OY | oi |
| | | | | |
| ear | | | EEr | îr |
| air | | | AIr | âr |
| marry | | | Ar | ăr |
| fur | | | Er | ûr |
| poor | | | OOr | o͝or |
| or | | | AWr | ôr |
| are | | | AHr | är |

# 3: A Brief Guide to Punctuation

| Punctuation | | Used for | Example(s) |
|---|---|---|---|
| **Apostrophe** | ' | to indicate omissions in contractions | doesn't, won't |
| | | to indicate possession | Mary's, the Joneses' |
| | | to indicate plurals of letters and numerals | 1870's, p's and q's |
| **Brackets** | [ ] | to indicate comment or question in quoted material | "He [Lincoln] was assassinated by a mad actor." |
| | | to indicate comment or question within material in parentheses | (Kuwait was liberated [was turned into a desolate battleground] by the U.N. forces in March,1991). |
| **Colon** | : | in writing clock time | 9:15, 2:47, 17:09 |
| | | to introduce a list | We need the following items: soap, toothpaste, and hand lotion. |
| | | after the names of speakers in a dialogue | Joe: Will you come, Honey? Sue: Are you nuts? No way! |
| | | before a formal quotation | The tall speaker began: "Four score and seven years ago,.... |
| | | after salutations in formal or business letters | Dear Sir: Dear Ms. Landsdowne: |
| **Comma** | , | after *yes* or *no* in a response | Yes, we have no bananas. |
| | | before the conjunction in a compound sentence except when the clauses are short | The oldest boy is going to school, and the youngest is going to work. He walked and she rode. |
| | | to separate the elements in an address | New Orleans, Louisana, U. S. A. They live at 418 Cedar Street, Winnetka, Illinois |
| | | to separate the elements in a date | He was born on Tuesday, January 25, 1944, in Chicago. |
| | | to separate equivalent elements in a series | Watch the stocks of Target, Ames, and Walmart. |
| | | to separate a speaker's words from the introductory statement | John asked, "May I leave?" |
| | | to group large numbers into thousands | 9,121; 1,268,421,135 |
| | | to set off the name of a person spoken to in direct speech | Mary, take this ring. |
| | | to separate an introductory clause from the sentence | When the party was over, I walked home. |

| Punctuation | | Used for | Example(s) |
|---|---|---|---|
| **Comma,** cont. | | after a mild exclamation | Well, I don't care. |
| | | before and after an appositive | George, a famous poet, spoke next. |
| | | to separate a tag question from the rest of the sentence | It's cold, isn't it? |
| | | before and after a non-restrictive adjective clause | Punctuation, which is essential for writing, seems complicated at first. |
| **Dash** | — | to indicate an interruption or an afterthought | We'll be there—at last—in an hour! I'll do it—at least, I'll try. |
| | | to indicate special emphasis in place of a comma | Give people what they want—money, fame, and power. |
| **Exclamation Point** | ! | to indicate strong feeling or emotion or for emphasis | Help! Watch out! She said she'd jump and she did! |
| **Hyphen** | - | in certain fixed expressions | person-to-person, matter-of-fact, station-to-station |
| | | in writing out compound numbers | twenty-one, ninety-nine, twenty-first, ninety-ninth |
| | | in expressions of clock time | It's seven-thirty. It's one-fifteen. |
| | | in joining a prefix to a proper name | pre-Columbian, post-Roosevelt, un-Christian |
| | | in joining a prefix to a noun whose first letter is the same as the last letter of the prefix | anti-intellectual, pre-existing, post-temperance |
| **Parenthesis** | ( ) | to enclose remarks, comments, explanations that interrupt the main thought | She invited the two men (they are cousins) to the party. If it rains (it usually doesn't this time of year), we'll postpone the picnic. |
| **Period** | . | at the end of a statement | I want to be alone. |
| | | after initials and abbreviations | Mr. P. T. Barnum. It's 7 p.m. |
| | | to indicate cents/decimals | $5.39; 257.0932; .00906 |
| **Question Mark** | ? | at the end of a direct question | Where does it all end? |
| | | after a tag question | You like to talk, don't you? |

| Punctuation | Used for | Example(s) |
| --- | --- | --- |

*Classic art deco seamless Aztec pattern*

**Quotation Marks** " " to enclose direct quotations — "Come here," Jim said.

around titles of chapters — "The Return to Witchwood"

articles in magazines or newspapers — "Wood Stove Madness," *Country Journal*

songs, poems, radio and TV programs — "Michelle, Ma Belle" "Hurt Hawks" "Music from the Hearts of Space" "I Love Lucy"

with other punctuation, as follows: — "Come, " he said. "I'm going." I said, "I will;" I followed. "Can you see?" he asked. Did I answer, "No?"

**Semicolon** ; in a compound sentence without a connective — The singular form is "mouse;" the plural form is "mice."

in a sentence with two main clauses joined by a conjunctive adverb. — The teacher was sick; therefore, the class was called off. Roseanne ran a good race; however, she failed to qualify for the finals.

**Underlining and *Italics*** Use underlining in handwritten or typed material and Italics in printed material:

for titles of periodicals and books — <u>Newsweek</u>, <u>A Farewell to Arms</u>

foreign phrases and words used in an English context — And then, *alors,* there she was. "<u>Cuidado,</u>" I warned myself, "You're a fool, but <u>que, sera, sera.</u>

words emphasized — I wanted *three* tickets, not four!

the names of ships, trains and airplanes — *Titanic,* <u>Orient Express,</u> *Constellation, Spirit of St. Louis*

# 4: Useful Spelling Rules

A. If a word ends in **y** preceded by a consonant, change the **y** to an **i** before every suffix except **-ing**.

| | | | |
|---|---|---|---|
| salary | salaries | copy | copying |
| marry | married | try | trying |
| lonely | loneliness | fly | flying |
| worry | worried | worry | worrying |

B. Write **i** before **e**, except after **c** or when sounded like **a**, as in *neighbor* and *weigh*.

| | |
|---|---|
| **i** before **e**: | *brief, piece, chief, yield* |
| **e** before **i**: | *receive, deceive, ceiling, freight, sleigh* |

Exceptions:     *either, neither, seize, leisure, weird, species, financier*

C. If a word has only one syllable and ends with a single consonant preceded by a single vowel *(hop, bat)* and you add a suffix beginning with a vowel **(-er, -ed, -ing)**, double the final consonant.

| | | | |
|---|---|---|---|
| stop | stopped | trip | tripped |
| bat | batter | drop | dropping |
| rub | rubbing | spin | spinning |

If the word has more than one syllable and the final syllable is stressed, double the final consonant.

| | | | |
|---|---|---|---|
| occur | occurring | confer | conferred |
| admit | admitted | omit | omitted |

D. If a word ends with a silent **e** and you add a suffix,

drop the **e** if the suffix begins with a vowel:

| | | | |
|---|---|---|---|
| love | lovable | move | moving |
| desire | desirable | use | usable |

but keep the **e** if the **e** is preceded by **c** or **g** and the suffix begins with **a, o,** or **u:**

| | | | |
|---|---|---|---|
| notice | noticeable | manage | manageable |
| courage | courageous | | |

Exceptions: words ending in **ee** never drop the final **ee**:

| | | | | | |
|---|---|---|---|---|---|
| agree | agreeing | flee | fleeing | see | seeing |

keep the **e** if the suffix begins with a consonant:

| | | | |
|---|---|---|---|
| use | useful | engage | engagement |
| love | lovely | move | movement |

Exceptions: words that end in **-ple, -ble** and **-tle,** drop the **-le** before **-ly:**

| | | | |
|---|---|---|---|
| simple | simply | probable | probably |

272

# 5: Differences between British/Canadian* and American (U. S.) Spelling

| American | | British | |
|---|---|---|---|
| **e** | *anesthesia* <br> *encyclopedia* | **ae** | *anaesthesia* <br> *encyclopaedia* |
| **-ection** | *connection* <br> *reflection* | **-exion*** | *connexion* <br> *reflexion* |
| **-ed** | *burned* <br> *learned* <br> *spelled* | **-t*** | *burnt* <br> *learnt* <br> *spelt* |
| **-ense** | *license* <br> *defense* | **-ence** | *licence* <br> *defence*** |
| **-er** | *center* <br> *meter* <br> *theater* | **-re** | *centre* <br> *metre* <br> *theatre* |
| **-ization** | *civilization* <br> *naturalization* | **-isation*** | *civilisation* <br> *naturalisation* |
| **-ize** | *criticize* <br> *memorize* | **-ise*** | *criticise* <br> *memorise* |
| **-ll** | *fulfill* <br> *skillful* | **-l** | *fulfil* <br> *skilful* |
| **-ment** | *judgment* <br> *argument* | **-ement** | *judgement* <br> *arguement*** |
| **-or** | *color* <br> *neighbor* | **-our** | *colour* <br> *neighbour* |

Note: **In British usage,** words ending in an l preceded by a single vowel usually double the l.

| quarrel | quarrelling | model | modelling |
|---|---|---|---|
| travel | travelling | signal | signalling |

**In American usage,** the consonant is doubled only if the last syllable is accented.

| signal | signaling | excel | excellent |
|---|---|---|---|
| travel | traveling | propel | propeller |

British spelling is often seen in the United States, and in some cases it is quite common; *encyclopaedia, centre, judgement, traveller, theatre,* for example, are frequently encountered. However, these spellings are not the normal, preferred spelling.

* In Canada, British spelling is generally preferred. However, newspapers often use U.S. spelling because it "saves space." In other words, although British spelling is generally considered the norm in Canada, Canadians often use U.S. spellings, particularly in the cases marked with an asterisk (*) above.

# 6: Some American - British Vocabulary Differences

| American* | British |
|---|---|
| aisle (theater) | gangway (theatre) |
| apartment | flat |
| baby carriage | perambulator, pram |
| bar | pub |
| bartender | barman |
| bathtub | bath |
| battery (automobile) | accumulator |
| bill (money) | banknote |
| broiled (meat) | grilled |
| can | tin |
| candy | sweets |
| candy store | sweet shop |
| checkers (game) | draughts |
| cookie | biscuit |
| corn | maize |
| derby (hat) | bowler |
| detour | diversion |
| druggist | chemist |
| elevator | lift |
| eraser | rubber |
| faucet | tap |
| flashlight | torch |
| French fries | chips |
| garbage collector | dustman |
| gasoline | petrol |
| generator | dynamo |
| groceries | stores |
| hood (automobile) | bonnet |
| incorporated (Inc.) | limited (Ltd.) |

* Canadians generally use U.S. American rather than British vocabulary.

| American | British |
|---|---|
| installment plan | hire-purchase system |
| internal revenue | inland revenue |
| janitor | caretaker, porter |
| john (toilet) | loo |
| kerosene | paraffin |
| kindergarten | infant's school |
| lawyer | barrister |
| line | queue |
| living-room | sitting-room |
| liquor | spirits |
| long distance(telephone) | trunk |
| mailman | postman |
| molasses | treacle |
| oatmeal | porridge |
| pants | trousers |
| paste | gum |
| period (punctuation) | full stop |
| phonograph | gramophone |
| potato chips | crisps |
| private school | public school |
| raincoat | waterproof, mackintosh |
| rooster | cock |
| second floor | first floor |
| sedan | saloon car |
| sidewalk | pavement |
| soccer | football |
| subway | tube |
| suspenders (men's) | braces |
| taxes | rates |
| thermos bottle | flask |
| truck | lorry |
| underpants | pants |
| vacation | holiday |
| vest | waistcoat |
| windshield | windscreen |
| wrench | spanner |

# 7: 600 High-Frequency Words:*
## (1-300-word level – roman; *301-600-word level* – **bold**)

AAAAAAAAAA

a/an
**about**
  (*approximately*)
**adjective**
**adverb**
after
afternoon
again
**age**
**agree(ment)**
**ago**
all
**almost**
**also**
**always**
and
another/the other
answer
any
**April**
**arm**
**arrive/arrival**
**article (*grammar*)**
**as**
ask
at
**August**
**aunt**
**auto(mobile)**

BBBBBBBBBB

**back - n, adj**
**(in) back of**
**bad/worse/worst**
bank
bathroom
be/am/are/is/was/
were
 /been
**beautiful**
**because**
**become/became**
**bed**

before
begin/began/begun
**behind**
**believe**
beside
between
big
black
blue
-body
   **anybody**
   **everybody**
   **nobody**
   **somebody**
book
**born**
**both**
**boy**
**break/broke
 /broken**
**break (*take a*)**
breakfast
bring/brought
brother
brown
**building**
bus
but
buy/bought
by (*near, beside*)

CCCCCCCCCC

**call (*what do
 you x this*)**
can - m
car
**careful/careless**
**carry**
**cassette**
cent
**center - n**
**chair**
**change - v, n**
change (*money*) -n

cheap
**check in/out**
child/children
**choose/choice**
city
class(room)
**clean - v, adj**
**clear - adj**
clock/o' clock
close - v/closed- adj
**close(ly) - adj, adv**
clothes
coat
coffee
cold
color - n
come/came
**consonant**
**continue**
**cool - adj**
**copy - n,v**
corner
**(in)correct - adj,
 v/correction**
cost - v, n
could - m
**count -v**
**country**
cup

DDDDDDDDD

**date (*today's*)**
daughter
day
**December**
**desk**
dictionary
**difficult**
different/difference
**dime**
dinner
**direction**
**discuss(ion)**
do/did/done - v, av

doctor
dollar
door
down
drink/drank/drunk
**drive/drove/driven**
**drop**
**drug/drugstore**

EEEEEEEEE

each
**early**
**east(ern)**
easy
eat/ate/eaten
eight
**either**
eleven
**else**
**end - n, v**
**enjoy/enjoyable**
enough
enter/entrance
evening
**ever**
every
**example**
excuse - v
**exercise (*textbook*)
 - n**
exit - n
expensive
**explain
 /explanation**

FFFFFFFFF

face
**fall (*season*)**
**fall/fell/fallen**
family
far
fast
father
**favorite**

**February**
**feel/felt**
few/ a few
**fill**
**fill out**
**find/found**
fine - adj
**finish - v**
first
five
food
**foot/feet (*12 inches*)**
**foot/feet (*body part*)**
for
forget/forgot
 /forgotten
**fork**
four
Friday
friend
from
**(in) front (of)**

GGGGGGGGG

**gallon**
**game**
get/got/gotten
 (*obtain, reach*)
**get in/out of (*a car*)**
**get on/off (*a bus*)**
**get up (*arise*)**
girl
give/gave/given
**glass (*of water*)**
go/went/gone
**go away**
**(be) going to**
good/better/best
goodbye/bye/bye-bye
**gray**
**great (*wonderful*)
 - adj, excl**
green
**guess**

*H H H H H H H H H*

half
**hand**
**hand in/out**
**happen**
**happy**
**hard (*difficult*)**
**hat**
have/has/had
**have got to - m**
have to/had to - m
he
**head**
hear/heard
**heavy**
hello
help - v, n
her(s)
here
**high/height**
him
his
**holiday**
home
**hope - v**
hospital
hot
hotel
**hour**
house
how
hundred
**hungry**
husband

*I I I I I I I I I I I*

I
**idea**
if
**(un)important**
in
**inch**
**interesting**
into
**introduce/intro-
duction**
it(s)

*J J J J J J J J J J J*

**January**
**job**
**July**
**June**
**just**

*K K K K K K K K K*

**keep/kept**
**key**
**kiss - n, v**
**kitchen**
**kind - adj**
**kind of**
**knife**
know/knew/known

*L L L L L L L L L*

**language**
**large**
**last - adj**
late
**laugh - n, v**
learn
leave/left
left (*direction*)
**leg**
**less**
**let**
let's
letter (*alphabetic*)
**letter (*correspon-
dence*)**
**light – n**
**light (*not heavy*)**
like - v
**like - prep**
listen
little/a little
little (*small*)
**live - v**
**look (at)**
**look (*appear*)**
**look up (*a word*)**
lose/lost
lots of/a lot of
**love - v, n**
lunch

*M M M M M M M*

make/made
man/men
many
**March**
**marry/married/
marriage**
**matter - v, n**
may - m
**May**
maybe
me
mean/meant - v/
meaning - n
**meet/met**
**meter/metric**
  **centi-**
  **milli-**
  **kilo-**
**middle**
might - m
**mile**
**million**
**mind - v**
mine - pro
**minute**
**miss - v**
Miss
mistake
Monday
money
**month**
more/most
morning
mother
**mouth**
**move**
Mr.
Mrs.
Ms.
much
**must - m**
my

*N N N N N N N*

name - n
near
**(un)necessary**

need
**neighbor**
**neither .. nor**
**nervous**
never
new
**news/newspaper**
next
nice
**nickel**
night
nine
no
**noon**
**north(ern)**
nose
not
note
**notice - v, n**
**noun**
**November**
now
number

*O O O O O O O*

**October**
of
off
**office**
**often**
OK/okay
**old**
on
**once**
one
-one
  anyone
  everyone
  no one
  someone
only
open - adj, v
**opposite**
or
**orange**
ought to - m
**ounce**
our(s)

out
**outside**
**over**

*P P P P P P P P*

**package**
page
**pair/pair up/off**
paper
**paragraph**
**parents**
**part(ly)**
**past (*half past one*)**
pay
pen
pencil
**penny**
**pepper**
**period**
  (*punctuation*)
person/people
**phone/telephone**
**photo/photograph**
**pick up**
picture
**piece**
**pint**
**place - n**
plane/airplane
**play - v**
please
police
**(im)possible**
**pound (*lb.*)**
**practice**
**preposition**
**pretty - adj**
**pretty - int**
**price**
probably
problem
**pronoun**
**pronounce
/pronunciation**
pull
push
put

*Q Q Q Q Q Q Q Q Q*

**quart**

**quarter**
  *(coin, fraction)*

question

**quick(ly)**

**quiet(ly)**

*R R R R R R R R*

**rain(y) - n, v, adj**

read/read

ready

red

remember

restaurant

return

**review - v, n**

right
  *(correct, direction)*

road

room *(place)*

**run/ran**

*S S S S S S S S*

**sale**

**salt**

**same**

say/said

Saturday

school

**season**

**seat**

second
  *(ordinal number)*

see/saw/seen

**seem**

**-self/-selves**

**send/sent/sender**

sentence

**September**

seven

**several**

**share - v**

she

shop - n, v

**short**

should - m

**show - v, n**

sick

**sign - v/signature**

since

**sing/sang/sung**

**single (unmarried)**

sir

sister

sit/sat

six

**size**

sleep/slept

slow(ly)

**small**

**so - conj**

**soap**

some

**sometimes**

son

**soon**

sorry

**sort (of)**

**south(ern)**

speak/spoke/spoken

spell

**spoon**

**spring (season)**

**stairs**

station

**stamp (postage)**

**start - v**

**stay**

**still (continuing)**

stop

store

**story**

**straight**

street

study/student

**such**

**summer**

Sunday

sure

*T T T T T T T T T*

table

take/took/taken

talk

**tall**

taxi

**tea**

teach/taught/teacher

**television/TV**

tell/told

ten

than

thank

the

then

there

there is/are

they/them/their(s)

thing

-thing

  anything

  everything

  nothing

  something

think/thought/
  thought - n

**thirsty**

this/that/these/those

thousand

three/thirteen/thirty
  /third

**through**

**throw**

**throw away**

Thursday

**ticket**

time

tired

to

today

toilet

tomorrow

tonight

too - int

**too (also)**

**top**

**toward(s)**

**towel**

**town**

train

try

Tuesday

**turn - v**

turn on/off

**turn up/down**
  *(volume)*

twelve

twenty

two

*U U U U U U U U*

**uncle**

under

understand
  /understood

**until**

up

use - v

**usual(ly)**

*V V V V V V V*

**verb**

very

**vocabulary**

**vowel**

*W W W W W W*

wait

**wake (up)/woke
  /woken**

walk

want

**warm**

**wash**

watch - v

watch - n *(clock)*

water

**way**

we

**weather**

Wednesday

week

weekend

welcome - excl

well - excl

**well - adv**

**west(ern)**

**wet**

what

when

where

-where

  anywhere

  everywhere

  nowhere

  somewhere

**which**

while

white

who/whom/whose

why

wife

will/won't - m

**winter**

**wish - v, n**

with

woman/women

**wonderful**

word

**work(er)**

**world**

**worry**

**would**

would like to - m

**would rather - m**

write/wrote/written

wrong

*X X X X X X*

*Y Y Y Y Y Y*

**yard (3 feet)**

**year**

yellow

yes/yeah

yesterday

**yet**

**young**

you(r)(s)

*Z Z Z Z Z Z Z*

zero

> **\* This word list is from**
> *The Learners Lexicon,*
> **published by Pro Lingua**
> **Associates.** The complete
> list contains 2,400 words.

# 8: Measurement Terms and Equivalents

## Non-Metric

**Linear measure**

| | |
|---|---|
| 12 inches | = 1 foot |
| 3 feet | = 1 yard |
| 5 1/2 yards | = 1 rod |
| 40 rods | = 1 furlong |
| 8 furlongs | = 1 mile |

**Mariner's measure**

| | |
|---|---|
| 6 feet | = 1 fathom |
| 1,000 fathoms | = 1 nautical mile |
| 3 nautical miles | = 1 league |

**Square measure**

| | |
|---|---|
| 160 square rods | = 1 acre |
| 640 acres | = 1 square mile |

**Avoirdupois weight**

| | |
|---|---|
| 16 drams | = 1 ounce |
| 16 ounces | = 1 pound |
| 2,000 pounds | = 1 ton |

**Liquid measure**

| | |
|---|---|
| 2 pints | = 1 quart |
| 4 quarts | = 1 gallon |

**Dry measure**

| | |
|---|---|
| 2 pints | = 1 quart |
| 8 quarts | = 1 peck |
| 4 pecks | = 1 bushel |

## Metric/English Measure Equivalents

**Linear and square measure**

| | |
|---|---|
| 1 centimeter (cm.) | = .3937 inch (in.) |
| 1 meter (m.) | = 39.37 in. |
| | or 3.28 feet (ft.) |
| 1 kilometer (km.) | = .62137 mile (mi.) |
| 1,000 m² | = 1 hectare (ha.) |
| | or 2.471 acres |

**Liquid measure**

| | |
|---|---|
| 1 centiliter (cl.) | = .338 fluid ounces (fl. oz.) |
| 1 liter (l.) | = .9081 dry quart (qt.) |
| | or 1.0567 liquid quarts |

**Avoirdupois weight**

| | |
|---|---|
| 1 gram (g.) | = .03527 ounces (oz.) |
| 1 kilogram (kg.) | = 2.2046 pounds (lb.) |

## English/Metric Measure Equivalents

**Linear and square measure**

| | | | |
|---|---|---|---|
| 1 inch | | = 2.54 centimeters |
| 12 in. | = 1 foot | = .3048 meters . |
| 3 ft. | = 1 yard | = .9144 meters |
| 16.5 ft. | = 1 rod | = 5.029 meters |
| 5,280 ft. | = 1 mile | =1.6093 kilometers |
| 4,840 yd | = 1 acre | = .4 hectatres |

**Avoirdupois weight**

| | | |
|---|---|---|
| 1 ounce | = 28 grams | |
| 16 oz. | = 1 pound | = .45 kilo (kg.) |

**Liquid Measure**

| | | | | |
|---|---|---|---|---|
| 1 teaspoon (tsp.) | | = | 5 milliliters |
| 3 tsp. | = 1 tbs. | = | 15 ml. |
| 8 oz. | = 1 cup (c.) | = | .24 liters (l.) |
| 2 cups | = 1 pint (pt.) | | = .47 l. |
| 2 pints | = 1 quart (qt.) | | = .95 l. |
| 4 quarts | = 1 gallon (gal.) | | = 3.81 l. |

279

## Fahrenheit/Celsius

(°F-32)x5÷9=°C
°Cx9÷5+32=°F

# Degrees

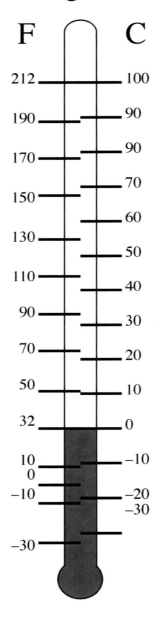

F       C

100°F = 37.8°C

90°F = 32.2°C

80°F = 26.7°C

70°F = 21.1°C

60°F = 15.6°C

50°F = 10.0°C

40°F =  4.4°C

32°F =   0°C

100°C = 212°F

40°C = 104°F

30°C = 86°F

20°C = 68°F

10°C = 50°F

0°C = 32°F

| F | C |
|---|---|
| 212 | 100 |
| 190 | 90 |
| 170 | 90 |
| 150 | 70 |
| 130 | 60 |
| 110 | 50 |
| 90 | 40 |
| 70 | 30 |
| 50 | 20 |
| 32 | 10 |
| 10 | 0 |
| 0 | -10 |
| -10 | -20 |
| | -30 |
| -30 | |

# 9: Common Elements*

| Atomic number | Symbol | Element Name | Atomic Number | Symbol | Element Name |
|---|---|---|---|---|---|
| 1 | H | hydrogen | 24 | Cr | chromium |
| 2 | He | helium | 25 | Mn | manganese |
| 3 | Li | lithium | 26 | Fe | iron |
| 4 | Be | beryllium | 27 | Co | cobalt |
| 5 | B | boron | 28 | Ni | nickel |
| 6 | C | carbon | 29 | Cu | copper |
| 7 | N | nitrogen | 30 | Zn | zinc |
| 8 | O | oxygen | 33 | As | arsenic |
| 9 | F | fluoride | 47 | Ag | silver |
| 10 | Ne | neon | 50 | Sn | tin |
| 11 | Na | sodium | 51 | Sb | antimony |
| 12 | Mg | magnesium | 53 | I | iodine |
| 13 | Al | aluminum | 56 | Ba | barium |
| 14 | Si | silicon | 78 | Pt | platinum |
| 15 | P | phosphorous | 79 | Au | gold |
| 16 | S | sulfur | 80 | Hg | mercury |
| 17 | Cl | chlorine | 82 | Pb | lead |
| 18 | Ar | argon | 83 | Bi | bismuth |
| 19 | K | potassium | 88 | Ra | radium |
| 20 | Ca | calcium | 92 | U | uranium |
|  |  |  | 94 | Pu | plutonium |

* This list contains only the commonly known elements.

# 10: Common Symbols

| | | | |
|---|---|---|---|
| ♂ | male | ' | foot (6') |
| ♀ | female | " | inch (6'2") |
| | | ✕ | by (2" x 4") |
| + | plus | | |
| — | minus | $ | dollar |
| ✕ | times | ¢ | cent |
| ÷ | divided by | £ | pound (£ 3) ) |
| = | equals | p | penny, pence (6p) |
| > | greater than | € | Euro (€5 or 5 EUR |
| < | less than | | |
| ≠ | not equal to | ~ | tilde (cañon) |
| √ | square root | ^ | circumflex (fetê) |
| π | pi | ¸ | cedilla (Français) |
| ∞ | infinity | ´ | acute accent (passé) |
| | | ` | grave accent (à la carte) |
| ° | degree (60°) | ¨ | dieresis (zoölogy) |
| ' | minute (60° 30') | | |
| " | second (60° 30' 15") | © | copyright |
| @ | at (@ 80¢ per quart) | TM | trademark |
| ≈ | approximately | & | ampersand (and) |
| o/a | on or about | * | a hypothetical or wrong form (he *drinked) |
| % | percent | * | asterisk for note |
| # | number (#10 nail) | † | dagger for note |
| # | pounds (80#) | ‡ | double dagger for note |

## 11: Proofreading and Correction Marks

∧ insert here *a word*

↑ insert comma

⊙ insert period⊙

⌐ delete ~~this~~

⊂ close up (foot‿ball)

¶ paragraph

N.¶ no paragraph

∿ transpose (a, b, /d⟩c,/e)

# insert # space
∧

.... let it stand

STET let it stand STET

≡ capitalize (washington) CAP

/ lower case (Ȼapital) l.c.

Awk awkward construction

Frag sentence fragment

Sp spelling error hear *here*

## 12: Roman Numerals

| | | | | | | | |
|---|---|---|---|---|---|---|---|
| I, i | 1 | VI, vi | 6 | XX | 20 | CD | 400 |
| II, ii | 2 | VII, vii | 7 | XL | 40 | D | 500 |
| III, iii | 3 | VIII, viii | 8 | L | 50 | CM | 900 |
| IV, iv | 4 | IX, ix | 9 | XC | 90 | M | 1000 |
| V, v | 5 | X, x | 10 | C | 100 | MM | 2000 |

| | |
|---|---|
| MCDXCII | 1492 |
| MDCXLVIII | 1648 |
| MCMXCIX | 1999 |
| MMI | 2001 |

# 13: Abbreviations (abbr., abbrev.)

## A. General (Gen.)

| | |
|---|---|
| A.A. | Associate of Arts (degree) |
| A.D. | *anno Domini,* in the year of Our Lord |
| a.m. | *ante meridiem,* before noon |
| Amer. | America, American |
| anon. | anonymous |
| assn. | association |
| assoc. | associate(s) |
| | |
| b. | born |
| B.A.,A.B. | Bachelor of Arts |
| B.C. | before Christ |
| B.S. | Bachelor of Science |
| bibliog. | bibliography |
| biog. | biography |
| | |
| c. | hundred (4c = 400) |
| c., ca. | *circa,* about |
| C.E. | common era = A.D. |
| cf. | *confer,* compare |
| ch., chap. | chapter |
| Co. | Company |
| Coll. | College |
| | |
| d. | died |
| D.D.S. | Doctor of Dental Science (Surgery) |
| dept. | department |
| | |
| E. | east |
| E., Eng., | English |
| ed. | edition, editor, edited by |
| e.g. | *exempligratia,* for example |
| esp. | especially |
| et al | *et alii,* and others |
| etc. | *et cetera,* and so forth |
| ex. | example |
| | |
| f.,ff. | and the following page(s) |
| Fr. | French |
| | |
| Gr. | German |
| Gk. | Greek |
| | |
| hist. | history |
| | |
| ibid. | *ibidem,* in the same place |
| i.e. | *id est.* that is |
| Inc. | Incorporated |
| intro. | introduction |
| It. | Italian |
| | |
| Jr. | junior |

| | |
|---|---|
| K | thousand |
| | |
| lang. | language |
| L., Lat. | Latin |
| L.C., LC | Library of Congress |
| Ltd. | Limited |
| | |
| m | thousand ($55m = $55,000) |
| M.A. | Master of Arts |
| M.A.T. | Master of Arts in Teaching |
| M.B.A. | Master of Business Administration |
| M.D. | Doctor of Medicine |
| misc. | miscellaneous |
| mph, m.p.h. | miles per hour |
| Mr. | Mister |
| Mrs. | married woman (Mistress) |
| Ms. | Miss, Mrs., Woman |
| ms. | manuscript |
| M.S. | Master of Science |
| | |
| N. | north |
| N.B. | *nota bene,* take note, note well |
| no. | number |
| | |
| p., pp. | page(s) |
| par. | paragraph |
| p.c. | politically correct |
| Ph.D. | Doctor of Philosophy |
| philos. | philosophy |
| p.m. | *post meridiem,* afternoon |
| pub. | published by |
| | |
| q.v. | *quod vide,* which see |
| rpm, r.p.m. | revolutions per minute |
| | |
| S. | south |
| Sr. | senior |
| sic. | thus |
| Sp. | Spanish |
| sp. | spelling |
| St. | Saint |
| St. | Street |
| | |
| T.M. | trademark |
| | |
| U., Univ. | university |
| vol. | volume |
| W. | west |

## B. Days and Months (Mos.)

| | | | |
|---|---|---|---|
| Jan. | January | Nov. | November |
| Feb. | February | Dec. | December |
| Mar. | March | | |
| Apr. | April | Mon. | Monday |
| May | May | Tues. | Tuesday |
| June | June | Wed. | Wednesday |
| July | July | Thurs. | Thursday |
| Aug. | August | Fri. | Friday |
| Sept. | September | Sat. | Saturday |
| Oct. | October | Sun. | Sunday |

## Measures

| | | | |
|---|---|---|---|
| in. | inch | mm. | millimeter |
| ft. | foot | cm. | centimeter |
| yd. | yard | m. | meter |
| mi. | mile | km. | kilometer |
| | | | |
| oz. | ounce | g., gr. | gram |
| fl. oz. | fluid ounce | c. | centigram |
| lb. | pound | kg. | kilo., kilogram |
| | | t. | tonnes |
| tsp. | teaspoon | | |
| tbs.,tbsp. | tablespoon | ml. | milliliter |
| | | l. | liter |
| c. | cup | | |
| pt. | pint | | |
| qt. | quart | | |
| gal. | gallon | | |

Many abbreviations are commonly used like words.  There are two kinds: Acronyms are pronounceable words.  Alphabetisms are pronounced by saying each letter, but they are usually written in capital letters without periods.  Some familiar examples:

| **Acronyms** | **Alphabetisms** | |
|---|---|---|
| ACTFL | AA | IRS, INS |
| AIDS | AAA | MIA |
| Laser | ATM | PC |
| NASA | ATV, SUV | RSVP |
| NATO | CBS, NBC, ABC, | TV |
| OPEC |   PBS, NPR, CNN | USA |
| PIN |   CBC, BBC | UN |
| Radar | EFL, ESL, ESP | UPC |
| Scuba | GED, GRE | UPS |
| TESOL | GPS | USA |
| UNESCO | HIV | WMD |
| UNICEF | | |

## Postal Abbrs.

| State | Traditional | New | State | Traditional | New | State | Traditional | New |
|-------|-------------|-----|-------|-------------|-----|-------|-------------|-----|
| Alabama | Ala. | AL | Maine | Me. | ME | Oklahoma | Okla. | OK |
| Alaska | Alas. | AK | Maryland | Md. | MD | Oregon | Ore. | OR |
| Arizona | Ariz. | AZ | Massachusetts | Mass. | MA | Pennsylvania | Penn. | PA |
| Arkansas | Ark. | AR | Michigan | Mich. | MI | Rhode Island | R.I. | RI |
| California | Cal. | CA | Minnesota | Minn. | MN | South Carolina | S.C. | SC |
| Colorado | Colo. | CO | Mississippi | Miss. | MS | South Dakota | S.D. | SD |
| Connecticut | Conn. | CT | Missouri | Mo. | MO | Tennessee | Tenn. | TN |
| Delaware | Del. | DE | Montana | Mont. | MT | Texas | Tex. | TX |
| Florida | Fla. | FL | Nebraska | Neb. | NE | Utah | Utah | UT |
| Georgia | Ga. | GA | Nevada | Nev. | NV | Vermont | Vt. | VT |
| Hawaii | Ha. | HI | New Hampshire | N.H. | NH | Virginia | Va. | VA |
| Idaho | Ida. | ID | New Jersey | N.J. | NJ | Washington | Wash. | WA |
| Illinois | Ill. | IL | New Mexico | N.M. | NM | West Virginia | W.V. | WV |
| Indiana | Ind. | IN | New York | N.Y. | NY | Wisconsin | Wisc. | WI |
| Iowa | Ia. | IA | North Carolina | N.C. | NC | Wyoming | Wyo. | WY |
| Kansas | Kan. | KS | North Dakota | N.D. | ND | Puerto Rico | P.R. | PR |
| Kentucky | Ky. | KY | Ohio | Ohio | OH | Guam | Guam | GU |
| Louisiana | La. | LA | | | | Virgin Island | V.I. | VI |

## North America

| | | | | | | |
|---|---|---|---|---|---|---|
| United States of America | U.S. U.S.A. | Canada | Can. | Central America | C.A. | |
| | | Mexico | Mex. | | | |

## Cities

| | | | | | |
|---|---|---|---|---|---|
| District of Columbia | D.C., DC | Miami | MIA | San Francisco | S.F., SF |
| Los Angeles | L.A., LA | New York City | N.Y.C., NYC | Seattle | SEA |

## Other Postal Abbrs.

| | | | | | |
|---|---|---|---|---|---|
| APO | Army and Air Force Post Office | Cir. | Circle | Jct. | Junction |
| FPO | Naval Post Office | Ct. | Court | Ln. | Lane |
| RFD | Rural Free Delivery | Cres. | Crescent | Pl. | Place |
| PO Box | Post Office Box | Dr. | Drive | Pt. | Point |
| | | Expy. | Expressway | Rd. | Road |
| | | Ext. | Extension | Rte. | Route |
| Ave. | Avenue | Fwy. | Freeway | Sq. | Square |
| Blvd. | Boulevard | Gdns. | Gardens | St. | Street |
| Byp. | Bypass | Hts. | Heights | Ter. | Terrace |
| Cswy. | Causeway | Hwy. | Highway | Tpke. | Turnpike |
| Ctr. | Center | | | | |

# 14: Computer/Internet Acronyms

**http**    hyper text transfer protocol

**html**    hyper text markup language (how you build web pages)

**ftp**    file transfer protocol

**ping**    packet internet groper

**ack**    acknowledgment

**url**    uniform resource locator (aka a web page address)

**ajax**    Asynchronous JavaScript and XML - a newer approach to building rich, interactive web pages (such as Gmail)

**dns**    domain name server

**ip**    internet protocol

**www**    world wide web

**ansi**    American National Standards Institute

**w3c**    world wide web consortium (www.w3c.org)

**ASCII**    American Standard Code for Information Interchange

**xml**    eXtensible Markup Language

**xsl**    eXtensible Stylesheet Language

**css**    Cascading Style Sheets

**wysiwyg**    what you see is what you get (the technology whereby the word processor screen looks just like what is ultimately printed, pronounced wiz ee wig)

**vm**    virtual machine

**usb**    universal serial bus

**tcp/ip**    transmission control protocol/internet protocol

**ssi**    server side include

**smtp**    simple mail transfer protocol

**sql**    structured query language

**ssl**    secure sockets layer

**ram**    random access memory

**dram**    dynamic random access memory

**eprom**    eraseable programmable read only memory

**rom**    read only memory

**p2p**    peer to peer

**pc**    personal computer

**pgp**    pretty good privacy

| | |
|---|---|
| **PnP** | Plug and Play |
| **pots** | plain old telephone service (as contrasted with digital phone systems) |
| **ppp** | Point to Point Protocol |
| **ppoe** | Point to Point Protocol over Ethernet |
| **os** | operating system |
| **mapi** | messaging application programming interface |
| **pop** | post office protocol |
| **mpeg** | motion picture experts group |
| **mp3** | mpeg third layer |
| **jpeg** | joint photographic experts group |
| **gif** | graphics interchange format |
| **lan** | local area network |
| **lcd** | liquid crystal display |
| **jvm** | java virtual machine |
| **faq** | frequently asked questions |
| **imap** | internet montage access protocol |

## Common Internet Slang Acronyms

| | | | | | |
|---|---|---|---|---|---|
| **k** | OK | **btw** | by the way | **moo?** | what? |
| **q** | question | **byo** | bring your own | **omg** | oh my gosh |
| **r** | are/our | **cuz** | because | **stfu** | shut up |
| **u** | you | **fyi** | for your information | **O RLY?** | oh really |
| **y** | why | **tmi** | too much informaton | **YA RLY!** | yeah really! |
| **am** | above mentioned | **g2g** | got to go | **NO WAI!!!** | no way! |
| **cu** | see you | **iaal** | I am actually laughing | **otp** | on the phone |
| **nm** | nothing much | | | **ppl** | people |
| **np** | no problem | **idc** | I don't care | **ROFl** | rolling on the floor laughing |
| **rl** | real life | **idk** | I don't know | | |
| **ty** | thank you | **iirc** | if I remember correctly | **RTFM** | read the fine manual |
| **wb** | welcome back | | | **SAL** | smiling a little |
| **yw** | you're welcome | **imho** | in my humble opinion | **tbh** | to be honest |
| **afaik** | as far as I know | | | **thx** | thanks |
| **atm** | at the moment | **l8r** | later | **TIA** | thanks in advance |
| **brb** | be right back | **LDR** | long-distance relationship | **ttyl** | talk to you later |
| **bbiab** | be back in a bit | | | **tyt** | take your time |
| **bbl** | be back later | **lol** | laughing out loud | **kewl** | cool, awesome |
| **bfn** | bye for now | **lmfao** | laughing my ass off | **ke** | OK |

# 15: Road Signs

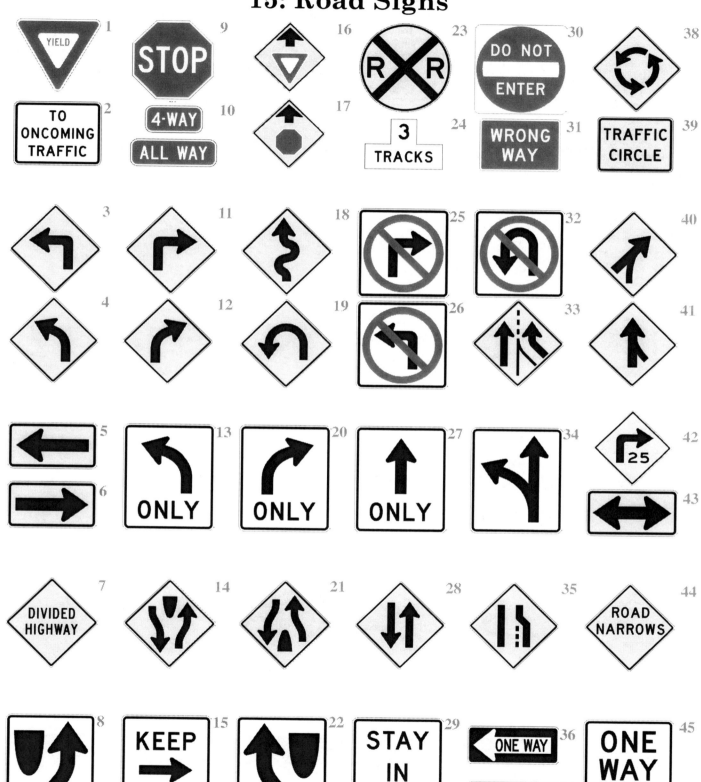

Explanations of the signs on page 292

 46

 52

 58

 64

 70

 76

 47

 53

 59

 65

 71

 77

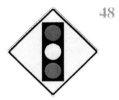 48

 54

 60

 66

 72

 78

 49

 55

 61

 67

 73

 79

 50

 56

 62

 68

 74

 80

 51

57

63

69

75

81

 82

 89

 DIVIDED HIGHWAY ENDS 96

 SOFT SHOULDER 103

 LEFT LANE ENDS 110

 PAVEMENT ENDS 117

 COMMERCIAL VEHICLES EXCLUDED 83

 TRUCKS USE RIGHT LANE 90

 HOV 2+ LANE ◇ AHEAD 97

 BIKE LANE AHEAD 104

 LEFT ON GREEN ARROW ONLY 111

 NO TURN ON RED 118

 SLOWER TRAFFIC KEEP RIGHT 84

 WALK ON LEFT FACING TRAFFIC 91

 PUSH BUTTON FOR GREEN LIGHT 98

 CROSS ONLY AT CROSS WALKS 105

 DO NOT BLOCK INTERSECTION 112

STOP HERE ON RED 119

 85

 92

 99

 106

 113

120

 EMERGENCY SIGNAL AHEAD 86

 BY-PASS 93

ALTERNATE 100

TEMPORARY 107

TRUCK 114

BUSINESS 121

 87

94

101

108

115

12'-6" 122

88

95

NO OUTLET 102

DEAD END 109

 DETOUR 116

 END DETOUR 123

291

124 — NO STANDING ANY TIME

126 — NO PARKING ANY TIME

128 — NO PARKING 8:30 AM TO 5:30 PM

131 — NO PARKING ANY TIME | ONE HOUR PARKING 9AM-7PM

133 — EMERGENCY PARKING ONLY

134 — (bus / no parking)

125 — NO PARKING LOADING ZONE

127 — EMERGENCY SNOW ROUTE NO PARKING IF OVER 2 INCHES

129 — RESERVED PARKING

130 — TOW-AWAY ZONE

132 — NO PARKING BUS STOP

## *Key to Road Signs*

1. Yield – *This shape is only used on yield signs.*
2. Yield to oncoming traffic – *Horizontal rectangles are used to give warnings, regulations or to supplement other signs.*
3. Warning left turn – *The diamond shape is only used for warning.*
4. Warning curve left
5. One way to left
6. One way to right
7. Divided highway
8. Keep right of divider – *This vertical rectangle shape is generally used to give regulations.*
9. Stop – *This shape is only used on stop signs.*
10. All cars must stop, used with stop signs.
11. Right turn
12. Curve right
13. Left turn only
14. Divided highway
15. Keep right
16. Yield sign ahead
17. Stop sign ahead
18. Winding road
19. Hair pin curve
20. Right turn only
21. Divided highway ends
22. Keep left of divider
23. Warning railroad crossing

24. Number of railroad tracks to be crossed.
25. No right turn – *This shape and symbol (a circle in a square barred from upper left to lower right) is used to say "no," to prohibit some activity.*
26. No left turn
27. Straight through only
28. Two way traffic
29. Stay in lane.
30. Do not enter
31. Wrong way
32. No U turn
33. Lane added
34. Left curve with optional lane going straight
35. Right lane ends; road narrows
36. One way going left
37. One way going right
38. Round-about or traffic circle ahead
39. Traffic circle
40. Entering roadway merge
41. Merge
42. Turn with speed advisory
43. Two way traffic
44. Road narrows
45. One way
46. Seat belts are mandatory
47. No bicycles
48. Signal light ahead
49. Hill
50. New speed limit ahead
51. Speed limit
52. School
53. Bicycles
54. Signal ahead
55. Hill

56. Speed limit, miles per hour
57. Minimum speed limit
58. Stop: children crossing
59. Playground
60. Be prepared to stop
61. Bump
62. Truck speed limit
63. Speed limit on exit
64. No pedestrians
65. Wheelchair warning
66. Stop ahead
67. Dip
68. Night speed limit
69. Speed limit on curve
70. Push button for pedestrian crossing signal
71. Pedestrian crossing
72. School bus stop ahead
73. Bridge ices before road
74. No turns
75. Do not pass
76. Cross only on signal
77. No hitch hiking
78. No trucks
79. Slippery when wet
80. Left land must turn left
81. Pass with care
82. Interstate route number
83. No commercial vehicles
84. Slower traffic keep right
85. Library – *Square signs are used for information.*
86. Emergency signal ahead
87. Emergency vehicles
88. Road work
89. Route number
90. Trucks use right lane
91. Walk on left
92. Hiking trail
93. By-pass
94. Horses in road

95. Flagman; work zone
96. Divided highway ends
97. HOV (high-occupancy vehicles) lane
98. Push button for green light
99. Hospital
100. Alternate route
101. Snowmobile crossing
102. No outlet
103. Soft shoulder
104. Bike lane; bike lane ahead
105. Cross only at cross walks
106. Airport
107. Temporary route
108. Deer crossing
109. Dead end
110. Left land ends
111. Left on green arrow only
112. Do not block intersection
113. Bus station
114. Truck route
115. Farm machinery
116. Detour
117. Pavement ends
118. No turn on red light
119. Spot here on red light
120. Train station
121. Business route
122. Clearance under bridge
123. End detour
124. No standing
125. No parking loading zone
126. No parking any time
127. No parking in snow
128. No parking time specified
129. Parking for handicapped
130. Tow-away zone
131. Two parking signs
132. No parking: bus stop
133. Emergency parking only
134. No parking: bus stop

The design of these signs are set by the U.S. government. These images are available in color for educational use from the *Manual of Traffic Signs*, by

Richard C. Moeur (http://www.trafficsign.us/) Copyright 2005 Richard C. Moeur. All rights are reserved.

# Pedagogical
# Atlas of the World
# 2014

with keyed outline maps
(see keys on page 306 to 308)

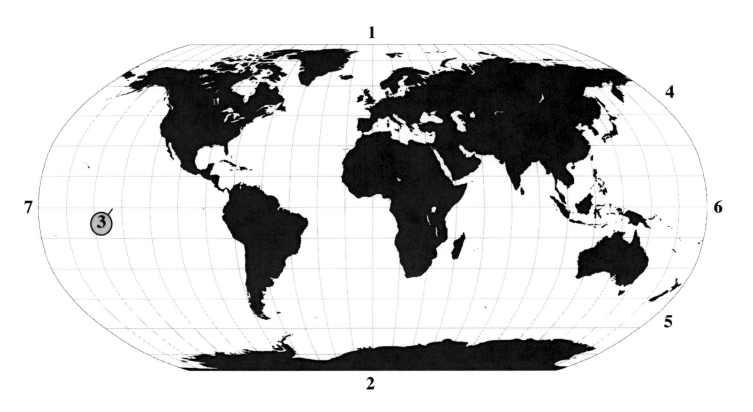

**Map 1 World**

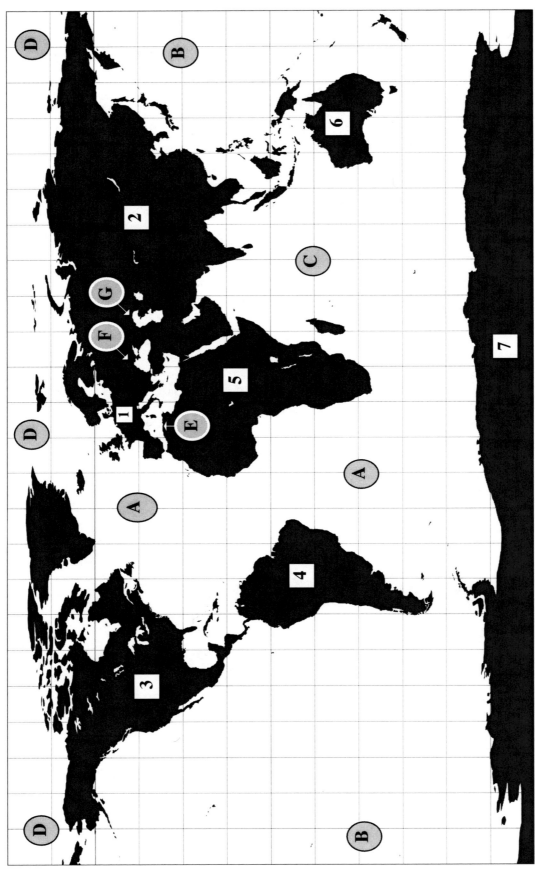

Map 2 Continents and Seas

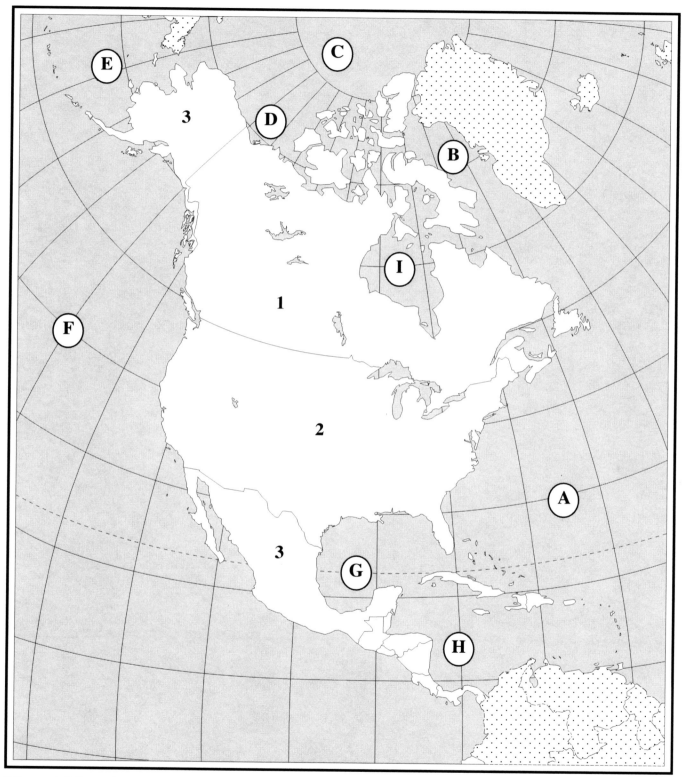

**Map 3 North America**

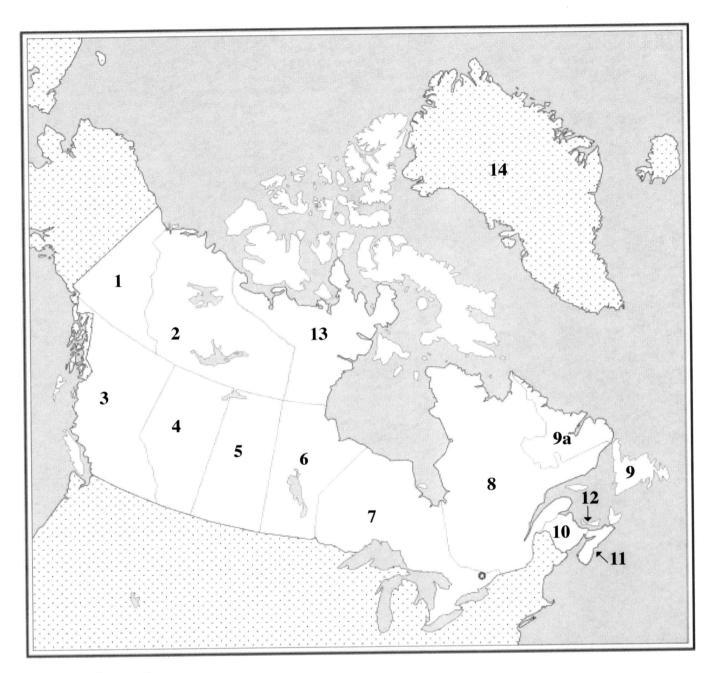

**Map 4 Canada**

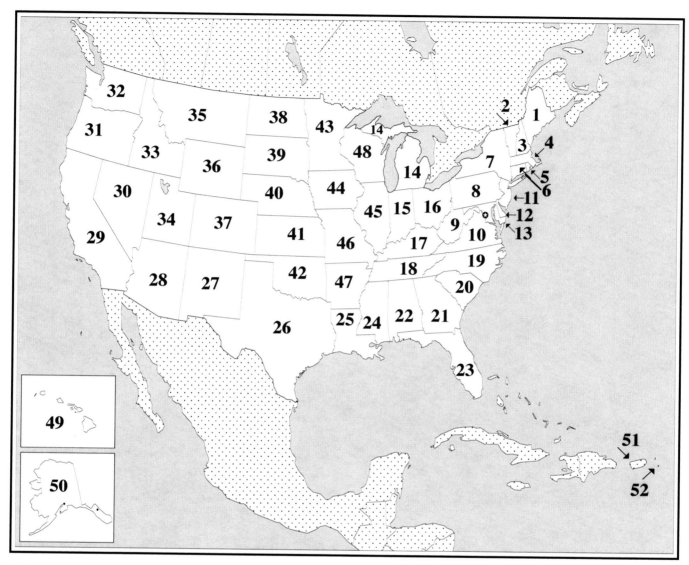

**Map 5 United States of America**

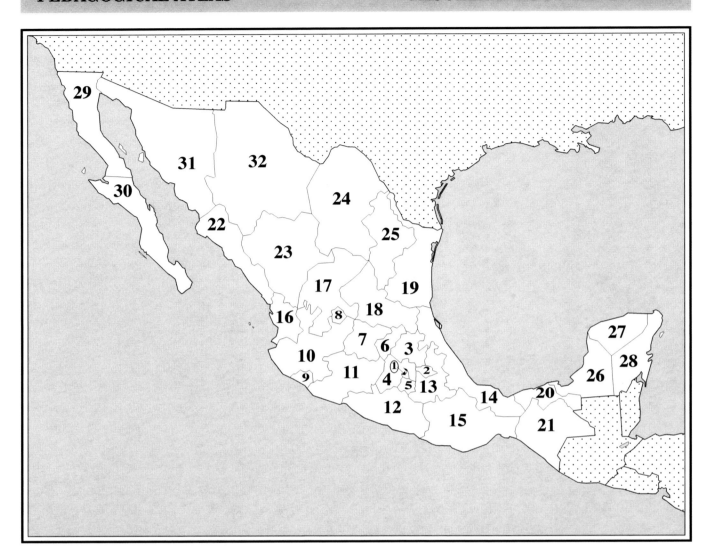

**Map 6 Mexico**

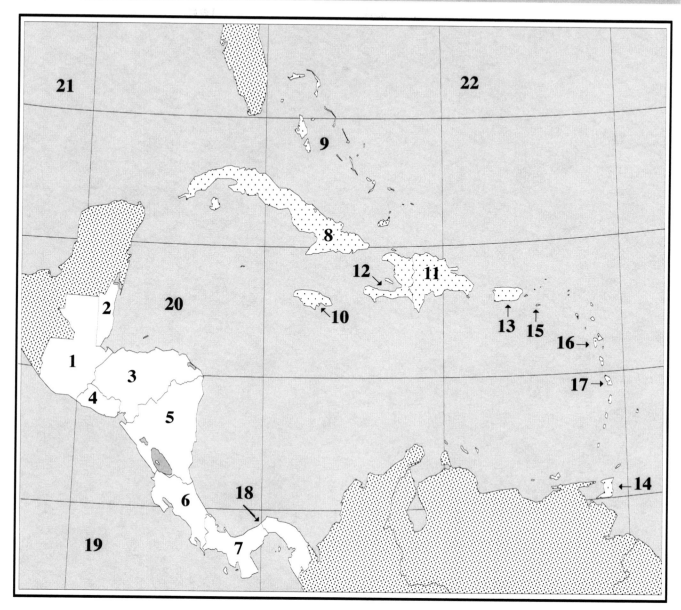

**Map 7 Central America and the Caribbean**

**Map 8 South America**

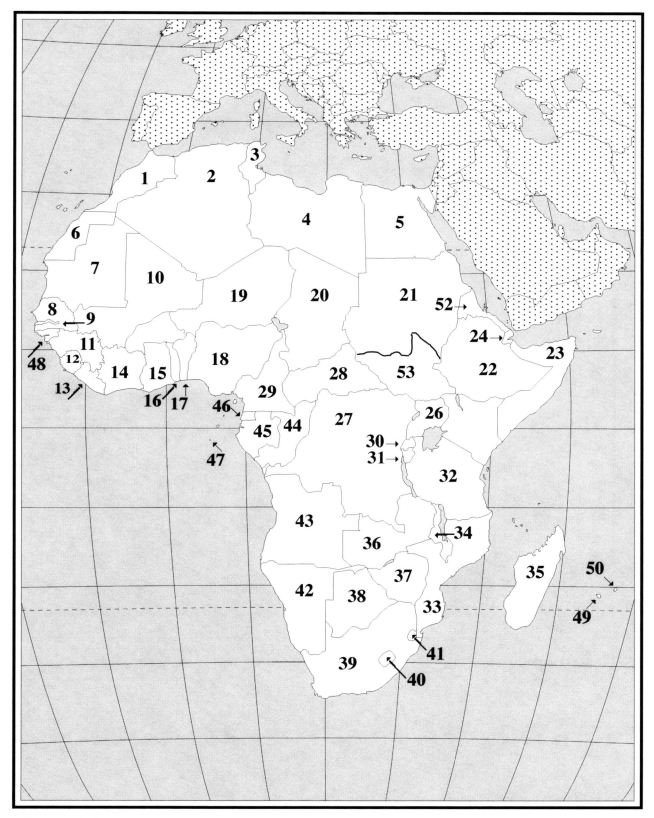

**Map 9 Africa**

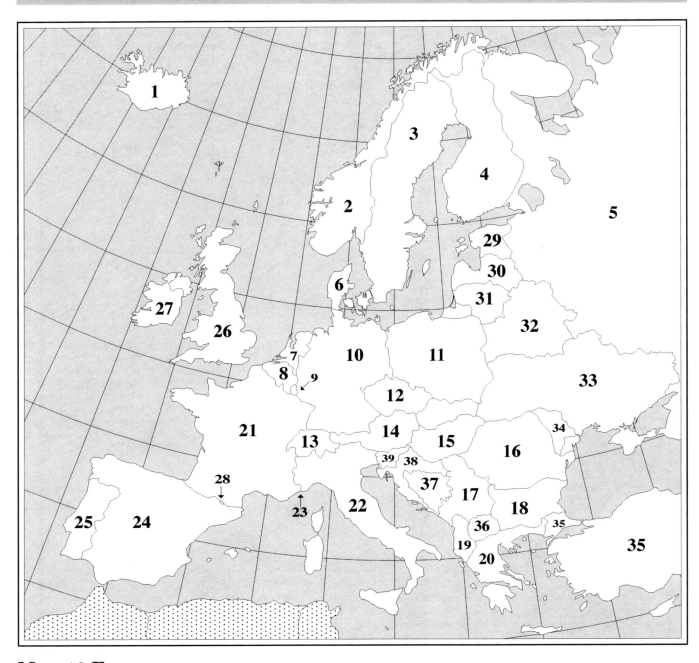

**Map 10 Europe**

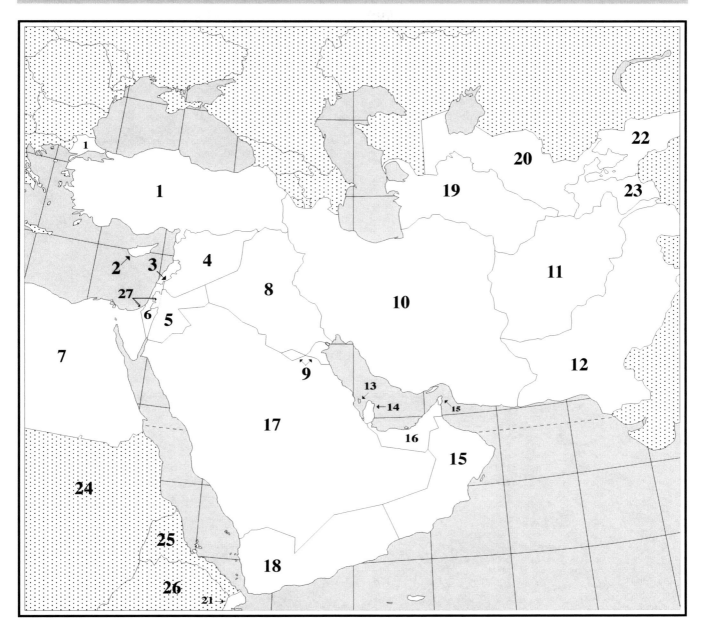

**Map 11 Middle East**

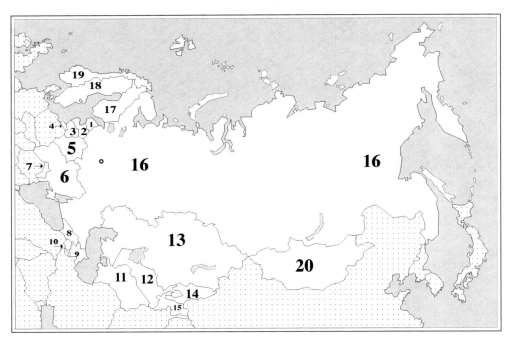

## Map 12 Northern Eurasia

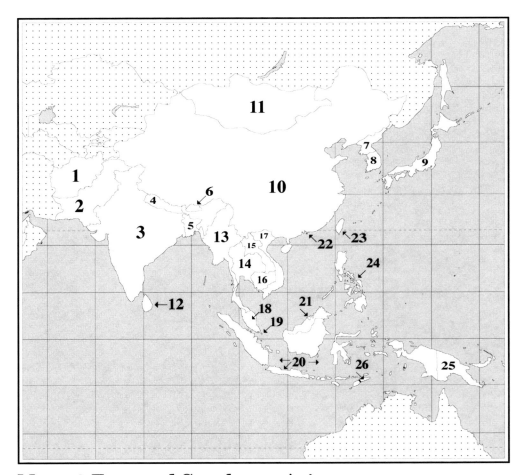

## Map 13 East and Southeast Asia

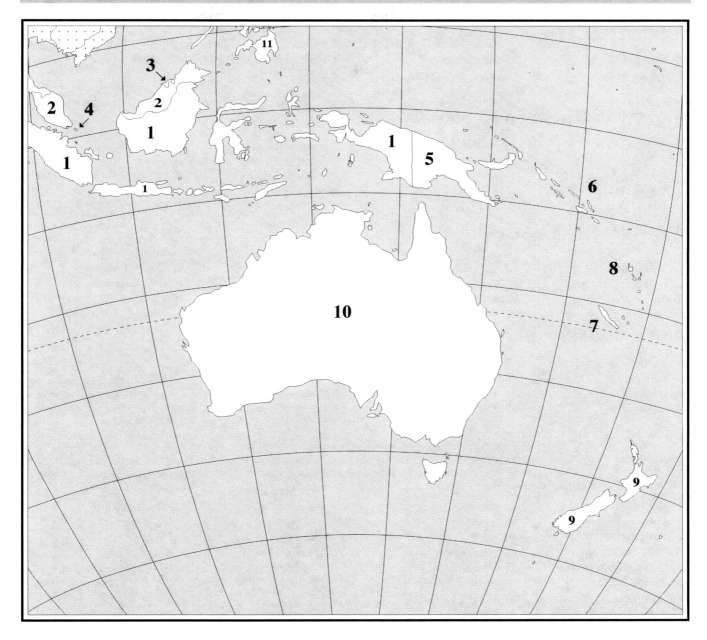

**Map 14 South Pacific**

## Map 1 World

1 North Pole
2 South Pole
3 Equator
4 Northern Hemisphere
5 Southern Hemisphere
6 East
7 West

## Map 2 Continents and Seas

1 Europe
2 Asia
3 North America
4 South America
5 Africa
6 Australia
7 Antarctica

A Atlantic Ocean
B Pacific Ocean
C Indian Ocean
D Arctic Ocean

E Mediterranean Sea
F Black Sea
G Caspian Sea

## Map 3 North America

1 Canada
2 U.S.A.
3 Mexico

A North Atlantic
B Baffin Bay
C Arctic

D Beaufort Sea
E Bering Sea
F Pacific

G Gulf of Mexico
H Caribbean Sea
I Hudson Bay

## Map 4 Canada

1 Yukon Territory
2 Northwest Territories
3 British Columbia
4 Alberta
5 Saskatchewan
6 Manitoba
7 Ontario
8 Quebec
9 Newfoundland
9a (including Labrador)
10 New Brunswick
11 Nova Scotia
12 Prince Edward Island
13 Nunavut
14 Greenland (Denmark)

## Map 5 United States of America

1 Maine
2 Vermont
3 New Hampshire
4 Massachusetts
5 Rhode Island
6 Connecticut
7 New York
8 Pennsylvania
9 West Virginia
10 Virginia
11 New Jersey
12 Delaware
13 Maryland
14 Michigan
15 Indiana
16 Ohio
17 Kentucky
18 Tennessee
19 North Carolina
20 South Carolina
21 Georgia
22 Alabama
23 Florida
24 Mississippi
25 Louisiana
26 Texas
27 NewMexico
28 Arizona
29 California
30 Nevada
31 Oregon
32 Washington
33 Idaho
34 Utah
35 Montana
36 Wyoming
37 Colorado
38 North Dakota
39 South Dakota
40 Nebraska
41 Kansas
42 Oklahoma
43 Minnesota
44 Iowa
45 Illinois
46 Missouri
47 Arkansas
48 Wisconsin
49 Hawaii
50 Alaska
51 Puerto Rico
52 Virgin Islands

## Map 6 Mexico

1 Distrito Federal
2 Tlaxcala
3 Hidalgo
4 Mexico
5 Morelos
6 Queretaro
7 Guanajuato
8 Aguascalientes
9 Colima
10 Jalisco
11 Michoacan
12 Guerrero
13 Puebla
14 Veracruz
15 Oaxaca
16 Nayarit
17 Zacatecas
18 San Luis Potosi
19 Tamaulipas
20 Villahermosa
21 Chiapas
22 Sinaloa
23 Durango
24 Coahuila
25 Nuevo Leon
26 Campeche
27 Yucatan
28 Quintana Roo
29 Baja California Norte
30 Baja California Sur
31 Sonora
32 Chihuaha

## Map 7 Central America and the Caribbean

1 Guatemala
2 Belize
3 Honduras
4 El Salvador
5 Nicaragua
6 Costa Rica

7 Panama
8 Cuba
9 The Bahamas
10 Jamaica
11 Dominican
   Republic

12 Haiti
13 Puerto Rico
14 Trinidad/Tobago
15 US Virgin Islands
16 Martinique
17 Guadeloupe

18 Panama Canal
19 Pacific Ocean
20 Caribbean Sea
21 Gulf of Mexico
22 Atlantic Ocean

## Map 8 South America

1 Colombia
2 Venezuela
3 Guyana
4 Suriname

5 French Guiana
6 Ecuador
7 Peru

8 Bolivia
9 Chile
10 Paraguay

11 Argentina
12 Uruguay
13 Brazil

## Map 9 Africa

1 Morocco
2 Algeria
3 Tunisia
4 Libya
5 Egypt
6 Western Sahara
7 Mauritania
8 Senegal
9 Gambia
10 Mali
11 Guinea
12 Sierra Leone
13 Liberia

14 Ivory Coast
15 Ghana
16 Togo
17 Benin
18 Nigeria
19 Niger
20 Chad
21 Sudan
22 Ethiopia
23 Somalia
24 Djibouti
25 Kenya
26 Uganda

27 Dem. Republic of Congo
28 Central African Republic
29 Cameroun
30 Rwanda
31 Burundi
32 Tanzania
33 Mozambique
34 Malawi
35 Madagascar
36 Zambia
37 Zimbabwe
38 Botswana
39 South Africa

40 Lesotho
41 Swaziland
42 Namibia
43 Angola
44 Republic of Congo
45 Gabon
46 Equatorial Guinea
47 Sao Tome/Principe
48 Guinea Bissau
49 Reunion
50 Mauritius
51 Burkina Faso
52 Eritrea
53 South Sudan

## Map 10 Europe

1 Iceland
2 Norway
3 Sweden
4 Finland
5 Russia
6 Denmark
7 Netherlands
8 Belgium
9 Luxembourg
10 Germany

11 Poland
12 Czech Republic
13 Switzerland
14 Austria
15 Hungary
16 Romania
17 Yugoslavia
18 Bulgaria
19 Albania
20 Greece

21 France
22 Italy
23 Monaco
24 Spain
25 Portugal
26 The United Kingdom
27 Ireland
28 Andorra
29 Estonia
30 Latvia

31 Lithuania
32 Belarus
33 Ukraine
34 Moldova
35 Turkiye
36 Macedonia
37 Bosnia
38 Croatia
39 Slovenia
40 Slovakia

## Map 11 Middle East

1 Turkey
2 Cyprus
3 Lebanon
4 Syria
5 Jordan
6 Israel
7 Egypt

8 Iraq
9 Kuwait
10 Iran
11 Afghanistan
12 Pakistan
13 Bahrain
14 Qatar

15 Oman
16 United Arab Emirates
17 Saudi Arabia
18 Yemen
19 Turkmenistan
20 Uzbekistan
21 Djibouti

22 Kyrgyzstan
23 Tajikistan
24 Sudan
25 Eritrea
26 Ethiopia
27 Occupied Territories:
   West Bank and Gaza

## Map 12 Northern Eurasia

| | | | |
|---|---|---|---|
| 1 Estonia | 6 Ukraine | 11 Turkmenistan | 16 Russia |
| 2 Latvia | 7 Moldova | 12 Uzbekistan | 17 Finland |
| 3 Lithuania | 8 Georgia | 13 Kazakhstan | 18 Sweden |
| 4 Kaliningrad | 9 Azerbaijan | 14 Kyrgyztan | 19 Norway |
| 5 Belarus | 10 Armenia | 15 Tajikistan | 20 Mongolia |

## Map 13 East snd Southeast Asia

| | | | |
|---|---|---|---|
| 1 Afghanistan | 8 South Korea | 15 Laos | 22 Hong Kong |
| 2 Pakistan | 9 Japan | 16 Kampuchea | 23 Taiwan |
| 3 India | 10 China | 17 Vietnam | 24 The Philippines |
| 4 Nepal | 11 Mongolia | 18 Malaysia | 25 Papua New Guinea |
| 5 Bangladesh | 12 Sri Lanka | 19 Singapore | 26 East Timor |
| 6 Bhutan | 13 Burma/Myanmar | 20 Indonesia | |
| 7 North Korea | 14 Thailand | 21 Brunei | |

## Map 14 South Pacific

| | | | |
|---|---|---|---|
| 1 Indonesia | 4 Singapore | 7 New Caledonia | 10 Australia |
| 2 Malaysia | 5 Papua New Guinea | 8 Vanuatu | 11 The Philippines |
| 3 Brunei | 6 Solomon Islands | 9 New Zealand | |

# The Paralinguistic Aspect

We are using the term paralinguistic to include a variety of acts that accompany language or are used in place of language to communicate a message. Sometimes sound itself is used, e.g. a "wolf whistle;" sometimes the body is used, e.g. a smile. In short, this Aspect is about non-verbal communication. But let us hasten to say, it is not about all kinds of non-verbal communication. Painting and sculpture, for example, could be considered non-verbal forms of communication, but because they are only very distant cousins of language, they are not of primary interest to the language learner and teacher.

We have not dealt with the entire spectrum of non-verbal communication partly because to do so would make the book overly long and partly because paralinguistic communication does not lend itself to exploration in a book such as this one. Such paralinguistic events as a whistle and a smile are not easily classified or captured and catalogued in print, as are nouns, verbs, and topical vocabulary. Paralinguistic communication is very important, however, and we want to give students and teachers a handle on the subject. To do this we have outlined the field of paralinguistics and non-verbal communication. This outline, in checklist form, as usual, is included as a reminder that at some point in the language program it would be useful to discuss and explore the various sounds and actions suggested by the list. Also, as usual, the outline is far from exhaustive; it is suggestive and is intended only as a start.

Because they do fit into the format of this book, we have chosen to present three forms of paralinguistic communication in some detail: the International Sign Alphabet, Classroom Gestures, and a selection or sampling of common American Gestures. The alphabet of the International Sign Language has been included because we feel it is of potential value to language teachers and learners. For example, it can be used in the classroom in instances where a teacher might want to avoid oral spelling. The signs for the vowels might be especially useful because of the discrepancy between the sounds and the names of English vowels (*A, E,* and *I* give students a lot of trouble). And in general, a sign alphabet might be a useful tool for teachers who try to keep their own verbalizations at a minimum.

The Classroom Gestures are included here only to suggest that there can be a pedagogical use for paralinguistic gestures. To a certain extent, such gestures are idiosyncratic, but our brief page of sketches is, we hope, illustrative of some rather widely used classroom gestures. We would like to suggest that teachers and students might be well advised to establish their own system of classroom gestures at the outset of the language program. Our illustration can be used as a starting point.

The sampling of common American Gestures speaks for itself. These gestures were originally collected, photographed, labeled, and categorized by Peg Clement in 1981. The images and some of the gestures became somewhat dated over the next twenty-five years, and so we have recreated her collection using new models and some new gestures. However, with a few minor changes, we have used her classification system in presenting the photos. We have also included additional information about the meanings and the sounds that might accompany the gestures.

The two children who demonstrated the American gestures are Veronica McKay and Cole Madden. The adults are Liza Aldana and  Adrienne Antrim Major. All the photos were taken by Mike Jerald.

# Contents

*Hopi Wolf Dancer
Kachina doll*

# 1: An Outline of Paralinguistic Communication

## A. Sounds

❏ 1. Individual sounds
    a. Fricatives—Shh!
    b. Nasals— Mmmm.
    c. Trills—Brrr.
    d. Clicks and stops—Tsk, tsk; Pst.

❏ 2. Emotional Intonation
    a. Surprise
    b. Fear
    c. Anger
    d. Irony
    e. Sarcasm
    f. Teasing
    g. Mockery
    h. Complaint
    i. Persuasion
    j. Pleading
    k. Flirtation
    l. Intimacy
    m. Pleasure

❏ 3. Exclamations and Interjections

❏ 4. Voice qualities and styles
    a. Whisper
    b. Baby talk
    c. Falsetto
    d. Command, stern and calm
    e. Command, gruff

❏ 5. Whistling

❏ 6. Humming

❏ 7. Yelling

❏ 8. Laughing

❏ 9. Crying

❏ 10. Coughing and throat clearing

## B. Body Language (Kinesics)

❏ 1. Facial expressions

❏ 2. Eye contact

❏ 3. Gestures

❏ 4. Touching (Haptics)

## C. Other Areas of Paralinguistic Communication

❏ 1. Silence

❏ 2. Time

❏ 3. Space and distance (Proxemics)

311

# 2: International Sign Alphabet

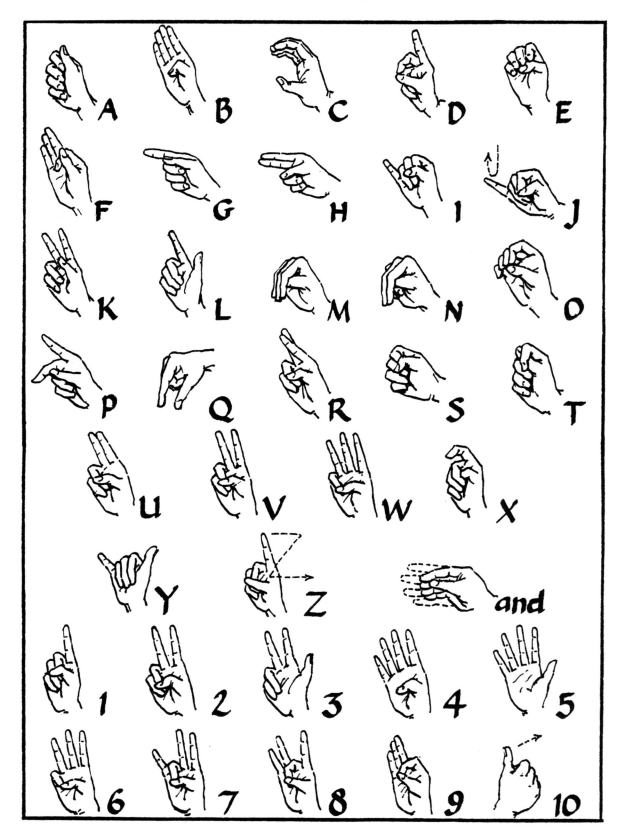

# 3: Classroom Gestures

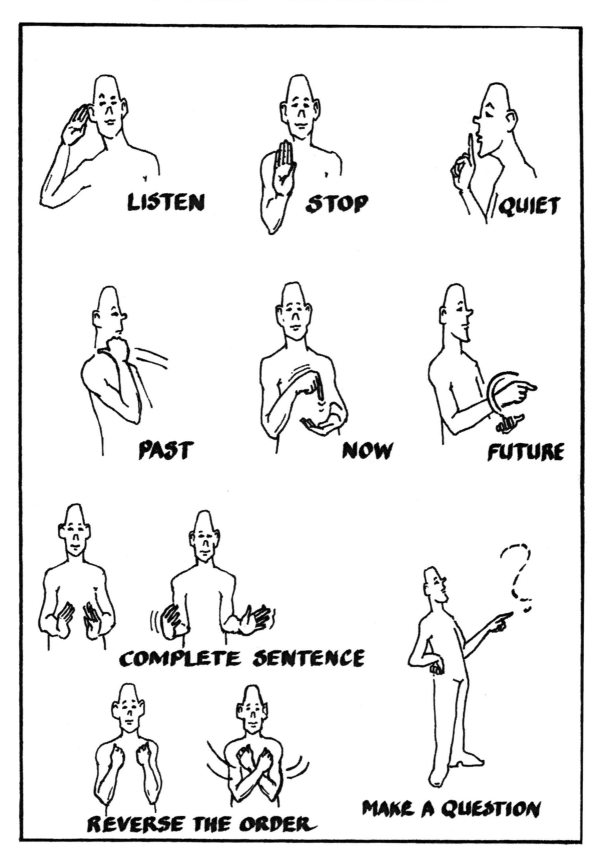

# 4: Selected American Gestures

## Checklist

| Classification: Children's Gestures | | | page 305 |
|---|---|---|---|
| **Number** | **What it means** | **What it's called, if anything** | **What sounds or words are used with it** |
| ❑ 1. | An act of defiance, often teasing, to someone giving orders. | Sticking out your tongue | Nnn, nnnn |
| ❑ 2. | Teasing ridicule meaning: "Ha ha! you got caught (and I didn't). It serves you right. You made a mistake. I'm right and you're wrong." | * * * | "Naa naa!" "Yaa yaa!" |
| ❑ 3. | Teasing ridicule meaning, literally, something or someone smells bad. It implies, "I don't like that. It is awful!" | Holding your nose. | "PU!" "Yuck!" "That stinks!" |
| ❑ 4. | Secretly giving a person who is having their picture taken "devil's horns" as a teasing joke or trick. This is very common childish behavior before a camera. | * * * | No noise, because the joke is secret; giggling is typical. |
| ❑ 5. | Crossing your fingers behind your back means that you really don't mean to do what you are promising to do. | Fingers crossed | No noise, because the joke is secret |
| ❑ 6. | Making the "L" sign referring to someone means that the person indicated is a "Loser." It is a secret signal. | * * * | No noise, because the message is secret |
| ❑ 7. | Making the "W" sign referring to someone means that the person indicated is a "Winner." It is a secret signal. | * * * | No noise, because the message is secret |

| Parental Gestures | | | page 306 |
|---|---|---|---|
| ❑ 8. | Beckoning by wiggling the index finger means: "Come here. I want you here, now!" It is not always imperative and not always done to a child, although the person beckoned is usually of inferior status. | * * * | "Come here." "Come on." – said encouragingly. |
| ❑ 9. | A reprimand or scolding gesture, often teasing, usually done to a child or inferior. The index/forefinger is pointed up and wagged back and forth. | Shaking your finger at someone. | "Naughty, Naughty!" "Bad girl! (or boy) "Tsk, tsk!" "No!" |
| ❑ 10. | Scraping your index fingers together at someone usually a child or inferior, often teasingly. | Reprimand | "Shame, shame." "No, no." |
| ❑ 11. | A signal to be quiet. | Shushing someone. | Sometimes done silently to avoid noise or with whispered "Shh" "Be quiet!" |
| ❑ 12. | A reprimand or scolding gesture, often teasing, usually done to a child or inferior. The index/forefinger is pointed at the child. | Scolding, pointing your finger at someone | 12. Same as 9 |

314

## Societal Gestures                    page 307

❑ 13. A civilian style salute most commonly used when pledging allegiance to the national flag or singing the national anthem. *See National Documents at the end of the* Topics *section.*

Holding your hand over your heart.

\* \* \*

❑ 14. The formal stance assumed while taking an oath. The right hand is raised, the left is placed on a Bible or other sacred book. Those who prefer not to swear to the truth using a book (which is forbidden in some religions) can affirm the truth putting a hand over their heart.

Taking an oath. Putting your hand on the Bible.

"I swear (on the Bible/on my honor) that I will...."

❑ 15. A military salute, a gesture of respect given to a superior commissioned officer and often returned. It is also used by others in uniform (such as police) as a formal greeting, and by most people in uniform during the pledge of allegiance or the national anthem, or to honor the raising or passing of the national flag, usually while standing stiffly at formal attention.

Saluting_____. (the flag, an officer, etc.)

\* \* \*

## Gestures of Greeting and Leave Taking        pages 307-308

There are many forms of greeting and leave taking used in North America. These vary regionally and between age groups and ethnic groups. A very informal "salute" or wave is most common. More formally people shake right hands. In some groups, an "air kiss" on one or two cheeks is typical among friends as is a quick hug, even among men. People say different things, such as "Hi." "Hey there." "Good to see you." How're you doing?" For somewhat formal introductions: "Hello." "How do you do." "It's nice to meet you."

❑ 16. Between two members of some cultural, ethnic, and age groups, elaborate special hand shakes are popular. "High five," clapping raised right hands is used, particularly by athletes, both as a greeting and as a celebratory gesture.

High five

"Slap me five, Brother!"

❑ 17. Elaborate "handshake" greetings go in and out of fashion. One purpose is to indicate that the people involved are initiates, "brothers." Groups which have typically invented and used such rituals include children, athletes, members of secret societies, and people who identify themselves with a specific ethnic group and/or a specific social or political philosophy. Knowing and using the ritual gesture is a way of identifying oneself and celebrating one's beliefs or success. The one pictured is very common. A "high five" is followed by a "low five," tapping palms or finger tips.

Low five

❑ 18. A wave of the hand with fingers extended is the most common gesture of greeting or goodbye used either informally or from a distance. It is also used to get someone's attention. Emotions or strength of feeling are indicated by the vigor of the gesture and the person's expression.

A wave.

"Hi." "Hello." "Bye." "Yoo hoo." "Here I am."

| | | |
|---|---|---|
| ❏ 19. To say goodbye to a loved one. Men or women kiss their finger tips and then either toss or blow the "kiss" to the departing person. | Blowing a kiss. | "I love you." |
| ❏ 20. The "Vulcan salute" (now often comical) is a leave taking and blessing. It originated with the character Mr. Spock, a Vulcan officer on space ship Enterprise, in the TV series *Star Trek*. It became popular with young people of the 1960's and remains so with fans today, perhaps because it is similar to a "Peace" gesture. | Vulcan farewell salute | "Live long and prosper." |

## Gestures of Complicity and Fraternity          page 309

| | | |
|---|---|---|
| ❏ 21. Tapping your temple with your forefinger or making a circular motion around your ear, usually while rolling your eyes towards someone and then pointing at them, means that you disapprove (good naturedly) of that person's behavior or opinions as being abnormal. | Crazy sign | "He's crazy." "...nuts." "...wacko." "...batty." "...loco." "...got a screw loose." "... out of his mind." and other such comic overstatements. |
| ❏ 22. Pointing with one's thumb, often while extending the lower lip and rolling one's eyes upwards, is a gesture generally of mockery, disapproval, or approval shared with someone who will agree with the opinion expressed. It is a common comic gesture. | * * * | "Get a load of this!" This expession is generally thought, not said out loud. |
| ❏ 23. This comic gesture suggests that you have a good and clever idea for some action. It is sometimes done simply to show anticipation, but when it is exaggerated (often with a grin of evil delight and a low chuckling sound), it suggests that you are being crafty. | Rubbing your hands (in glee). | "Oh, boy!" "Hee, hee, hee!" "Oh, just wait 'til I ..." |
| ❏ 24. A wink is a friendly facial gesture. It may mean many different things depending on the context and the people communicating. It may mean that you are taking someone into your confidence and that you agree with them: Don't let on, but I agree with you. Don't really believe me; I was only kidding. A wink may also be a gesture on quiet congratulations: I won't make a fuss, but, between us, you did a great job! Or it may be a gesture of greeting or invitation. A politician may wink to say: I see you are with me and I like you! Others may wink to say: You're attractive to me, Handsome (or Beautiful). Come over and get to know me! People are generally careful who they wink at. | Winking. | Nothing is usually said. Winks are often combined with a slight nod of agreement or encouragement. There is an old saying: "A wink's as good as a nod." |
| ❏ 25. A gesture of resignation or non-involvement meaning: So, don't ask me, it's not my problem, how should I know? I know nothing about it. What can I do? Who cares? | A shrug | "Damned if I know." "Who knows?" "So what?" |
| ❏ 26. A dramatic gesture showing shock or disappointment, particularly with oneself. Variations are clutching your forehead, covering your eyes, or slapping yourself on the forehead. It is often used when you have made a costly or stupid mistake. | *** | "No!" " Daaah!" "Stupid me!" "How could I?" |

## Gestures of Identification    page 310

❑ 27. Pointing to yourself.                                          ***        "Me?"

❑ 28. Pointing to, recognizing or acknowledging someone else.        ***        "You!" "It's you!"

## Gestures of Hope or Good Luck    page 310

*The following gestures were originally magic rituals addressed to the powers of Fate or the goddess Fortune. To some strongly religious people these are gestures of pagan superstition and evil, while some true believers in magic take such rituals very seriously. However, most people practice these gestures, or at least refer to them, as good-natured jokes. Such rituals and other superstitions may amuse people, but they often make them slightly nervous as well. For this reason, some hotels do not have thirteenth floors, and many people will not walk under ladders, and they avoid black cats.*

❑ 29. This gesture, knocking on wood, is done to avoid tempting fate, to avoid bad luck, when someone says something very positive about you or when you or someone else has just predicted some good luck or fortune. A common joke is to knock on your head, making gentle fun of the ritual and ridiculing yourself as having a wooden head – a block head – stupid enough to go through with the ritual, which, of course, you always do, religiously. | Knocking on wood. | "I hope so — it is going to work – knock on wood."

❑ 30. Traditionally, the believer looks for something made of wood to knock on.

❑ 31. A gesture expressing the hope that some specific good thing will happen. This gesture is also sometimes used with arms crossed over the chest (heart), particularly by children, as a pledge of truthfulness: "It's true! Cross my fingers, hope to die, if it's not!" | Crossing your fingers. | "I think we're in luck, but I'm keeping my fingers crossed – just in case."

❑ 32. The crossed fingers gesture may also express concern that something will go wrong. A worried look suggests that the person would prevent bad luck it they could. | | "Oh, I'm so afraid it won't work, but I've got my fingers crossed!"

## Gestures of Jubilation    page 311

❑ 33. Shaking your hands enthusiastically above your head, like pumping a person's hand enthusiastically, is a gesture of enthusiastic approval. | Cheering. | Hooray

❑ 34. Putting your hands on your cheeks, showing surprise. | Surprize | Wow

❑ 35. Raising your arm, making a fist, jerking your fist down fast to waist level is an expression of exultation. | Cheering | Yes!!!.

## Gestures of Congratulation and Self-Congratulation     page 312

❏ 36. Shaking your hand with the palm out, thumb and index finger touching, and the rest of the fingers extended is a quiet, happy sign of approval and encouragement. *However, it should be noted that Americans from some non-U.S. cultural backgrounds may mistake the meaning of this gesture; elsewhere it is a vulgar gesture with strongly sexual implications.*

\* \* \*

"All right!"
"That'a way!"
"That's A OK!"
"Right on!" said with a smile.

❏ 37. A comic gesture of self-congratulation. Dampening your nails with your breath and then rubbing them on your chest is interpreted variously as polishing a prize, medal. or apple.

\* \* \*

The gesture speaks for itself.

❏ 38. A gesture meaning that you or someone else has scored a point, either literally, in a game, or figuratively, in a discussion, argument, or some other competitive situation. You wet you finger and then make a motion as if you were making a wet mark on the air.

Chalking one up.

"OK, that's one for me" (you, him, her, them, etc.)

## Gestures of Nervousness, Impatience, Worry, and Boredom     page 313

❏ 39. Americans from many ethnic groups chew their fingernails when they are anxious or nervous. This gesture refers to the habit meaning that you are, or should be, nervous. It is often done dramatically for comic effect.

Biting your nails.

\* \* \*

❏ 40. Hands on hips, foot tapping, head tilted. This full-body gesture shows that you are impatient and most probably angry.

Tapping your foot.

\* \* \*

❏ 41. All humans and even monkeys yawn when they are tired, bored, or impatient. Usually Americans politely stifle or hide their yawns, but they may gesture, pretending to yawn, to show their feelings.

A fake yawn

A loud intake of breath, like a yawn

❏ 42. Drumming with your fingers, tapping a surface with one finger after another, is another gesture showing boredom, impatience, and probably anger.

Finger drumming

\* \* \*

❏ 43. Baring your teeth, wrinkling your forehead with your eyes to one side is a gesture showing worry or concern. It is often done with your arms folded, suggesting a hug.

Grimace

\* \* \*

❏ 44. Putting your hands together with the fingers linked while rolling ("twiddling") your thumbs is a common gesture of impatience. When it is done openly while someone is talking, it is rude. It is often done covertly to tell someone that you are bored with what someone else is saying or with the situation you are in. Although it can show real annoyance, it is generally a comic or mocking expression.

Twid-dling your thumbs.

A sigh. "Ho hum!"
"Really!"
"I'm just bored to death!"

## Miscellaneous Gestures Showing Other Emotions    pages 314-315

❏ 45. A gesture meaning "stop" or "slow down." It can be a command or an expression of concern, depending on your facial expression and the authority of your movement.

\* \* \*

"Whoa!" "Slow down!"
"Just a minute!"
"Hold it right there!"

❏ 46. Making and sometimes shaking a fist while frowning shows anger and threatens retaliation.

\* \* \*

"I'll get you!"
"You just wait!"

❏ 47. Frowning is a facial gesture of anger or concern

Frowning

Generally silent

❏ 48. Standing with your weight on your back foot, your hands on your hips, and aa expression shock suggests outrage.

\* \* \*

"No way!" "You're wrong!"
"That's terrible!"

❏ 49. Turning away from someone while holding up you hand as if to block them is a gesture meaning "stop" or "wait."

\* \* \*

"Just wait a minute!"
"Stop it, now!"

❏ 50. The gesture of snapping your fingers along with an expression of delight and surprise means that you have just thought of or remembered something you have been trying to think of. Snapping your fingers with a stern, impatient, or angry expression generally means that you want someone to do something immediately. Snapping your fingers to get someone's attention (a waiter in a crowded restaurant, for example) is often effective but is considered to be very offensive; it will often get the waiter's attention but bad service as well.

Snapping your fingers.

"I've got it!" "That's it!"
"Ah, ha!" "Eureka!"

"Now, this minute!"

"You, over here! Come here! I want you now!"

❏ 51. Scratching your head is an expression of puzzlement or bewilderment.

Scratching your head.

"What?" "I don't get it!"
"Huh?" "What's that supposed to mean?"

❏ 52. Brushing your forehead with your fingers while blowing air through your pursed lips is a gesture of relief after avoiding a serious misfortune. The same gesture is also used to complain about the heat.

Wiping your forehead.
Wiping your brow.

"Phew!" "That was a close call!"
"Oh, that was too close for comfort."

❏ 53. Covering your ears, gasping, and staring is a gesture of horror or fright, suggesting that you don't want to hear.

\* \* \*

"No! It can't be! I don't want to hear it! I don't want to look!"

❏ 54. Covering your mouth, gasping, and staring is a gesture of of horror, suggesting that you don't want to speak or scream.

\* \* \*

Aaah! I want to scream! What should I do?"

319

## Miscellaneous Gestures With Specific Meanings          page 316

❏ 55. Measurement gestures are common to most languages and cultures. The one shown means the object or person was about as high or tall as the woman's hand. Length is shown by holding the thumb and forefinger apart the right distance or by holding the two hands apart with the fingers extended and the palms held inward.

\* \* \*

"Oh, it (he or she) was about this high (tall, deep)."

❏ 56. The gesture of holding your hand up when you are in a group of people is the accepted way of indicating that you want to be called on or recognized to speak next. It is polite when it is silent. Children may raise their hands high and even wave. Adults generally make the least gesture necessary to get attention.

Putting your hand up

Silent, except when done comically to get attention and show enthusiasm with expressions like "I'm ready!" "Call on me!"

❏ 57. Gesturing to get the attention of a waiter is extremely difficult in American English, unless the waiter is attentive. You may wave discreetly or lift your index finger as shown here. You may even say "Excuse me," very softly and politely, as he or she passes close by. However, these gestures often go unseen in a busy restaurant, and snapping your fingers, clapping your hands, whistling, and shouting out for service are all considered to be very objectionable. They are outdoor behavior, suitable for hailing taxicabs in heavy traffic, an art which may also look like the gesture pictured when practiced by a master.

Catching a waiter's eye.

Done either silently or with very quiet, polite noises like a gentle cough, "um," or "oh." "Excuse me, please." "Ah. Could we please...."

"Taxi!" or a loud whistle

❏ 58. Gestures of approval and disapproval, dating back to ancient Rome, when "thumbs up" meant 'let the gladiator up; let him live." Gesture made with a smile.

Thumbs up

"I'm for it." "Great!" "That's good!"

❏ 59. "Thumbs down" meant "let them die without mercy." In America, the signal means "my reaction is negative. I don't like it, him, or her. No, I vote against it. The gesture is often made while sticking out your lower lip or frowning.

Thumbs down

"No, I'm against it!" "Bad!" "That's no good!" "That's awful!"

❏ 60. This gesture with your thumb stretched back next to your ear and your little finger stretched forward in front of your mouth means "call me on the telephone: A similar gesture, putting your thumb to your lips and then tipping your hand up like a bottle with your little finger raised, means you want a drink.

Call me

A silent signal, though sometimes the person mouths, "Call me."

❏ 61. This signal is a request for a break in the action. Originally it was used in team sports asking the officials for "time out." It is now used to ask for or suggest that a class or meeting should be stopped for a few minutes so that the participants can "take a break." The hands are raised to form a T for "Time."

Time out

Generally silent, but in sports particularly the person may reinforce the gesture by yelling, "Time out."

320

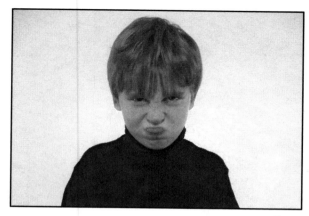

1

2

3

4

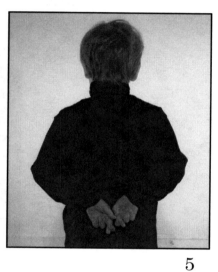

5

6

7

Meanings: page 298

8

9

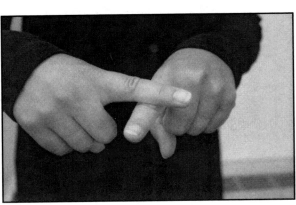

10

11

12

Meanings: page 298

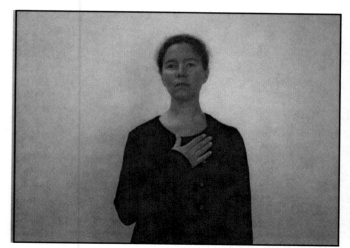

13

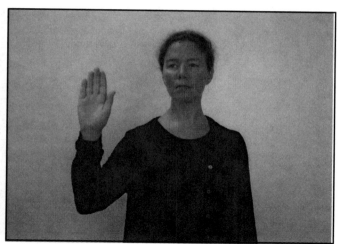

14

15

## GESTURES OF GREETING

16

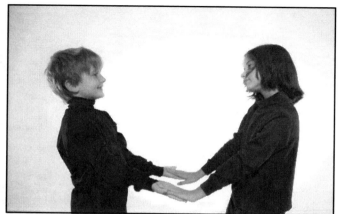

17

Meanings: page 299

18

19

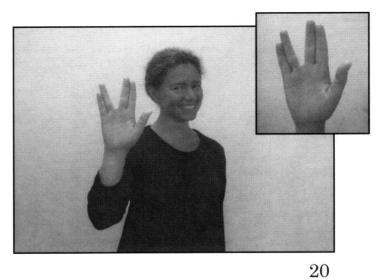

20

Meanings: pages 299 - 300

21

22

23

24

25

26

Meanings: page 309

27

28

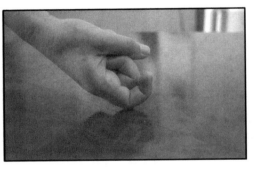

30

29

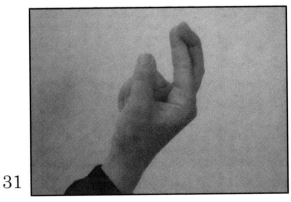

31

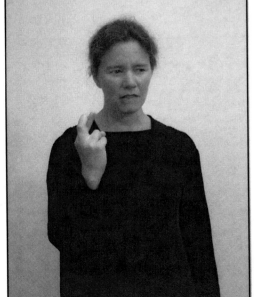

32

Meanings: page 310

33

34

35

Meanings: page 301

36

37

38

Meanings: page 302

39

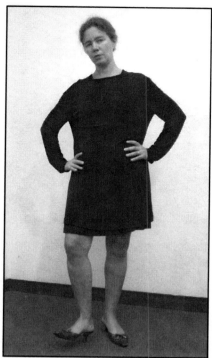

40

41

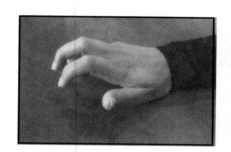

42

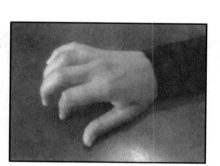

43

44

Meanings: page 302

329

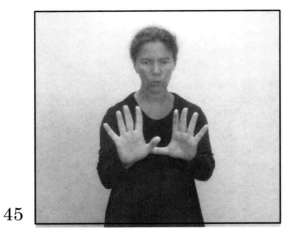

45

46

47

48

49

Meanings: page 303

50

51

52

53

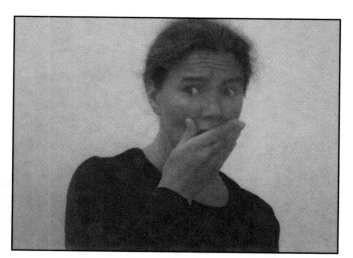

54

Meanings: page 303

55

56

57

58

59

60

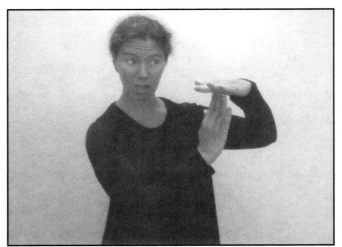

61

Meanings: page 304

# SOURCES

Allison, Alexander W., Herbert Barrows, et al. *The Norton Anthology of Poetry,* Third Edition. New York, N.Y.: W. W. Norton & Co., 1986

Boone, Eleanor; Rick Gildea, and Pat Moran. *Resources for TESOL Teaching* (Program and Training Journal 26). Washington, D.C.: ACTION/ Peace Corps, 1978

Beilenson, Evelyn, and Ann Tenenbaum, eds. *Wit and Wisdom of Famous American Women.* White Plains, N.Y.: Peter Pauper Press, Inc., 1986

Burrows, Arthur A. *Bumper Sticker,* Brattleboro, VT: Pro Lingua Associates. 2013

Carruth, Gordon, and Eugene Ehrlich, eds. *The Harper Book of American Quotations.* New York, N.Y.: Harper & Row, 1988

Celce-Murcia and Diane Larsen-Freeman. *The Grammar Book, 2nd edition.* Boston: Heinle and Heinle, 1999

Chase, William D., and Helen M. Chase. *Chase's Annual Events: Special Days, Weeks, and Months.* Chicago, Ill.: Contemporary Books, Inc.

Clark, Raymond C. *The Learner's Lexicon,* Brattleboro, VT: Pro Lingua Associates. 2002

Clark, Raymond C. and Janie L. Duncan. *Getting a Fix on Vocabulary,* Brattleboro VT: Pro Lingua Associates. 2009

Clark, Raymond C. and Janie L. Duncan. *Teaching Languages for Communication and Accuracy,* Brattleboro, VT: Pro Lingua Associates, 2013

Clark, Raymond C. and Richard Yorkey. *Teaching North American English Pronunciation,* Brattleboro, VT: Pro Lingua Associates. 2011

*The Concise Columbia Encyclopedia.,* New York, N.Y.: Avon Books (Columbia University Press), Hearst Corp., 1983

Crystal, David. *The Cambridge Encyclopedia of Language.* Cambridge: Cambridge University Press, 1987

Dobler, Lavinia. *Customs and Holidays Around the World.* New York, N.Y.: Fleet Publishing Co., 1962

*The Encyclopaedia Britannica.* Chicago, Ill., 2014

Encyclopedia of Knowledge. Danbury,CT.: Grolier, 1991

Evans, Bergen. *Dictionary of Quotations.* New York, N.Y.: Delacorte Press, 1968

Frank, Marcella. *Modern English: A Practical Reference Guide.* Englewood Cliffs, N.J.: Prentice-Hall, 1972

Gunterman, Gail. "Purposeful Communication Practice: Developing Functional Proficiency in a Foreign Language." *FLAnnals (NI No.3),* 1979

Hacker, Andrew. *U.S.:A Statistical Portrait of the American People.* New York, N.Y.: Viking Press,1983

*The Hammond Almanac.* Maplewood, N.J.: Hammond Almanac, Inc.,2014

*Indian and Northern Affairs Canada* website: www.ina.gc.ca 1999

Internet Sources
    adherents.com (major religions) 2005
    allyoucanread.com (Canada News Sites) 2014
    familyeducation.com (names) 2014
    franchisedirect.com 2014
    infoplease.com (US Cities) 2010
    lifesmith.com (surnames) 1990
    Pew Forum on Religion and Public Life, 2014
    psaresearch.com (magazines) 2011
    SSA.gov (names) 2014
    Wikipedia (various sources) 2103, 2014

Jacquet, Constant H., ed. *Yearbook of American and Canadian Churches, 1987,* Nashville, Tenn.: Abington Press,1989

Kehoe, Alice B. *North American Indians: A Comprehensive Account.* Englewood Cliffs, N.J.: Prentice-Hall,1981

Keller, Charles. *Tongue Twisters.* New York, N.Y.: Simon and Schuster,1989

Key, Mary Ritchie. *Paralanguage and Kinesics.* Metuchen, N.J.: The Scarecrow Press, 1975

Kin, David. ed. *Dictionary of American Proverbs.* New York, N.Y.: Philosophical Library

Moeur, Richard C. *Manual of Traffic Signs.*
www,trafficsign.us

Murdock, George P. "The Common Denominators
of Culture" in *The Science of Man in the World
Crisis,* Ralph Linton, ed. New York, N.Y.:
Columbia University Press,1945

Munro, David. *Oxford Dictionary of the World.* New
York: Oxford University Press, 1995

*The New American Desk Encyclopedia.* New York,
N.Y.: New American Library (A Signet Book), 1989

*2007 Census / Statistics Canada*
website: www.statcan.ca 2007

*The New York Times Almanac.* New York, N.Y.
Penguin Books,  2013

Parnwell, E. C. *Oxford Picture Dictionary of
American English.* New York: Oxford University
Press, 1978

Quirk, Randolph. *A Concise Grammar of Contemporary
English.* New York: Harcourt, Brace, 1973

Radford, E. and M.A. *Encyclopaedia of Superstitions.*
New York: Philosophical Library, 1949

*Reader's Digest Almanac, 1987.* Pleasantville,
N.Y.: The Reader's Digest Association, Inc., 1986

Richards, Jack C., John Platt, and Heidi Platt.
*Longman Dictionary of Teaching and Applied
Linguistics.* London: Longman 1992

Silber, Irwin and Fred. *The Folksinger's Word Book.*
New York: Oak Publications, 1973

*Time Almanac with Information Please.*
Boston: Time, Inc. Pearson Education, 2014

U. S. Census Bureau 2014
U. S. Department of State. *Background Notes*

Untermeyer, Louis, ed. *Golden Treasury of
Poetry.* New York, N.Y.: Golden Press, 1989

Wallechinsky, David, and Irving Wallace.
*The People's Almanac.* Garden City, N.J.:
Doubleday & Company, Inc., 1975

Whitford, Harold C. and Robert J. Dixon.
*Handbook of American Idioms and Idiomatic
Usage.* New York: Regents, 1953

*The World Almanac and Book of Facts, 2014.*
New York: World Almanac Books 2014

*Classic American scrimshaw found on Bequia Island in the Grenadines*

# INDEX

*Modern African American triptych, a classic*
*African tradition*

# *Photocopyable Resources from Pro Lingua Associates:*

- **The Great Big BINGO Book.** 44 varied, creative, and *photcopyable* BINGO games make it fun for students to learn about grammar, vocabulary, writing, pronunciation, and cultural topics.

- **The Great Big Book of Crosswords.** Working independently, in pairs, or in triads, students solve these 66 fun **photocopyable** puzzles rich with vocabulary and culture.

- **Potluck**: Exploring North American Meals, Culinary Practices, and Places, including a culinary tour of Canada and the United States.

- **Grammar Practice**: Worksheets for 212 Interactive Grammar Activities.

- **Pronunciation Practice**: The Sounds of North American English. 70 basic lessons. Expansion activities. Contrasting pairs. Syllable stress flashcards. 5 audio CDs.

- **Teaching North American English Pronunciation**. The basics of English phonology and a collection of photocopyable handouts.

- **The Modal Book**. Exploring the form, meaning, and use of the American English modal verb system. Each of the 14 units also explores the colorful culture of a variety of countries from Egypt to Thailand.

- **Go Fish.** 7 speaking and listening games for learning languages. 126 everyday objects from around the home are pictured in color on large playing/flash cards. Students practice conversation and learn vocabulary in any language. English word lists are in the book. Many other languages are free at Pro Lingua's web site.

- **Match It!** 83 *photocopyable* sets of cards for playing the index card game, Matched Pairs (Concentration), a grammar/vocabulary game for beginning to high intermediate students.

- **Shenanigames:** Grammar Focused ESL/EFL Activities and Games. A *photocopyable* teacher resource with 49 easy-to-understand-and-play game exercises that practice specific, clearly indicated grammar points appropriate for low to high intermediate students at the middle school, high school, university, and adult levels.

- **Index Card Games for ESL.** A new edition of one of Pro Lingua's all-time best sellers. The 7 card game techniques explained are easy to prepare and play using 3x5 index cards. These are student-centered, group activities which provide practice with vocabulary, structure, spelling, questioning, and conversation. Sample games for beginning to advanced students are all *photocopyable*. •*Also available,* **More Index Card Games**, with 9 techniques.

- **Conversation Inspirations.** Over 2,400 conversation topics and 9 distinctive conversation activities. The topics range from lighthearted fun to serious subjects for discussion, from the universal – human nature and interpersonal relationships – to the culturally vital – cutting edge issues in North American society and how people from other cultures feel about them and deal with them. All *photocopyable*.

- **Writing Inspirations:** A Fundex of Individualized Writing Activities for English Language Practice. The book includes 176 *photocopyable* masters for topic cards. Each topic has several variations, so that student have over 600 writing tasks to choose from.

- **Got It!** A game for building vocabulary and conversation skills.

- **The Idiom Book**. 101 two-page lessons featuring idioms in the context of informal conversation.

- **Surveys for Conversation.** 64, 0ne-page handouts in the format of a questionnaire. The students form their personal answers and then compare with their classmates.

- **In My Opinion**. Thought-provoking topics are presented in two formats: A questionnaire and opinion cards.

- **Faces**. 50 Drawings to prompt conversation. The students choose a face (character) and then day-by-day create a character for the face and interact.

# *Cultural Resources from Pro Lingua Associates:*

• **Cultural Differences**. This high-intermediate/advanced text focuses on the confusion, misunderstandings, and misconceptions that can occur when learners don't understand each other's culture, A Supplementary Activities book is also available.

• **Living in the United States:** How to feel at home, make friends, and enjoy everyday life. This is a brief introduction to the culture of the United States for visitors, students, and business travelers.

• **Teaching in the United States**. A handbook for international educators to help them understand and appropriately respond to the experiences as a teacher in the Unied States.

• **All Around America: The Time Traveler's Talk Show.** American history and geography are made vivid as students listen to and participate in 18 talk shows visiting sites from the ancient pueblos of the Anasazi to the skyscrapers of Chicago and meeting historical figures from Lincoln and Lee at Gettysburg to Vitus Bering in Alaska and Queen Liliuokalani of Hawaii. .

• **Legends: 52 People Who Made a Difference.** *Graded readings from American History.* Brief bio-sketches for reading, retelling, listening, writing, and research. There are 13 groups of legendary Americans each represented by 4 biographies; these range in length and difficulty - 100 words long to 250. Pages can be removed and used as story cards, each with a timeline on the back for retelling and discussion and a web site reference for research.

• **Celebrating American Heroes.** *13 brief plays* about significant historical figures. Written to be read aloud dramatically, each play has a few main characters and a chorus. The heroes are Betsy Ross and Washington; Dolley Madison; Sacagawea; Stowe; Lincoln; Edison; Muir; Jackie Robinson; Salk; Frost; Cesar Chavez; Astronauts Armstrong, Aldrin, and Collins; and Jaime Escalante – all people who contributed to making this a better nation.

• **Heroes from American History,** an ESL/Civics text. This companion to Celebrating American Heroes can be used independently. An integrated-skills reader, it covers the same great Americans plus Eleanor Roosevelt, Maya Lin, and the average American citizen.

• **Plays for the Holidays:** Historical and Cultural Celebrations. In each play a few characters (stars) are supported by a chorus (the rest of the class) which comments, advises, warns, and cajoles the stars while at the same time giving the big picture behind the drama. Most of the plays have historical subjects relating to the traditions and origins of the holidays; the author adapts *Scrooge* for Christmas and *The Headless Horseman* for Halloween.

• **American Holidays**: Exploring Traditions, Customs, and Backgrounds: Readings about our American national holidays is not only fun, it is a way of exploring our diverse culture and values. How do we celebrate Memorial Day and Kwanzaa? What is the history of Cinco de Mayo and Thanksgiving? What does "Be my valentine" mean? How are Ramadan, Chinese New Year, Easter, and Rosh Hashana celebrated.

• **North American Indian Tales** – *Story Cards*. 48 animal stories collected from American Indian tribes across North America, from Canada, Mexico, and the United States. The tales explain how the world came to be as it is. The illustrations, by a popular Native American artist and story teller, draw on symbols and motifs from the many cultures represented to impart the wisdom and mystery of the great oral tradition of the "animal people" tales.

• **Potluck**: Exploring North American Meals, Culinary Practices, and Places, including a culinary tour of Canada and the United States.

• **Aesop's Fables.** – *Story Cards*. The classic stories in a format for telling and listening.

• **Bumper Sticker**. A collection of 363 bumper sticker sayings about an odd, fascinating, and funny side of American culture. Great discussion prompts.

• **Real Life Stories,** Twenty-one fascinating stories about people and animals from a variety of cultures for interactive telling and listening.